Studies in Society: 20
Series editor: Ronald Wild

Women, Social Welfare and the State in Australia

edited by
CORA V. BALDOCK
Associate Professor in Social & Political Theory,
Murdoch University, Western Australia

BETTINA CASS
Senior Research Fellow, Social Welfare Research Centre,
University of New South Wales

Sydney
George Allen & Unwin
London   Boston

First published in 1983 by
George Allen & Unwin Australia Pty Ltd
8 Napier Street, North Sydney, NSW 2060 Australia

George Allen & Unwin (Publishers) Ltd
Park Lane, Hemel Hempstead, Herts HP2 4TE, England

Allen & Unwin Inc
9 Winchester Terrace, Winchester, Mass 01890 USA

National Library of Australia
Cataloguing-in-Publication entry:

Women, social welfare and the state in Australia.
  Bibliography.
  Includes index.
  ISBN 0 86861 158 1.
  ISBN 0 86861 166 2 (pbk.).
  1. Women — Services for — Australia.   2. Public welfare — Australia.
  3. Australia — Social policy. I. Baldock, Cora V. (Cora Vellekoop), 1935-.
  II. Cass, Bettina. (Series: Studies in society (Sydney, N.S.W.); 20).
362.8'3' 0994

Library of Congress Catalog Card Number: 83-70996

Set in 10 on 11 pt Times by Setrite Typesetters

Printed in Singapore by Richard Clay (S.E. Asia) Pte Limited

Contents

vi   *Contents*

Contributors

Cora Baldock, Associate Professor in Social and Political Theory and Women's Studies Coordinator at Murdoch University has written three books, including *Australia and Social Change Theory* (1978). She continues to be involved in research on the political economy of the 'voluntary' sector and has recently embarked on a study of labourmarket prospects of mature age students. She is also engaged jointly with other Western Australian feminists on research concerned with feminist critiques of social and political theory.

Dorothy H. Broom, Research Fellow, Social Justice Project, Research School of Social Sciences, Australian National University. She is currently interested in the sociology of domestic work, women's health, and socioeconomic factors in health and illness. She is co-author of a first-year sociology text and joint editor of a special issue of *The Australian & New Zealand Journal of Criminology on women and crime*.

Lois Bryson, Associate Professor, University of New South Wales, is co-author of *An Australian Newtown*. Her research interests are in issues of inequality and social policy.

Bettina Cass, Senior Research Fellow, Social Welfare Research Centre, University of New South Wales, previously lecturer in Sociology at the same university. She is co-author of *Why So Few? Women Academics in Australian Universities* (1983). Her recent research is concerned with social welfare and the tax system, unemployment and public policy, and family policies in Australia in the post-war period.

Eva Cox, Social Policy Consultant, has had over a decade of involvement in lobbying to improve the supply of children's services. She is a founder member of WEL. She has published articles and reports on many areas of women's employment, social welfare, social research and social policy. She is currently working on an analysis of voluntarism and its implications for welfare policy.

Sara Dowse, former head of the Federal Government's Office of

Women's Affairs, is a writer. Her chapter won the 1982 Women and Politics Prize and the 50th Anniversary Foundation Prize of the Australian Institute of Political Science. She is currently working on her first novel, to be published in 1983.

Elizabeth (Liz) Harman, Lecturer, Social and Political Theory, Murdoch University. Co-editor of *State, Capital and Resources*, U.W.A. Press, 1981. Her two major research interests are urban social theory and the role of the state in mineral development in Australia and Canada.

Paige Porter, Senior Lecturer, School of Education, Murdoch University, is the author of a variety of journal articles relating to both the sociology and politics of education. Her current research is concerned with the relationship between the state, the family and education policy.

Rosemary Pringle, Senior Lecturer in Sociology at Macquarie University, is a co-author of *Gender at Work*. She is interested in feminist analyses of capitalism and the labour process, and the history of gender relations, sexuality and 'everyday life' in twentieth century Australia.

Jill Roe, Senior Lecturer in History in the School of History, Philosophy and Politics, Macquarie University, edited *Social Policy in Australia* (1976) and *Twentieth Century Sydney* (1980). She works in the areas of modern social and cultural history.

Jocelynne A. Scutt, Lawyer of Canberra and Sydney, currently Research Scholar at the Max-Planck-Institut, Freiburg im Breisgau, West Germany, is editor of *Rape Law Reform* and *Violence in the Family* and co-editor of *Women and Crime*. She is currently researching in industrial relations, as well as women's right to equality in the public and private spheres.

Sheila Shaver, Senior Lecturer in Sociology, Macquarie University, is a co-author of *Who Cares?* She is currently working on a study of the social wage in Australia since 1942.

Tables

Figure

Introduction

BETTINA CASS AND CORA V. BALDOCK

This book explores the ways in which public policies at the levels of political parties, government, administration and the judiciary intervene in the lives of Australian women. Each chapter discusses, in the context of a particular area of policy, the social, economic and political processes which have constructed women's position of relative dependency in the family and their concentration in those segments of the paid workforce characterised by low pay, insecurity and the absence of job autonomy. The interconnections between the domestic, the 'public' and the paid working lives of women have been the subject of vigorous debate in the literature of the 1970s, since the emergence of a new feminist paradigm in social theory and research. But what has been less well addressed, in terms of both empirical work and theory, is the arena of state activity: those governmental, bureaucratic, judicial interventions through the development of wage-fixation and employment policies; social security and tax policies; health, education and urban planning policies which have a significant impact on the distribution of economic resources, social services and amenities, and the opportunities for political participation of women and men.

The basic question addressed in each chapter is: to what extent do various state interventions reinforce, challenge or transform some elements of the enduring but changing pattern of women's unequal access to economic security and social autonomy? One of the clear conclusions of the book as a whole is that this question cannot be addressed, let alone answered, by abstract theory at the level of 'the advanced capitalist state'. The book, then, brings together studies of particular social policies, particular sets of state activity, based on carefully collected evidence, usually situated in a historical perspective and informed by an understanding of the class structure and gender order of Australian society.

Recent feminist accounts concerned with the position of women in the advanced capitalist states tend to agree on several basic assumptions, even if there are some differences of emphasis. They recognise that women are defined officially in terms of the prevailing sexual division of labour, as mothers, first and foremost, responsible for the bearing and rearing of children, and as wives responsible for the care of husbands, and the maintenance of a 'private' domestic space separate from the competitive labour market and the non-intrusive state. Feminist critiques of the ideology of the non-instrusive state reveal that state policies (e.g. through social security and income tax policies and through industrial and family law) actually regulate the social and economic relations of normal domestic life. The institution of marriage in its current form is seen to locate women in unequal relations of production, distribution and authority which disadvantage them (McIntosh, 1978) and in a labour contract by means of which unpaid labour is extracted from them (Barker, 1978). Income tax and social security policies in Australia and Britain are seen to assume and reinforce women's dependency and to provide disincentives to their paid labour force activity (Land, 1978; Edwards, 1980a, 1980d; Keens and Cass, 1982; Bryson, Chapter 6; Shaver, Chapter 7).

Women's unpaid domestic labour advantages not only their husbands, but supports the whole structure of wages and profits in the labour market and subsidises public expenditure in the state sector. Women's work in the household provides uncosted goods and services for family use and consumption which supplements the value of wages (Cass, 1978b), while women's care of children, and of aged and sick relatives provides an informal and private welfare system which allows the cost of state provision of welfare services to be minimised (Waerness, 1978; Land, 1978; Rose, 1981). As argued by Baldock in Chapter 14, the extension of women's unpaid caring work in the provision of voluntary services in non-government welfare organisations also allows for the minimisation of public expenditure on formal welfare provision.

Women's position in the institutions of marriage and motherhood is very likely to render them dependent, deprived of personal economic security as unpaid domestic workers and disadvantaged in a competitive labour market by their domestic responsibilities. As a result, they become potential recruits into the large category of persons maintained as welfare beneficiaries (and usually maintained in poverty) if they do not have the support of a male-breadwinner (Summers, 1975; Roe, 1975; Land, 1976), but they are deprived of access to the more lucrative systems of welfare which flow through the tax system and through the occupational system (Rose, 1981).

There is a contradiction which cuts across the primary emphasis in social policy on women's role as unpaid workers in household and community, legitimated by the ideology of women's reliance on a male income earner (Wilson, 1977; Land, 1976; McIntosh, 1978). Despite the presumption of women as privately 'supported', the reality of the situation in Australia in 1982 is that of all women over the age of fourteen, only one in three could be presumed to be fully supported by a male partner. Thirty five per cent of Australian women are not currently living in a marriage or a de facto relationship, and of those who are living with a partner, 48 per cent are in the labour force[1]. At any one point in time then, two-thirds of women do not fit the stereotype of total dependence on a male breadwinner; hence labour market, wage fixation and social security policies based on the premise of women as 'supported' are seriously misguided. At the same time an analysis of the typical life-cycle pattern for women who become mothers shows that the years of early child rearing are associated with women's withdrawal from paid work, or reduced hours of work and, that as a result of their persisting childcare and domestic responsibilities, women's subsequent employment history is often characterised by intermittent, part-time, low paid employment (Rein, 1980; Cass, Keens and Wyndham, 1983). This pattern interacts with the sex-segmented labour market which has been consolidated in the post-war period (and which affects women without children as well as those with) to reinforce women's relative impoverishment (Baldock, Chapter 2, and Bryson, Chapter 6).

The presumption of women's dependency, and its reinforcement in labour force, income, social security and tax policies, entails a complementary presumption of men as necessarily bread-winners: conjugal relations in the current domestic division of labour reinforce 'work incentives' for men (Land, 1978). Since the time of the *Poor Law Amendment Act* in England in 1834, the maintenance of men's work incentives has been officially defined as a necessary adjunct to a system of 'relief', so that men would be deterred from adopting the habits of the 'work-shy' and from abandoning wage-labour (Fraser, 1973). An identical concern infuses the history of Australian welfare provision throughout the twentieth century, when advocacy for the introduction of various pensions and benefits and cash transfers (like child endowment) engendered the fear that such provisions would undermine men's work incentives (see Cass, Chapter 3). The Australian system of income-tested pensions, benefits and allowances, and the definition of the married couple (whether dejure or de facto) as the income unit to determine eligibility for benefit, continue to be based on the fundamental policy that men's work incentives must be maintained. The treatment of *women's* work incentives however is problematic and contradictory. On the one hand social security and tax policies create disincentives to women's paid work, as does the scarcity of childcare provision (see Cox, Chapter 9); on the other hand developments in education policies (Porter, Chapter 12) in wage fixation (Baldock, Chapter 2) and the growth of consumer capitalism (Pringle, Chapter 4) provide very strong incentives for women to seek paid work.

Most of the feminist accounts (previously cited) of the relationships between women, the family, the labour market and the state conclude that social policies which reinforce the division of labour in the household and in the workplace disadvantage women and tend to maintain class and gender inequalities. The nub of the argument is that state policies which maintain the unpaid labour of women as a cheap system of private welfare services to the young, the old, the ill, the disabled, and to able-bodied men legitimate an official emphasis on the 'family' as the private and informal provider of services for its members, the provider of first and last resort. In the 'long boom' of economic buoyancy when collective provision of social services through public expenditure was politically acceptable, the family was seen as the *partner* of the state in bearing responsibility for the welfare of its members (Moroney, 1976). In the current period of economic crisis and public sector stringency, emphasis on the family as the *primary* provider of welfare services and of income support is used to legitimate cuts in state welfare expenditure (Rose, 1981; Cass, Chapter 8).

Such official emphasis on the 'family' as the provider of a private welfare system presumes that all individuals may call upon family support, and that all families have equal financial capacity to provide it. Both of these presumptions are mistaken: firstly, 1.5 million people (almost 10 per cent of the population) were living alone or in a household of unrelated persons in 1982 (ABS, 1982e) and *their* capacity to call on the support of family is at best problematic. Secondly, the capacity of families to provide income support and services for their dependent members is determined by their class situation–by their access to income and wealth. Class inequalities ensure that the official encouragement of private, family welfare provision disadvantages most severely working class people with the least financial resources.

Feminist accounts of the welfare state, while usually recognising the interplay of class inequalities and gender inequalities, differ in their emphasis. McIntosh (1978) saw the welfare state as a set of institutions which support and regulate capitalist class relationships but which could not be said to dominate women directly. Domination of women occurs only in so far as social policies maintain a family-household system of male authority and female domestic servicing: a family system which predated capitalism and became, in the capitalist period, the major institution providing for the care and subsistence of the working class family.

For Summers (1975), Wilson (1977) and Land (1978) and for most of the contributors to this book, the sexual division of labour is central to the development of the welfare state: the maintenance of women as intermittently dependent mothers, wives and low paid workers is a key element in the maintenance of class inequalities, the containment of class unrest, and the social control of women. Public policies which 'protect' the dependency of women and legitimate men's domestic authority result in the vulnerability of women and their children to poverty. Social policies delegate financial care of women and children to their husband/father when the man is in work and also when he is a welfare beneficiary. The social security system assumes responsibility for the income maintenance of women and their dependent children when there is no co-resident male (and subject to an income test) under an ideological umbrella which explicitly emphasises that the state is 'taking over' responsibilities belonging properly to men (see Bryson, Chapter 6; Shaver, Chapter 7). There is little official recognition that the provision of income maintenance for mother-headed single parent families is necessary because of women's reduced labour market power, the inadequacy of childcare facilities and the strength of the ideology of women's dependence.

Perhaps the most succinct summary of the conjuncture of the maintenance of class inequalities and sex inequalities is provided by Land:

> Why then do the state's income-maintenance schemes still only support men in the role of chief bread-winner and women as man's dependent housewife? The answer must lie in the fact that there are enormous advantages to the economically powerful groups in our society in sustaining the belief that men are breadwinners and women, at most, are supplementary earners, whose primary duties be in the home. In this way work incentives for men are preserved even among low wage earners whose wives also have to work to support the family. At the same time it justifies paying women lower wages than men. Women when they enter the labour market do so in the belief that they do not need as high a wage as a man. Moreover, their paid employment must take second place to their unpaid work in the home... at the same time, they continue to care for husbands, children, the elderly and the infirm at minimum cost to the state. (Land, 1978: 142).

Certain accounts of the nature of the welfare state (e.g. Wilson, 1977; McIntosh, 1978) see it as a package of social policies and their administration which are designed to ameliorate the hardships and problems created by urban industrial capitalism; to support with cash transfers and social services those who are disadvantaged by class race, sex and age in a competitive labour market. They see such policies constituting an apparatus of social control and class containment—reproducing existing class and gender inequalities, and justifying them by dividing the 'deserving' from the 'non-deserving', by dividing 'productive' taxpayers from 'unproductive' welfare recipients.

Such accounts of welfare which assume that *all* state interventions have the effect of maintaining the existing system of productive relations and existing class and gender inequalities tend to ignore the essentially dynamic nature of public policy negotiations. There are other accounts however (e.g. Roe, 1976; Land, 1975; Rose, 1978; Hicks, Friedland and Johnson, 1978; McIntosh, 1981) which examine specific social policies as the outcome of contested class and interest group demands and resistances.

Roe (1976) insists that social policies which confer benefits are only introduced by Australian governments when they are subjected to the organised political action of claimant gròups. Hicks, Friedland and Johnson (1978) maintain that government redistribution of income to the poor in the USA is partially determined by conflicting class forces, with corporate and labour union organisations acting as the basis for the mobilisation of class interests. Land (1975), Rose (1978) and McIntosh (1981) outline various ways in which feminists have mobilised in Britain to demand income maintenance policies (e.g. family allowances, the treatment of women as individuals in the social security system) and social services (e.g. women's refuges) which redistribute income to women and provide a greater potential for social and political participation.

Such feminist conceptions of social policy do not see all state interventions as inevitably supportive of existing inequalities. On the contrary, they develop the concept of the 'social wage': public expenditures through the taxation/social security system and through social service provision, which redistribute income and distribute services outside of the paid labour market (cf. Gough, 1979). Women in particular may derive benefits from such public provision precisely because of their disadvantages in the labour market, and their consequent total or partial reliance on private support, i.e. on transfers of income within the family. In the Australian welfare system, the winning of widows' pensions, supporting parent benefit, family allowances, childcare centres and women's refuges, represent gains which redistribute explicitly to women and which extend the sphere of women's freedom.

Most of our contributors adopt a similar conception of social policy and explore the role of the women's movement which (in various groups and in different periods) has organised to secure legislative changes, the provision of cash transfers and social services which will promote women's economic security, their social autonomy and their capacity for political participation. The chapters outline the history of women as determined, professional providers of social services and the concerted efforts of women's groups to gain widows' pensions

(Roe, Chapter 1). They discuss the mobilisation of women in the labour movement and in feminist groups to demand equal pay (Baldock, Chapter 2); state provision of child endowment for mothers in recognition of their right to an independent income (Cass, Chapter 3); the provision of childcare services (Cox, Chapter 9 and Dowse, Chapter 10); anti-discrimination legislation and reform of family law (Scutt, Chapter 11) and non-discriminatory education policies (Porter, Chapter 12). Dowse outlines the particularly significant period of the mid 1970s when the voices of the women's movement gained expression and influence inside the Commonwealth government bureaucracy. But her chapter also shows the formidable, organised resistance to women's movement aspiration and projects.

Other chapters on health policy (Broom, Chapter 13), population policy (Cass, Chapter 8), on the spatial limits to women's equitable access to urban services and occupational opportunities as enforced in the planning of cities and regions (Harman, Chapter 5), and chapters on the patriarchal values embodied in Australian taxation and social security policies (Bryson, Chapter 6; Shaver, Chapter 7), on the material and symbolic manipulation of women as the managers of consumption (Pringle, Chapter 4) and the extension of women's unpaid work into volunteer work for the welfare state (Baldock, Chapter 14) demonstrate the structural and ideological constraints which continue to enforce women's dependency.

The emphasis in the book as a whole then is on the *contest*: on the aspirations of women's groups, the demands they have made and the concessions they have gained, as well as on the constraints in the labour market, in the domestic division of labour and in public policies which provide resistance to these aspirations and demands.

Note

1 Australian Bureau of Statistics (1982) *Australian Families, 1982* unpublished tables supplied by ABS.

1 The end is where we start from: women and welfare since 1901

JILL ROE

On 11 November 1980 in Melbourne, 137 delegates from about 80 charities assembled for the first Australasian Conference on Charity, organised by the Melbourne Charity Organisation Society to promote the principles and practice of scientific charity. This meant coordination, case work, and the exclusion of imposters, who were known to cross colonial borders to prey on indiscriminate almsgivers. At this and a second conference in 1891 a philanthropic élite from private and state charity canvassed new approaches to poor relief; exchanged information on remedies like refuges, ragged schools and labour colonies for the unemployed; and shared common problems, such as those presented by deserting husbands. It was a high point for the charity organisers. It was also a high point for philanthropic women, as suggested by the presence of Lady Windeyer and Catherine Helen Spence.

By 1890 the stereotype of women as dispensers of charity seemed to have real substance in Australia. In foundation days governors' wives had set an example in benevolence to women of 'the best circles', who supported ventures like Lady Darling's Female School of Industry (1826) and, less self-interestedly, the Tasmanian Maternal and Dorcas Society (1835) formed 'to assist destitute married women during . . . their confinement'. From the mid-nineteenth century, following responsible government in the eastern colonies, middle-class women of the towns were increasingly active in both Christian and secular charity as advisers, fund-raisers and visitors. The powerful Melbourne Ladies' Benevolent Society, for example, was establishing dominance over outdoor relief there. Also, as the Hill sisters emphasised in *What we saw in Australia* (1875), there would be places for professionals in the newly established institutions to rescue 'neglected and perishing' children. By the 1880s charities for women run by women, such as the Queen's Fund (1888), were proliferating. The new breed took even larger initiatives, most effectively the boarding-out of orphaned children previously incarcerated in barrack-line asylums, resulting, in New South Wales in 1881, in the creation of the State Children's

Relief Board. In all the colonial cities there were bourgeois women experienced in works of salvation, succour and rescue, especially of their less fortunate sisters. (Nine of the eighteen papers delivered at the 1891 conference were by women.) The next step seemed to be public recognition of their expertise.

Women had gained an unusual degree of public prominence in charitable activity. This was not only because it seemed their natural role; their presence was also required in the interests of delicacy and decency, so that they could deal with what were otherwise embarrassing cases of female need and distress. In colonial society the bulk of the poor were female, generally women with children—impoverished wives, widows, deserted wives, 'magdalens' (unmarried mothers)— but also young girls exposed to moral danger by colonial circumstance.[1] The Charity Conferences touched often on their plight, as was inevitable given the ground rules of charity, which the Charity Organisation Society sought to strengthen. The way the rules worked meant that charities were particularly concerned with women.

The charitable believed that poverty was caused by intemperance and idleness, and that it was useless to relieve moral failures, i.e. the undeserving poor. However, moral failure was largely (though not entirely) masculine. Women were rarely 'undeserving', much less children. For undeserving women, such as wayward girls who transgressed the code of respectability, reform, not relief, was required; and late nineteenth-century Australia was equipped with up-to-date reformatories, where the necessary discipline came from the state. Hence, both ordinary and scientific charity found itself with cases of 'deserving' women swelling the books, and ways of tightening the laws of maintenance were sought.

It is not too much to say that women have been moulded by the canons of nineteenth-century poor relief, more so than by other historic sources of low self-esteem, by fear of the poor-house, horror of the laundries in the lying-in hospitals, and (as with Shasta in Summer Locke Elliott's novel *Water under the Bridge* and also in *Caddie*) distress at the sight of orphan asylums: by the distinction between deserving and undeserving, and its consequences. Indeed the colonial context gave new life to the ancient distinction.

Able-bodied men suffered, and still suffer, moralism and attendant harassment, but in the 1890s they objected to its application, challenging the determination of the state to leave outdoor relief to charitable hands for fear of pauperising the people. Women were poorly placed to protest; in the last resort too much depended on meriting aid. Petit bourgeois beliefs and sexual stereotyping sustained the distinction. To be married was to be respectable, but to be respectable was not to be secure. The economic support of a male breadwinner, though he be the best of husbands, could still be uncertain. Furthermore, men could not be made to stay put. Despite increasing concern for the legal rights of married women, even they were insecure and vulnerable to the withdrawal of male support (and with the movement and danger in colonial economic life it happened often). There was no royal road to independence, given the limited range of female employment. And only very advanced women like Maybanke Wolstenholme were sufficiently emboldened to ask what good charitable effort was when hundreds of women were barely able to earn a living, to 'keep within the narrow line, outside which lies starvation or prostitution' (Kingston, 1977:136).

The charitable approach to women's needs continued in the twentieth century. The new forms of social security, developed out of the 1890s depression and shaped by Federation, emerged without much reference to women. Women bore equally the distress and guilt of the 1890s, but it was the male workforce which generated new responses. Charity lost the initiative as statutory benefits became the main method of support, and the focus shifted from charitable to collective provision. As a side effect, historical perspective on women and welfare in Australia was lost.

Four main historical reasons for the invisibility of women in social welfare debate now present themselves. First, the new turn-of-the-century liberalism disregarded gender distinctions, as in age and invalid pensions. They were male-oriented, but women benefited equally with men. The needs of women were apparently submerged in the statutory provisions pre-1914. Second, the new federal constitution, constructed to further national business interests, allocated very limited welfare powers to the commonwealth, and most of the support most relevant to women remained with the separate states: education, health, housing and the like. In effect it split provision between cash benefits (the commonwealth) and services (the states). As the commonwealth has gained power and prestige through the twentieth century, more attention has been paid to increasing commonwealth provision (and expenditure) than to the states; but for women's welfare the states were the crucial areas. The states retained their powers acquired in mid-Victorian times relatively undisturbed until World War II. This historical reality, it may be noted, is another reason why there has been such a carry-over of nineteenth-century attitudes in so many areas affecting women. Third, reform-minded women often worked at states level, fragmented and subordinate. And fourth, given that women have been excluded from political power, and confined at low levels in both commonwealth and state bureaucracies, all this has lowered the profile on women and welfare. Whereas nineteenth-century women like Lady Windeyer are relatively well known, the names of the first women bureaucrats, political organisers and social workers do not spring to mind. In summary, the complicated Australian version of a federal liberal democracy created in the early twentieth century marginalised women, fragmented effort, and reduced visibility.

Nevertheless, there has been a certain amount of selective amnesia. Australian women have always been involved in the creation and operation of welfare systems, both as agents and recipients, for the simple reason that so many women have needed help in this crude laissez-faire economy. Nor have they always beaten haplessly about the bush. The newly formed Country Women's Association in 1922 announced what it aimed to do for 'the Women of the West', and 'Meantime, the cry of the Country Women is "Aeroplanes! Aeroplanes! Give us aeroplanes that we may cover the big distances and reach the women of the outback in their need!"' (Kingston, 1977:37). Perhaps there has been some success, too, at least in the austere terms of social administration. As will be shown, the last 80 years tell a story of widening eligibility for help. On the other hand, there is the inescapable fact that a majority of the poor are female in contemporary, as in colonial, Australia and the overwhelming majority of people working to relieve poverty are now, as then, also female. The 'femocrats' of the 1980s are heirs to a long tradition, as substantial as the only comparable claimant of women's energies in Australian history, that is, literature. Today's single mothers on supporting parents' benefits bear witness to other continuities.

In so far as the male-dominated political system has been concerned with women's welfare, it has been concerned with strengthening the family in a nationalistic way. Support for 'deserving' women, that is wives-and-mothers, has been forthcoming, albeit fitfully; also, the categories have been loosened. Beverley Kingston, in calling her documentary history of Australian women *The World Moves Slowly* (1977), has emphasised the wisdom of feminist Vida Goldstein who wrote in 1903: 'The world moves slowly, my masters, women's world especially, but it does move.' In what direction?—is another vexed and crucial question, sharply focused by contradictions in the position of women today. But perspective is being recovered, no matter how unmanageable the sources initially. The real problem is to bring together feminist historiography and welfare history. A brief historiographical diversion suggests how far apart they still are.

Feminist historiography

It is no criticism to note that at first the relevant issues were touched on but not much explored. The balance of Kingston's *My Wife, My Daughter and Poor Mary Ann* (1975) shifts to 'my wife' by 1939, where the argument rests. 'The poverty of dependence', as sharply phrased by Anne Summers in *Damned Whores and God's Police*

(1975), is related mainly to the 1970s. Miriam Dixson, in pursuit of *The Real Matilda*, emphasises the impoverished stock of role models available in colonial Australia for female identity formation, and asks why élite women lacked initiative by the late nineteenth century (1976: ch. 6). Recent collections like *In Pursuit of Justice* (Mackinolty and Radi, 1979) and *Women, Class and History* (Windschuttle, 1980) contain new information, especially about legal and ideological restraints. And the evidence is mounting from the descriptive bibliography *Women in Australia* (Daniels et al., 1977) and recent documentary collections, as to how women actually fared historically in welfare systems. *Uphill All the Way* (Daniels and Murnane, 1980) begins with evidence of women as 'Outcasts of Society'. Overall, there is now a vital sense of complexity and of the hostile continuities in Australian history, especially late nineteenth-century Australian history, which kept most women marginal, and many women poor.

In Australian welfare history there is as yet no survey like Elizabeth Wilson's *Women and the Welfare State* (1977), an influential and vigorous Marxist-feminist polemic which works selectively over the long tradition of historical research on the British 'welfare state'. Public records of the operation of the ancient and unitary British Poor Law have also ensured insights into provisions for women, for example, Pat Thane's account (1978) of the backward-looking arrangements pre-World War I. In Australia the sources are more fragmented (there was of course no Poor Law in Australia) and the tradition is thinner. Nor have the spate of publications on social policy in the 1970s departed far from it. Though women's welfare issues were at last effectively politicised then, and, as inadvertently illustrated by Michael Jones's unexamined proposition that women are indeed the key to the modern welfare state (1980: 209), they remain marginal. Even Patricia Tulloch's *Poor Policies* (1979) does not escape the marginalising effect. The chief pressure has come from the new encyclopaedists of social policy who paradoxically have almost succeeded in refining gender considerations out of the problems of policy formation.

In this situation it is merely trivial to note that the people on the cover of the latest history of social welfare in Australia, *No Charity There* (Dickey, 1980), are all men, especially since the author makes an effort to include the main historical categories of welfare recipients, which means much on women and children. Nevertheless, feminists and feminist historians have a long way to go in reshaping an unresponsive administrative approach, newly refurbished with academic expertise.

There are then many reason—from both the past and present—why the balance between continuity and change in women and welfare in modern Australia is difficult to strike, even before admitting that any such balance would be wide open to a variety of interpretations. What follows is an account of the main trends affecting women since 1901, with emphasis on widows, regarded as the strategic historical category; and a brief look at the Australian social work tradition since the 1920s. Taken together, these twin themes suggest what happened to nineteenth century prescriptions and how far they have been recast in the twentieth. The overall theme is powerlessness, and its effects. If, on balance, it is a negative theme, it is also a provisional one. As T.S. Eliot put it in 'Little Gidding':

What we call the beginning is often the end
And to make an end is to make a beginning
The end is where we start from.

Women as welfare recipients: main trends since federation

The early years
The pattern of social security was set at commonwealth level prior to World War I, for women and men, with age and invalid pensions (1908) and the regulation of wages (first by state arbitration courts and wages boards, and then also from 1904, by the Commonwealth Concilation and Arbitration Court). Non-contributory pensions and a 'basic' wage, the latter fragile until the 1920s but not superseded until the late 1960s, were the new liberals' contribution to the longstanding problems of the dependent and labouring poor. White working-class women benefited—indeed some feminists claimed women voters were responsible for the speedy introduction of pensions—but they were primarily directed at the male workforce.

Age pensions, means-tested but available as of right, went to both men and women (and it is interesting to note, five years earlier to women, presumably to ensure support for wives, usually somewhat younger, when the breadwinner retired). They also served as an incentive to, and control over, the workforce, since statutory age limits for eligibility established a fixed age of retirement. As it happened, life expectancy had improved dramatically by the early twentieth century, and more so for women, so that women have always been the chief recipients of age pensions. Much amended, and liberalised extensively since the 1960s, non-contributory pensions were designed to rescue the deserving and dependent poor from (costly) indoor relief (see Roe, 1981).

Wage regulation, in so far as it regulated welfare as well as industrial conflict, was directed at the labouring poor by Justice Higgins's symbolic Harvester Judgement (1907). With the aid of budgets compiled by trade unionists' wives, Higgins determined a 'fair and reasonable wage' for an unskilled worker, seen as the breadwinner with a wife and three children to support. He was influenced by the 1890s' anti-sweating campaign in Victoria, directed mainly against exploitation of women out-workers (and Chinese), and contemporary wage levels. Although only the male worker came within his jurisdiction, the humane Higgins invented the notion of the basic wage, in reality a family wage, working within the assumptions of his day. It had of course permanent consequences for the independent remuneration of women. Thus issue is discussed in more detail in Chapter 2.

This was at a time when the participation of women in the paid workforce was expanding. By 1910 females constituted from a fifth to a quarter of Australian wage-earners (by 1973, a full third) (Ryan and Conlon, 1975: 79, 174; see also Chapter 2).[2] Other women were sustained by the much-underestimated 'female economy': laundry, sewing, cake-icing, taking lodgers, for example. More still welcomed the prospect of marriage, increasingly popular in Australia, and were protected by diminishing family size, and above all by comparatively high male wages. In the early twentieth century female dependency was taken for granted, and reinforced. Philanthropic feminists fought for moral and industrial protection for working women, but unsuccessfully for equal pay or better employment opportunities; thus the scope for charitable action was undiminished.

The eminent British Fabian Beatrice Webb, originally against votes for women, recanted in 1906 with the observation that increasing state intervention in family life justified the vote. In effect Australian women agreed; and in this, the first phase of female citizenship, were primarily concerned with securing their natural power-base, especially Motherhood. They both reflected and advanced dominant imperial concerns with national efficiency and race propagation, the latter particularly sensitive in Australia. The only pre-1914 commonwealth provision which recognised women independently, as citizens with sex-specific claims, was the universalist maternity allowance (1912). In effect a one-off medical benefit to minimise the still formidable hazards of childbirth, it came at the end of a long period of concern about declining birthrates, when birth-control was a selfish middle-class affectation lamented especially by eugenicists; 'populate or perish' had begun a long life as vital slogan; and the scourge of infant mortality remained. A premium was placed on 'viable' births. As the tag 'baby bonus' suggests, the survival of babies rather that mothers was stressed. The allowance was directed to mothers because of constitutional limitations—'The Commonwealth has no control over public health, and has not the same power to deal with children that the States have,' said Labor prime minister Andrew Fisher—and it was not until the 1920s that the high rate of maternal mortality was independently stressed. The nationalist, natalist drive is apparent from the disregard in this legislation of marital status, and whether beneficiaries were therefore 'deserving' or 'undeserving'.

Despite international attention to antipodean 'state experiments', little enough had been achieved. The limit was nowhere more obvious than in health, constitutionally a states matter, where access to both medical and hospital services rested on a charitable base. Even a determined reformer like NSW Labor Health Minister Fred Flowers had limited success prior to World War I in the face of autonomous hospital boards, the friendly societies which delivered some general practitioner services to the respectable working class, and a still insecure medical profession. If women's health improved, and the steadily increasing size of Australian girls tabulated by Ronald Mendelsohn (1979) suggests that it did, it was because of environmental factors, improved sanitation, diet and living conditions; and to local effort, like charitable dispensaries and the campaign to encourage breast-feeding in Edwardian Sydney. On the other hand, reticence, ignorance, and hostility to women doctors by the medical profession perpetuated widespread gynaecological disorders; and the stress on venereal disease by women's organisations, while realistic, focused concern too narrowly. It should be reiterated that the efforts of women's organisations were focused mainly on the state sphere; and unlike today, where much campaigning revolves pragmatically around more/better commonwealth benefits, dominant concerns were then structural (though not necessarily radical or egalitarian): representational, legal, industrial, and moral, as with raising the age of consent.

If recognition of the costs of motherhood and effective child-rearing were the new issues, widowhood was an old one, well known to charity workers. In measures to relieve the poor, it might be thought, widows' pensions were a prime category, and widows the most deserving. Relief for widows reached the political agenda in 1913 when the conservative Cook government proposed the first of many commonwealth contributory schemes, all of which failed more because of opposition from vested interests like life insurance companies than hostility from below. The non-contributory precedents set in Australia by pensions and maternity allowances now became a stumbling block to further provision of welfare.

Indeed it seemed as if change would come only when the established methods of provision were changed from a non-contributory to a contributory basis, along the lines of Bismarckian social insurance or, later, Lloyd George's 1911 *National Insurance Act* in Britain, establishing contributory sickness and unemployment benefits. Although more comprehensive, such schemes were seldom welcomed by women, very few of whom could easily afford the compulsory contributions.

The effects of World War I
World War I changed all that—not instantly, but decisively, and in unpredictable ways, but four aspects stand out.

First, as an immediate response to the realities of trench warfare, to death and loss, war widows' pensions were introduced in 1914, on the same non-contributory basis as age and invalid pensions, administered by Treasury.

Second, support for mothers and children gained ground; and the argument for family allowances was extended beyond recognition. Originally advanced by British feminist Eleanor Rathbone and the Fabians, who recognised the liberation of wives and the relief of child poverty in large families through their husbands' army allotments, it was relevant to the soldiers' wives gathered up in social centres in Sydney by Dr Mary Booth, and quickly became another premium on motherhood at a time when the prospect of the next generation seemed sadly diminished. The first legislative proposal came from eugenicist Dr Richard Arthur to the New South Wales Legislative Assembly in September 1916. 'Family allowances' became 'child endowment' in Australia, and after complicated manoeuvring, this was successfully introduced in New South Wales by Jack Lang in 1926, by which time yet another and more significant rationale had been added. Child endowment, restricted by income, enabled a cut-back in the size of the unit of calculation of the basic wage, thus discriminating between single and married men, and between married men on the basis of family size. At least, however, the money went to their wives, as Rathbone (1924) and A.B. Piddington (1921) had argued all along (cf. Chapter 3 in this volume).

Third is the post-war clamour for improved health services. The patriotic efforts of women as sock-knitters and charity-workers in World War I have often been derided; and women's organisations seemed more anxious to attack the demon drink than the axis enemy. But the female Anzacs have also had their defenders; and it was not only vice and disorder in the streets they feared. The great fact of social medicine in World War I was the exposure to and detection of venereal disease, the Great Scourge faced at last. For a variety of reasons (the cost of invalid pensions, war, new responsibilities post-war) the commonwealth took new interest in public health.

It was not, however, effectively sustained into the 1930s, largely owing to the resistance of the medical profession intent on retaining economic independence via charitable service to the poor. The development of collective responsibility for health care in the inter-war years was painfully slow (Thame, 1974: 237; Read and Oakes, 1977: Chapt. 3) Again victims of the charitable approach, and even more vulnerable to the social and moral arguments which bedevilled post-war attempts to control infections and contagious diseases like venereal disease and tuberculosis for example (Thame, 1974: 105 n. 155, 180-1), women probably suffered more than men from inadequate provisions, especially given the familial orbit of tubercular infection, and the relative neglect of venereal disease in women.

(Contemporary research in Melbourne, notably at the Queen Victoria Hospital, revealed latent syphilis in 7 to 10 per cent of confinements.)

Greater success attended deepened concern about maternal and infant mortality rates, though the newly formed Royal Society for the Welfare of Mothers and Babies found the going hard:

> Politicians of all shades seem agreed that the problems which we are endeavouring to grapple with are of the greatest national import- ance. The raising of a virile, native-born population is freely acknowledged on paper; but when it comes to action, we find our- selves blocked at every turn (Royal Society for the Welfare of Mothers and Babies *Annual Report* 1919-20 cited in Thame, 1974: 213).

There was good cause for concern. War exposed the weakness of the social fabric. Behind the rhetoric of 1919 that 'next to winning the war the nation's first duty is to save the babies', lay the statistical realities of the early twentieth century. Maternal mortality actually rose between 1910 and 1930, accounting in the 1920s for one-sixth of married women's deaths in early and mid-adult life, declining to inter- nationally respectable levels only in the 1940s. Infant mortality, also unacceptably high, dropped dramatically over the period, but not mortality in the first week of life, the rate of which, paralleling maternal mortality, remained high until the 1940s. Reproduction- related disorders may have increased with the medicalisation of child- birth. In 1928 one estimate has it that 50 per cent of all mothers experienced some weakening of bodily function following childbirth (Thame, 1974: 160, 164, 200, 209). Generally, conditions of domestic labour weakened women, traditionally the smallest eaters in the family. This writer's mother died of tubercular complications shortly after her fourth successful childbirth in 1942, the second female in her family to fall victim of tuberculosis, and the third in a family of eight to die relatively young.

In fact, there probably was improvement in women's health post-1918. It came, not from commonwealth effort, but rather from extensive voluntarism, and at state level. It was due to consensus on the importance of effective motherhood ('babies make the best immigrants') and the cheapness of the necessary paramedical services, plus scientific advances. More elusive, the new emphasis on domestic and family consumption in the inter-war years saw the elevation of Motherhood to new heights. Claudia Thame's conclusion was that its enhanced status was very influential by the end of the 1930s:

> The campaign to make motherhood fashionable could only be described as a triumph, and was crucial to the development of the role of women in Australian society in the post-war period (Thame, 1974; 184).

Fourth, unpredictably, Australia emerged from the World War I with an entirely new and separate welfare system for soldiers and their dependants, under the *Australian Soldiers' Repatriation Act* administered by the commonwealth Repatriation Commission established in 1920. Although successive governments hoped that charitable effort would suffice, and there was much tragic buck-passing subsequently, the task of repatriation and resettlement was immense, inevitably collective. The Western Australian Council of Women, for example, in March 1917 called on the government to introduce 'proper taxation to provide necessary funds for the repatriation and assistance for Soldiers and their dependants' (Daniels et al., 1977: I, 99).

So, not only were welfare services vastly extended, but they were extended on established principles. The contributory principle was absolutely irrelevant. The outburst of generosity occurred at a time of great need, when no other provisions for sick soldiers sufficed (voluntary hospitals being scarcely equipped for the treatment of war casualties) and there were no state supports for dependent women and children beyond 'boarding-out'. The sacrifices of war created new deserts, *en masse*, a new system, and new divisions among women, as among men.

Some women are more equal than others: The case of widows' pensions

War widows headed the hierarchy of women welfare recipients until the 1960s—no great honour in itself, and a struggle for the War Widows' Guild (founded in 1945). The embattled Mum of Clive James's *Unreliable Memoirs* (1980) made do on a war widow's pension; and James himself was saved for higher things by the intervention of 'Repat', the Commonwealth Repatriation Scheme, which sent him to Sydney University, despite his self-destructive school experience at Sydney Boys' Technical School. At least it showed the benefit of having powerful male friends, that is the support of the Returned Services League. Pensions for civilian widows, first paid in New South Wales in 1926, which presumably owed something to heightened consciousness of widowhood post-war, but more to the old New South Wales 'boarding-out' provisions of 1896, were on the old relief basis. Significantly, New South Wales widows' pensions were at first means-tested and paid to women with children under fourteen (they were later amended and extended in scope). In all other states except Victoria no specific provisions were made for widows with dependent children, who might receive limited assistance from child welfare or sustenance departments.

When commonwealth provision came at last in 1942, five years after Victoria's characteristically skimpy scheme, it too bore the marks of poverty relief, although its introduction coincided with the deployment of women in the war economy and a fresh anxiety about the loss of a generation through war. The case for non-contributory civilian widows' pensions was buttressed by war rhetoric. Recommendation 32 of the first interim report of the Commonwealth Joint Committee on Social Security, made in September 1941, recommended pensions for widows and children because 'In caring for their children, widows are performing a national service, and are entitled to community assistance.' They were also victims of that 'lack of unity' in Australian provisions, so evident in emergency. But basically, it was agreed, widows with dependent children had been too long 'in a particularly unhappy position'.

The extent of relief envisaged is obvious from the scope of the Act, which created three classes of widow pensioners, and included de facto as well as de jure wives. As Jean Aitken-Swan remarked in the pioneering survey *Widows in Australia* (1962), the term 'widow' lost its meaning. By the time of the consolidating *Social Services Act*, 1947, a very wide class of dependent women had been encompassed.

As Aitken-Swan also remarked, there was still in the 1960s 'an ambivalent attitude towards women without men', reflected in the hierarchy of widowhood (and now in the distinction between 'widows' and other unsupported women). An Association of Civilian Widows was formed in the 1950s, no doubt well aware that 'the Commonwealth government discriminates in favour of women whose husband's death is attributable to war service'; and, supported by the National Association of Apex Clubs, agitated for equality (Aitken-Swan, 1962: 2, 119). The position of civilian widows improved owing to the more selectivist approach of the Menzies administration, culminating in the additional mother's allowance of 1963. Nevertheless, not until the 1970s were widows' pensions rates standardised, the base rate for both being $148.30 per fortnight in June 1982. The chief difference between war and civilian widows' pensions is that the former are not means-tested.

It was inevitable that Aitken-Swan should stress the number of children for whom this 'small but vulnerable sector' was responsible. From the very beginning social security benefits paid to women have been in aid of their children, primarily. Very few, if any, have been directed at women independently of their relationships to men and children. Even as the pace of provision quickened in the 1940s, there were dependent daughter/housekeeping benefits for male support; wives' allowances for pensioners' wives too young or healthy to share their husbands' eligibility; and of course child endowment, in Australia from 1941 paid again to the mother. Aboriginal people, including women, attained eligibility across a wide range of benefits.

Since World War I, however, an important shift had occurred. There was now a significant distinction between 'widows' and other unsupported women. The widening of the term 'widow' emphasised by Aitken-Swan, whilst expanding the numbers of deserving women, did so on the basis of marital and quasi-marital status. Women unable to fit that category became once again undeserving, emphatically so in the period after World War II. Despite anxiety over the birthrate in the 1940s, the subsequent increase in population through immigration and the post-war baby boom made it possible once more to regard the unmarried mother as morally defective and thus undeserving.

It was therefore a remarkable breakthrough when in 1973 the Labor government introduced the supporting mother's benefit, extended to lone fathers in 1977, to cover women previously ineligible for support under widows' pensions. Earlier, in 1968, the *States Grants (Deserted Wives) Act* offered commonwealth grants to assist a wide range of needy mothers of families without breadwinners and ineligible for widows' pensions (because the commonwealth did not grant aid during the first six months of a male's desertion, or imprisonment, not wishing to impede reconciliations and restorations) (see Kewley, 1980: 111). What the 1973 legislation did was to strip away another sex-related stigma, and widen the categories of women eligible for, or deserving of, state assistance. Thereafter motherhood alone sufficed regardless of marital status; and with the extension to supporting parent's benefit, mothering by men was endorsed.

Even more remarkable, from November 1980 the supporting parents' benefit was available without the notional six-month wait. This relieved the states entirely of an historic responsibility—when and where it was accepted, and not left to charity. It regularised the ancient need for 'outdoor' relief, along the same lines as laid down in 1908 for age and invalidity. It also exposed a new and growing group of women to surveillance, under the notorious cohabitation rule. If a New Zealand survey of female welfare recipients conducted in 1978 is any guide—and it may not be—most were anxious, stigmatised as solo parents, but nonetheless grateful to be judged deserving (Schlesinger, 1979: 5-7).[3] And since all this coincided not only with changing sexual habits but also with increasing female unemployment, the outcome must be regarded as belated and ambiguous, whilst also historic. Nearly a century elapsed before the Charity Organisation's coercive prescriptions were finally eliminated. Meantime, dependency remains. Will the state prove more reliable as a provider than its menfolk?

Women as dependants on 'the Social Services', or women as paid workers
Elizabeth Wilson has argued that the British welfare state has always been connected with the development of the family, and that the social services represent 'a set of ideas about society, about the family, and

... about women' (1977: 9). Unlike Beatrice Webb, she regards 'the State organization of domestic life' as repressive, though paradoxical and contradictory in effect. In Australia, where state intervention on behalf of women has been meagre, fitful, moralistic and preoccupied with children, the story seems to be similar. Supports have always been directed at the family, and eligibility determined until very recently by derived and dependent status, that is by relationships with men.

In reality, there are only two other options, dependence on the state and gainful employ. The position of women in the paid workforce in twentieth century Australia has hardly been gainful; nor has their right to work even as the breadwinner been secure. Not until 1958 were there significant moves in the states towards equal pay. More important, as recent historical discussion suggests, women workers have been confined within the workforce by a sexual division of labour, in low-paid, unskilled jobs. In times of unemployment women workers have often been the first to be attacked. The location of female employment, its distribution, and also the marital status of women workers, has changed; but for the majority of women, paid employment has been an uncertain proposition, with low status, low pay, and attendant insecurity.

For the Depression of the 1930s the evidence is incomplete and contradictory. If women in the workforce had a separately stressful experience, as first outlined by Anne Summers, and unskilled women workers fared better than men in other depression-hit industries, others were regarded as dispensable (like married women teachers in New South Wales); and unemployed girls were often ineligible for unemployment relief, to the distress of some women's organisations like the Women's Service Guild in Western Australia. Today there is little specific concern about female unemployment, and women are still regarded as problematic, subsidiary, perhaps even dispensable. Certainly there have been contradictions for women themselves, as workers and houseworkers, and collective concern has not been directed effectively at lightening the dual load, nor at estimating the economic worth of housework and childcare. Even where independent working women have been eligible for alternative forms of social security, they have been discriminated against in favour of the male workforce, as recently documented regarding the NSW Public Service Superannuation Scheme launched in 1919 (Turtle, 1979). Conditions in the private sector are almost certainly worse, and remain unregulated.

T. H. Kewley in *Australian Social Security Today* suggests that the Australian social security system is 'not far removed in practice from a guaranteed minimum income system', though making little contribution to the situation of the working poor (1980: 219), of whom large numbers are women workers. Despite the extension of benefits to women in the twentieth century, there have been meagre supports for poorly paid female jobs and stereotyped roles. The significance of a fully articulated, guaranteed minimum income is that it would strengthen those very stereotypes and transferred dependencies. Even now, with the contraction of 'undeserving' categories, more and more women are supported by the state; at the same time mass unemployment threatens. The imprisoning effects of the social service system are plain to see, and may intensify the contradictions and rigidities of the position in which increasing numbers of women are placed by wider social and economic arrangements.

Women as welfare workers

The other side of the evolution of female welfare dependency in twentieth century Australia is the rise of social work as fit work for women. This was not just a matter of those women playing 'My Lady Bountiful', whose activities have continued unabated as fund-raisers and party-givers. Until the 1960s there were very few qualified social workers in employment in Australia: 368 in 1954; as recently as 1940 the five training institutes established since 1929 had trained only 112 social workers, almost all of whom were women (Lawrence, 1965: 33, 66, 168). The previously mentioned Joint Committee on Social Security in 1941 made no such qualification. Recommending that the newly established Department of Social Services employ social workers to investigate 'the general social effects' of commonwealth provision, and advise people on 'the wise expenditure of pensions, allowances, and endowment payments' (recommendation 23), it said straightforwardly: 'Social workers are women who have been trained at a school of social study such as those now working in collaboration with the Universities of Adelaide, Melbourne and Sydney.'

Nor was professionalisation straightforward 'from charity to casework', a theme derived from Anglo-American sources, where the Charity Organisation Society was much stronger. Rather, the doctrine of 'separate spheres' shaped the Australian social work tradition. Of course, the Charity Organisation Society was influential, especially in Victoria. But so too were women. The National Council of Women promoted the first Australian Board of Social Study and Training (in Sydney, 1929). Philanthropic women on the Melbourne Hospital Board were effective in establishing the first Institute of Almoners (1930), and employing Australia's first qualified social worker, the British-trained almoner, Agnes Macintyre (1930). In the 1920s, university-educated women also sought new openings, notably the Westralian, Norma Parker, at the Catholic University of America, and the redoubtable Kate Ogilvie, secretary of Rachel Forster Hospital, Redfern (Lawrence, 1965: 34).[4]

Social workers gained a foothold in Australia in the 1930s through medical social work in the largest charities of all, the voluntary hospitals. Despite heavy case-loads—Ogilvie interviewed 2849 patients in her first year as almoner at Rachel Forster, over half about their eligibility for free service—they worked to establish professional standards, training and associations, and the coordination of employers, first achieved in 1936 with the formation of the NSW Council of Social Service and thereafter run on a shoestring for four decades by Helen Halse Rogers, executive secretary 1939–74.[5] Later, the professionals were prime movers in federal coordination, the forerunner of the Australian Council of Social Service being promoted in 1956. With respectable frontmen, doctors and professors, they brought social work to professional status by the early 1940s, when the appropriate State universities assumed training responsibilities. However there was no training in Queensland until established in 1956 by the university.

By then the social worker's sphere of activity had expanded considerably, from administering mainly the sick poor to community work, as recognised by the Canadian, Elizabeth Govan, first 'acting' woman director of social studies at Sydney University (1940–45), and also evidenced by the rehabilitatory work of the Red Cross (Govan, 1942). Unfortunately for a female profession dedicated to service, its maturation coincided with the decisive shift to commonwealth provision via cash benefits in the 1940s: a development in which social workers played a minor policy role (submissions to the Joint Committee on Social Security 1941–45), and which in practice offered small scope for women. The Commonwealth Department of Social Services thereafter employed very few social workers under Lyra Taylor, who headed a Social Work and Research Section until 1959. Furthermore, the very thing social workers struggled to make professional, the delivery of services, was rendered subsidiary, supposedly vestigial, by advances of the 1940s. R.J. Lawrence, writing in the 1960s, saw part of the problem perhaps in the long run the lesser part:

> There was, then, a cleavage in Australian social administration. On the one hand, there was an approach through broad legislative measures, sponsored by political parties and administered by government, largely male, officials; on the other was an approach through numerous small voluntary organizations, catering for individual needs, sponsored by a wide variety of citizen groups or churches, with detailed work largely in the hands of unpaid women in the higher income groups. (1965: 29).

The Australian system did develop a cleavage, between the provision of benefits and the provisions of services, and social workers were caught in the middle.

Although the reluctance or inability of the commonwealth to enter the field of statutory services, as for example, in housing, childcare, health, may be diminishing (and social workers have been increasingly utilised at all levels of the bureaucracy for the allocation of cash benefits), the cleavage remains. It is a cleavage which affects women directly: all too often a woman's need will be for support services, for food, furniture, blankets,childcare, as well as for cash benefits. At that level women social workers, employed perhaps by the Smith Family, and women claimants come face to face in their respective subordinations.

Both in the making of the profession and in its relationship with the wider world, social work has been a victim and expression of the traditional doctrine of separate spheres. As an appropriate group to rectify the most obvious deficiencies of an ad hoc system geared to men not women, women social workers have been not only confined but powerless, the victims of both custom and constitution—and the fragile expertise of caring casework. No doubt improved statutory services may be introduced by men. Insofar as they have been, it has been in response to pressure from without, often from social workers, as happened with meals on wheels and widows' allowances.

The low status of women in Australia, so marked in social work despite all the stereotypes, where even the most capable women have been remote from dominant political and bureaucratic structures and dependent on male advocates, has had a detrimental effect on provision overall. Marie Coleman, the most successful inheritor of the tradition as chairperson of the Social Welfare Commission 1973–76, brought it to the end of the road. The regional-based Australian Assistance Plan promoted by the Social Welfare Commission was not so much 'an idea before its time', but an historic impasse for the profession. There was no way around the dominant political structures. Synthesis was not effected.

Of the ability of the women who created the profession there can be no doubt. More could—and should—be said of the first professionals. The conflict between academic status and professional expertise likewise proved a new and tricky field for women. The first academic social workers were never directors, always acting directors, of their departments, at least in Sydney where Norma Parker spent nine years on and off in 'acting' positions. The cry for more men in social work, for male recruitment and promotion, was buttressed with some specious and sexist argument, which neither resolved the cleavage nor recognised the true abilities of some of the women who were victims of it.

Lest this interpretation be thought extreme, consider the situation in child welfare by the inter-war years. Women workers who pioneered boarding-out and ensured its workings as voluntary (and no doubt judgemental) lady visitors were eliminated by the NSW Child Welfare bureaucracy, so that according to Brian Dickey 'care for state children took an increasingly bureaucratic air, in the inter-war years, and saw a reassertion of some of the punitive characteristics of institutional care (1980: 153). Later it was, apparently, Elizabeth Govan and Norma Parker who investigated the recurrent deficiencies of Parramatta Girls' School in 1944. (Parker 'lived in' in 1943, as part of the work for the Delinquency Committee's *Report*, 1945, which led to the re-organisation of the NSW Child Welfare Department; 'to its great benefit', she noted).[6] There is, then, a nice historical point in the renaming of the school in May 1980. It is now the Norma Parker Centre, on the initiative of Dr Tony Vinson, originally a social work student who attained real significance in the New South Wales bureaucracy as chairman of the NSW Corrective Services Commissions from 1979 to 1981.

Final comment

The transition from charitable allowances to statutory benefits has indeed been full of paradoxes. With every extension of statutory benefits in the twentieth century, there has been a noticeable transfer of needy women from one category to the other. The work of the late nineteenth century Queen's Fund changed when age and invalid pensions were introduced. The strain on charitable and state services was diminished in the 1940s when lone mothers transferred to widows' pensions and/or received child endowment. The focus of single mothers' dependency changed in the 1970s. Furthermore, discrimination against women on the basis of marital status is diminishing as the twentieth century closes in. On the other hand these have been but transfers of dependency from the supposed male breadwinner to the state. And some categories of dependency, especially young single mothers, have expanded; whether this is due to economic dislocation or social change is uncertain. Nor is it certain that the old classification of deserving or undeserving will not be now applied to the quality of mothering provided by these dependants of the state. Within the overall estimate of unemployment at 14 per cent of the workforce, female unemployment is now the largest single category, perturbingly disaggregated by area, family and class (Cass and Pedler, 1980). The needs of married women entering the workforce have not been met by adequate childcare services. Neither social security nor social service have proven sufficient to maintain a 'fair and reasonable' wage for the women who need it most. That, rather than further articulation of a guaranteed minimum income, would place women in Australia in the 1980s on a par with unskilled labour in 1907.

Richard Titmuss used to say to first-year students of social administration at the London School of Economics, 'When we study welfare systems in other countries, we see they reflect the dominant cultural and political characteristics of their societies' (Titmuss, 1974: 22). That is certainly true of Australia, where the subordinate, dependent and powerless state of women is reflected in a system which has diminished and thwarted women's efforts at alleviation while at the same time sustaining female dependency.

Acknowledgement

I should like to thank Sydney researcher Barbara Dale for assistance and support in the preparation of this article.

Notes

1 For example, the Sydney Charity Organisation and Relief Society *Report* for the year 1 October 1897 to 30 September 1898, p.5, classification of applicants: 1048 married couples, 344 widows, 100 deserted wives, 22 single women, 588 single men, 2673 children (Mitchell Library).

2 The discrepancy between Ryan and Conlon's and Baldock's estimates reflects the problems of definition of women's paid labour.

3 Solo parents perceived themselves as the bottom rung of the female beneficiary hierarchy, seen in descending order as widowed, divorced, separated, single.

4 See also L. O'Brien and C. Turner (1979); R.J. Lawrence (1969) *Norma Parker's Record of Service* Sydney: Mitchell Library; Department of Social Work, University of Sydney (n.d.) *Katharine Ogilvie, Social Work Educator: An Appreciation by her Colleagues.*

5 'Helen Rogers and the Council of Social Service 1937–1974' *Social Service* 25, 5-6, March/June, 1974.

6 See *Katharine Ogilvie*, p. 13 and *Norma Parker's Record of Service*, p. 4. For an account of the School at an earlier period, see S. Willis (1980).

2 Public policies and the paid work of women

CORA V. BALDOCK

Throughout this book we maintain that capitalism and patriarchy are mutual reinforcements in the production of public policies which affect the lives of women in Australia. This general theoretical viewpoint has a special pertinence to the issue of women's work. It is, indeed, a direct consequence of the close connection between the structures and ideologies of capitalism and patriarchy that within our society distinctions are made between public and private sphere, work and home, productive and non-productive labour, or paid and non-paid work, and that public policies are based on these distinctions (Hamilton, 1978; McIntosh, 1978; Eisenstein, 1979; Smith, 1980).

Most writers now recognise that such distinctions were not meaningful to the lives of people in pre-industrial, pre-capitalist society (Hamilton, 1978; Stacey, 1980). However, few acknowledge that the dualism exemplified in concepts such as productive and non-productive, paid and non-paid, public and private, and related pairs of adjectives such as rational and non-rational, scientific and non-scientific, objective and subjective, culture and nature, is embedded in the ideology of capitalism in conjunction with—and supported by—the patriarchy (Foreman, 1977; Thornton, 1980). That patriarchy has had a special significance in shaping this dualism is clear by the fact that every one of the set of concepts expressing the dualism divides *men and women*.

The patriarchal expression of the dualism pervades the structure and ideology of western society, and is reflected in the writings of philosophers and social scientists theorising about the human condition in the western world (Clark and Lange, 1979). For instance, should not Engels' views on the difference between productive and non-productive labour, incorporated in his theory of the 'liberation' of women through entry into productive labour, be seen as an example of the grip dualism has on the consciousness even of those who are the most fervent critics of capitalism (Engels, 1884)? Could the distinction made by many feminists between capitalism and patriarchy and the ongoing debate about the relevance of each for the oppression of women be a further example of the power of dualistic thinking?

The patriarchal expression of the dualism has a profound effect on our everyday lives. For example, members of the labour movement who may have an acute awareness of the mystifications of capitalism, are generally oblivious to the fact that the structure and ideology of the nuclear family are historical phenomena produced by capitalism in the same context as the organisation and power structure of the workplace, or the ideologies of individualism, competitiveness and private enterprise. When active unionists say—as many do—'A man should be able to provide for his family on a 40-hours-a-week job,' 'Women should not have to work,' 'Women's natural role is in the home,' 'Some women were greedy in the 1960s and wanted a job,' and even 'People should not live beyond their means,' they seem unaware that they are in fact expressing the values and ideologies of capitalism and not (just) the ideologies of the patriarchy.[1]

In this chapter I attempt to bracket the dualism of capitalism and patriarchy. I assume that women *work* whether they are paid or not, that the specific division of labour which allocates women to a position of economic dependence as 'limbo workers' (Thornton, 1980) is an historical phenomenon and product of the dialectical relation between capitalism and patriarchy, and I assume further that public policies, whether oriented to the home and family *or* to the workplace, need to be seen as furthering the same ends, those of the mutual accommodation of patriarchy and capitalism (Hartmann, 1976; Curthoys, 1979; Smith, 1980).

This chapter focuses on paid work but the relationship between paid and unpaid work is always acknowledged. It is especially important in this context to remember that there are no policies or expressed ideologies in Australian history directed to home and family which define paid work for women as an activity which makes a *positive* contribution to home life in the same manner as occurs with men, whose paid work defines them as 'breadwinners' and 'providers' and gives them privileges regarding family finance, housing loans and family property in that capacity. And vice versa, there are, to my knowledge, no public policies in Australia which divert the male from his breadwinner's role and focus on his participation in home and family life as a positive contribution. Although part-time work is available it is not seen as appropriate for males except when very young or near retirement. A supporting father's benefit is available but the numbers of fathers requesting custody of their children is still very small and those who do are on the whole financially better off with paid work than on benefit (while the reverse appears to be the case with women on supporting parent benefit (see Chapters 6 and 7 in this volume). The only policy which has ever encouraged males to take on the role of homemaker, that of paternity leave, existed only for a few years during the Whitlam government.

While this chapter,then, focuses on policies directed to the paid labour force, readers are asked to see these in conjunction with the evidence provided in later chapters which illustrates the extent to which public policies directed at home and family deter women from paid work, encourage males to maintain their traditional role as breadwinner, and prevent males from performing anything other than a marginal task at home.

The paid work of women and class segmentation

Women's position within the paid labour market has been described with the use of concepts such as 'sex segregation', 'industrial reserve army', or 'dual labour market'. For a full understanding of the theoretical relations between these concepts it may be useful to centre on an analysis of the notion of class segmentation.

Reich, Gordon and Edwards (1973) have defined labour market segmentation as the

> historical process whereby political-economic forces encourage the division of the labor market into separate submarkets or segments, distinguished by different labormarket characteristics and be-havioral rules. (Reich et al., 1973: 359).

This segmentation or fractioning of the labour force operates along several lines (Reich et al, 1973; Freedman, 1975; Brennan, 1977; Collins, 1978). Divisions usually emphasised are those between industrial and service workers, between manual and non-manual workers, and between workers at different levels of skill and job hierarchy. Cutting across these divisions is the fractioning of the working population in a 'dual labour market', with categories of permanent, well-trained workers with relatively high wages and good working conditions in the primary sector, contrasted with insecure, low-paid, poorly-trained expendable workers in the secondary sector (Freedman, 1975; Barron and Norris, 1976; Brennan, 1977; Cass, 1978b) and between and within each of these 'markets' a segregation based on gender and race or ethnicity (Collins, 1978; Power, 1979).

Labour market segmentation is usually defended by arguments about alleged differences in skill, experience and authority, and the increased productivity and efficiency created by job differentiation and bureaucratisation (Cass, 1978b; Amsden, 1980). At the same time, it tends to be supported by ideological expressions stereotyping racial, ethnic, gender and other ascribed characteristics of workers employed in the various segments of the labour market (Power, 1976; Boon and Jones, 1979). 'Women don't want to achieve,' 'Blacks are lazy,' 'Young people don't want to work,' are the typical forms such stereotyping may take. It is important to note that such ideologies of racism, sexism and nationalism are internalised by workers themselves. The agony of some married women in paid work over the question whether they are causing unemployment, even if they themselves provide essential support for the family income, is sad to see.[2]

In reality labour market segmentation has the economic effect of allowing the maintenance of wage differentiation and a flexible labour market, thereby contributing to the creation of surplus value (Reich et al, 1973; Collins, 1978). Politically it helps to maintain a divided labour force unable to develop a sense of class solidarity (Gordon, 1972; Reich et al 1973; Rubery, 1980). Ideologically it creates categories of 'superior' and 'inferior' workers as a legitimation for inequalities in authority and control and as a justification for the maintenance of industrial reserve armies as expendable, flexible pools of workers within particular segments of the labour force who can be called on in time of economic expansion and withdrawn during recessions (Milkman, 1976; Brennan, 1977; Power, 1979; Boon and Jones, 1979).

Labour market segmentation based on gender is a particularly powerful device of dividing the workforce. The deeply ingrained ideology of motherhood which asserts that women's prime responsibility is to the care of children, provides a 'natural' justification for women's low status in paid work (Boon and Jones, 1979; Wearing, 1981). Such ideologies include myths supported by health and medical authorities about the vital role of mothers in the upbringing of children, the importance of bonding, breast-feeding and intensive baby and toddler care by the mother, or the negative consequences of the phenomenon of 'latch-key' children. This preoccupation with motherhood and home life in the socialisation and training of young women leaves them ill-prepared for paid work, not only because they have been imbued with myths about female inferiority in the workplace, have been socialised into non-assertive, non-competitive roles and lack the self-confidence to go out into paid work (Safilios-Rothschild, 1976), but also because they suffer from excruciating feelings of guilt for any real or imagined wrongs done to their children if they give priority to activities which do not relate directly to home and family (Harper and Richards, 1979; Wearing, 1981). Thus, unequal job opportunities and income levels between women and men are legitimated because of women's domestic responsibilities (Cass, 1978b; Curthoys, 1979).

Labour market segmentation on the basis of race and ethnicity is also often justified by strongly held ideologies, i.e. of assumed 'natural' inferiority of certain racial or ethnic groups. However, it is only in the case of segmentation based on gender that such an ideology about 'natural' characteristics of workers has found material expression, firstly and fundamentally, in the separation of domestic and productive labour, and secondly, in the effect that women's domestic role has on their earning capacity and general marketability in the paid labour market. As Curthoys puts it:

> given that women's domestic responsibilities will mean that the woman's income is likely to be intermittent, casual, or indeed often completely absent, the man's income must be the staple family income. It is more important, therefore, for the male than the female worker to acquire and protect skills, and to organise for increased pay and better working conditions. (Curthoys, 1979: 62).

Once women's low status in the paid labour market has been established it helps to obscure other divisions between workers such as between the primary and secondary sector, or between industrial and office or service workers. As Freedman points out, industrial workers, who are mostly male, are 'involved in the production of material goods and are aware that they are responsible, in some measure, for the daily reproduction of the life of the population' (Freedman, 1975: 59). Office workers, who are mostly female, work under privatised conditions that reinforce an 'individualistic and passive relation to the job' (Freedman, 1975: 59). The purpose of office work is often hidden to the workers, and their loyalty is more likely to be to the firm than to the product they create (Women's Employment Rights Campaign, 1979). Service workers, again mostly female, often produce a direct service to the public in positions that help to legitimise bourgeois ideology. They, like the office workers, work under privatised conditions and the ideology of 'service' and 'caring' implied in their job tasks acts against their interests as workers.

Because divisions between, for example, industrial, office or service workers coincide with sex segregation, it is all too easy for the properties of the jobs to become confused with, and obscured by, alleged characteristics of the job holders (Barron and Norris, 1976). Thus, women workers are said to be 'passive' and 'docile', whereas in fact the properties of the jobs in which most women are employed may demand strict obedience to machine tempos, subservience to other personnel, and low initiative. This issue is especially pertinent with the increased use of advanced technology in office and service work in as much as this leads to deskilling of (primarily female) workers and to an increased transfer of control of the pace of work from workers to management (Kipnis, 1980).

The theory of labour market segmentation, then, helps to explain the position of women in paid work, when read in conjunction with an understanding of the particular role the patriarchy plays within the process of labour supply and demand. Patriarchy through the ideology of motherhood, which assigns the duties of childcare solely to the mother, creates the material and ideological conditions which limit women's opportunities to compete in the paid labour market (Cass, 1981b). This applies in principle to all women, because of the limited educational choices available to women, and the subsequent stereotyping of their motivation and career orientation.[3] In practice, it has a special applicability to the job opportunities of mothers who at all times need to juggle the demands of paid work with their responsibilities for children and other aspects of domestic labour, and usually need to vary their commitments to paid work according to the stage of their family life cycle (Young, 1974). The mystifying effect of ideologies about motherhood and home life is revealed clearly by the fact that married women who opt for part-time work do so often to disguise to husband and children that they are involved in paid work at all (Harper and Richards, 1979).

There has been some debate in the literature about the applicability of the concept of 'industrial reserve army' to the position of women. It is now generally agreed that given the segmented nature of the labour force an industrial reserve army thesis which assumes that women are at all times 'the last hired, the first fired', cannot be maintained (Milkman, 1976; Power, 1979; Curthoys, 1979; Boon and Jones, 1979). Employers prefer to employ women in particular segments of the paid labour market because the workings of the patriarchy make them a cheaper and more expendable labour pool and more easily manipulated than male workers (Baldock and Thiele, 1979). Age, marital status, race and ethnicity then interact with gender in creating further segmentation of the female labour force leading to differential opportunity structures for each specific group of workers (Power, 1976; 1979). Although women may be hired last in times of an expanding market, they may retain their jobs in those areas where sex segregation ensures that they are not competing within the male job market. A recession, then, puts some women's paid work in jeopardy, while not touching job markets in other areas. For employers the further advantage of the segmentation of the labour force according to ascribed characteristics such as gender is that it limits workers' sense of class solidarity. As Frankenberg explains:

The responsibility of women for housekeeping and childrearing, the solidarity of the male peer group reinforced by shared work hazards, . . . led to a situation in which men reacted to exploitation by fighting not as a class against capitalism, but as a gender group against women—or rather within a framework of sex solidarity against a specific woman chosen and caged for this express purpose. (Frankenberg, 1976: 40).

Trends in women's participation in paid labour: an overview

Australia has during the last half-century gone through profound changes in its economic structure. Prior to World War II it was predominantly a small-scale rural society, isolated from the mainstream of international politics and economically dependent on Great Britain (Baldock, 1978). As may be expected in a generally stable economy, the participation rate of women workers did not change a great deal during pre-war years (Richmond, 1974). Women made up about one-fifth of the workforce in 1901, a situation which had not changed substantially by 1933, the last census taken prior to the war (see Table 2.1). The paid work done by women prior to the 1940s took place mostly in a sex-segregated labour market with the majority of women confined to 'women's occupations' (Power, 1975b). Concomitant with this was a substantial pay differential between weekly wages of men and women, with women's pay scales set on average at about 54 per cent of those of males (Power, 1974; Ryan and Conlon, 1975). The war itself set the scene for potential changes when due to the scarcity of male labour more women were brought into paid employment and especially into work previously done by men. Between 1939 and 1944 the number of women in full-time paid work increased threefold. I return to a discussion of pre-war and war conditions for female workers in the next section on public policy.

Post-war years brought major changes through rapid industrial developments, a dramatic expansion of mineral exploration and extraction and increased government control over finance, health, welfare and education (Baldock, 1978; Cass, 1981c). Post-war needs for the supply of industrial workers were met by active immigration policies which brought large numbers of unskilled women and men to this country. The forced labour mobilisation practised during the last years of the war was now applied to migrants who were directed to specified work areas during their first two years of settlement, a policy which assured sufficient supply of workers to key industries. In post-war years, women on the whole lost the hold on the employment market they had gained during war years, and a comparison of census data for 1933, 1947 and 1954 shows only small improvements in their overall participation rates (Richmond, 1974: 269). In 1933, for example, 27.8 per cent of women were in paid employment; in 1947, the percentage was 28.4 and in 1954, 30.5 per cent.

These overall figures, however, obscure substantial variations in the participation rates of different categories of labour. Migrant women, most of them married, filled the needs of the burgeoning industries producing textiles, clothing and food. Thus, the labour of Australian-born women was withdrawn from the workforce in the decade following World War II, but migrant women had a high involvement in paid

Table 2.1 Participation of women in paid labour, 1901-76

	Percentage of women at work	Women at work as percentage of total workforce	Percentage of married women at work	Married women at work as of total workforce	Married women at work as percentage of female workforce
1901	30.7	20.5	N/A	N/A	N/A
1911	28.5	20.1	6.1	2.2	11.1
1921	26.7	20.3	4.4	1.9	9.2
1933	27.8	21.8	5.4	2.4	11.0
1947	28.4	22.4	8.6	4.4	19.8
1954	30.5	22.8	13.6	7.0	30.5
1961	33.8	25.1	18.7	9.6	38.3
1966	40.9	29.5	28.8	14.1	47.8
1971	37.1	31.7	32.8	18.0	56.8
1976	43.0	35.9	41.2	22.5	62.5

Source: Data for 1901-66, Richmond (1974: 269) as derived from census statistics; for 1971, Australian Department of Labour (1974: 4-6); for 1976, ABS (1976) and calculated from ABS (1979). Comparability from census to census is reduced by the number of changes in the definition of the workforce.

work. For example, in 1954 10.9 per cent of Australian-born married women were in paid employment, as compared with 15.1 per cent of married women born in the United Kingdom, and as many as 29.2 per cent of married women from all other birthplaces (Richmond, 1974: 296).

It was not until the late 1960s that the overall participation rate of women began to increase more rapidly, with a recorded rate of 39.6 per cent in 1970, and eventually 45.1 per cent in 1980, a trend that is generally explained by the growing demands for women workers in the expanding tertiary sector (Jamrozik and Hoey, 1981). Participation rates for males have dropped over the last decade, from 83 per cent in 1970 to 78 per cent in 1980. Although this is mainly due to a decline in male participation at the extreme ends of the age structure, i.e. young people staying in school longer and elderly workers opting for early retirement, some have tried to gain political mileage out of these facts by arguing that women have made excessive gains during the last decade at the expense of male workers. It is crucial, though, to remember that throughout the entire period when women's participation rates improved, most women worked in sex-segregated jobs under conditions not suitable or desired by men. Sex segregation still signifies lower average wages for women than men (Power, 1976; Cass, 1981c). Women still cluster in a small range of jobs, with about one-third of all women workers concentrated in three occupations: clerical work, sales work and stenography/typing (Windschuttle, 1979: 138).

Table 2.2 Distribution of employed persons in various industries: men and women, 1966-80, in pecentages

	1966 M	1966 F	1971 M	1971 F	1974 M	1974 F	1978 M	1978 F	1980 M	1980 F
agriculture, forestry, fishing and hunting	11.0	4,0	9.0	4.0	8.6	3.5	8.0	3.5	8.0	4.0
mining	1.6	—	2.0	0.4	1.8	—	1.9	.2	1.9	.3
manufacturing	27.0	21.0	27.0	20.0	26.0	18.0	23.0	15.0	23.0	13.0
construction	12.0	1.0	12.0	1.4	12.0	1.3	11.5	2.0	11.0	2.0
wholesale and retail trade	18.0	26.0	18.0	24.0	17.0	25.0	19.0	24.0	18.0	24.0
transport and storage	7.0	2.0	7.0	2.0	7.0	2.0	7.0	2.0	7.0	2.0
finance, real estate and business service	5.0	8.0	6.0	9.0	6.0	10.0	6.0	10.0	7.0	10.0
community services	6.0	20.0	7.0	21.0	7.0	23.0	9.0	27.0	9.0	28.0
entertainment recreation restaurants, etc	5.0	12.0	4.0	11.0	4.0	11.0	4.0	10.0	4.0	10.0
other	9.0	5.0	9.0	6.0	0.0	6.0	10.0	6.0	10.6	6.0
total	100	100	100	100	100	100	100	100	100	100

Source: Cass, 1981c: 12. These data are derived from ABS *Labour Force Surveys*

It should also be noted that a substantial number of them work *part-time*, and that the major increase in women's employment during the last decade has been in part-time rather than full-time work (Eadie, 1977; Jamrozik and Hoey, 1981). In 1979, for example, 44 per cent of all employed married women were in part-time work (Prosser, 1981: 101).

Also, participation figures include unemployed workers. It is clear from the data that on the whole the rate of unemployment is much higher among females than males (Women's Employment Rights Campaign, 1979; Scotton and Ferber, 1980). Cass (1981c) reports official unemployment rates for women of 2.6 per cent in 1966, and 7.5 per cent in 1980, as compared with 1.1 per cent and 5.0 per cent for men in the same years. She notes that if various forms of hidden unemployment were considered, then in her estimate real unemployment figures would have amounted to 18.5 per cent for women, and to 7.5 per cent for men in 1980 (Cass, 1981c: 37). These figures include 'between one-quarter and one-third of women regarded as housewives and thus outside the workforce who should be counted as among the

Table 2.3 Part-time workers as percentage of all employed adults: 1964-80

		Males	Females	Persons
May	1964	3.6	21.7	8.4
	1965	3.5	21.8	8.7
	1966	3.5	23.0	9.2
	1967	3.7	23.5	9.7
	1968	3.6	25.1	10.2
	1969	3.9	26.1	10.7
	1970	3.4	25.6	10.4
	1971	3.4	25.9	10.7
	1972	3.0	25.6	10.2
	1973	3.4	27.4	11.3
	1974	3.5	28.8	12.1
	1975	3.8	30.4	12.8
	1976	4.5	32.9	14.3
July	1980	5.0	35.4	16.1

Sources: Eadie (1977); Jamrozik and Hoey (1981).

hidden unemployed' (Windschuttle, 1979: 146). Another aspect of women's paid work is its *discontinuity*; for example in 1979, 85 per cent of males in the paid labour force worked for the entire year; this applied to only 65 per cent of the female labour force (Prosser, 1981).

General trends of women's participation in paid employment, then, hide a considerable amount of underemployment, due to the incidence of part-time work, part-year work, and unemployment. In her analysis, Cass adds as another form of underemployment,—so far hardly assessed,—the employment of workers *below* their level of qualifications and skills (Cass, 1981c: 39). Relatively speaking women have fewer educational or trade qualifications than men. However, there is abundant evidence to show that even when qualifications of men and women are comparable, women are relegated to positions of lower rank and pay (Australian Department of Labour, 1974; Power, 1976). Also, differentials in formal qualifications and experience have limited relevance to real *potential* if: (a) women are barred or discouraged from gaining formal qualifications needed to compete in the labour market; (b) women are unable to gain experience (or find their experience is not taken into consideration) because of dis-continuous occupational services; and (c) unpaid work carried out by women in domestic or volunteer labour is not taken into account as a form of job experience.

I indicated earlier the existence of differential participation rates of migrant and other working women. What in fact occurred in post-war years was the development of a distinct labour segmentation within the female workforce (Denis, 1980). While migrant women have been concentrated primarily in manufacturing and some service areas,

Australian-born women are found mainly in professional, clerical and sales jobs, and 'Australian-born women are five times less likely than Southern European born women to work in manufacturing as a process-worker' (Cass, 1981c: 3). The effects of this labour segmentation on job security, wage levels, unemployment rates and general work conditions of migrant women, has been well documented (Richmond, 1974; Collins, 1978; Power, 1979). Even more disadvantaged than migrant women have been Aboriginal women workers; they are employed mainly in agriculture, in personal services and as process-workers, and earn consistently low wages in insecure, often seasonal jobs, and have an official unemployment rate vastly exceeding that of non-Aboriginal women (Power, 1976; Cass, 1981c: 3).

Table 2.4 Employed persons, occupation by sex: 1966-80: August (percentages)

	1966		1970		1974		1978		1980	
	M	F	M	F	M	F	M	F	M	F
professional, technical	8.3	13.3	9.3	13.0	10.8	15.1	11.7	17.6	12.1	18.8
administrative, executive and managerial	8.4	3.3	8.1	2.2	8.5	2.1	8.4	2.1	8.6	2.4
clerical	8.6	30.1	9.1	32.4	8.4	33.7	8.2	33.5	7.8	32.4
sales	6.0	13.4	6.0	13.5	6.0	13.0	6.8	12.7	6.7	13.1
farmers, fishermen, timbergetters	11.8	4.4	10.4	4.0	9.5	3.2	8.8	3.6	8.8	4.1
transport and communication	7.9	2.5	7.8	2.5	7.6	2.4	7.5	2.1	6.9	2.1
tradesmen, production-process workers and labourers	44.5	16.0	45.0	15.2	44.4	14.0	43.4	11.3	43.5	10.2
service, sport and recreation	4.4	17.1	4.4	17.2	4.8	16.5	5.3	17.1	5.5	16.9
total	100.0		100.0		100.0		100.0		100.0	

Source: Cass, 1981c: 15, as derived from ABS *Labour Force Surveys*

Much attention has been given in the literature to the fact that postwar years saw a dramatic increase in the number of *married* women in the workforce. In focusing on this trend, writers have often spent much time explaining the specific factors motivating married women to seek paid work. Demographic changes, such as family size or spacing of children, economic necessity, and improved educational qualifications, are mentioned in these accounts (e.g. Richmond, 1974; Cass, 1978b). The relevance of these factors for individual choices made by women to enter paid work can indeed be demonstrated. For example, responsibility for pre-school children is still an important reason for women to stay out of the labourforce; in 1979, 85 per cent of women without dependents in the 20—24 age group were in paid work, compared with 30 per cent of women with dependents in that age group. Also, women who are lone parents are less likely to be in the labour force than wives (Prosser, 1981: 6). However, a preoccupation in research with the characteristics of women moving into paid work may well obscure what really happens. On the one hand such research may be based on an unexamined assumption that women's participation in paid work always requires a special explanation, different from and not determined by the same factors as apply to men. Richmond (1974: 294) notes that women in clerical jobs have relatively small families but that the same appears to apply to men in clerical jobs; she suggests that in this case the social class background of workers may be more important than their gender. If more research were conducted along these lines, it may well be that the characteristics of male and female workers are found to show more similarity than has generally been assumed.

On the other hand, present research also glosses over the fact that married women would not have entered the labour market in such substantial numbers if there had not been a demand for their labour. In making this point I am not suggesting that all married women would take up paid work if the demand for their work were there. Nevertheless, it may be assumed that many more women would engage in full-time or part-time employment if the opportunities (and these include the availability of childcare) were given to them. This is illustrated by the substantial numbers of part-time workers who would prefer to work full time, and of unemployed persons who have given up looking for jobs but would actively look for and accept employment if they felt it were available (Prosser, 1981: 15; Scotton and Ferber, 1980: 35; Cass, 1981c: 35-6).

The early 1970s saw a severe economic recession in Australia leading to high levels of unemployment, especially in the manufacturing field, as a consequence of the introduction of new technologies and the relocation of some industries to the cheaper labour markets of Southeast Asia (Short, 1979; Women's Employment Rights Campaign, 1979). Cass (1981c), Scotton and Ferber (1980), and Jamrozik and Hoey (1981) have conducted in-depth studies of the labour market trends of this last decade. Their research evidences a serious intensification of labour market segmentation since the economic recession of the early 1970s. Data show a slight reversal in the general post-war trends of increased participation for married women, with virtually no new full-time job options for married women at present (Prosser, 1981: 12). Sex segregation has increased further as women have become more and more concentrated in wholesale and retail trades and in community services and have decreased in numbers within production-process work and skilled trades. At the same time there has been a general loss of jobs for young women and a tendency to substitute part-time and casual work for full-time job opportunities, and this mainly in those areas where women's participation has increased: wholesale, and retail trade, finance, insurance, real estate, business services and community services. In other words, what appears to be an improvement is in fact a shift towards positions with low pay and limited job opportunities for career advancement, positions thus typical of the secondary sector of the dual labour market, and contributing to considerable profits for the employer due to lower labour costs (Cass, 1981c: 19).

Also in those areas where women have made some gains, e.g. the professional and technical fields, sex segregation has the effect of creating a hierarchy of authority and control in which males dominate (Cass, 1981c; Deacon, 1981). The movement of women workers out of private industry into the public sector (a shift of 23 per cent between 1966 and 1980) should also be seen in this light. That women now participate in about equal proportions with men in the public sector has limited relevance if most women involved be subordinate to males, or if a substantial number of women work part-time. Beyond this, the threat of increased unemployment because of technological innovations, and/or the drastic cuts in public expenditure for health, education, and welfare, should not be underestimated.

Until now migrant and Aboriginal women, older women (over the age of 45), and very young women have been the hardest hit by unemployment and underemployment, while opportunities continue to exist for well-educated Australian-born and middle-class women. As Cass outlines:

> The decline in the proportions of employed women in production process jobs reflects the decreasing job openings for unskilled migrant women; the increasing proportions in the 'community services' reflects the growth in job opportunities for tertiary educated Australian-born and other English-speaking women. (Cass, 1981c: 5)

However, the present movements within the tertiary sector, and the severe cuts in public expenditure, make one wonder how long this growth in job opportunities in the 'community services' will persist (Power, 1981).

Data on the participation rates of women in the paid labour force then confirm the general thesis on labour market segmentation I reviewed above. The overall trends in women's labour force participation within Australia suggest that women did provide a supply of labour in expanding sectors of the economy in post-war years, first in the 1950s and 1960s in production-process work, later in the 1960s and 1970s in the growing tertiary sector. Women also continued to fill traditional 'women's occupations' in the secondary sector of the dual labour market. The ensuing labour segmentation based on gender, and on birthplace and race, guaranteed flexible pools of labour which could be manipulated into low-level jobs and an ever accelerating spiral of underemployment and unemployment.

It appears that such labour market segmentation can be maintained only because of the presumed primary role of women in domestic labour and their alleged dependence on a male breadwinner. Wages earned by women make an important contribution to *reducing* the incidence of poverty in two-income families (Jamrozik and Hoey, 1981) and in many cases where women are also parents or main bread-winner, to supporting entire families. It remains a sad fact of life, though, that notwithstanding the large number of women in paid work, only a very small proportion of them, mainly women in pro-fessional careers, earn an income that can by itself sustain a family at a decent standard of living (Rein, 1980). Lois Bryson (Chapter 6 in this volume) provides some telling data on income distribution which illustrate this point.

Public policy and women's paid work

To what extent have governments and private enterprise actively encouraged or discouraged the persistence of sex-segregated labour markets and unequal opportunities for women and men in Australia? In order to answer this question adequately, no doubt a full parliamentary inquiry would be necessary as has been undertaken in other countries such as the United States or Canada (New York City Commission on Human Rights, 1970; Committee on Education and Labor, 1970; Royal Commission on the Status of Women in Canada, 1976; Cahn, 1979).

The aim of the present discussion will have to be more modest. I have chosen to review wage fixation policies as an area which appears most crucial to the development of sex segregation, with some attention to the issue of maternity leave, and the question of working hours, as two policy areas of considerable importance to women who need to combine the dual responsibilities of paid and unpaid work. These are all issues in which changes have occurred over the years. Although economic factors seem to be crucial in explaining the changes in policies, in each case women's rights groups and trade unions have played an important role in lobbying for change.

Before embarking on this review, I should note that most public policies which affect women in employment are based upon and created by the interplay of government, private enterprise and unions. In 1974, the latest date for which I have figures, only 7.3 per cent of women in Australia were not covered by awards (Burbidge, 1981: 157). Women who are affected by awards tend to settle their disputes via arbitration rather than through strike action and collective bargaining. This means that most policies regarding the paid employment of women are the outcome of negotiations by the three major interest groups involved in arbitration. It should also be remembered that men usually act as 'gatekeepers' to the paid employment of women, whether in the construction of policies or in the actual process of hiring and firing (Denis, 1980). For example, there have been only a few occasions where women have presided over arbitration cases, one of the most notable being Commissioner Mary Gaudron who presided over the 1974 National Wage Case. And, in the absence of affirmative action programs no policies exist which stipulate that job selection should be monitored by female supervisory staff.

Men's work and women's work, the prewar setting
One of the most striking features of the Australian labour market has been the *deliberate* maintenance of sex segregation as a major national policy. When, in 1907, three years after the establishment of the Commonwealth Arbitration Court, Justice Higgins introduced—in his now famous 'Harvester judgment'—the notion of a 'living wage' based on the 'normal needs of the average employee regarded as a human being living in a civilised community' (Ryan and Conlon, 1975: 90), he provided the Australian working class with a guaranteed minimum income, a provision at that time not yet granted in any other country (Hutson, 1971; Roe, 1976). However, at the same time he set a policy which legitimated and enshrined in law existing practices of sex segregation for a period of at least 60 years. He did this by stipulating that the living wage was to be a family wage for male workers sufficient to keep a man, his wife, and a family of three children in reasonable comfort. All unskilled male workers received this basic wage (with a variable margin added) even though at the time of the Harvester Judgment 45 per cent of the male workforce were single (Whelan, 1979: 55). No basic wage for women was established at the time, but there was general agreement that their wage as single women not assumed to have dependents should be not less than 50 per cent but not more than 54 per cent of the male basic wage, a practice set in 1919 for the Clothing Trades and adopted as a standard by the court (Ryan and Conlon, 1975; Ryan and Rowse, 1975; Beaton, 1980). It is quite apparent from the scholarly literature that the amount set for a living wage was inadequate; one can imagine the austerity of the lives of women (who in many cases were not single and had dependants to support) trying to survive on 54 per cent of that living wage (Baker, 1966; Ryan and Conlon, 1975).

Because in practice decisions of the Arbitration Court were concerned with awards for specific industries and jobs rather than with general wage fixation based on marital status or other such criteria, Justice Higgins decided in 1912 that clear demarcations were required regarding male and female work, thereby providing an additional legal basis for women's lower wages and for protection of male wages against competition by women. This in fact meant exclusion of women from many occupations, and similarly exclusion of male workers from the women's sector of the labour market.

In deciding which occupations were men's work or women's work, Justice Higgins apparently accepted existing customs. In his 1912 decision which dealt with pay rates in the fruit-picking industries he declared that men and women should be paid at the same rate, because at present 'men and women were fairly in competition as to that class of work' (Ryan and Conlon, 1975: 99). However, equal pay was not granted to fruit packers because that work has been carried out mostly by women and girls 'who offered no competition to men' (Ryan and Conlon, 1975: 99). The 1912 Judgment then set the scene for separate pay rates for women's work regardless of productivity; when women were in 'women's work' they were paid a woman's wage, but if in 'men's work' (that is when they competed with males) a male rate should be granted to avoid pushing men out of work (Ryan and Conlon, 1975: 100).

The existence of differential pay rates for women and men encouraged employers to hire women as cheap labour power and the Court was approached on a number of occasions with requests for reclassification of a particular job as woman's work. Also, in several cases where equal pay was requested because workers were deemed to be involved in similar duties, the Court in fact set different rates for men and women (Ryan and Conlon, 1975; Ryan and Rowse, 1975). The implied threat for male workers gave the trade unions only two options: to insist on the maintenance of rigid sex segregation, or to advocate equal pay (Beaton, 1980).[4]

The record shows that in most cases the support by male-dominated unions for equal pay was based on attempts to safeguard males from competition by women. It is possibly significant that trade unions looked more favourably upon equal pay principles during the Depression as a mechanism of keeping women from competing for men's jobs. At that time the Commonwealth Arbitration Court negated the basic principles of the Harvester Judgment for the first time by stipulating that from now on the guiding principle in fixing wages was the 'capacity of industry to pay' (Ryan and Conlon, 1975: 120). Wages were reduced by 10 per cent in all industries as the outcome of that decision, but also in several instances jobs that had been classified as men's jobs and which had provided women in those jobs with equal pay now were reclassified as women's jobs, which meant that women were no longer paid at men's rates. Although this led to severe cuts in women's wages in those industries (fruit-picking, interestingly, was one of them) it must also have had the effect of safeguarding women's work, vis-à-vis men. Power (1979) has argued—against other theorists defending an 'industrial reserve' thesis—that in the Depression unemployment was less severe for women than for men, because the highest rates of unemployment took place in industries where few women were employed. However, she does not mention the reclassification of jobs which took place during the Depression and the effect this had on unemployment rates of men and women. It is quite clear, though, that whatever the degree of competition between women and men for paid work, it was the outcome of deliberate policies implemented to reduce costs to the employer by maintaining cheap female labour. While the reaction of male unionists was often blatantly sexist, traditional union principles were also at stake. The introduction of female workers sometimes gave employers the opportunity to introduce other measures as well, such as piecework, or an accelerated pace of work, which were to the disadvantage of all workers (Stone, 1976: 10).

As said, decisions on classification of jobs as women's or men's work were based on custom. In dubious cases and where reclassification was requested, the nature of the job was taken into account, and when work was seen to be very heavy, or involving the lifting of heavy weights, and as dangerous or dirty, the position would be defined as men's work to the exclusion of women. Jobs seen as suitable to women were often those requiring manual dexterity, limited skill, and work seen to be of a somewhat repetitive nature. An interesting example of the manner in which jobs were stereotyped occurred in 1941, during a dispute within the metal trade about the question whether women were allowed to enter that trade. During the hearings one union representative described the kind of workers needed for the machinery in question as 'men who can become automatons with very little exercise of mentality because all that is required is the operating of the handles of the machines', to which the arbitration court judge replied 'that sounds like a woman's job' (School of Behavioural Science, 1980: 83).

Women in men's jobs?—the war years
The above illustration concerns a dispute which took place during the Second World War. At that time the shortages of male labour especially in war-related industries called for drastic measures. Women were now drawn into paid labour in increasing numbers; the kind of policies implemented to facilitate their entry, however, show clearly that the traditional rights of male workers were guaranteed and that the model of a sex-segregated labour market was at all times

maintained. Government action began in 1940 with so-called 'dilution' agreements, allowing the admission of non-tradesmen to particular trades as a *temporary* measure, under the condition that tradesmen were assured of the preferential right to return to their jobs and that normal standards of training, temporarily suspended, would then resume (Ryan and Rowse, 1975). An urgent demand for telegraph operators in the Royal Air Force brought the government to accept the formation of the Women's Auxiliary Air Force but again on a temporary basis, and at a salary of two-thirds of that of males (Beaton, 1980; 69). When the Japanese entered the war and an even greater war effort was required, the Labor government established a Women's Employment Bureau (WEB) to regulate the employment of women in men's work. The main object of the Bureau was, as stated at the time, 'to secure the maximum release of men for war purposes, to achieve, by the utmost legitimate use of female labour, the maximum war effort' (Foenander, 1943: 110). That the WEB's activities were to be conducted as a crisis measure and with full regard for traditional male privileges is clear from the Prime Minister's declaration:

> as a war measure to approve of the principle of extensive employment of women in industries where men are not available in sufficient numbers to attain the scale of production approved as a war objective...

and

> all women employed under the conditions approved shall be employed only for the duration of the war and shall be replaced by men as they become available. (Beaton, 1980: 69-70).

In principle women employed under the auspices of the WEB were to be paid male rates; however, employers argued again and again that the productivity of women was lower than men because of an alleged higher rate of absenteeism, lesser strength and other assumed differences between males and females. In practice this meant that women's pay rates under the WEB ranged from between 80 to 100 per cent of male rates (Larmour, 1975). For example, tram conductresses, electrical workers, telegraphists, mail officers, clerks in public service, but also hotel barmaids and confectionary workers, were paid at 100 per cent of male rates, while female wool-classers and lorry drivers were paid at 80 per cent (Foenander, 1943). No doubt the threat of competition as well as differential demand played an important part in these variations in pay rates. Justification for entry of women in many industries was, even within this crisis situation, still given in terms of sex-specific job abilities. For example, Foenander, an academic writing as a contemporary, reveals the biases current at the time when he states that the influx of women into industry has been:

> rendered receptive by the strong and vigorous growth in the mech-
> anisation of industry that made available in increasing amounts
> machine and process tasks of a simplified, repetitive or highly mani-
> pulative character suitable to female capacity (Foenander, 1943:
> 110).

The Women's Employment Bureau had only powers to deal with work:

a) which is usually performed by males;

b) which was, during the period from the third day of September
1939, to the date of the employment of, or proposal to employ,
females, performed by males ... or

c) which was not, during that period, performed in Australia by
any person (Foenander, 1943: 113).

By 1943 only approximately 85 000 women had been affected by the
WEB with about 800 000 working women still in traditional female
jobs at 54 per cent of male rates. The manner in which women were
manipulated for the benefit of the war effort and the profit motive is
described vividly by Beaton (1980). She relates how in 1943, when the
entry of US forces in the Pacific region created a need for consumer
goods, the demand for female labour shifted from war-related industries to those in which women had been employed traditionally at very
low pay, such as the food and clothing industry. Beaton says that
when employers were unwilling to raise the pay level in these industries, women were conscripted under the threat of heavy fines by the
Manpower Committee (set up by the federal government at the
beginning of the war) which was now allowed to direct any person to
engage in any specific employment. Most women strongly resisted this
involuntary movement toward poorly paid jobs, but they received
very little support. The conscription of women to lowly paid jobs was
apparently by no means as worrisome as the encouragement of women
into well paid jobs had been earlier during the war years.

Post-war policies to restore the status quo
At the end of the war policies were instituted immediately for the
restoration of pre-war labour market conditions. The Re-establish-
ment and Employment Bill 1945, ensured service personnel automatic
preference in employment and reinstatement in their previous
positions where possible (Ryan and Rowse, 1975; 27). Although many
women remained in paid employment, nearly all were forced out of
men's jobs and those who remained saw their wages reduced from 90
per cent to about 75 per cent of male rates. This percentage was set in
1950 as the outcome of a test case for equal pay taken to the High

Court by the Australian Council of Trade Unions (Ryan and Conlon, 1975: 140-1).[5] The principle of differential wages was maintained on this occasion in a majority judgment which stated that: 'it was socially preferable to provide a high wage to the male because of his social obligation to fiancee, wife and family' (Nieuwenhuysen and Hicks, 1975: 77). As Ryan and Conlon comment:

> Only six years after being told their labour was essential, efficient and highly productive, adult women workers could be made to work for 75 per cent of the male basic wage and on a junior's margin! One would scarcely credit women workers could lose their efficiency so quickly. (Ryan and Conlon, 1975, p.144).

At this time the concept of the basic wage was finally formally recognised through an Act of Parliament, when it was defined as:

> that wage, or part of that wage, which is just and reasonable for an adult male, without regard to any circumstances pertaining to the work upon which, or the industry in which, he is employed, or the principle upon which it is computed. (Hutson, 1971: 9).

This, of course, was only a formality; over the years the principles of sex segregation had become firmly established in most state and federal awards.

Domesticity, suburbia and the consumer society became the ideals held up to women in post-war years (Ryan and Rowse, 1975; Game and Pringle, 1979). Their removal from men's work rendered them again economically invisible (Beaton, 1980). When many, indeed, responded to the ideological pressures to return to home and kitchen, their places were taken by migrant women as a new pool of labour even less likely to challenge the traditional orders of the sex-segregated labour market.

Equal pay?
The 1960s, however, saw a vast expansion of the public service sector and a demand for new recruits. Australian-born women reappeared in the paid labour force to take up positions in the areas of education, social welfare, and other community services newly created as part of this development in the public service. While, ironically, after World War II the entry of large numbers of migrant women in the paid work-force did not lead to any specific policy changes, the recruitment of well-educated, middle-class, Australian-born women into paid work quite clearly set the scene for some reforms. One of the issues to come under attack in most States was that of the continued inequalities between male and female wages.[6] The principle of equal pay which was established eventually was the outcome of decisions laid down in various State awards and handed down by the Commonwealth Con-

ciliation and Arbitration Commission in the equal pay cases of 1969, 1972 and 1974. In fact, it was a victory 'that was won again and again' (Gaudron and Bosworth, 1979: 161).

The 1969 equal pay case initiated by the Liberal government established the notion of equal pay for equal work. Coming within the context of a rigidly defined demarcation between the sexes, it ensured equal pay for only a very small number of female workers estimated at about 18 per cent of total numbers (Nieuwenhuysen and Hicks, 1975: 78). After all, to accept that those who do the same work should receive the same pay has little relevance if women do not do the same work as men. As Ryan and Conlon remark with reference to the first equal pay amendment reached in New South Wales in 1959: 'the fortuitous division between work that was mainly men's work and work that was mainly women's work saved the day for the employers' (Ryan and Conlon, 1975: 148).

The case for equal pay was reopened by the new Labor government in 1972 and the notion of equal pay for equal *value* which was applied then in the National Wage case had a much more profound effect. For the first time it was now recognised that women should receive the same rate of pay as males, whatever work they were doing. However, one more issue had to be resolved, the longstanding policy of granting to males a special wage based on the understanding that they had a family to support. The original notion of a basic 'living wage' plus margins had already been challenged, and was replaced in 1967 by the concept of a 'total wage' *and* the notion of a male minimum wage. That problem was tackled in 1974, and one minimum wage for men and women was adopted. This national wage case was a follow on from the ratification by the Australian government of the International Labour Office Convention No. 100, on equal pay for work of equal value.

An important new development in the 1974 case was the effective intervention of women's rights groups in the arbitration procedures. Representatives of three women's movement groups made submissions in the case on behalf of low-paid women. These were the Union of Australian Women, the National Council of Women, and Women's Electoral Lobby. In addition a submission was presented by a woman advocate of the Department of Labour in the Australian Labor government (Ryan and Conlon, 1975: 170). WEL played an especially prominent part in this equal pay case by providing evidence in court of the number of families in Australia without a male breadwinner, where women as sole breadwinners required the benefit of a minimum wage equal to that paid to males.

What was accomplished in 1974 was 'theoretical equality in pay rates' (Gaudron and Bosworth, 1979: 169). This was certainly a significant advance for Australian female workers as is shown clearly in the wage increases women in specific trades now received. However, overall equality in incomes between women and men had not been accomplished by these changes. For example, 'the weighted average minimum weekly pay rates for females rose from 70.9 per cent in 1960, to 77.4 per cent in 1972, to 88.5 per cent in 1976 of the weighted average for males' (Gaudron and Bosworth, 1979: 169). As Gaudron and Bosworth note:

> Equal pay can only be reality when it is accompanied by the extension of equal access to jobs, by affirmative action to end discrimination in employment and by constant effort by women's organisations and women in the trade unions to safeguard and extend the gains already made. (1979: 169).

Equal pay is not just a matter of minimum award wages. Differentials in over-award payments, restrictions on the access of women to certain jobs, and generally the distinction between women's jobs and men's jobs, with most women's jobs in the secondary sector of the labour market, were still maintained. A range of other policies was required to resolve the remaining basic inequalities in opportunities between male and female workers.

Equal opportunity?
During the 1960s and 1970s advances were made in eliminating some of the factors contributing to inequality of opportunity. These include the removal in 1966 of the so-called marriage bar in the public service, the establishment of various mechanisms to further anti-discrimination legislation in the 1970s, and the *National Maternity Leave* case in 1978-79.

The reason for the removal of the marriage bar appears to have been purely economic; the demand for female recruits to the expanding public service made it essential that trained women workers be retained after marriage. Changes in the political scene in the 1970s brought deliberate policies on the part of government to reduce inequalities, including the appointment of women to several key positions in the public service.[7] The greater number of women in permanent positions within the government sector provided the networks necessary to keep a watching brief on the development of new policies and their implementation. (See Sara Dowse elsewhere in this book.)

The marriage bar. Potentially one of the most important policy changes was the removal of the marriage bar which had excluded married women from permanent positions in the commonwealth public service from its very beginning.[8] As Deacon points out, the *Public Service Act* of 1902 institutionalised the normative expectation that married women should not work outside the home, and effectively sealed women in to the secondary labourmarket and its spiral of disadvantage. (Deacon, 1981: 8).

Although there were no formal barriers to single women, in practice women in the public service were not granted the opportunities for training and promotion that would have given them access to more senior positions. Thus, effectively they remained in the lower-level clerical jobs in the Fourth Division without any movement to the higher ranks. It was not until 1949 that they were admitted to the examinations for the Third Division (Deacon, 1981: 18).

The lifting of the marriage bar in 1966, which was accompanied by a resolution providing for maternity leave for women in the public service, considerably increased employment opportunities for women. However, as Deacon demonstrates, it did not have the effect of eliminating sex segregation within the public service. Competition for jobs is still between women, not with men. The majority of women are still in the Fourth Division, and have very little opportunity for promotion to the top positions from there. Although women have increased their share of the Third Division (now about one-third of workers in this division) they are mostly located in 'non-management' categories, thereby being excluded from the 'pool of eligibles for the executive positions of the Second and First Divisions' (Deacon, 1981: 19). If eligible for promotion, women still have many formal and informal barriers to scale. For example, seniority is an important factor in assessing eligibility for advancement. However, women can only count their seniority from 1966 when married women were admitted to permanent positions. It is also apparent that many other decisions are required to eliminate discrimination against women in specific job categories. For example, in 1976 a policy change in the Foreign Service for the first time allowed women diplomats to be posted overseas. The Australian Navy instituted integrated officer training in 1978; the Air Force had similar arrangements as early as the 1960s. However, women are not yet admitted to any units which may be engaged in combat during war time.

The issue of anti-discrimination. In 1973 the Whitlam government ratified the ILO Convention No. 111 on Discrimination in Employment and Occupation, and in 1974 the government became party to international conventions concerned with promoting civil rights of women, the United Nations Convention on the Political Rights of Women to Take and Hold Public Office on Equal Terms with Men, and the ILO Convention No. 100 on equal pay which I mentioned earlier. Also, International Women's Year in 1975 marked the occasion for a number of valuable projects initiated with government support which further encouraged women's participation in public life.

Ratification of the ILO Convention No. 111 on Discrimination led in 1973 to the establishment of national and state committees on Discrimination in Employment and Occupations, as a first step in a program intended by the Whitlam government to combat discrimination. Although well intentioned, the sanctions available to these committees have been limited (Ronalds, 1981).

Anti-discrimination legislation which proscribes discrimination on grounds of sex and marital status has been instituted in New South Wales, Victoria and South Australia since the late 1970s; this has given women access to *legal* channels in fighting discriminatory practices in hiring, firing or career advancement. A few spectacular successes have been gained such as in the Wardley case, but great emotional burdens are placed on individual complainants and the costs involved in taking legal action are prohibitive (Thornton, 1979a). Also, it is not always certain whether women working under federal awards in these States have access to state anti-discrimination legislation (Ronalds, 1980). The *Human Rights Commission Act* (Com) established in 1981 with the aim of ensuring that Australian 'laws conform with various United Nations instruments dealing with human rights that have been ratified by the Commonwealth Government' (Thornton, 1981), is formulated in very general terms, and deals with the operation of the Human Rights Commission itself rather than with specifications of what human rights are. As Thornton notes, the Act defines the commission only as a last resort if all other avenues of action fail.

Anti-discrimination legislation in Australia is, thus, still in its infancy. 'Class action', instituted by one or two persons on behalf of a group, is being discussed as a possible procedure, but has not yet been used.[9] The traditional rights of employers to choose their employees and to dismiss workers at short notice which are still entrenched in Australian labour laws, although affecting job security of all workers, are especially damaging to women's rights.[10] Anti-discrimination legislation does not have the teeth to overcome such problems. And when it concerns long-term trends such as the movement toward part-time work for women, or decline of employment opportunity because of technological change, present anti-discrimination legislation may in specific cases deal with the *result* of such long-term trends but it cannot anticipate future situations which may show to be discriminatory. Jocelynne Scutt takes up the issue of anti-discrimination again in Chapter 11.

Maternity leave. In recent years women unionists have gained greater opportunities for action to improve the access of women to equal job opportunities. This is the case with specific unions, such as the Teachers Federation in some states, but also, and most significantly, in the context of the Australian Council of Trade Unions. In 1977 a working women's charter was adopted unanimously by the ACTU Congress, and a Women's Charter Committee appointed by the ACTU executive began its work in early 1978. The priorities for action set by the first conference called by this Committee were maternity leave, childcare and equal pay. The first case in fact to be taken up by the ACTU was that of maternity leave.

As with many other policies, Australia 'was a latecomer to the idea of maternity leave' (Lynch and Tiffin, 1979). The ILO had issued a convention recommending paid maternity leave for 12 weeks as early as 1919, with more extensive legislation following in 1952 (ILO Convention 103). Although many countries had ratified these conventions, Australia did not. Instead the Liberal–Country Party coalition government introduced maternity leave without pay only within the public service in 1966. In 1972 this policy was changed by the Labor government into a provision for 12 weeks paid maternity leave with guaranteed re-employment after confinement. Various awards in the public and private sector established some provisions for maternity leave, most, however, without proper job protection. It has been estimated that at the end of the 1970s about 42.4 per cent of working women were covered by some kind of maternity leave provision (Lynch and Tiffin, 1979: 34).

At the end of 1978 the ACTU mounted a test case for maternity leave in federal awards which was argued by the ACTU advocate Jan Marsh. The main provision contained in the final decision on the case (handed down in 1979) was for unpaid leave up to a period of 52 weeks, with 6 weeks compulsory leave prior to confinement, and for the leave to be only available after a 12-months eligibility period. Absence during maternity leave was not to be counted toward seniority, and although re-employment was to be guaranteed, job offers after return to work could be at a lower pay rate if the previous job no longer existed. It was not a decision that would cause employers much hardship (Ryan, 1980).

Representatives of five women's organisations intervened in support of the case, as well as representatives of three state Labor governments, with the Women's Electoral Lobby taking a prominent place in the debate. It is interesting to note that the defence placed considerable emphasis on the importance of the role of mothers in child-rearing as evidence for the leave claim. As Lynch and Tiffin comment, this:

> reinforces the division of family responsibility and undermines the possibility of securing parental leave, whereby the father would also

have the opportunity to leave the paid workforce and care for his infant children. (Lynch and Tiffin, 1979: 35).

The fact that the leave granted is unpaid means that in fact only middle-class women, who have the support of a male breadwinner, can take full advantage of it. Working-class women have gained little from the provisions of this maternity leave case, as they need to return to paid work as soon as possible, something they are unable to do under the regulation that 12 weeks of leave are to be compulsory. Also the qualifying period of 12 months, which was included in the provisions upon the recommendation of the Women's Electoral Lobby[11], is a serious disadvantage to working women in lower paid jobs where turnover rates are high. Notwithstanding these drawbacks, 'the overriding ideological significance of the judgment is its recognition of a woman's right both to remain in the paid workforce and bear children' (Lynch and Tiffin, 1979: 40). It is clear then that maternity leave encourages women's participation in paid labour while at the same time reinforcing their ideological identification with mothering.

Current trends
Female unionists continue to act upon priorities set at the first conference organised by the ACTU Women's Charter Committee. Surveys have been conducted on the issue of *equal pay* which have shown that considerable sex-based differences in over-award payments and superannuation provisions still exist. (See Bryson, elsewhere in this volume). At present efforts are being made to rectify these inequities for all awards in question. Union awareness has been raised on the importance of *childcare* as a public responsibility and as a right of both parents to be involved with the care of children. At the same time the ACTU Women's Committee has taken initiatives to provide better protection of the health of female workers, to provide training courses for women unionists interested in union leadership positions, and to protect the rights of women engaged in part-time work (ACTU, 1979b). Recently the ACTU congress adopted a policy in support of women's access to free abortion as a measure deliberately intended to improve women's employment opportunities. The Australian Labor Party, in opposition, continued to argue for more effective anti-discrimination legislation, improved childcare, availability of unemployment benefits regardless of marital status, and other measures which would promote equality of women in paid work.

Since coming to office in 1976, the Fraser government established a twelve-member National Women's Advisory Council to advise the government through the Minister of Home Affairs (Pringle, 1979). This council has given special attention to the problems experienced by migrant women, unemployment problems in rural areas and general issues of employment and training for women. It has argued for flexible work patterns and arrangements providing greater opportunities for part-time work. It has also acknowledged the consequences for women's employment of increased technological change and has taken a firm stand on the need for more extensive legislation to combat discrimination in employment (National Women's Advisory Council, 1979). In 1980 the council organised a National Women's Conference with, as its main purpose, the drafting of recommendations to government for discussion at the International Mid-Decade for Women Conference held in Copenhagen later that year.

Through its Department of Employment and Youth Affairs the Fraser government initiated campaigns for equal employment opportunity guidelines to employers and on apprenticeship training for women.[12] These were generally public relations exercises which, although useful in bringing the problems of high unemployment of women and girls to the attention of the public, did not lead to any clear directives to industry such as found in affirmative action or equal opportunity programs in other countries. At the same time there is, as documented elsewhere in this book, a renewed emphasis on pronatalist policies, and a push toward private home-based solutions for problems of health, welfare and unemployment.

Future prospects

The women's movement has on the whole attacked government policies which have the effect of reinforcing the role of women as homemakers. However, there are two issues on which the movement appears internally divided. One concerns the implementation of policies allowing pay for housework, the other the encouragement of part-time work. It is quite clear that the more conservative women's groups would like to see the 'status' of housework improved and expect that some form of payment for housework would ensure recognition of women's responsibility as homemakers. From time to time representatives of employers' organisations and of some of the established churches have made newspaper headlines with suggestions along the same lines, such as for increased tax rebates for dependent spouses or homemakers' allowances. The government has kindled these interests by its proposals for income splitting as a tax incentive for single-income families but has always distanced itself from any demands for wages for housework because of the expense involved (Windschuttle, 1974). Radical women's groups overseas have at times supported the notion of paid housework (Dallacosta and James, 1972); they have generally been motivated in this by the desire to ensure economic independence for women and to create a common class base for male and female workers. However, others, overseas and in Australia, have pointed to the dangerous implications such a wage for housework would have (e.g. James, 1975: 28; Windschuttle, 1974). In the words of Windschuttle:

> If the government supports the idea of a mother's wage, it contributes in a small way to the enormous institutional and ideological forces that cause women to see themselves (falsely) only as housewives and mothers... (Windschuttle, 1974: 22).

The feasibility of a wage for housework is small. A much more contentious policy, because easier to implement, is the one concerning part-time work. It is apparent that not only the Women's Committee of the ACTU, and the National Women's Advisory Council, but also employers' organisations *and* federal and State governments, favour the provision of part-time work. The ACTU's emphasis has been on regulation of part-time work in order to prevent exploitation (ACTU, 1979a), but it is significant that even in the case of the ACTU Women's Committee the introduction of part-time work provisions is encouraged, and that the emphasis is on part-time work for the benefit of *female* workers, who need to combine part-time work with home duties. On the other hand, traditional unionists seem to have ignored the existence of large numbers of part-time workers. Instead they have centred attention on provisions for a shorter working week (Bielski, 1981). In so doing they have not taken any notice of the needs of women workers operating in a society in which they continue to be seen as the main caretakers of their children. Just to provide one example, current trade union proposals for shortening of working hours through the introduction of a nine-day fortnight or a nineteen-day month, do not make reference at all to any changes in the scheduling of school hours. If present practices continue women workers who have to fit their work routines to the timetables of their children will be severely disadvantaged if and when shorter working hours are introduced, because it will be even more difficult than it is already to synchronise their *new* work rosters with their home-related duties (Baldock, 1981). There is considerable danger that present policy trends in this area will reinforce the sex segregation of the labour market and put women further back in their attempts to job equality (Power, 1981). It is after all quite likely that by the time the unions have reached their agreement with employers over the reduction of working hours to 35 hours a week, many women who could have benefited from the continuity and security of a full-time job on reduced hours would have been transferred to part-time jobs on reduced wages, or made redundant altogether (Baldock, 1981: 14).

Students of policy trends in overseas countries have predicted an increased emphasis on public policies oriented toward homemaking. They have argued that governments are motivated to encourage such policies for three reasons, (a) to reduce unemployment; (b) to curb inflation; and (c) to hold down social welfare spending. For example, specific policies that are envisaged for the USA are changes in pensions and property laws to recognise housework, financial support for so-called 'displaced' homemakers, that is women left without financial support after divorce, and provisions for supporting mothers' benefits (Adams and Winston, 1980).

The short-term benefits of such measures for women caught in the role of homemaker may be considerable. Such short-term benefits appear indeed to be the main incentive for actions by the ACTU Women's Committee and other women's groups to increase opportunities for part-time work. As stated in a recent report from that committee:

> There is continuing need to remind the trade union movement and society generally, that although women work for exactly the same reasons as do men, the demands upon their time and energies are substantially different. (ACTU, 1979b: 3).

However attractive in the short term, the long-term effect of any policies emphasising the special obligations of women toward home and children is to act as a trap, keeping women forever locked in their dependent positions within an ever continuing sexual division of labour.

The future of technology
The most severe threats at present to women's job opportunities are, in my view, found in the effect of technological change[13] and in reductions of government spending on community services. Women are heavily concentrated in the areas of employment vulnerable to these changes. Power has suggested that the only possible remedies for this situation of present and future unemployment lie in the provision of unemployment benefits for married women and in effective programs for job creation, *not* geared toward traditional areas of female employment but towards the opening of traditionally male areas to women workers (Power, 1981). There is, however, one further matter to be considered, and that is the overall change in the nature of work, due to advanced technology. One recent study has noted the following trends within factory organisations (School of Behavioural Science, 1980):

1   A narrowing in the range of skills with a reduction in the number of highly skilled jobs and deskilling in the others.

2   Work becoming less heavy, involving less physical exertion, because of use of lighter materials and automatic transfer equipment.

3 Work getting less dirty and dangerous in the traditional sense, although possibly subject to new health hazards associated with automation.

4 Work becoming increasingly boring, with focus on machine minding and the use of simple push buttons.

5 Less physical mobility with people's movement controlled by machines.

Such trends, it has been argued, erode the basis for distinguishing between men's and women's jobs, because all jobs become increasingly like women's jobs as they were traditionally defined. With proper programs of affirmative action and anti-discrimination this kind of development could lead to a breakdown of sex segregation. In the absence of such measures, and while ideological pressures continue on women and men to define women's task as primarily focused on home and family, it is more likely that *new* distinctions will develop between men's jobs and women's jobs. Women may be allocated to the simple or outmoded machines, whereas males are given the more up-to-date and more complex equipment. In that way 'the sense that men have better jobs than women can be maintained' (School of Behavioural Science, 1980: 103).

There appears little likelihood, then, within the near future of the resolution of the sexual division of labour. Even if the grounds on which segmentation of the labour force is defended shift, there is no indication of any change in the ideological commitment to the maintenance of the patriarchy as it is reflected in policies reinforcing women's dependent status and men's non-participation in childcare and home care.

Home and work in the capitalist economy: a final comment

Most writers seem to be in agreement that women fulfil two important functions for the capitalist economy to operate effectively and efficiently. In the first place women act as members of flexible and expandable pools of labour in a segmented labour market. But secondly, and equally important, women maintain the social relations of reproducing the workforce through the institutions of the family and the unpaid labour in it (Eisenstein, 1979; Kuhn and Wolpe, 1978; Curthoys, 1979). Women bear children, they keep husbands and children in a state of fitness and health, cater for their emotional wellbeing and socialise their children into the values and ideologies, work habits and behaviour patterns of the market economy, thereby maintaining the present and future labour force.

In addition, women's domestic labour is said to contribute directly to the profits of capitalism. The organisation of individual home units in which women preside over the privatised needs of their families stimulates consumption and guarantees the capitalist enterprise a ready market for its products (see Pringle, elsewhere in this book). Also, unpaid domestic labour adds to the profit of the capitalist by reducing the wages of the wage earner. At one time such unpaid domestic service, e.g. cooking, washing, sewing, childcare, may be said to have been contained in the 'family wage' paid out to male workers under the assumption that they had a family to maintain. But now the concept of a family wage is no longer adhered to, the unpaid labour in the home adds significantly to the value extracted from the paid labourer. Finally, the unpaid domestic and volunteer work of women reduces costs incurred in professional social welfare for the elderly, or the sick (Baldock, 1980, see also Chapter 14).

It is, again, generally agreed that the state plays an important part in facilitating women's contribution to the capitalist economy, through labour market policies which reinforce women's role as expendable workers, and as MacIntosh has put it, through its support for a specific form of household, i.e. dependent largely upon a male wage and upon female domestic servicing (McIntosh, 1978). My review of Australian public policies on paid work has confirmed that the state has played this part consistently within this country.

It is also generally assumed that the role of women in domestic and paid labour are mutually reinforcing. The continued importance of domestic labour and the allocation of women to it reduce women's opportunity to participate fully in paid work. As Curthoys says:

> the basis of the unequal sexual division of labour in paid work is the sexual division of labour in unpaid childcaring which in turn is reinforced by the unequal sexual division of labour in paid work. (Curthoys, 1979: 61).

If this is so, there is very little hope for any improvement in the situation of women. However, it could be argued that the two main aims of the capitalist economy satisfied by the work of women, i.e. the maintenance of productive forces (labour power) and the maintenance of the social relations of reproduction, are not always mutually supportive. In fact, it could be suggested that changes in women's position occur at those times that these two main aims of the capitalist economy become mutually contradictory.

As we have seen in this overview, capitalism, in its search to maintain its productive forces has itself freed women from the 'chains' of domesticity. The entry of women in the paid labour force during war years, and, again—but under different conditions—in the 1960s was not a concession to women's demands but instead a direct response to the need for labour power in private enterprise and public service. On the other hand, there continues to be strong ideological support for the maintenance of the family and the unpaid domestic labour in it. Thus we find side by side pressure on women to support the ideology of motherhood and home life, and at the same time to fight for equal opportunity in the workplace. What are the material conditions under which these two sets of contradictory ideologies continue to coexist? Will one prevail at any one time, thereby clearing the path for social change? Could capitalism, for example in a period of vast economic expansion and labour shortage, condone or even support socialisation of household and childcare duties in order to free women for full participation in paid work? Experiences during World War II suggest that this is so. On the other hand, is it feasible that in a period of economic recession accompanied by a financial crisis of the state, all or most welfare services hitherto provided by professionals employed by the state are handed over to volunteers,

Table 2.5 Material and ideological relations between domestic and paid labour

material conditions		policy change	
paid labour	domestic labour	paid labour	domestic labour
increased demand for women's paid work	decreased availability of women's unpaid labour	facilitation of entry and participation of women in paid workforce	measures to socialise household duties provision for professional service for care of sick and elderly
decreased demand for women's paid work	increased availability of women's unpaid work	hindrance of entry and participation in paid work force	desocialisation of household duties encouragement of volunteer services
decreased availability of paid labour	increased demand for women's domestic labour	discouragement of entry and participation of women in paid work	facilitation of women's active involvement with home duties facilitation of involvement of women's volunteer tasks
increased availability of women in paid labour	decreased demand for women's domestic labour	encouragement of women to participate in paid labour	discouragement of women's involvement in home duties discouragement of women from taking up volunteer labour

available for unpaid labour in a domestic setting because they have been ousted from the paid job market? The present economic crisis appears to provide examples of this.

A systematic answer to these kinds of questions is not possible given the data we have available. It would require an analysis of all the dynamic forces involved in the material and ideological relations between domestic and paid labour along lines suggested in Table 2.5. That such an analysis would contribute to our understanding of the relationships between the material and ideological demands for paid and unpaid labour, and thus of the complex connections between capitalism and patriarchy cannot be doubted.

Acknowledgements

I acknowledge with thanks help given with this chapter by David Baldock, Kathy Brown, Ann Holden, Anna Kanaris and Beverly Thiele.

Notes

1   These were actual comments made to me by shop stewards during informal discussions following a shop stewards' training session.
2   Unpublished interview data collected by Cora Baldock and Beverly Thiele, Perth, 1979.
3   See also Paige Porter's chapter on education elsewhere in this book.
4   It should be noted that the Federal Public Service has recognised equal pay since 1902; by 1923, however this principle had been abolished completely and been replaced by those implied in the Harvester and Fruitpickers judgment (Ryan and Conlon, 1975: 100).
5   The ACTU had adopted a statement in support of equal pay for the first time in 1938.
6   The Australian government had supported the ILO convention No.100 on equal pay but had not ratified it.
7   These included Elizabeth Reid, adviser on Women's Issues to the Prime Minister; two women judges to the Arbitration Commission, Elizabeth Evatt and Mary Gaudron; a woman Australian Ambassador, Ruth Dobson; and a woman to direct an Australian Government Commission, Marie Coleman (McKinley, 1979: 274).
8   State regulations had varied with regards to the Marriage Bar. MacKinolty (1979) reports, for example, on a policy change in Victoria during the depression (1932) when married women *lost* the right to permanent employment in the State teaching service, unless there were charitable reasons for them to continue. In order to assess women's eligibility for continuation of permanent service they had to complete a form each year with income details. As MacKinolty says: 'for those retained on charitable grounds, continued employment was now dependent on the failure of their husbands to support the family unit' (MacKinolty, 1979: 146).
9   The principle is accepted in the New South Wales *Anti-Discrimination Act*, but has not yet been used (Thornton, 1981).
10   Senator Patricia Giles addressed this issue in her maiden speech in Senate, on 16 September 1981.
11   It is possible that the 12-months qualifying period would have been included

anyway; even if so the WEL recommendation was an unfortunate concession to employers' demands.

12 Per 30 June 1980 there were about 137 000 apprentices in training in Australia; excluding hairdressing, only 535 of these were *women*.

13 In a recent article it was predicted that between 17 and 23 per cent of people in the typist/secretary category in 1976 would be displaced by word processors by 1982 (McDonald and Mandeville, 1980). It is interesting to note that the authors of that article did not consider this cause for alarm.

3 Redistribution to children and to mothers: a history of child endowment and family allowances

BETTINA CASS

A study of the development and introduction of child endowment and family allowance policies in Australia must be placed within the history of the doctrine of the 'living wage', its implementation in the Commonwealth Court of Conciliation and Arbitration and in the various state arbitration tribunals in the early years of the twentieth century, and the concerted efforts made to revise, redefine or discredit the concept and its application. Advocacy for the introduction of child endowment or family endowment provisions gained political momentum from the end of World War I, at the same time as attacks on the legitimacy of the 'living wage' concept. The history of attempts to introduce child endowment as a 'social policy' illustrates well the contention that social policy cannot be separated from economic policy, and that the political definition of a measure as 'social' very often hides its economic purpose (Roe, 1976). The interconnections of the economic (in the shape of wage fixation policies) and the social (in the shape of a welfare measure to redistribute income to the mothers of dependent children) are manifestly clear in the child endowment debates.

Child endowment and the living wage: class relations

The principle of the 'living wage' in Australia was formulated by members of the labour movement and by liberal politicians, judges and churchmen in the late nineteenth century in a period of unemployment and strikes which seriously weakened trade union strength and the bargaining power of labour. It was a demand for an 'ethical' wages policy which would use the power of state tribunals to intervene in 'free' labour market mechanisms in which labour and capital met on unequal terms. The 'living wage' debate was surrounded by notions of 'social justice', and the protection of low wage-earners from being driven below subsistence levels. This was translated into the rights of *adult male* workers to a basic minimum wage which allowed them and their families to be maintained in reasonable comfort (Higgins, 1920; Sawkins, 1933; Macarthy, 1967; Ryan and Conlon, 1975).

In the Commonwealth Court of Conciliation and Arbitration in 1907 this concept was made concrete by Mr Justice Higgins in the 'Harvester Judgment', as that minimum wage which would be 'fair and reasonable' to meet the needs of an unskilled labourer, his wife and three dependent children. in the New South Wales Arbitration Court in 1914, Mr Justice Heydon redefined the domestic unit for ascertaining the 'living wage' to a man, his wife and two dependent children. Wage fixation tribunals in the commonwealth and the states formally accepted the needs of a domestic unit of either five or four members (headed by an unskilled male breadwinner) as the stated formula for fixing a 'living' (later called a 'basic') wage for all unskilled adult male labour (Hutson, 1971).

From 1919, the trade unions' endorsement and utilisation of the 'family needs principle' in their wage bargaining strategy came under increasing challenge from the opposing concept, 'the capacity of industry to pay', the ideological nub of the employer case which gained ascendancy from 1934, but not without continuing contestation from the unions (Hagan, 1981). The importance of the size of the actual domestic unit on which the basic wage was determined has been disputed by later commentators (e.g. Anderson, 1939), with the claim that the 'capacity of the state to pay' had more bearing on actual wage determinations from the inception of the Harvester equivalent in 1907. This may well be an accurate reflection of the dominance of employer claims in arbitration tribunals dating from well before the 1930s, but it ignores the bargaining significance of the 'family needs' principle in the trade union case for the preservation of the Harvester equivalent and the protection of the gains won in 1907.

Although the principle of a 'family wage' was not institutionalised in centralised wage fixation tribunals or in collective wage bargaining in the United Kingdom and the United States, the demand for a 'living wage' with a family component for adult male labour was also utilised as a strategy by the British and the American labour movements. Demands made from 1919 by organised labour for wage increases which would keep pace with inflation and maintain adequately a working man and his dependants (a standard family of five), were met with the counter-attack that not all the produced wealth of industry, if distributed equally amongst working men, would be sufficient to meet union demands for adequate family subsistence (Piddington, 1921; Rathbone, 1924; Douglas, 1925).

Arguments for 'child endowment', 'motherhood endowment', 'family endowment' or 'family allowances', as the policy was variously named and widely publicised by its advocates A.B. Piddington in Australia, Eleanor Rathbone in the United Kingdom and Paul

Douglas in the United States in the first half of the 1920s, were framed within the living wage debate. Although their writings, in particular those of Douglas, can be interpreted as providing ideological support for attacks on the legitimacy of the living wage and its family component, their arguments also introduced issues which broadened the terms of that debate. These were firstly, issues of the separate rights of children and their mothers to an independent income: rights which inhered in them as citizens, not rights which they derived from their status as dependants of a husband/father/breadwinner. Rathbone argued that organised labour's principle of a 'family wage' provided mothers and children with only secondary, mediated rights which were, moreover, unenforceable because no authority was vested with the power to ensure that working men distributed to their wives and children that margin of the wage which was their due. In her conception (1924: 263), only 'direct provision' to mothers in respect of their children 'implies the recognition of wives and children as persons whose claims on the community arise out of their own reserve value to it and not out of the husband's and father's contribution to industry' (Rathbone, 1924: 263).

Similarly, Piddington extended the notion of rights to 'fair and reasonable' standards of subsistence which had been accorded to male employees by Higgins in the Harvester Judgment and spoke of the separate rights of children as individual citizens and the more severely limited rights of their mothers:

> a strict and even-handed canon of plain justice will recognise that the children of those engaged in industry have a right to maintenance from industry and that the mother who rears children for the future of industry and the State has a right to receive the only wage she ever asks—enough to enable her as society's trustee for nurture and education to discharge the duties of her trust (Piddington, 1921: 29-30).

A related issue these advocates addressed was that of family poverty, which they saw as arising from the mismatch between adult male wage rates and family size: between the wage and the demands made upon it. It was contended that minimum wage rates for adult male labour were more than adequate for a single man; sufficient for a man, wife and one child, but quite inadequate when family size increased. In Australia where the Harvester equivalent had been operating since 1907, evidence presented to the Royal Commission on the Basic Wage in 1920 had demonstrated that the 'living wage' as declared had never been adequate to meet the needs of reasonable comfort and subsistence for a family of more than husband, wife and one child (Piddington, 1921). Only family endowment i.e. separate transfers of income to the mothers of dependent children, would sever the connection between wage-fixation and family size; allowing adult male wage rates to be based on the needs of either a man and his wife (as argued by Piddington and Rathbone) or a single man (as argued by Douglas).

Income transfers to mothers in respect of their dependent children would not only provide social recognition of the value of motherhood, alleviate poverty in families where the numbers of children outstripped their father's earning capacity and ensure that the money was spent on children since mothers were considered to be 'naturally' committed to their children's welfare, but would also solve the problem currently confronting industry and the state. This was the problem of the 'living wage' based on a standard family of five: a flat wage rate for all adult male employees which was being asked to support a very large number of 'phantom' wives and 'phantom' children. Statistical evidence was produced to show that the average family size of male employees was in fact not five but three (man, wife and one child) while a significant proportion of male employees (in Australia about 62 per cent) had neither wife nor children, or had a wife but no dependent children. If consideration of dependent children was to be removed from living-wage declarations, then savings would be made on the wages bill; sufficient savings to allow for a certain portion to be transferred to mothers for the benefit of *existing* children, either through state-organised taxation or through voluntary, employer-organised schemes.

There was debate over the size of the unit to attract the adult male basic wage. Piddington and Rathbone argued for a man and his wife on the grounds that single men would be able to save for marriage; that single men incurred extra costs in paying for services which wives rendered free of charge (laundry, cooking, cleaning etc.); and so that employers would not be given an incentive to discriminate against the employment of married men which they might do if their wages were higher. Douglas however argued that the single man should constitute the wage standard, not only because it was cheaper for industry, but also because this individual-based wage could be applied to female labour, thus ending wage discrimination based on the premise of men's family obligations. One of the major elements in Rathbone's systematic critique of the 'family wage' concept was that the case for equal pay for women could only be fought by removing the issue of men's family obligations from wage-fixing consideration:

a system of direct provision or family allowances ... will, once and for all, cut away the maintenance of children and the reproduction of the race from the question of wages and allow wages to be determined by the value of the workers' contribution to production, without reference to his family responsibilities. (Rathbone, 1924: 116).

All the advocates argued that direct provision for children should be made not by employers paying their employees according to their family size (since this would result in discrimination against employees with dependants) but by 'pooling the provision for them and pooling the obligation to make that provision' (Piddington, 1921: 30). This might be done either through state-organised transfers from taxation revenues or through voluntary schemes organised by industry. Piddington and Rathbone favoured the former: Piddington recommending a tax on employers according to the numbers of their employees and Rathbone arguing that the state method would allow for more efficient and equitable distribution of national resources and more effective recognition of the value of maternity and childhood independently of other forms of productive services. Douglas pointed out that various voluntary schemes organised through associations of employers (which already existed in France, Germany and Belgium) enabled various employer federations, grouped on either a regional or an industrial basis, to 'equalise' the costs of supporting their employees' dependants. Douglas clearly favoured such schemes which provided efficient means of wage control and labour discipline, by allowing for the standard male wage rate to be kept relatively low and through cessation of payments for children in the case of strikes, lockouts and workers' absences (Rathbone, 1924). It is significant also that in most cases the French and German employer-based funds made child-related payments to the wage earner and not to the mother. It was considered preferable by some critics of these schemes that separate payment be made to mothers so as to reduce the animosity of childless workers towards the fathers of families who appeared to be provided with a 'bonus'. As the trade unions recognised, increased wages for employees with children, while not leading to discrimination against them because of the operation of 'equalisation funds', nevertheless produced divisions and conflict of interests between the childless and those with children.

Most trade unions in England, France, Germany and Australia were united in arguing that family allowances be paid out of state funds and organised on a centralised state basis, because the allowances would be paid during strikes, lockouts and unemployment; because the basic wage would not be lowered to the same extent as it was in employer-based schemes; and because the raising of revenue through taxation would shift the burden to the rich through income and inheritance taxes, rather than by allowing employers to shift the burden to the workers by increasing the price of commodities.

In Douglas's conception of the problem, the mode of provision of family allowance was clearly a class issue:

The advocates of state allowances want the allowances to be given as net additions to existing wages. They do not want them to be used to lower the basic wage to the needs of the single man, or to transfer the sums paid out in allowances from the pockets of the bachelors to those with dependents. They want to increase, at the expense of the employer and owning classes, the share received by labour as a whole. (Douglas, 1925: 215).

Despite their discussion of the uses of family allowances to recognise the individual rights of children and to a lesser extent of mothers, to alleviate family poverty and to remove one of the major bastions of wage injustice for women, Piddington, Douglas and Rathbone situated their analyses and their polemics squarely within anti-labour attacks on the legitimacy of the 'living wage' concept. Rathbone and Douglas defined the question to be asked as 'Could the redistribution of the nation's wealth, so as to provide the largest possible share to wage-earners, meet labour's demands for a living wage?'

Both staunchly denied that the provision of a legal minimum to support a family of five was a practical possibility. Piddington was more circumspect, but he pointed out that even if nominal wage increases could be made, they would soon be overtaken by inflationary pressures caused by the consequent increase in prices and he cautioned labour against making excessive wage demands. Because labour continued to make their claims for a living wage, in the face of what Rathbone saw as incontrovertible evidence that such a wage was unattainable, Rathbone stated that they were both class-blind and sex-blind:

'I suggest that the leaders of working men are themselves subconsciously biased by prejudice of sex as well as class, when they cling persistently to the ideal of a uniform adequate family wage, even when acknowledging that its attainment belongs to a distant and speculative future. Are they not influenced by a secret reluctance to see their wives and children recognised as separate personalities ... instead of being fused in the multiple personality of the family with its male head.' (Rathbone, 1924: 37).

The policies of child endowment which Piddington, Rathbone and Douglas helped to popularise had their immediate prototypes in schemes which had been introduced in state-sector employment (in the public service, in state authorities and in the army) in most European countries and in Australia either just before, during or immediately after World War I and in employer-organised schemes in France, Belgium and Germany (Rathbone, 1924; Douglas, 1925; Rathbone, 1940; Vadakin, 1958). Australia had a scheme of allowances (called, as in England, separation allowances) for the wives and children of men serving in the army in World War I. These allowances were increased towards the end of the war to encourage renewed enlistment (Piddington, 1922; Turner, 1974). The scope for wage control and labour discipline which these schemes provided were well understood by both their supporters and their critics (Land, 1975).

It is not surprising therefore that child endowment schemes were introduced on the wage-fixation and legislative agendas as a way out of the alleged impasse created by labour demands for an adequate living wage which kept pace with the cost of living. These demands increased along with industrial and political unrest from 1915 in the context of rapid wartime price rises and even in the post-war boom of 1919-20, workers' struggle to maintain the value of their wages continued (Turner, 1974; Radi, 1974).

The *Report* of the Royal Commission on the Basic Wage (1920), established by Nationalist leader Hughes to fulfil an election promise to investigate wages and prices, after a rigorous investigation of the costs involved in maintaining an 'average worker's' family of five, found that the cost was approximately 36 per cent higher than the current commonwealth Harvester equivalent. The commonwealth statistician, H.G. Knibbs, having been asked by the prime minister to comment on the feasibility of increasing the 'living wage' according to the commission's findings, asserted that such a wage could not be paid to all adult male employees because the whole produced wealth of the country, including all that portion of produced wealth which went in the shape of profit to employers, would not, if divided up equally amongst employees, yield the necessary weekly amount. Piddington's response to Hughes' request for a way out of this impasse (a wage rise of such magnitude was unacceptable to employers and to the government) was his Memorandum (1920) setting out the terms of his proposed family endowment scheme. The flat-rate basic wage for all adult men could be reduced (or at least not increased in its real value) by reducing the domestic unit for wage-fixing purposes to a man and his wife. This would result in wage restraint and cheaper labour costs, allowing for redistribution of revenue from a direct levy on employers, to provide maintenance for workers' actual children. A major political and economic role was thus forged for family endowment: the fostering of wage restraint and its legitimation.

Labour and the principle of child endowment

Organised labour in Australia envisaged a different role for allowances paid to mothers in respect of their dependent children. The principle of child endowment, conceived as a universal transfer based on the inherent right of the child and independent of the wage of the parent, to be financed from consolidated revenue from a graduated tax on incomes, was adopted into the programes of the All Australian Trade

Union Congress and the various state and federal branches of the Australian Labor Party in the early 1920s (*Monthly Labour Review*, 1929; Heagney, 1935). Taken together with pensions for the aged and the invalid (introduced by the commonwealth government in 1908), the endowment of dependent children represented redistribution of income to those periods of the life-cycle which, by the necessities of modern industrial production and the state regulated labour market, are typically spent outside of income-earning activity. Policies of this nature, envisaged by the labour movement as both horizontally and vertically redistributive through the parallel operation of a progressive taxation system, were intended to subsidise, or at best, fully cover the periods of apparently natural dependency associated with childhood, youth, old age and incapacity for labour. Contrary to the opposing view of child endowment as a strategy for wage restraint, this was a vision of the complementarity of a redistributive cash transfer to the mothers of dependent children, linked with a living wage doctrine which would establish a floor for the remuneration of labour (*adult male* labour) according to family needs and in pace with the cost of living. Child endowment would supplement the basic wage and be of particular advantage in low income families with more than two or three children. The most succinct statement of this position was given by trade union witnesses to the Royal Commission on Child Endowment or Family Allowances, which reported in 1929. These witnesses urged that over and above the basic wage as then determined (using the original Harvester domestic unit) a commonwealth scheme of child endowment should be introduced to cover the full costs of a child's maintenance, the scheme to be funded from commonwealth taxation (Royal Commission on Child Endowment or Family Allowance, 1929: 15).

Feminist issues

The principle of the 'living wage' for men had become institutionalised as a 'family wage' in commonwealth and state arbitration tribunals since the years 1905 and 1907. However, when it came to fixing the living wage for women, different principles were assumed to be operating. Mr Justice Higgins justified the decision he had made in the *Mildura Fruit Pickers* Case of 1912 to lay down a separate and lower minimum rate for jobs normally carried out by women, on the ground that women were not usually legally responsible for the maintenance of a family (Higgins, 1915).

Similarly, Mr Justice Heydon, making the first declaration of a 'living wage' for women in the New South Wales Board of Trade in 1918, decided that the court could not consider that the female worker had any other responsibilities besides supporting herself. The female minimum was to be determined on the presumed typical case of the woman with no responsibility for dependants, just as the male minimum was to be based on the presumed typical case of the man with legal responsibility for wife and children (Ryan and Conlon, 1975).

As a result of such decisions, the female living wage was maintained in commonwealth and state industrial arbitration jurisdictions at 50-54 per cent of the male rate until the 'abnormal' industrial conditions of World War II interrupted this pattern.

Only in occupations where women's cheaper labour might lead to the displacement of men was equal pay a real consideration. Ironically, a wage concept designed to protect the low-paid unskilled male worker from being forced down below subsistence level in the 'higgling of the market' was defended by the trade union movement at the expense of that other low paid segment of the workforce, women. State intervention into wage determination served to consolidate the domestic division of labour, to legitimate the financial obligations of men as breadwinners (and hence to maintain the incentives for men to labour) and to legitimate the role of women as secondary workers for only a limited period of their adolescent and young adult lives. The family needs of a high proportion of women wage-earners were ignored as exceptional. That it was not exceptional for women workers to have dependants was demonstrated by Dr Marion Ireland's survey of women in Victorian manufacturing industries in 1928. The survey found that almost 30 per cent of the women interviewed were helping to keep, or were wholly supporting other family members (Ireland, 1928). This proportion was seen by the author to understate the real incidence of women's support of dependants because 46 per cent of the employees surveyed were juveniles, most of whom did not earn a wage sufficient to assist in the support of others.

The labour movement's support for child endowment since the early 1920s, but failure to fully support and make active representation for equal pay on a centralised basis until the late 1930s, suggest that the two issues were not seen in all their interconnections. Muriel Heagney, Labor Party and Labor Women's activist, research worker and organiser for the Clothing Trades Union, the Federated Clerks Union and the Amalgamated Engineering Union, and founder of the Council of Action for Equal Pay in 1937, saw the provision of a system of child endowment as an essential prerequisite for the introduction of equal pay. It was only when dependent children were maintained by state redistribution of income from consolidated revenue that 'men and women in industry would meet on more equal terms than is possible under present circumstances' (Heagney, 1935: 106). She indicated this when she appeared as a witness for the Australian Council of Trade Unions to present the case for equal pay in the 1937 Basic Wage Inquiry (Commonwealth Arbitration Court, 1937).

Similarly, Jessie Street in the late 1920s, at that time outside the labour movement and speaking for the feminist United Associations of Women, saw payment of child endowment to mothers as a just recognition of their economic contribution as child-rearer and housewife; a payment which was necessary to remove them from debilitating dependency on their husbands' income. Later, after her conversion to socialist ideas in the late 1930s, Street continued her energetic advocacy for both equal pay and child endowment, believing that the provision of equal pay required an accompanying social welfare scheme to provide for the maintenance of dependent mothers and their children (Street, 1966; Sekuless, 1978).

Again, the women of the Labor Women's Central Organising Committee, who doggedly lobbied New South Wales Labor leader Lang to include family endowment and widows' pensions in Labor's 1925 election policy, were influenced by considerations of income redistribution to mothers to make better provision for the welfare of women and children (Melville, 1954). They favoured a more equitable computation of the basic wage which a system of child endowment would facilitate (*Labour Daily*, 1924).

Arguments for the introduction of child endowment were not only encapsulated within the living wage struggle which involved the labour movement, employers, conservative and labor politicians and arbitration tribunal judges and commissioners. There were other related interests at stake which became the focus of organisation and lobbying by women. Piddington articulated these interests in 1921 when he declared that women and children had *rights* to income separable from the husband/father's *right* to a living wage. But Piddington was more forthright about children's rights than about women's rights. Various women, with either a feminist consciousness, or a working class consciousness, or both, took the issue further. Motherhood and child endowment were seen as:

(a) A just recognition of the rights of women and children to an income, separate from the concept of the male 'living wage'—and to supplement the inadequacies of the basic wage, particularly for large families.

(b) Recognition of the economic contribution made by women's non-market work of motherhood and domestic labour.

(c) As a pre-condition for equal pay, which would arise when adult males' assumed greater financial obligation to support their children could no longer be used to promote the 'family wage' concept, and with it wage injustice for women workers.

The conservative response

The liberal and labour elites carried the case for child endowment (usually disappointing, if not betraying, the hopes of trade unionists and Labor women that child endowment provisions should not be used as a strategy for wage restraint). Conservative elites argued the case against child endowment on the basic premise that allowances to the mothers of dependent children would undermine the parents', and in particular the father's, obligation to maintain his own children. The case was put succinctly by T.R. Bavin, Nationalist member of the New South Wales Legislative Assembly, debating against Piddington in the pages of *The Forum* in 1922. The thrust of Bavin's argument was that state-funded provision of allowances for the mothers of dependent children would undermine the primary responsibility of fathers. Any hardship which might result from this system was best dealt with by the current legislation which provided 'charitable relief' for those children whose parents could not or would not discharge their responsibilities. But the intention of child endòwment was quite different because it ignored the primary responsibility of parents and assumed that the state, or the industries of the state had an obligation to provide maintenance for every child born. Even the certain amount of hardship and suffering which might accompany such individual parental obligation was more uplifting than a system which subordinated parental responsibility to that of the state (Bavin, 1922).

The position was reiterated in the *Majority Report* of the Royal Commission on Child Endowment or Family Allowances in 1929 which declaimed, in support of the decision that a scheme of child endowment should not be adopted:

> 'By removing from parents all financial responsibility for their children, parental responsibility would be weakened, incentive to effort reduced and the sense of unity of interest between parents lessened.' (Royal Commission on Child Endowment or Family Allowances, 1929: 9)

The potential uses of child endowment as an adjunct to and legitimation of wage restraint were not sufficiently powerful to overcome conservative interests in protecting the system of individual parental responsibilities, and in particular, individual paternal responsibilities. These private responsibilities underpinned the principle of the free labour market with its individually motivated free labourers, the principle of patriarchal obligations and rights, and the selective, residual system of welfare provision which was a legacy of the colonial period. Direct provision to mothers was depicted as a threat to traditional conjugal relationships (by alleviating women's economic dependency) and to men's work incentives (by lightening their burden of responsibility).

Child endowment, new liberalism and social welfare

By the 1920s, strong challenges had been made to the colonial conception of welfare as a residual, selective system of charitable dispensation. Various developments at commonwealth and state government levels had clearly demonstrated the capacity of governments to centralise, regularise and standardise welfare provision through the disbursement of public revenues. What had occurred in the period from 1890 to the 1920s was a shift in public expectations about welfare provision: 'What once was regarded as charitable dispensation subject to moral discretion came to be perceived as a right inherent in citizenship' (Macintyre, 1981: 44).

The role of governments in regularising welfare provision and divesting it of some of its stigma and discretionary zeal was made clear by the introduction of Age and Invalid Pensions (1908) and Maternity Allowances (1912) at commonwealth level; and in New South Wales by amendments to the *State Children's Relief Act* in 1896 which permitted the payment of a boarding out fee to destitute mothers on behalf of their own children (Dickey, 1980). In addition, the early 1920s saw debate in the states about government provision of maternal health and infant welfare services (Thame, 1974).

The role of the state in regulating the wages system and in redistributing public revenue to improve the 'condition of the people' was a key element in the 'new liberal' approach to the political regulation of class relations. In the two and a half decades before World War I, the precepts of classical liberalism were fundamentally reformulated in Australia and Britain (Freeden, 1978). The imperatives to protect the inviolable 'free' contract between capital and labour and with it the theory of the fixed wages fund which were the ideological nub of *laissez-faire* capitalism and classical liberalism, were replaced by the doctrine of an ethical wages policy. This was the 'social minium' or the living wage which would allow not only for workers' subsistence, but civilised subsistence. Classical liberalism was characterised by distrust of the state, except in providing a framework of laws which would protect property rights and the free play of the market. New liberalism saw a role for the state in promoting 'equitable distribution' through a wages policy and social reforms. Classical liberalism was concerned with defining *political* rights: new liberalism extended this notion of citizenship to include *social* rights, thus providing the guiding ideology of the universalist approach to government social welfare provision. Although the policy of child endowment was developed at official level in opposition to the living wage doctrine, in more fundamental ways the principle was an extension of the ethical precepts of the living wage. From the rights of men, as representing their families, the rights of men to live as civilised human beings and to be relied upon to extend these benefits to their dependants, were formulated a new and separate set of rights, those of children and those of their mothers. Feminists extended the notion of mothers' rights to income (albeit income in trust for their children) by recognising the connection with women employees' rights to wage justice.

It was in the contested interplay of class and interest group politics that the implementation of various child endowment policies proceeded. At one level of explanation, it might be possible to agree with Brian Fitzpatrick (1969) that the redistribution of revenue to subsidise some of the costs of children's maintenance was made necessary by the refusal of capital to reward labour adequately. The combination of state interventions and market processes, which resulted in one adult male income-earner becoming legally and morally responsible for total maintenance of several dependent family members, and the failure of the wages system to take adequate account of these obligations, required still further state intervention to ensure the reproduction and adequate maintenance of future labour: the implementation of a horizontally redistributive (i.e. an intra-class) cash transfer to families with dependant children, which also served to reinforce the domestic division of labour (cf. McIntosh, 1978).

However, a closer examination of the processes of contest between the labour movement, women's groups inside the labour movement and independent feminist groups on the one hand, and employer interests on the other mediated through political/judicial elites, demonstrates the contradictory potential of a child endowment scheme. Endowment could be used an an adjunct to wage restraint, or it could be used to supplement existing wage rates to redistribute income to mothers in respect of their dependent children and thus establish a precondition for equal pay demands. As a tansfer of income through the taxation/social welfare system, based on the criterion of social rights inhering in children and their mothers, endowment represented one aspect of the 'social wage', receipt of which did not depend on having a job, i.e. on the sale of labour power in the market. In addition, endowment intervened in the traditional conjugal relationship, providing mothers with income independently of transfers from their husbands. As the conservative critics of family endowment recognised clearly, the policy had very progressive potentialities.

The events

This account will focus on the major attempts to enact child endowment legislation in New South Wales and the Commonwealth and on the political and economic conditions surrounding these legislative initiatives.

Child endowment bills in New South Wales: early 1920s
The first determined attempt to introduce a child endowment bill in

New South Wales was made by the Holman Nationalist government in 1919. The Maintenance of Children Bill provided for child endowment to be paid in respect of each child in a family while an accompanying amendment of the *Industrial Arbitration Act* would alter the unit of calculation of the living wage from man, wife and two children to a man and wife (Whalley, 1972). The endowment was to be paid for the children of employed wage-earners but not small business people, domestic servants, rural workers and workers covered by federal awards, and it was to be paid directly to the mother. Endowment was not to be paid to a wife whose husband was on strike, or where income exceeded £400 per annum (Jelly, 1977:91). The scheme was to be financed by contributions from employers in amounts based on the number of their employees, and if these contributions were insufficient, they would be augmented from consolidated revenue.

The bill was a response by the Holman government to the Board of Trade's recent declaration of the adult male living wage at £3/17/0 a week, an increase of 28 per cent over the existing wage. Holman's biographer, H.V. Evatt, asserted that not only was the wage increase more than warranted by the increased cost of living, but that Holman's response was an attempt to protect the industries of New South Wales from the imposition of an additional financial obligation of £14 000 000, which, it was believed, might force many of them to close or to relocate in another state (Evatt, 1979). It is clear from the circumstances surrounding the bill, and the various exclusions from the criteria of eligibility, that wage restraint was the principal intention—an attempt to reverse the gains recently won by labour in the Board of Trade's declaration. That the savings to employers would be considerable was demonstrated by Holman's own estimate that the maintenance of children scheme would cost £6 500 000 compared with the projected £14 000 000 increase in the wages bill.

The initiative to use child endowment to facilitate changes to living wage declarations did not spring only from outright political party activity: a prior suggestion about the feasibility of dividing up the elements of the living wage had come from within the Board of Trade. In the course of the living wage declaration, the board's statistician, D.T. Sawkins, having pointed out that the average number of dependent children for male wage-earners was not two but a little more than one (i.e. 1.6), suggested a formula by which the living wage might be divided into a component for a man and wife, and components for children's maintenance. Employer contributions would be paid into a government administered fund from which the necessary payments to mothers would be made. The adoption of this formula would have enabled the Board of Trade to declare the living wage at £3, i.e. at the existing rate. But the board did not adopt this proposal since it was beyond its powers, and declared the living wage at £3/17/0. It was this proposal which Holman incorporated into the Maintenance of Children Bill (Campbell, 1927).

The bill was opposed on all sides: by Labor and the trade unions who understood it as an attack on the living wage—a device to 'filch the increase of 17 shillings from the workers'; and by the majority of employers in secondary industry and the rural interests. Employers saw child maintenance on so vast a scale (it was expected to affect nearly 80 per cent of wage-earners) as a revolutionary plan whose ultimate effects would outweigh the 'ephemeral advantages of the smaller wages cost' (Sawkins, 1933:24). Having been passed by the Legislative Assembly but rejected by the Legislative Council, the bill was finally dropped. The increased wage was made applicable to all industries under state awards, and the industries of New South Wales did not collapse.

This attempted orchestration of political activity in the legislature and wage-fixation in the wages tribunal was a process which was to be repeated in later, successful attempts to enact child endowment.

Several other unsuccessful attempts to introduce child endowment schemes in the early 1920s were motivated by intentions other than wage restraint. McGirr, Minister for Public Health and Motherhood in the Labor government, introduced a Motherhood Endowment Bill in 1921 which shifted the emphasis from reduction of the living wage to fertility inducement and the alleviation of children's poverty. The bill provided for payment of 6 shillings per week to mothers in respect of every child after the first two, subject to a means test. In addition, widows were to be endowed in respect of all children in their care, with an additional 10 shillings per week for their own use. Mothers might only be endowed if they were of British stock, or wives of men of British stock, or naturalised British subjects (Whalley, 1972:4).

The rationale of the bill was the alleviation of poverty caused by the failure of the living wage to meet the needs of families with more than two children, and also the alleviation of poverty caused by the loss or absence of a male breadwinner. McGirr's rhetoric in support of the bill was largely concerned with official recognition of the value of motherhood, incentives for increasing the quantity of children, and social welfare transfers to improve the 'quality' of children—as a response to the social problem of 'race suicide'. Motherhood endowment might encourage women to cease shirking their national duty, by recognising the noble work of the mothers of large families who were 'rearing an Australian race'.

In support of an earlier Motherhood Endowment Bill (1920) McGirr had intermingled social welfare issues, pronatalism and the 'race suicide' bogey:

> ... the black races are breeding ten to one of the white races. The civilized races are being over educated. Women try to avoid the

hardship of bearing and breeding children. They want to enjoy life and the bearing of children is looked upon as an encumbrance and a hindrance.... The only way to alter the balance in favour of the white races is to ensure that the women who are prepared to do their duty should not be penalised, as is the case today. We know that under the conditions that prevail children are born into homes of workers for whom there is absolutely no provision for food, clothing or upkeep. (New South Wales Parliamentary Debates, 1920:4087).

The bill of 1921 was rejected in the Legislative Council. Major opposition to it consisted of arguments against the costs which would be incurred, and apprehension that cash transfers to mothers would create work disincentives. It was held that citizens might come to rely increasingly upon the state rather than on their own exertions to support and maintain themselves and their dependants, and thus slacken in their 'incentives to effort' (Whalley, 1972: 27-33). It is significant that child endowment, introduced as a measure to combat poverty by redistributing income to the mothers of more than two children and to widows, was justified as a pronatalist policy, glorifying motherhood, invoking racist fears, and endowing only the mothers and children of British stock. The invocation of 'race suicide' is similar to the earlier advocacy of the Fabian, Sydney Webb, who used race suicide rhetoric in support of motherhood endowment in England in 1907 (Land, 1975).

This unsuccessful attempt to enact a Motherhood Endowment Bill which was not intended to facilitate wage control placed the issue within a social welfare framework, and was opposed by conservative interests who were protecting individual effort and work incentives (even for widows!). However, social welfare issues were closely associated with an ideology of pronatalism which sought to encourage white women's 'natural' role and their national duty.

The federal Basic Wage Commission 1920

Shortly after the Maintenance of Children's Bill was rejected, Prime Minister Hughes set up a Royal Commission to inquire into the cost of living according to reasonable standards of comfort, including all matters comprised in the ordinary expenditure of a household, for a man with a wife and three children under 14 years of age.

This commission fulfilled an election promise and was a response to repeated requests from federal arbitration judges for a statistical investigation of the actual cost of living on which the living wage might be calculated. Its *Report* was tabled in 1920, in an atmosphere of 'fear of economic crisis' (in the words of the contemporary participant, Sawkins, then statistician to the New South Wales Board of

Trade) (Sawkins, 1933:27). The commission deliberated on its evidence and presented its report in a context of industrial unrest and increasing labour militancy after a long period of war and its aftermath in which inflation had lowered the real value of wages (Hagan, 1981).

The commission found that the cost of living for the 'standard' family of five was £5/16/0, roughly 36 per cent higher than ruling basic wage rates. It had been expected in many quarters (particularly amongst trade unionists) that the commission's findings would become the basis of the federal Arbitration Court's wage awards (Campbell, 1927). Commenting on the Commonwealth Statistician's claim that such a wage rise would be economically impossible, the chairman of the commission, A.B. Piddington in his Memorandum to the Royal Commission Report, agreed that the implementation of a wage rise of such magnitude would impose a crippling burden on industry, leading to the ruin of the exporting manufacturing industries, to inflationary price rises, and to a greatly increased wages bill in the public sector. Piddington's memorandum drew attention to the 'anomalies' created by a living wage actually based on the needs of a family of five: all families with more than three children would suffer privation; all families with less than three children would receive more than was necessary; all unmarried men would receive sufficient to support a wife and three children. Australian industry was therefore paying for '450 000 non-existent wives and 2 100 000 non-existent children' (Royal Commission on the Basic wage, 1920).

The desired result of meeting the needs of families, and at the same time preventing the wages bill from crippling industry, could be achieved by calculating the living wage on the basis of a man and wife and declaring it at £4 per week. Wives' dependence was assumed, and single men would be able to marry and support a wife at an early age. Child endowment at the rate of 12 shillings per child could be paid to mothers from a tax on employers (per head of their employees). This proposal to endow the existing 900 000 children of employees (rather than to extract payment for two million non-existent children) would represent a saving for industry of £65 000 000 (Royal Commission on the Basic Wage, 1920:91).

The federal government chose to implement Piddington's proposals in a modified form in the commonwealth public service in 1920 (Sawkins, 1933). The basic wage rate was set at £4 per week, but the allowance for each child was reduced to 5 shillings and was made subject to an income ceiling. At first the endowment was a direct addition to wages and its cost was borne by the government, but from 1923 until the scheme ceased in 1941, it was financed by the public service officers themselves. The necessary fund to meet it was created by deducting the average value of the payment from the basic wage of all adult officers at a fixed rate of from £10 to £12 per annum (ABS, 1935:78). The Commonwealth Public Service Arbitrator, Mr Atlee Hunt, pointed out to the Royal Commission on Child Endowment in 1929 that the scheme cost the country practically nothing because the general scale of wages had been reduced sufficiently to pay the cost of the allowance. This enabled wages and salaries in the service to be kept lower than the basic wage outside the service, while still meeting the needs of public servants (with children) on low salaries. Mr Hunt informed the commission that he found general acceptance of the system in all grades: even those younger, childless men who might be critical nevertheless realised that they would probably also benefit in the fullness of time (Royal Commission on Child Endowment, 1929:32-34).

This was clearly a scheme which redistributed income amongst public service employees, from the childless to those with children: a scheme which reduced labour costs, legitimated wage restraint and acted as an incentive to job stability. As in many European countries, this government-implemented system of child endowment for its employees demonstrated the potential of the scheme for enforcing wage restraint. A system of child endowment was also introduced into the army in 1924, by means of which every serviceman who was married or widowed and responsible for dependent children was entitled to receive £13 per annum for each child, again subject to an income-test (Whalley, 1972:6). What is significant about these public sector schemes is that they were conceived as additions to employees' wages, in respect of dependent children—not as redistribution to mothers. A statutory scheme applicable to all children regardless of the place of their parents' employment was not introduced at this stage, despite Piddington's advocacy.

The savings argument which he used to commend his scheme to government and employers was not sufficiently compelling because the Royal Commission on the Basic Wage had no wage-fixation powers, and the government was quite free to ingore its findings (Sawkins, 1933). Not even in New South Wales one year previously, where a statutory wage-fixing authority had declared a flat rate wage increase of relatively high magnitude, had the spectre of rising labour costs been sufficient to overcome conservative opposition to the use of the state to redistribute large sums of money to the mothers of dependent children.

The Family Endowment Act: New South Wales, 1927

There are conflicting interpretations of the nexus of events which surrounded the enactment of *Family Endowment* by the Lang Labor government in New South Wales in 1927. In later years, Lang wrote about family endowment and widows' pensions (introduced in 1926) as if they had been his personal contributions to Labor Party policy (Lang, 1956). He depicted himself as having fought staunchly against trade unionists who feared that child endowment would be used as a 'lever to reduce the basic wage'. Lang claimed that endowment would provide income for the mothers of poor children, no matter what happened to the breadwinner.

The introduction of such schemes into Labor Party policy has been attributed to other advocates, namely Labor Party women (Kingston, 1975). Women of the labour movement had recommended that mother's endowment be adopted from 1918. The Labor Women's central organising Committee had fought for this reform and for widows' pensions through the 1920s. Gertrude Melville, looking back to this period when she spoke at the Golden Jubilee Conference of the LWCOC in 1954, corrected Lang's claim that he had championed the measure.

In Mr. Lang's policy speech delivered at Auburn 1925, he made no mention of either Widows' Pensions or Endowment.

The W.C.O.C. called a special meeting and sent the following ladies, Mesdames Dwyer, Seery, Maincke, Melville, McDonald, and Misses Golding and Matthews to Coronation Hall, Bondi Junction, where he was to deliver his second address.

Mrs Dwyer, leading the deputation, was very indignant, and after threatening to ask questions from the floor of the meeting, he agreed to make a statement, which was he would bring in legislation to help women and children.

Following on that after the elections, the Committee kept on with deputations and used every means in their power to have these bills introduced.

I well remember Mr Lang telling us we were as bad as Dr Evatt (then M.L.A.) who was like a yapping terrier at every caucus meeting demanding widows' pensions and endowment and firmly believe R.E. O'Halloran, Dr. Evatt, Bob Greig, with other members, and constant pressure from W.C.O.C. was responsible for those Acts.' (Melville, 1954 : 7-8).

However, there were other more powerful interests which continued to utilise child endowment for wage-fixation ends.

The Industrial Arbitration Act (1926) established an Industrial Commission (replacing the Board of Trade) empowered to determine a standard of living and declare a living wage, but without reference to a specified domestic unit. Although the employer and employee representatives on the commission agreed to accept the 1920 Basic Wage Commission's findings, including the five-member family, they did not agree to adopt these as the basis of a living wage. The subsequent finding of £5/4/- for a family of five was regarded by the commissioner, Piddington, as economically impossible. He advised that the only thing to be done was to declare the living wage at its present ruling rate of £4/4/- (which he believed, would provide the required standard of living for a man, wife and one child) and to record the decision that early legislation was imperative to secure family allowances (Sawkins, 1933). Piddington's judgment implied that a sum of 10 to 11 shillings per child was required for an adequate rate of endowment.

The Family Endowment Bill was introduced into the Legislative Assembly in early 1927, providing for endowment to be paid to mothers in respect of all their children under the age of fourteen, at the rate of 5 shillings per child. The payment would not be confined to wage-earners' children, but would be subject to an income ceiling. The family endowment tax would be raised by a 6.5 per cent pay-roll tax on employers, including the crown. The bill had a stormy passage through the Legislative Council where Nationalist members forced amendments which lowered the income ceiling, thereby excluding approximately 150 000 children from eligibility, and reducing the tax levy to 3 per cent of the private wages bill (Campbell, 1927).

An accompanying *Industrial Arbitration Amendment Act* (1927) instructed the Industrial Commission to fix the living wage on the basis of a man and wife only. Piddington declared the living wage at £4/5/- per week, a slight rise in the current ruling basic wage rate, arguing that it would be economically unacceptable to reduce the wage to £3/13/- which might have been the rate for a man and wife based on the commission's previous calculations. Conservative interests declared that the first child was now being provided for twice, once in the living wage and once by child endowment, even though it was generally recognised that 5 shillings endowment was inadequate to meet the costs of a child (Campbell, 1927). Piddington however saw the declaration as 'respect for vested rights', i.e. for ruling wage rates.

The Labor caucus's original Bill was planned to establish the independence of child endowment from wage fixation, by endowing all children and keeping the income ceiling above the living wage. Similarly, the Trade Union Congress of 1927 supported the principle of child endowment, but demanded that the basic wage be increased in accordance with the standards required for a family of five (Jelly, 1977). The resulting combination of child endowment and wage fixation legislation however had altered the basis of living wage declaration and had reduced eligibility for endowment to the poorest families whose income did not exceed the living wage. The labour movement reacted with anger to these events, identifying them as effective wage reduction with the rate of endowment set too low to provide families with adequate compensation (United Front Committee of the Unemployed, 1932).

Lang, in his memoirs, justified the compromise legislation by stating that it had established a 'principle', a principle of transfers to mothers (Lang, 1956: 224). Among contemporary opinion, Charteris, Professor of Law at Sydney University, saw child endowment as the most important measure of its kind to find a place on a British statute book (Charteris, 1927). The long contested issue of the domestic unit for wage-determination had at last been clarified and rationalised; the rate of endowment, although set at a 'modest' level, was capable of being altered to the advantage of labour by any Labor government with a working majority in both Houses of Parliament; and the separation of maintenance of children from considerations of wage determination allowed for separate provision to be made for 'necessitous children'. Charteris anticipated the possible introduction of a federal system of family endowment which would allow the domestic unit for wage determination to be reduced to man and wife, thus reducing the living wage for unskilled labour throughout Australia—removing 'one of the principal impediments to the intensive development of Australia's resources.'

Persia Campbell, in a paper read to the Australian and New Zealand Economic Society in 1927, placed endowment within a social welfare perspective, comparing it with allowances to soldiers' children during the World War I, with old-age pensions and maternity allowances: as a question of 'a social right or a national safeguard'.

What is significant, however, about the severance of children's maintenance from wage-fixation is that while the latter was subjected to routinised bargaining and advocacy in wage tribunals, the rate of provision of child endowment was indexed only to election promises. The Bavin Nationalist government in 1929 made several changes to the previous legislation which further reduced the position of labour. The domestic unit for wage fixation was defined as man, wife and one child. Subsequent wage decisions continued to be made at existing rates, on the grounds that Piddington had previously been setting the wage too high for a man and wife. This was followed by exclusion of the first child from endowment provisions. What had occurred effectively was consolidation of the machinery for wage restraint and reduction in the payment made to mothers.

The levy on employers to provide the funds for child endowment was discontinued in 1934, and the cost was then met from consolidated revenue. According to Brian Fitzpatrick (1969) the burden of payment was transferred from employers to taxpayers, at a time when most wage-earners were being drawn into the tax-paying class. While the class argument is compelling, highlighting the intra-class nature of the child endowment transfer, it does not do justice to the feminist argument. What had been instituted was a cash transfer from wage-earners and taxpayers to the mothers of dependent children, to women who were likely to be either totally or partially dependent because of wage inequalities and their family obligations.

It was in the Depression that the practical possibilities of child endowment were made manifestly clear to working class families and the organised labour movement. The United Front Committee of Unemployed (1932) recognised the major importance of endowment as the economic crisis deepened. When endowment was introduced in 1927 it represented an offensive against labour, but the unemployment rate was then 7 per cent and in 1932 it was 33 per cent. Under such conditions, the regular fortnightly payments to mothers meant sustenance for the families of the unemployed (Heagney, 1935). The United Front Committee and the militant women's publication *Working Woman*, called for mobilisation to defend endowment against the threat of its abolition, to restore endowment for the first child and to carry on the fight until the original 12 shillings per week per child was achieved (Daniels and Murnane, 1980:130).

The Royal Commission on Child Endowment or Family Allowances 1929
The Majority and Minority Reports of the Royal Commission on Child Endowment illustrate the class nature of the arguments marshalled in support of and in opposition to the introduction of a federal scheme. The commission was established by the Bruce/Page government following a meeting of the premiers of several states and of commonwealth ministers convened in 1927 to consider the question of child endowment from a national standpoint. The federal government was unwilling to establish a national endowment scheme while wage regulation rested with the states, and, as a way out of the impasse, appointed a royal commission (Beyrer, 1961). The Majority Report, signed by Chairman O'Halloran, Ivor Evans and Stephen Mills, made their attitude to a federal scheme of child endowment quite clear in their introductory statement. They were not in favour of the adoption of such a scheme because:

1 They did not accept the claim that child endowment was necessary on the grounds that wages were insufficient.
2 They feared the disastrous reactions which would be caused by additional taxation.
3 They feared the injurious results to industry if a levy were imposed.
4 They saw the current basic wage system containing sufficient elements of child endowment to provide for all existing dependent children. If child endowment were introduced, and the basic wage not reduced, the commissioners feared that the results would be: extravagant spending, a sharp rise in the cost of living,

a check in prosperity, a more or less severe collapse in values and serious unemployment.

5 They believed that if all financial responsibility for children were removed from parents, their 'incentive to effort' would be reduced and with it their unity of interests as parents.

6 They argued that available public money, in much smaller sums, could be used to assist the 'residual cases in the community', by extending social services.

7 Because of the grave problems which were expected to flow from the awarding of child endowment without changing the basis for wage fixation, the Commissioners held that the essential precondition for the establishment of any scheme was the Commonwealth Parliament first obtaining full and exclusive power to control wage fixation and other industrial matters. In addition, the basic wage must be reduced by eliminating the provision for children. (Royal Commission on Child Endowment, Majority Report, 1929)

The Majority Report totally rejected the proposals of many witnesses, chiefly trade union representatives, that the commonwealth introduce a scheme of child endowment to provide for the full cost of maintaining children under the age of 15, who were not included in the terms of the basic wage.

Without exception the Trade Union representatives urged that over and above the basic wage as determined in accordance with present methods, the rate of endowment should be sufficiently high to cover the full cost of maintenance of the child and that funds required should be provided by Commonwealth taxation. Stated in money, the majority of such witnesses considered that 10s. per week per child (or more) should be paid. (Majority Report, 1929:15).

The commissioners saw this as highly impractical because of the sums of money entailed, which would have to be raised by taxation at a time when the economic climate of public debt, high interest rates and growing rates of taxation made such a proposal untenable.

In their Minority Report, Mildred Muscio (vice-president and international secretary of the National Council of Women) and John Curtin (then editor of the *Western Australian Worker*) went halfway towards meeeting trade union proposals. They rejected the Majority Report conclusion that the commonwealth should not institute a child endowment scheme until it had complete control of wages and industrial regulation. Their arguments for a system of child endowment, without reduction of the basic wage or change in the nature of the domestic unit, were directed mainly toward the economic welfare of large families. They held that social services alone could not meet the needs of large families; cash transfers were required to supplement the provisions of the basic wage which provided only a frugal standard of comfort for a man, his wife and two children. They argued for benefits of £10 per child per annum after the second child, to cut out when family income exceeded £300 per annum. (This was two-fifths of the amount suggested by the majority of trade union representatives, who wanted child endowment to meet the full costs of children's maintenance.) It is an index of the social welfare orientation of their proposals that specific arguments were marshalled supporting the value of child endowment as a regular source of income for the children of the unemployed, widows, deserted wives and women otherwise without a male-breadwinner. Mothers were the preferred recipients of child endowment payments because they were seen as the direct provider for the child and were also thought to be in charge of expenditure in the home.

The scheme was to be financed by a progressive system of taxation, envisaged as one which would redistribute income through the lifecycle, from those without dependent children to those with, and one which would redistribute income from those with the greatest capacity to pay tax to those families with the greatest need. It was held that not only could the country presently afford to inaugurate a 'moderate' system of family allowances, but that such an expenditure of part of national income would be a good investment for the community (Royal Commission on Child Endowment, Minority Report, 1929).

The commonwealth government agreed with the Majority Report that child endowment could not be separated from the issue of total control of wage-regulation, a power which the commonwealth did not possess and which the states were not prepared to relinquish. It was generally agreed at the Conference of Commonwealth and State Ministers in 1929 that schemes which would increase costs to industry would be unwise at that time (Whalley, 1972). The government also stated that any system of child endowment it was likely to adopt would involve a reduction in wages (Kewley, 1977).

A federal child endowment scheme, 1941

As occurred in England in the war years (c.f. Land, 1975: 195-196), a scheme of child endowment became acceptable as one element in the government's wartime economic and political policies for raising taxation, controlling inflation, restraining wage increases, maintaining some of the essential purchasing power of families, and introducing some of the welfare legislation which would be a vouchsafe and a foretaste of post-war reconstruction.

When Holt, Minister for Labour and National Service in the Menzies United Australia Party/Country Party government, introduced the Child Endowment Bill in March 1941, he invoked the rhetoric of Australia as the laboratory of social experiment—left behind—but ready to enter a new 'fruitful period of social progress', of 'reconstruction', aided by the national unity of the war effort. The circumstances of war made a child endowment scheme more necessary and appropriate than in time of peace, because the expansion of the war programme called for a necessary reduction in consumption levels ('we are all called upon to make sacrifices'). Child endowment would ensure that the exigencies of war did not take necessary food and clothing from children, even while high levels of taxation to meet the war effort were raised (Commonwealth Parliamentary Debates, 12 March to 3 April 1941:336-342). Holt did not remark that the introduction of a scheme of child endowment had been a major plank in the Labor Party's election campaign in 1940. Child endowment was clearly used as a strategy for engineering political consensus by adopting the welfare concerns of the opposition.

Holt quoted from Keynes' booklet *How to Pay for the War* to justify introducing an expensive scheme in wartime, which would ensure that 'no matter how the war pinches our incomes, the basic needs of children will be satisfied'. The thrust of Keynes' argument was that a particular package of economic policies was required to finance the war effort: restrictions on civilian consumption, taxation at high rates, increased borrowing, wage restraint on the part of the working class, control of inflation. The general restraints entailed in this package should not be allowed to undermine the maintenance of adequate minimum standards, therefore Keynes proposed the introduction of family allowances: a scheme which he believed would compensate for the necessary imposition of wage restraints (Keynes, 1940:1-33). His arguments are believed to have similarly influenced English considerations of a family allowance scheme as part of wartime political and economic policy (Land, 1975: 190).

The scheme as introduced was to pay child endowment, universally without an income test, at a rate of 5 shillings per child after the first under the age of 16. The first child was excluded on economic grounds (because of the costs involved) but also on the ground that the existing basic wage was considered to provide for the needs of two parents and one child. In the original legislation, tax deductions in respect of endowed children were to be abolished (a measure favoured earlier by Scullin to remove the tax benefits favouring higher income groups) but in 1942 the Labor government introduced tax rebates at the same rates as had previously applied under the separate state and commonwealth laws (Kewley, 1977:199). Unequal fiscal treatments were much extended in 1950 when rebates were replaced by deductions, which remained in force until 1975.

What was the relationship between this scheme of child endowment and wage-fixation? In August 1940, the Full Commonwealth Court of Conciliation and Arbitration commenced the hearing of an application by the combined unions for an increase in the existing basic wage. The court unanimously refused to grant any increase and decided that the application should be stood over for further consideration after 30 June 1941. The refusal to grant an increase was justified with reference to the uncertainty of the economic outlook under existing war conditions. The Chief Judge, Beeby, in determining the basic wage, stated that he found problems in establishing the 'real average family unit' and the cost of living of an average family, and noted that: 'in the end, economic possibilities have always been the determining factor'; that wage determinations are made according to the general wage-paying capacity of the total industry of a country and more than ever before 'wage fixation is controlled by the economic outlook' (Commonwealth Arbitration Reports, 1940: 42-49).

The Chief Judge also drew attention to the inadequacy of the basic wage to maintain more than three people, and stated that he had been impressed by new evidence of the hardships experienced by families of more than four. He went on to allude to the scheme of child endowment which the commonwealth government had signified its intention to introduce, and hailed it as a scheme which would greatly simplify future basic wage fixation and reapportion national income to increase the wages of men and women with more than one dependent child (CAR, 1940:50).

It was not timing alone which linked Menzies' announcement of the intention to introduce child endowment (made in January 1941) and the judgment upon the *Basic Wage Inquiry* (made 7 February 1941). By this planned orchestration of wage tribunal decision and social welfare legislation, the inter-related policies of wage restraint, increased taxation, control of consumer spending and engineering of political consensus were realised.

Did women take an active interest in the Child Endowment Bill? Jessie Street, in her autobiography (1966), pointed to the concerted advocacy of the United Associations of Women who lobbied trade unionists and politicians on the issue from 1936. When the bill was first placed before Parliament in 1941, a deputation of women's organisations converged upon Canberra to signify their support, and to make a number of requests. Among these were the request that the bill should provide that endowment be paid to the mother and that endowment be paid to widows in respect of all the children maintained by them. Street recalled that the government consented to amend the bill to provide that endowment be paid to the mother, unless she proved to be an unsuitable person (Street, 1966:128). There is some evidence to corroborate Street's claim: the existence of an ealier draft of the bill in which the sex of the recipient of endowment is not specified.

It is not impossible to believe that the original legislation did not specify mothers as recipients. The Report of the Victorian Select Committee on Child Endowment, published in 1940, had recommended that a scheme of child endowment be commenced in Victoria, to provide payment for children after the third, the payment to be made 'at the same time as wages or salaries are being paid by employers' (Victorian Select Committee, 1940:41). Payment to *mothers* was not mentioned among the recommendations.
Street (1966:128) commended the final commonwealth legislation:

> We realised the enormous difference it would make to mothers, not only to have extra money, but to have it paid to them. For many mothers this was the only money that they were entitled to in their own right and it gave them the first taste of economic independence.

This taste of economic independence, small as the payment was, nevertheless elicited some opposition. The Victorian office of the Department of Social Services reported in 1960 that of the complaints raised by recipients, one of the main issues was the husband's objection to his wife's receiving and having the money (Beyrer, 1961: 56).

The 'rediscovery' of poverty and family allowances

During the post-war 'boom', advocacy for the extension and increase in the rate of child endowment left the province of wage fixation debates and was firmly located in social welfare arguments. After the endowment of the first child in 1950, child endowment advocacy remained predominantly with the Australian Council of Trade Unions who in 1955 and 1960 sought substantial increases in the rate of benefits; with women's groups (e.g. the Union of Australian Women); and with the National Catholic Social Welfare Committee which argued in 1962 for increased endowment for third and subsequent children to alleviate poverty in large families (Beyrer, 1961; National Catholic Welfare Committee, 1962).

Child endowment payments for two children were at their peak value in 1950 when they represented 11 per cent of the basic wage and 7 per cent of average weekly earnings. Their value was eroded through the two decades to 1971 when transfers for two children represented 3 per cent of the basic wage and 2 per cent of average weekly earnings (National Population Inquiry, 1978:165). At the same time tax deductions for dependent children were extended in the tax system in ways which provided substantially greater benefit to higher income-earners (Harper, 1972). What was pertaining from 1950 to 1975 (When tax deductions were converted to rebates) was a system of regressive redistribution through the tax system which provided highest benefits for high income-earners, usually for fathers; and a system of cash transfers to mothers: transfers whose value was allowed to erode, almost into insignificance.

It was the 'rediscovery' of poverty at the end of the 1960s, and in particular the work of the Poverty Commission, which brought the issue of child endowment or family allowances back on the political agenda. The First Main Report of the Poverty Commission (1975a) noted the poverty of 254 000 children living in families below the poverty line and a further 207 000 children in families whose income was less than 20 per cent above the austerely set poverty line. To alleviate child poverty immediately, as an interim measure pending the introduction of a guaranteed minimum-income scheme, the commission recommended an increase in cash transfers to the mothers of dependent children and the abolition of regressive taxation deductions. Increased, universal, non-income-tested transfers to mothers was seen as an effective strategy for alleviating poverty in large families, for maintaining horizontal equity between families of different sizes in the same income class, and for establishing and maintaining income differentials between low-paid families with a breadwinner in the workforce and low-income pensioner and beneficiary families. This social welfare advocacy, and the Asprey Committee's Report on the Australian taxation system (1975) received special mention as factors contributing to the introduction of the Family Allowance Scheme in 1976.

Before the introduction of family allowances, the system of regressive tax deductions had been replaced in 1975 by the Labor government which reinstated a less regressive system of tax rebates which benefited equally most tax payers with dependent children. But this 'fiscal welfare' had two inherent problems: firstly, parents on low incomes which incurred little or no tax received either limited or no benefit from the tax rebate; secondly, rebates in respect of dependent children directly benefited the taxpayer who was usually the father, rather than the mother of the children. The tax rebate scheme did not have as its guiding principle redistribution to *mothers* caring for children, but concessions to taxpayers to recognise their reduced capacity to pay tax in the period of childrearing. Large groups of mothers, particularly those who were welfare beneficiaries, were excluded from its benefits.

In May 1976, the coalition government announced that the existing system of assistance for families by child endowment and taxation rebates for dependent children would be replaced: tax rebates would be abolished and the resultant additional revenue disbursed in the form of large increases in child endowment, henceforth to be known as family allowances. This change was heralded as benefiting in particular 800 000 children in 300 000 families who had been disadvantaged under previous child support schemes:

> the children of widow and invalid pensioners, of workers close to the minimum wage or in intermittent employment, of self-employed people unable to earn an adequate income and of Aborigines, recently arrived migrants and other disadvantaged groups. (Commonwealth Parliamentary Debates, 1976:2343).

It was noted that in most households men would lose some take-home pay but women would gain it through the system of cash transfers, i.e. a redistribution of income would take place 'from wallet to purse'. In the national accounting system, expenditure on the increased value of cash transfers would be offset by the savings on revenue previously foregone through the operation of the rebate.

This cash transfer policy was accompanied by substantial cuts in public expenditure in the areas of housing, health, community amenities and Aboriginal services (seen as essential to the attack on inflation and unemployment and returning the private sector to its 'rightful role') and the decision to make unemployment and sickness benefits, widows and supporting mothers' benefit subject to tax. In addition, the introduction of family allowances was used to justify a decision in the National Wage Case of August 1976 not to implement full wage indexation (Cass, 1981d). It has also been noted that if assistance to dependent children had remained in the taxation system, it is very likely that the rebates would have been indexed. The savings made to revenue by moving from an indexed system of 'fiscal welfare' to an unindexed system of social welfare have been estimated at $254 to $458 million for the period 1976/77 to 1980/81 (Cass, Keens and Moller, 1981). Clearly, a highly praised social welfare reform was used to justify a range of economic policies the rationale of which was reduction of public expenditure for social purposes.

As in 1927 in New South Wales and in 1941 in the federal Parliament, no decision was made in 1976 to index family allowances to rises in the cost of living. Despite their historical origins as elements of the market wage, direct transfers to mothers have remained without a regularised procedure for maintaining their real value. Intermittent political considerations, and lobbying by welfare organisations and women's groups constitute the unpredictable means by which increases in the rate of benefit are obtained. The case for indexation of family allowances is carried by women's groups across a broad political spectrum; they continue to argue that redistribution to mothers is necessary to augment family income, to recognise the costs of children's maintenance, to recognise that mothers forego earned income in caring for their children. The case continues to reflect early feminist concerns with establishing and defending the rights of mothers and children to an independent income, and gains a particular sense of urgency in the current period of economic crisis when rates of unemployment and family poverty have increased.

Conclusions

The 'living wage' and child endowment debates were contested within a framework of conflicting class interests in the context of wage fixation in arbitration tribunals and in parliamentary statutes. In this class contest, child endowment was seen by labour as an addition to the living wage but used by employers and political/judicial elites as a replacement of the child maintenance component of the living wage in order to legitimate wage restraint. In the social welfare discourse of 'new liberalism', child endowment was conceived primarily as redistribution of income in respect of dependent children whose individual rights had been delineated and separated out from the father's right to a living wage with a family component.

Feminists in the labour movement and in women's groups outside the labour movement sought to change the terms of this debate. They defined 'family endowment' as containing a component of 'motherhood endowment' in recognition of the separate rights of mothers to an income to relieve their dependency and in recognition of the economic contribution provided by women's unpaid childcare and housework. Their advocacy for child endowment contained a critique of the 'family wage' concept which they saw as legitimating wage injustice for women. If the maintenance of dependants were to become the responsibility of state-directed redistribution, then the arguments supporting the family wage could be undermined and the case for equal pay strengthened.

The introductions of all three child endowment schemes (in the commonwealth public service in 1920; by the New South Wales government in 1927; and finally by the commonwealth government in 1941, by which enactment the other schemes were superseded) were the outcome of explicit wage-fixation and wage restraint concerns. From the mid 1940s child endowment issues became less associated with wage fixation policies and came to be seen and used as an instrument of social welfare policy. This role for child endowment became apparent during the Depression of the early 1930s in New South Wales when members of the labour movement organised to defend the allowance because it represented a regular payment to families with children in a period when unemployment, under-employment and reduced rates of pay were endemic. From the 1960s, child endowment and family allowances became associated with welfare policy for the alleviation of family poverty. However, the introduction of family allowances in

1976 was used as an adjunct to containment of public expenditure on social services, to increased tax liabilities for low-income recipients and to wage restraint.

At a higher level of analysis, after child endowment became universal and non-income-tested from 1941, the allowance represented a component of a 'social wage', a regular, state-organised redistribution of income through the tax-welfare system to the mothers of dependent children, a cash transfer which is not tied in any way to the labour market situation of the recipient or of the children's father. As an element of the 'social wage', these allowances left the arena of organised contest in arbitration tribunals, and lost the element of regularised adjustment to the cost of living which came to characterise the system of wage fixation from the 1920s. Attempts to maintain the real value of the allowance have come to rely on the effectiveness or otherwise of the political mobilisation of welfare groups, and, with greater conviction, of women's groups across a broad political spectrum.

Appendix

In 1980, the value of family allowances for two children represented 4 per cent of average earnings, and for four children, the value of allowances was 9 per cent of average earnings. In comparison with the countries of the European Community, Australia ranked with the United Kingdom, Denmark and Germany in providing relatively parsimonious child support; Belgium, France, Luxembourg and the Netherlands were the most generous in their level of support; Italy and Ireland were the least generous (Bradshaw and Piachaud, 1980). What is significant about this listing is that in Belgium, France, Luxembourg and the Netherlands, family allowances are increased in line with an index, either on prices or earnings—*and* in all but Belgium, allowances are paid to the father. Of the less generous countries, allowances are not indexed and in all countries but Italy are paid to the mother. It would appear that in very few countries of western and northern Europe, and certainly not in Australia, is there a significant government commitment to the redistribution of income to mothers with dependent children.

4 Women and consumer capitalism
ROSEMARY PRINGLE

Consumption provides a fruitful starting point for reconceptualising the relationship between 'patriarchy' and 'capitalism' and for understanding the specific forms of sexual oppression in advanced capitalist countries such as Australia. We live in a society that is conventionally labelled 'consumer capitalist' and we have long known that our oppression as women is tied to our role as consumers and the use of our bodies to sell commodities. Yet the connections remain obscure and consumption has rarely been the focus of theoretical debate. Its elements (economic, symbolic, emotional, sexual) are usually discussed separately or appear in the context of other debates. It is argued here that the changing relationship between consumption and production is of central importance for periodising male domination and understanding the particular forms it takes under late capitalism.

Why then do we find it so difficult to focus our analysis on consumption and to develop these connections? It is partly moralism. As Williams points out (1976: 68-70), the term still has connotations of waste and extravagance. This is reinforced by the economists' distinction between 'necessities' and 'luxuries'. Baran and Sweezy, in their influential book *Monopoly Capital* (1966), were concerned with 'under-consumption'. The main problem for capitalism, as they saw it, was not the tendency for the rate of profit to fall (as Marxists had traditionally argued), but an ever-growing surplus which was difficult to get rid of. Oligopolies, controlling prices and output as small, competitive firms never could, used advertising to exploit people's sexuality and persuade them to buy goods they did not want.

In this context, anyone who admitted to enjoying consumption was to be either condemned or pitied as a victim of media manipulation. Marcuse argued that sexual desire no longer has to be sublimated but is allowed more direct expression. Far from being liberating, this is merely functional to the requirements of expanding consumption. While this was a useful start, it overemphasised passivity and gullibility and denied the possibility of opposition and contradiction. That these issues were not taken up must be related to some unspoken assumption that they belonged to a female, hence trivial or subordinate area. There was certainly a recognition that *women* do most of the consumption work. Friedan (1963: 181-204) was the only one to give a gender-specific analysis of the process. She too was caught up in the 'manipulated victims' approach, and it was to be several years before the women's movement took up her ideas and gave them currency.

In the Marxist urban sociology of the early 1970s, particularly that associated with Castelles (1976a & b) it is 'collective' rather than 'individual' consumption that has featured. By this is meant such things as schooling and health services, restaurants and football stadiums, as against household consumption. The distinction between these areas is problematic and the boundaries fluid. Lojkine for example, sees 'individual' consumption as 'dehumanised by the objectification of the use value in a commodity' (1976: 122). As Cass pointed out (1978a) though this work points to the importance of the spatial separation of consumption in the urban environment, it completely failed to look at the sexual division of labour or to consider the importance of domestic labour. Castells, in a later work (1978) pointed out that the capitalist urban structure, in separating production from consumption, also rested upon the subordination of 'women consumers' to the 'men producers'. He claimed that the feminist movement, in challenging the unpaid work of women in maintaining housing and urban services, actually threatened the very logic of the contemporary city (Castells, 1978: 177-8). However, he did not produce any systematic analysis or explanation of the specific nature of the sexual relations of consumption, either individual or collective.

The taboo on discussing consumption is a result of some fundamental patriarchal biases, which have affected even feminist thinking on the subject. Consumption stands for destructiveness, waste, extravagance, triviality and insatiability—in fact for all the things that men traditionally hate or fear about women. It is only safe to talk about it in appropriately negative or *passive* terms. Accordingly it must be subordinated to production, as women are to men, and reduced to a role in 'reproducing' labour power. Baudrillard (1975) though hardly a feminist, has made the most thoroughgoing critique of this framework. He talks of the 'unbridled romanticism of productivity' which, even amongst anarchist thinkers, leaves no space outside itself. It is thus only through the 'mirror' of production that each and every moment of our lives become intelligible. This ignores the complexity of the *symbolic* exchange that takes place in consumption. It is not merely a matter of devouring or destroying an object but of communication and exchange. Mary Douglas (1979) takes up similar ideas when she talks of goods as part of a live information system. Consumption activity makes stable and visible the categories of culture. But the meaning is in the relations between all the goods rather than their individual or inherent properties.

Such insights are of profound importance for feminists caught in the categories of production and reproduction. After some incisive analyses in the early days of the women's movement (Friedan, 1963; Tax, 1970; Willis, 1971), feminist writers have either concentrated on descriptive material (Comer, 1974; Oakley, 1974, 1976), or been swept up in the debate about whether housework produced surplus value, either directly or indirectly.[1] Thereafter, it became part of the orthodoxy, for Marxists and non-Marxists alike, that housework was *productive*—if not of surplus value, then at least of *use* values. It seems now a measure of our oppression that we felt we *had* to do this in order to be taken seriously by the male left. Cass, in an important paper on consumption, immediately redefined it as 'the *production* of goods and services for use in the domestic economy' (my emphasis) (1978a: 1). The analysis of Curthoys and Barbalet (1976), which locates housework within the circuits of capital, suggests another line of development entirely. They remind us that the economic base of capitalism consists not only of the production of commodities but also of their consumption and exchange. This analysis makes it clear that housework is not a remnant of an older mode of production, nor a subordinate mode, nor a part of the capitalist production process. It is a fundamentally new category, the development of which is central to the growth and complexity of the consumption sphere.

This continuing preference for talking about production is part of the feminist tendency to see capitalism and patriarchy as separate and only loosely related systems. It was, of course, important to assert that male domination was not merely a function of capitalism. But in avoiding this type of reductionism we saw the alternative danger of setting up 'patriarchy' as a universal and ahistorical category (Beechey, 1979; Barrett, 1980). In attempting to provide a materialist account, feminists have frequently treated patriarchy as a separate mode of production outside capitalism (Delphy, 1977) or as a subordinate mode within it (Rowbotham, 1973). Quite apart from the vagueness of definition, this makes it very difficult to account for historical changes in family form or the nature of housework or domestic production.

Alternately, those who want to link capitalism and patriarchy more tightly have merely echoed the notion that consumption is the sphere of reproduction. This seems both too broad, too narrow and too reductionist to be useful. There are all kinds of problems in separating out the different *kinds*: reproduction of the conditions of production, reproduction of the labour force and biological reproduction (Edholm, Harris and Young, 1977). And in the midst of this, consumption per se seems to get lost.

Juliet Mitchell (1971) offered an interesting alternative framework in which patriarchy was treated as essentially ideological and capitalism as primarily economic. At least in this account they were part of the same social structure, functionally interconnected, even if they remained almost entirely separate. Mitchell (1971: 31, 35) noted that 'Without a highly articulated, ramified ideological world, a consumer society could not exist' and went on to argue that 'in a consumer society, the role of ideology is so important that it is within the sphere of ideology that the oppressions of the whole system sometimes manifest themselves most apparently'. However, she said little more about the system of consumption and left housework almost entirely out of account.

English feminists, in particular, have debated the usefulness of the concept of 'patriarchy' (particularly in the journals *M/F* and *Feminist Review*). The conclusion seems to be that the concept is of little analytical value, but is important as a reminder of the fundamental quality and longevity of male domination. If we wish to periodise the latter we must develop stronger feminist analyses on capitalism as well, analyses which extend beyond 'ideology', alone. Those doing this in terms of discourse analysis are explicitly rejecting any priority being given to the economic (e.g. Coward, 1978). The argument put forward here is that it is not the primacy of the economic, but the primacy of *production* that is the problem. If we are to understand the changing position of women under capitalism we must understand the changing relation between production and consumption. The expansion of the consumption sphere has created new forms of work, largely performed by women, largely unpaid, and ostensibly relegated to 'private' life. Despite the illusion of free choices, this world is as structured and controlled as that of production.

Consumption in patriarchal ideology: nature passified

How are we to conceptualise the relation between production and consumption? This question probably only has meaning in relation to capitalist and post-capitalist formations. In pre-capitalist societies, even where a market had already been established, enough remained of the personal quality of the exchange to make it difficult to distinguish production and consumption as two separate functions: 'The artisan lives his work as a relation of symbolic exchanges. . . . There is something that eludes, the law of value and bears witness to a kind of reciprocal prodigality (Baudrillard, 1975: 98-9).

The development of capitalism has involved not only the creation of ever-expanding markets but the separation of men (and in some senses women) from nature and the subsequent conquest of nature. There is a definitive split between man/subject and nature/object, an inability to recognise the subjectivity of the object world, to recognise self in nature. This was always implicit in the Judeo-Christian tradition (dominion over the birds and the fishes and so on in Genesis 1) but it has taken on a new force since the period of early capitalism. It has important implications at the level of sexuality and subjectivity, the creation of the male self as autonomous and the female self as relational. Significantly this is achieved by female mothering, in an increasingly child-centred environment (Chodorow, 1978).

As the Ewens (1978) have pointed out, the creation of markets required an abolition of the world view that militated against consumption. The new markets, by necessity, had to present a worldview in which *nature* was not merely separated from humankind, but was portrayed as inhospitable and/or a harmless anachronism (p.48). Baudrillard (1975: 55) claims that 'Nature is the concept of dominated essence and nothing else'. In the eighteenth century nature was 'discovered' as a potentiality of *powers* to be conquered. That is, labour power was applied to extract 'values' from nature. The political economists were obsessed with productivity, the wresting from nature of her (sic) riches, and assumed that all societies could be analysed in these terms. As Baudrillard points out (1975: 58-60), our concepts of necessity and abundance would have made little sense in earlier times. He suggests that Marx takes over the concepts of capitalist political economy unquestioningly and is caught within the very framework he is trying to criticise.

Marx himself spoke of labour as the father and the earth the mother of produced wealth. Baudrillard (1975: 55) notes this but does not appreciate its significance as *patriarchal* ideology. Capitalist relations are patriarchal at the core. They involved, simultaneously, the creation of 'autonomous' (male) subjects; the separation between 'man' and 'nature'; the division between ('active') production and ('passive') consumption and forms of female subjectivity which left women in a profoundly ambivalent position. They were half-way between 'man' and 'nature', mediating between production and consumption, both consumer and consumed. Women and commodities constitute the new consumption sphere which represents nature dominated and by-passed. In place of 'nature' we were offered commodity consumption. We can see an advanced form of this in Rainwater's (1959) study of working-class housewives in the 1950s, for whom the 'modern' signified the whole new world of better things. These women enthusiastically accepted the consumer ethic and saw their primary responsibility as spending money wisely.

Has consumption become so separated from production that it is completely autonomous from it, or that the relations of determinance have been changed? Baudrillard (1975) believes so, for the code of meanings no longer has to refer to anything beyond itself. And as long as the code remains, consumption can be indefinitely extended. I maintain here that production *is* primary, but only in the sense that you cannot consume what has not been produced. The system of monopoly capitalism itself determines the growing dominance of the consumption 'sphere'. And it is this historical development that makes it possible to do a full critique of political economy and productionist ideology.

Consumption is as *active* an exchange as production. What is consumed is not simply a material object which satisfies a physical need, but a symbolic meaning. This is *not* to be confused with the psychological aspects of consuming particular goods. The symbolic refers to the laws of the world, which we internalise through language. We need to examine the 'language of consumption', considering consumption goods as interrelated parts of an overall text. Under monopoly capitalism words no longer correspond to what they purport to. While this probably always holds true, it has a particular poignancy for consumer capitalism which 'detaches the signifier from the signified, making the signifier its own signified' (Baudrillard, 1975: 9). Consumption ultimately defies classification, for it cuts right across out existing categories. The divisions that follow are therefore somewhat arbitrary, and must be considered as a preliminary attempt to cover the range and complexity of the issues.

Growth of the consumption sphere

The separation between production and consumption proceeded gradually with the extension of capitalist relations into every aspect of life, and has reached its peak under monopoly capitalism. It is, of course, true that production always involves consumption and vice versa. Marx speaks of the production process as 'productive consumption' and also of consumption 'consummating' production, completing it. (The sexual symbolism is well to the fore, though unrecognised.) But he makes an important conceptual distinction between 'productive consumption' and 'consumption proper'. The development of capitalism has seen the expansion and progressive separation of the two spheres, to the extent that we experience ourselves as having different and conflicting interests as producers and consumers.

As production was gradually removed from the home, the space was filled with *new* consumption activities. The development of capitalist markets depended on the promotion of consumption as a 'way of life' and the superiority (and relative cheapness) of the 'bought' over the homemade. The home itself was, of course, the commodity par excellence, a spur for male paid labour and the site of female unpaid labour. The wage labourer and the housewife became the typical figures of modern capitalism. The split between production and consumption was immediately paralleled by the split between public and personal life. Consumption assumed emotional, and later sexual, connotations as the arena of personal fulfilment and individual meaning.

Fairly obviously the expansion of production has implied the expansion also of consumption. But under monopoly capitalism the proportion of workers involved directly in production has declined and the proportion of consumption workers has accelerated. The nineteenth century had already seen the expansion of domestic servants, and particularly *female* domestic servants, to meet the growing consumption capacities of the new 'middle class'. By the twentieth century we have what Galbraith (1973) calls the transformation of women as a whole into a 'crypto-servant class'. Galbraith notes that beyond a certain point the possession and consumption of goods becomes burdensome unless the associated tasks can be delegated. In the twentieth century,

> rising standards of popular consumption combined with the disappearance of the menial personal servant, created an urgent need for labour to administer and otherwise manage consumption. In consequence a new social virtue came to attach to household management. (Galbraith 1973: 31).

In the neo-classical model this is disguised in the 'household', distributing 'its' income to various uses so that the satisfactions are roughly equal at the margin. Yet the basic authority lies with the male, and the woman acquiesces in this as part of the 'natural' responsibilities of her sex.

In articulating women's position as that of unpaid personal servants, Galbraith is making important connections between gender and class. He is also aware that we have to move beyond economics for an explanation of how and why women are made to acquiesce in this situation and subordinate themselves to male authority. Though he plays down the class differences between women, he does draw attention to the importance of housework in *all* classes under monopoly capitalism. In a sense it is true that there *has* been a growing uniformity of women's experience. Women of *all* classes are substantially occupied with consumption activities centred around their own homes, and the associated relational skills have become a defining characteristic of femininity.

Consumption activities may be considered in terms of three different phases: acquisition or purchase; transformation and servicing; destroying, appropriating or 'using up'. These phases have undergone different types and rates of change. In practice, of course, it is not always easy to make this distinction, and they do not always follow in neat chronological order. With consumer durables, for instance, the second and third tend to happen together. One is 'using up' a washing machine at the moment of transforming dirty clothes into clean. All items have their display function, which may be even more important than their 'final' use. A television set is a piece of furniture as well as a screen; a power boat is a phallic symbol and general status object as well as a boat. And, obviously, the service elements of clearing away and washing up have to follow the actual 'final' consumption of a meal.

In addition, a great deal of confusion arises from the fact that many writers refer to the third phase only as 'consumption'. Since most of what we regard as 'housework' actually takes place during the first two phases, this effectively leaves most of women's work in the home out of account. This explains why Douglas (1979) for instance, is able to be so gender-blind in her analysis. Although she talks about 'goods' in general, she actually concentrates on the much narrower area of who socialises with whom and particularly who eats with whom. We shall come back to this after we have considered the earlier phases.

The buying phase

There are certain facts of life so obvious and mundane that no one talks about them... Why is it never said that the really crucial function, the really important role that women serve as housewives is *to buy more things for the house*? (Friedan, 1963: 181)

In the first instance then, consumption 'is the work of acquiring goods and services' (Weinbaum and Bridges, 1979: 194). This takes up a much higher proportion of women's time in recent years: — according to Vanek (1974: 116), one full day a week, compared with two hours in the 1920s, and it has undergone fundamental changes in structure and meaning. As capital removes production from households, it also expands market relations and increases the necessity of *purchasing* the means of life. Selling is organised by capital, increasingly on its own terms. By 1962 self-service establishments had 71 per cent of the grocery trade, with only 16 per cent of the outlets (Johnston and Rimmer, 1969: 41). A woman's value as housewife and mother is reflected largely in her success as a *shopper*, which has replaced the older emphasis on such productive skills as food preservation and home sewing. In addition, the housewife now performs services which were once carried out by the retailer: searching the supermarket shelves, selecting items, filling the trolley, packing, grinding the coffee, even, in some stores, herself marking the price on the goods selected. In this way capital demonstrates its:

> ability to increase its own profit by rearranging the labour process and working conditions of shopping and service centres. Those employed there find their work increasingly reduced to detail labour.... Both those who are employed and those who are shopping or seeking services suffer a speedup. (Weinbaum and Bridges, 1979: 1960).

The time spent on marketing and record-keeping has actually

increased. For example, freezers, which were supposed to decrease shopping time by enabling bulk purchases to be made, have frequently had the opposite effect. The housewife has to buy large amounts of items when they are on special—increasing the complexity of planning and record-keeping. Inflation, and constant rapid changes in price, make 'careful shopping' still more difficult. Yet successful housekeeping *and* personal worth depend on being able to stretch the household income by bargain-hunting. While the centralisation of shopping centres and services may make distribution more efficient, it is frequently at the expense of the housewife's time, the time she must spend travelling between centres, or waiting in queues for services which once came to her. She might have the illusion of 'being her own boss' but her hours are actually determined stringently by the need to fit in with other people's schedules (Weinbaum and Bridges, 1979: 194).

The housewife is not simply buying 'goods and services'. She is operating a highly symbolic process. The goods that she buys have a social meaning which comes from the relation between goods and is not inherent in the individual goods themselves (Sahlins: 1976). The immediate point to make is that in this overall use of goods as a *code*, the actual *buying* process has become much more important. 'Values' which are supposedly extracted or created in the production process are actually sold back to us as part of the process of forming our identities. As Berger (1972: 134) puts it, 'the publicity image steals her love of herself as she is, and offers it back to her for the price of the product' (1972: 134). Shopping has become more and more of a drama (McQuade, 1980).

Because it is believed that women make (or at least implement) most consumption decisions, a great deal of advertising is directed at them. They have to shop not only on their own behalf but on behalf of their families, whose needs they have to identify with, almost as an extension of themselves. Particularly notable is the development of separate children's markets. To be a 'good mother' now includes creating them in an appropriate image, by consuming on their behalf.

An example of distortions in the coding process is the setting up of a pet-food market literally from nothing, to become the fastest growing sector of Australia's grocery trade, with a turnover of $116 million a year by 1971 (*Australian Financial Review*, 16 March 1971). That is, spending on pet-food was equivalent to the combined spending on baby foods, detergents and breakfast cereals (*Bulletin*, 7 February 1970: 46). Animals were once fed scraps, but since the 1950s they have joined the affluent society and acquired their own unique diets. Since women are mostly responsible for the care of pets it is the *housewife*, we are told, who 'is vitally interested in the look, texture and smell of pet food as she takes it out of the can' (*Bulletin*, 7

February 1970: 47). One study suggested that 'pets offer the opportunity to give and receive a totally involving kind of love, a kind which husbands or children often do not want or cannot tolerate' (Whiteside, 1978).

Shopping is work although not often acknowledged as such. Until very recently, most advertising directed at housewives represented them as people with leisure (*Australian Financial Review*, 10 September 1980). As it expanded to take up more time, shopping took on a sexual and symbolic significance, purporting to offer fulfillment and identity.

'The emotionalisation of housework'

It might be thought that with this growing emphasis on the purchase of commodities the work actually carried out within the home might have been reduced. This has not been the case, although there has been a shift from what might loosely be called 'productive' work to work associated more closely with the transformation or servicing of commodities. Even activities like growing vegetables or sewing clothes, which might be seen as having a larger 'productive' component, are now dependent on *bought* seeds and plants, fertiliser and garden equipment; or material, thread, paper patterns and sewing machines. Skills like baking bread and cakes, bottling fruit or making jams are still admired, but are relatively marginal.

By way of illustrating this, Paul Fine (1971) notes that many American women operate on as few as seven basic meals. They are no longer taught to cook by their mothers but only learn after marriage. By this time the family has become accustomed to a few basic dishes and great pressure builds up to keep within this safe framework. It may, alternatively, be interpreted as passive rebellion against the deskilling process, as cooking is largely reduced to a process of turning commodities into consumable form.[2]

New technology in the home has reduced the amount of heavy repetitive chores but it has done little to reduce work frequencies and in some cases has increased them. For instance, probably no aspect of housework has been lightened so much as laundry, yet time spent on it has actually increased (Vanek, 1974: 117). Women may be expected to wash daily instead of weekly, and to prepare a series of individual meals instead of just one (not to mention the dog and the cat!). Since the value of household work is not clear, non-employed women feel pressure to spend long hours at it, to ensure that an equal contribution is being made. Since rising standards of housekeeping have created new forms of drudgery, it may be more accurate to speak of the 'deskilling' of housework (Game and Pringle, 1979: 9).

Housework is not a remnant of an older mode of production, nor a

subordinate mode. The 'industrialisation' of housework is not, therefore, about the reduction of housework but about its *extension* as
consumption activity. If we saw housework as 'productive' we might
have expected it to become more specialised, less time-consuming and
less emotionally involving. Instead, as Ruth Cowan (1976) points out,
the reverse has been true. Housework, in middle- and even upper-class
homes has become *less* specialised. Where once it might have been
divided between a cook, butler, housemaid, parlourmaid and
nursemaid, now all these functions are usually performed by one
person. The extension of single-family dwellings (whether owned or
rented) and increases in the housework performed in working-class
homes has changed the nature of house work: including the loss of
managerial categories among homeworkers, since housewives are their
own servants.

Middle-class women may have hoped that 'mod. cons' would
enable them to get through their work and out of the kitchen.
Working-class women had fewer expectations. Those in Rainwater's
study (1959) wanted, above all, 'an up-to-date house with a
modernised up-to-the-minute kitchen'. While relieved to be freed
from domestic slavery they 'do not anticipate that they will ever
accomplish so easy an escape from the kitchen. Nor are they quite that
eager to escape'.

Labour-saving devices were not intended to reduce the amount of
time spent on household labour but to improve its quality and increase
the time available to provide for other family needs (Vanek, 1978:
367-8). Most obviously, there has been a big increase in the time spent
on childcare. This was partly due to the suburban environment
becoming more hostile to children (traffic, high rise buildings, fewer
places to play safely, etc.) so that they needed more supervision. But
there was also a concern with personal development and the discovery
of a whole series of *new* children's needs, which more than counter
balance the reality of smaller families.

Most important of all, the emotionalisation of housework (the
phrase is Cowan's, 1976: 22) occurred to an extent apparently quite
out of proportion to its own inherent value (Friedan, 1963). This
development has a long history, but a key period was the 1920s, the
decade of electrification and the rapid spread of appliances. This
'industrial revolution' did not increase the divorce rate or married
women's participation in the workforce. Any increase in divorce peti-
tions was counteracted by a rapid rise in the marriage rate and a
declining age at marriage (McDonald, 1975: 144-5). The proportion of
women in the workforce actually declined, due largely to a reduction
in the proportional number of full-time domestic servants, who had
made a substantial contribution to the total of women workers.

Women's domestic role was given a high status during this period, which is reflected in the setting up of the Housewives' and Country Women's Associations (Game and Pringle, 1979: 7).

> Laundering was not just laundering but an expression of love.... Feeding the family was not just feeding the family but a way to express the housewife's artistic inclinations and a way to encourage feelings of family loyalty and affection. Diapering the baby was not just diapering, but a time to build the baby's sense of security and love for the mother. Cleaning the bathroom sink was not just cleaning, but an exercise of protective maternal instincts, providing a way for the housewife to keep her family safe from disease. Tasks of this emotional magnitude could not possibly be delegated to servants, even assuming that qualified servants could be found. (Cowan, 1976: 18).

'Emotionalisation' thus provided a rationalisation for the middle-class woman who was in most parts of the advanced capitalist world now doing her own housework. It also provided a justification for many working-class women to leave the workforce and do their own domestic work instead of someone else's. Women frequently had to work to be able to buy things, and the consumer economy provided increasing numbers of low-paying 'women's' jobs to juggle with their household duties as wives, mothers and consumers, But, most importantly, the ideal of the non-working wife was consolidated, and treated as the norm. Housework thus became not just a job but an expression of love and warmth, performed by each woman for her own family.

The inter-war period was one of transition. It was the time when housework had its highest status and dignity. At this conjuncture it still retained enough of the old skills to make the new emotional dimensions convincing. After World War II images of domesticity and maternal love were not sufficient settings for consumption and it became more directly sexualised.

Sexuality and consumption

The sexualisation of consumption of course began much earlier. In the post-war period it has merely become more direct and all-encompassing, as advertising has become more blatant and central to our everyday lives. A new interest in sexual pleasure for women as well as men was apparent in the 1920s. For America at least, there was a proliferation of surveys, one of which showed that 61 per cent of middle- and upper-class women born after 1891 had sexual experience outside marriage, compared to only 24 per cent of those born earlier (Ryan, 1975: 271). Kinsey suggested that sexual practices in the 1920s were more sophisticated, with more foreplay and a wider range of positions used. It is difficult to find much information directly about Australia, but what there is suggests that we followed a similar pattern. The range and availability of contraceptives increased (Game and Pringle, 1979: 7) as did the resort to abortion by both married and unmarried women (Allen, 1982). The divorce rate increased—only slightly, but the reasons are more interesting than the absolute increase. Whereas in the earlier period women usually divorced men, for adultery and desertion, in the 1920s more men started to divorce their wives for adultery (Allen, 1982). While divorce rates are only the tip of the iceberg, the man dressed in 'co-respondent shoes' for a quick getaway became a figure of fun during this period. At a more macabre level, the incidence of wife murder also increased, with sexual jealousy being offered as a main motive (Allen, 1982). These figures suggest quite widespread changes in sexual practice, perhaps most significantly in the behaviour of married women.

At the same time, women's bodies became more directly sexualised. "Girlie" pictures began to appear in such newspapers as *Truth, Smith's Weekly* and the *Labour Daily*. The flapper was given strongly sexual connotations by advertisers becoming bolder in associating commodities with love and romance. They were acceptable because they corresponded to and were part of the new preoccupation with sexual attractiveness. Men were enticed by more undisguised sexual stimuli, and offered women as objects of consumption. Women were encouraged to consume in order to make themselves attractive to men. It would appear that women cooperated enthusiastically in becoming 'sex objects'. Coming from a background where their sexuality was either denied completely, or their right to sexual pleasure ignored, this is hardly surprising. Women were permitted sexual pleasure, but it had to be experienced in a *feminine* way, through passivity and responsiveness.

Though there were big shifts in the overall structure of sexuality they did not threaten the domestic sphere. In fact, advertisers linked sexuality to the emotionalisation of housework and the establishment of private life as the place where we 'find our real selves'. 'Subliminal promises of sexual fulfilment, love and a happy home life—all the prizes at stake in the marriage competition—were attached to anything from automobiles to toilet paper in the hope of engendering compulsive buying habits' (Ryan, 1975: 295).

The insatiability of the market presupposes the insatiability of desire. Rather than seeing people as manipulated by the media, we need to consider the construction of subjectivity in concrete social relations. This has involved a radical restructuring of sexuality, a process that has its own separate development but is linked at every point with the expansion of consumption (Game and Pringle, 1979: 10-11). Sexuality is not a biological given but a social and cultural creation that is open to historical change. While biology undoubtedly sets some limits, the possibilities are *almost* limitless, and we have still only utilised a relatively narrow band. Sexual desire is not merely repressed, but *created* in a set of social relationships. In our society it is constructed out of lack, which can never be satisfied (Marcuse, 1965). There is an immediate connection here with consumption, since we believe that the consumption of commodities will fill the gap and complete our sexual identities. Of course it never does so we are always in a state of 'desire'. In this sense, consumption is directly sexual, for we are offered back a 'complete' masculine or feminine identity through consumption patterns. We are under pressure to constantly 'produce' ourselves through consuming commodities. This relates back to what was said earlier about the establishment of consumption as a 'way of life', the superiority of the artificial over the natural, the 'bought' over the 'homemade'. (The recent discovery of the 'homemade' compares with the discovery and worship of 'nature' at the beginning of this process—indulgent romanticism.)

The system works rather differently for men and women. This is true not only in the obvious sense that masculinity and femininity have a different content, but, because of the power differential, different processes are evident. Masculine identity assumes that the denial of need for the other is the route to independence (Benjamin, 1977: 51). Where the little boy develops as separate and autonomous, the little girl has a tendency to boundary confusion. Her sense of self develops much more in relational terms (Chodorow, 1978). Thus, where the male presence is emphatic, the female presence expresses her own attitude to herself. She must be particularly aware of how she appears, especially to men. Willis puts it:

> To convince a man to buy, an ad must appeal to his desire for autonomy and freedom from conventional restrictions; to convince a woman, an ad must appeal to her need to please the male oppressor. (1971: 662)

Does consumption always involve sexuality? It seems to us difficult to find an advertisement which does not refer to our sexual identity—in fact this is almost axiomatic since our society is organised so heavily around gender differences. Clearly though, the sexual attractions of some advertisements and some products are much more obvious than are others. The attractions of clothes and make-up are of a different order from those of washing machines or vacuum clearners. Yet both kinds of goods have a place in the construction of femininity: the first through self-adornment and the second through being a good wife and mother, taking care of home and family. And women are particularly vulnerable to all this because our 'lack' is supposedly made good by the approval of others, and particularly men.

The male 'lack' is somewhat different. As possessor of the phallus, he can treat the world as his rightful inheritance. Though he may have little control over his conditions of existence he is constantly addressed as the subject of 'his' world. 'What the budget means for YOU', screams a newspaper headline, and 'you' always turns out to be a man (with or without a wife and kids, whom he is taken to 'represent' in some way). Pornography similarly constructs the (heterosexual) male view as its subject (Pringle, 1981). In these circumstances advertising and consumption cannot be of complementary importance for the construction of masculinity. Willis (1971: 662) suggests that while advertisers do stress the 'virility' of 'male' products 'it is never claimed that the product is *essential to masculinity* (as make-up is essential to femininity), but only *compatible* with it' (1971: 662). To dictate would be to undermine male subjectivity.

Despite some shifts, sexuality remains organised around the heterosexual couple and the polarity of masculine and feminine. Nevertheless it constantly threatens to break out of these strictures and we must ask whether consumer capitalism does any longer 'need' gender as an organising principle. Homosexuality is a case in point. It is a cliche now that homosexuals are the 'ideal' consumers. They are stereotyped as self-centred, narcissistic and without dependents. Certainly the business world has been quick to respond to this new market. Interestingly the 'ideal consumer' is thought of almost *entirely* in sexual terms. Tolerated as consumers but discriminated against in every other way, homosexuals are well placed to expose the limitations of sexual 'liberation' under capitalism. The gay liberation critique of consumer capitalism is already a powerful one, and will grow in strength as it comes to terms with the issues surrounding narcissism and gender. Lasch's (1979) recent attack on consumer capitalism is made in terms of narcissism. This is inadequate because it frequently descends into a 'blame the victim' approach. The possibility of resistance tends to be denied:

The unity of consumption

So far we have concentrated on the early phases of consumption—the acquisition and transformation of commodities—rather than on 'consumption proper', the 'using up' of the object, or the appropriation of the image. I have argued that it is somewhat arbitrary to separate out the economic and the ideological, or to give one primacy over the other. This becomes very clear when we consider the final phase.

Mary Douglas (1979) defines consumption activity as 'the joint production, with fellow consumers, of a universe of values. Consumption uses goods to make firm and visible a particular set of judgments in the fluid processes of classifying persons and events'. In this view, physical consumption is only part of the service yielded by goods. More significantly they perform 'marking services'. Our place in the overall social structure is defined by whom we can include in, and exclude from, a range of consumption rituals. A household that can afford to entertain frequently, and on a large scale, will be in much closer contact with the centres of power and influence than a poor household, which is relatively isolated. A pattern of life based on different periodicities automatically acts as a barrier to free social intercourse, since the reciprocity rule is the principle of exclusion.

Douglas is at pains to separate the symbolic aspects of consumption from the material and physical. She is also trying to make general propositions about consumption which hold true for any society. She is also extraordinarily 'gender-blind', given her subject matter. Nevertheless, we can build on her analysis and use it to draw together what has already been suggested as the basis for a more gender-specific analysis of this phase of capitalism.

Goods have a meaning which comes from their place in a symbolic system rather than from some essential nature or their capacity to satisfy a material need. Consumption cannot be seen merely in individualist or economic terms. It involves the appropriation of meanings, and it is part of an information system operating between rather than within households. This still leaves open the question of the relationship between the goods and the meanings we ascribe to them. It seems useful here to consider goods not as material objects but as *signs*. The object (the signifier) at no stage exists separately from its meaning (the signified), and they are only divided for purposes of analysis. That is to say, the analyses and decoding of advertisements in these terms need to be extended to consumption overall (Williamson, 1978). It is no accident that the discussion of 'consumerism' frequently gets collapsed into a discussion of advertising. Advertising clearly links into a network of systems or languages which together make up consumption.

The gender-blindness can be attributed partly to the tendency to be concerned only with the last phase of consumption, and chiefly as it relates to eating, drinking and general hospitality. Though consumption is not a private matter, it *is* organised predominantly around individual households. We therefore need a way to analyse patterns that operate simultaneously between *and* within households. Here the notion of 'consumption periodicities' can be usefully extended. For it is clear that not only do different classes have different patterns and lifestyles, but so do men and women within these categories. That is, not only are class and status marked out in separate consumption rituals; the separate statuses of women and men are marked out by their activities in what *appears* to be the same consumption space.

Women as consumers are principally involved in repetitive, high-frequency household routines. These carry low status, not inherently because they are performed by women but because those who operate this pattern have limited access to or control over information. Housewives tend to be more isolated, to spend their time with smaller groups of people, and share their consumption rituals with relatively few people. Their household obligations tie up their time in such a way as to exclude them, frequently, from wider social gatherings. At the same time they tend to be facilitators of other people's consumption rather than (or as well as) active participants. If consumption is about symbolic exchange, there is considerable ambiguity as to whether women are to be seen as objects of consumption or as participants in it. Their position as servants/objects in the consumption sphere also restricts their access to jobs in the paid workforce, through again locating them in jobs with the highest periodicity constraints. This, incidentally, has an important function in obscuring the sources of surplus value—a point which the underconsumption theorists have by and large overlooked.

The specific forms of male domination and female oppression in our society are crucially linked to the development of the consumption sphere, which has a high degree of autonomy from production and an ability, in turn, to influence it. Once we reject the absolute dominance of production, the categories fall into place. The old dichotomies of economic/ideological, public/private, physical/mental, and materialist/idealist have little applicability. If theoretical and political primacy were given to the consumption area, we might find that the analysis of capitalism and the analysis of male domination *could* proceed simultaneously as one and the same process, without any reductionism taking place.

Consumption and social policy?

If the previous analysis is correct, it seems unlikely that sexual oppression will disappear under capitalism, though male domination *is* under threat and its forms change constantly. There is a strong case for the left shifting its priorities away from production and towards consumption. Not that production should be ignored: it would be insane to replace one set of blinkers with another. This is a time when drastic restructuring and a high level of investment in new technology are taking place almost entirely on capital's terms. Workers have been relatively powerless to protect jobs or working conditions let alone to transform capitalism. And that prompts the question, what, if anything, would? I have argued that there are numerous contradictions at the level of sexuality, gender relations, consumption work and the broader division of labour which must in the long term be central to any major transformation. In the meantime we have to try to prevent things getting worse.

Any social policy designed to 'help' may simply trap women even further into their existing patterns. Consumption workers are required to be almost permanently on call, and they have to do a large number of repetitive chores which are spread out in such a way that it is difficult to get blocks of free time. The only escape has been through having servants (hence the desperate struggle of middle-class women to retain servants described by Kingston, 1975), or having a high level of technology in the home. The latter is highly problematic as we have seen. In many ways it has tied women down even more. There are also signs that it is being used as an *alternative* to breaking down the sexual division of labour (Bose, 1979).

The left, and most of the women's movement, have been pessimistic about organising with housewives. While the difficulties are immense I see no reason to assume that housewives are inherently more conservative than anyone else. If they appear so, it may simply mean that their needs and grievances have not been adequately analysed. The 'conservatism' of women voters was in some measure an indication of the extent to which all parties ignored them (Goot and Reid, 1975). When the ALP updated its image a little, it attracted their support. Women are responsible for 'nurturance' and it is this that conditions their confrontation with commodities so that 'the contradiction between private production and socially determined needs is embodied in the activities of the housewife' (Weinbaum and Bridges, 1979: 194). We cannot afford to see struggles in the consumption sphere as inherently and inevitably reformist. Consumption boycotts have not been notably effective in Australia, but then they have not been well organised or coordinated. At a time when retailers are sighing with relief at any signs of increased spending, consumers hold a great deal of power to extract concessions. Consumption strikes are not beyond the realms of possibility. They would need to be combined with a decoding of consumption imagery. Billboard Utilising Graffitists Against Unhealthy Promotions could provide the model of what is needed, to intervene at all levels of consumption discourses.

The right in Australia has benefited from the support of housewives' associations and, most recently, groups such as Women Who Want to Be Women. Similar groups appear to have contributed to Reagan's victory in the US. Massive demonstrations against strikes in Auckland and Sydney (*Daily Mirror*, 9 March 1981) were strongly supported by women who identified themselves as housewives. Their motivation or immediate interest is not clear. The left needs to develop its understanding of the grievances and frustrations behind such actions and develop policies accordingly.

As we have seen, the relation between 'individual' and 'collective' consumption is problematic. It is not at all clear how it is constituted, or how it can be broken down. Finally, we need to find ways of resolving our schizophrenic existence as producers and consumers. This will not be achieved just by translating consumption back into production. It does not involve a romantic 'return to nature'. But it does involve a recognition that the 'rationalisation' that has accompanied capitalism is patriarchal at its core in the subject/object, man/nature distinctions that were created. Capitalist relations involved simultaneously a new and very extreme form of male domination. Women, in so far as we are located half way between 'man' and 'nature', are well placed to challenge both sides of the split. We must expose this 'rationality' for what it is and not throw in our lot with it. Our aim should not be to escape from the world of consumption (which is only nature transformed), but to use the relational skills and identities that have been imposed on us to work out a saner way of relating to our environment. 'Patriarchy without the father' (Benjamin, 1977) is not what we want.

Acknowledgements

I should like to thank the following for critical comment and discussion: Judith Allen, Bob Connell, Jean Curthoys, Graeme Duncan, Ann Game, Barbara Smith, Lesley Stern.

Notes

1 An important exception is Ryan (1975), who *does* discuss women's *new* occupation as consumers.
2 This suggestion comes from Joan Greenbaum.

5 Capitalism patriarchy and the city

ELIZABETH J. HARMAN

Urban theorists from Alonso to Castells are almost universally blind to the interrelationship between capitalism, patriarchy and urbanisation, especially where the latter is defined in terms of the spatial and built form of the city. That such a nexus exists is most obvious in the extent to which the city has been shaped to keep women confined to their traditional roles in the family as wives and mothers. Suburbs are built expressly for the family; job opportunities are few for many; the public transport system is geared for the movement of commuters in peak periods and it is difficult for women at home to cross between suburbs; public places equipped with revolving doors or turnstiles render the woman with a pram or pushchair a 'handicapped person' (Weisman, 1981: 6). But the patriarchal nature of the city is not defined solely in terms of women and the family. The distribution of jobs across the city mirrors the segmentation of the labour market. Male and female job opportunities are concentrated in different places; hence the laboursheds and journey to work patterns typical of working women are significantly different from those of men (Manning, 1978; Howe and O'Connor, 1981).

Given the male dominated bias of general urban theory, it is not surprising to find that much Australian urban research also renders women largely invisible. This is not only true of texts written in a noncritical tradition (e.g. Neutze, 1977; Burnley, 1980) but also of those adopting an explicitly radical stance (e.g. Stilwell, 1980; Kilmartin and Thorns, 1978). Both Neutze and Stilwell do make brief references to women but only with respect to their role in the paid labour force as employed or unemployed workers. A few studies recognise the existence of all women. Bryson and Thompson in their study *An Australian Newtown* take some care to define the roles of women in the community but accept their situation uncritically (Bryson and Thompson, 1972). Stretton in his book *Ideas for Australian Cities* says he is 'for women' but his support is basically a celebration of the traditional role, and his proposals to organise cities are made in ways which facilitate this role (Stretton, 1970). (Both Bryson and Stretton have since recognised the weaknesses of their early positions.)

Williams' analysis of the lives of women in an Australian mining town is a notable recent exception to the general trend (Williams, 1981). But Williams treats the links between patriarchy and capitalism much more effectively than she does their combined interaction on the built form of the community she is discussing. This is not because she sees the latter as irrelevant or unimportant. The manner in which class is manifest in housing and the spatial organisation of residential areas in the town is considered in detail (Williams, 1981: 122-15), but the way in which patriarchy is also embedded in the planning and form of the settlement is not recognised to the same extent.

Feminist writers who are more self-consciously urban theorists take the nature of patriarchal capitalism as their starting point in looking at cities. This is true both overseas (e.g. MacKenzie, 1980; Markusen, 1980) and in Australia (e.g. Cass, 1978a; Young, 1980). Such studies are a vast improvement on the main body of urban literature which ignores the effects of patriarchy even when it does perceive the capitalist basis of urban form (Szelenyi, 1981). Be this as it may, this paper is basically a critique of feminist urban studies. I argue that feminist theorists have (perhaps unwittingly) limited their analyses to a description of the patriarchal basis of the city of the 1950s. There has been little real attempt yet to build the implications of contemporary urban trends into feminist theorising. Most of the existing work portrays the relationship between urbanisation, patriarchy and capitalism in terms of dualisms implicit in such dichotomies as work and home; city and suburb; public and private; male and female; production and consumption; labour and the reproduction of labour; market and domestic spheres. While this approach may usefully depict the industrial city, it has restricted and distorted our conception of the city and the problems of women under monopoly capitalism. For this we need to recognise changes which have been made in the workplace (which have had differential effects on men and women) and changes in the domestic sphere. The organisation of urban space and female activity patterns have been transformed by the emergence of a *non-residential* domestic sphere. By not taking greater account of the specific nature of the corporate city, feminist urban theory remains one step behind macro-social changes, while tendencies associated with economic restructuring, energy crises and neo-conservatism threaten to put them still further behind.

My critique of feminist writings on the city hinges on their widespread acceptance of this basic dualism. The patriarchal logic behind the division of labour in many cultures and its expression in gender-based roles predates capitalism. It persists within capitalism as the means for accommodating the division of labour between those involved in selling labour for wages as a basis for commodity production (predominantly males) and those who maintain the household as the locus for reproducing labour (predominantly females). Since these activities generally take place in different locations within contemporary western cities, it is reasonable that urban feminists should start by distinguishing between the male and female dimensions of spatial organisation. Suburbs are female in that they are the centres for home life, families, domestic activities, social reproduction and consumption (including schools, retail services, recreation, etc). Males spend much of their work life outside the suburb and are associated with activities in public places or production centres. They must necessarily move as commuters between home and work. Dichotomous categories to describe the organisation of the city have been used by Markusen (1980); Hayden (1980); Palm and Pred (1977), and appear also in several essays in the special urban issues of *Signs* (1980 5:3) and the *International Journal of Urban and Regional Research* (1978 2:3) to reveal how patriarchy is embedded in the organisation of urban space. In doing so however, they are adopting a conceptual apparatus which is itself patriarchal in that such categories not only describe the way in which cities divide men and women; they are the basis of an ideology which helps maintain and perpetuate such divisions.

The patriarchal nature of dualistic thinking in general has been explored by Foreman (1977) but is given special treatment in the context of urban studies by Saegert (1980). As she so acutely perceives, the basic dichotomy between 'masculine cities and feminine suburbs' is culturally based; a symbolic system of ideas which informs and guides our thinking of the city and our personal lives in terms of polar opposites. More than this she suggests it is a fictional view—a false consciousness. There are echoes of the same critique in Stacey's contention that the domestic sphere and the lives of women cannot be easily categorised on the 'private' pole of the public-private dichotomy (Stacey, 1980), and likewise in Cass' attack on those who 'facilely' split discussions of production from consumption in ways which are insensitive to the nature of sex roles (Cass, 1978: 13). (See also Chapter 4). While such writers appear to agree that the existing categories straitjacket our thinking, they disagree on the cause of this. Stacey, for example, suggests the problem has always existed, since the categories were themselves devised by males operating in and concerned with the public sphere. Saegert, on the other hand, contrasts what she calls the fictional nature of the dualism with a contemporary reality in which the lives of women, occupational structures and the demographic composition of urban areas are all undergoing change and hence are making dichotomous categories increasingly inappropriate.

Both explanations may, in fact, be right. The popular dichotomies have put some limit on our conceptions of the lives of urban women, but they have been useful. The problem is that the categories are now becoming so restrictive that they are obscuring the processes which are restructuring urban space in response to changes in both the nature of contemporary capitalism and patriarchy. Two quite dissimilar examples should make the point clear. Gentrification is basically a movement of middle-class, often childless households back into the inner-city residential areas, although it can be described in more complex terms than this (Kendig, 1979). It is explained on the one hand as an outcome of the process of accumulation in capitalist cities where it represents a recent discovery by capital of a high profit investment opportunity (Williams, P., 1981). On the other hand for Markusen (1980) gentrification is a consequence of shifts in patriarchy—the outcome of a decline in fertility and the rise of the two-career couple. The two effects obviously interact.

The rise and fall of the welfare state has affected the provision of a whole range of services and facilities within the city (e.g. health centres, family planning clinics, homes for the aged and handicapped, etc.). After having been established in periods of commitment to social welfare, many of these services are now being closed or moved from state-based institutional care back to residential, private and community-based care in the changed climate of economic recession and neo-conservative political philosophies. The welfare state altered the domestic role in the first instance by causing much domestic activity to be done *outside* the home. The complexities introduced by non-residential activities associated with social reproduction are difficult to handle in an analysis of urban form limited to home-work. The state is now pushing some services back into the home. The contradictions inherent in the current retreat from welfare funding is recognised as affecting the patriarchal bases of spatial organisation (Foord, 1980), but there is little substantial research yet done on the specific nature of the effects on the city.

There is a clear imperative to rethink the basic categories used in urban feminist theory, though not necessarily to devise totally new ones since there are advantages in building on what has already been achieved.

Insights based on dualistic concepts

Manifest in the patriarchal city are a whole set of social and spatial inequalities which generally disadvantage urban women (whether at home or employed) more than men (Palm and Pred, 1977; Madden, 1977; Forer and Kivell, 1981; Zelinsky et al., 1981). Inequalities are evident in access to transport, jobs, services and facilities, and in the social and psychological pathologies which plague women isolated in suburbia. Hence, men and women perceive and use urban space in different ways: for example, the symbolic meaning of home varies between the sexes, as Davidoff et al. (1976) and Saegert (1980) illustrate in their descriptions of the meaning of suburban community and home for men as the retreat or haven from the rigours of a hostile and competitive world of work. These inherent inequalities have led feminist commentators on architecture and planning to recognise that an egalitarian community must not only change the nature of social relations, it must restructure the physical environments in which we live. Hayden has been a pioneer in this area, exploring both the attempts to overcome patriarchy in past utopian communities, and in proposals for future urban reform (Hayden, 1976; Hayden, 1980; Hayden and Wright, 1976).

Feminist theorists have not only used the basic home-work dualism to understand the nature of cities, they have also turned their focus on urban research itself. Burnett (1973) shows how the patriarchal nature of urban space was reflected, implicitly in the assumptions made in the urban models (of Wilson, Forrester Muth and the urban factorial ecologists): models which assume, the dominance of the nuclear family, a traditional division of roles between the sexes, the separation of residence and employment, and the importance of the journey to work in determining residential location. Such models cannot cope with changing family structures or sex roles and their effect on urban spatial structure. Recent studies are attempting to build the activities of women into urban transportation models (Zelinsky et al., forthcoming; US Department of Transport, 1978). White (1977) has developed a utility model which relates residential location to women's journey to work preferences.

Much of this literature treats the separation of home and work or male and female daily lives as an *intellectual device*, a dualism which has been either consciously adopted in theory and research to help order a chaotic reality, or which is taken for granted as part of the dualistic cognitive systems of western culture. Yet it is equally clear that the urban dichotomies may be viewed as having a *concrete expression* in the actual organisation of daily lives and spatial form. After all, as a part of the dominant ideology, dichotomous concepts have helped to shape our material environment. As a result, categories like home-work, suburb-city are not only subject to paradigmatic shifts, they are subject to changes in the material organisation of life. The relationship between home and work or public and private can then be traced not only in the history of ideas (as for example by Stacey, 1980, or Foreman, 1977) but also in the historical evolution of sex roles, the household, the economy and urbanisation.

In pursuing the latter, theorists have been more intrigued by changes in the past than those of the present. There has been considerable historical interest in locating the particular period and conditions which produced the initial physical separation of home and work in western societies. Periods in which dichotomous concepts do *not* seem appropriate have been identified as (1) pre-state; (2) pre-mercantile; (3) pre-industrial and (4) pre-mass transit and therefore, pre-suburban.

Stacey (1980) contends that public and private domains were fused in the Carolingian period and it was only when the central state developed that a public (political) sphere emerged and women were excluded. The medieval period as a whole is often depicted as having no real spatial separation. The medieval family, while still patriarchal, was large and extended—a neighbourhood unit as much as a household, in which domestic, productive and political activities were all represented. Women played an active part although considerable variation occurred between cities and classes. In Genoa (Hughes, 1978) the desire of rich merchants (male) to consolidate their power in trade led directly to the loss of female rights to property, and hence the beginning of their economic dependence on husbands and fathers. The needs of merchant capital for credit were also identified by Weber (1923) and underly the separation of commercial and domestic accounting in the household. This in turn, laid the ground for the development of two separate spheres—a process which began in the middle ages but which was not complete in England until the mid nineteenth century (Cass 1978a: 13).

For many commentators, the spatical break came with industrialisation when factories moved the production of commodities out of the home and family-based craft work. This is the point at which the family moved from being a production unit to a consumption unit (Rothblatt et al., 1979: 37). Cass (1978d: 14) has criticised this view as 'arid technological determinism', a criticism which the more superficial analyses probably deserve. Nonetheless, industrialisation did introduce a myriad of significant changes which directly bear on the relations between patriarchy, capitalism and urban form.

Pred (1981a), using the concepts of time-geography has shown that the rise of the factory and large-scale shop production broke up the unity of home and work and the integration of male and female lives in artisan households in nineteenth-century America. Basing his ideas on Thompson's (1967) analysis of time use, Pred argues that the organisation of production in factories simultaneously restructured the meaning and use of time during the day for each member of the household; the nature of urban space; and of family life (including the definition of roles, authority relations and interpersonal contacts between males, females, parents and children). Pred describes the artisan household as one in which all members of the household were together at home for most of their day. Artisans were able to interrupt production 'to undertake marketing, meal preparation, child-care, household repairs, wood or coal retrieval, or other home-based

Figure 5.1   Daily time-space paths under artisan and factory mode of production

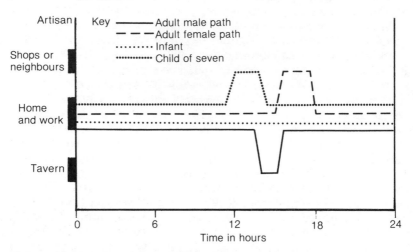

Notes: Members together much of the day.
Activities can be shifted to other times.

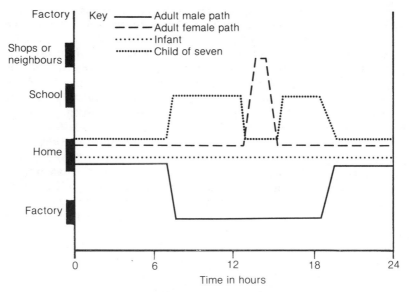

Notes: Only mother and infant together much of the day.
Flexibility for trips greatly reduced

Source: After Pred, 1981a: Figure 1, 11.

projects outside the realm of production, (Pred, 1981a,: 11). The factory changed all this by forcing workers to schedule their movements in time and space to meet the fixed working hours and spatial location of the factory. This work discipline put immediate constraints on their ability to participate in home projects or to make home-related trips, at any time other than in the short periods available before and after work (see Figure 5.1).

Under these conditions, one partner (normally the wife) was forced into taking on most, if not all, domestic responsibilities including the socialisation of children, while withdrawing from production for money income. Consequently she lost relative authority and power since in the market system value is expressed in terms of exchange and wage income. Domestic life was itself restructured to accommodate the coupling constraints imposed by the fixed operating hours of factories and schools. Opportunities for free-time for all members of the house were also restructured since the possibility to take time off throughout the day under the artisan mode were restricted under the new mode to 'prisms' (time-space limits) before and after dinner and on weekdays.

Yet another breakpoint in the separation of home and work has been identified at the point when mass transport (rail and train) in the second half of the nineteenth and early twentieth centuries encouraged a boom in suburbanisation. Suburban expansion exacerbated a separation which was already in motion and which culminated in the 1950s in a characteristic urban way of life associated with suburbia, home-based consumption and the female suburban neurosis popularised by Friedan (1963).

Corporate capitalism, the state and patriarchy

There has been little attempt yet to build the implications of contemporary urban trends into feminist theorising. This is not to deny that publications like Saegert (1980), Zelinsky et al. (forthcoming) and US Department of Transport (1978) have recognised that changes in female roles have effects which are resonating through the organisation of urban space. The problem with the work which now exists is that firstly, there is an overemphasis on single variables. Thus there has been a single-minded focus on the increase in the female labour force participation rate, which loses sight of the complex inter-connectedness of the many changes now occuring. Secondly, some of the most valuable empirical studies on the actual trip behaviour of urban women are those being done on the basis of time-space budgets (Forer and Kivell, 1981; Palm, 1981). But much of this work is atheoretical in that it uses the budget as a technique for empirical data collection and neglects to interpret the results in the context of a broader social theory integrating sex roles, domestic and market economies (Pred, 1981b).

Since about the 1920s in the USA and the 1950s in Australia, four major tendencies have helped to break up the simple work-home and hence male-female differentiation of urban space and daily life.

1 The logic guiding the urban (or for that matter, the regional or international) location of corporate capital in advanced capitalism is not the same as that of competitive capital. Production sites in the city have shifted in response to the increased concentration of capital; to its international organisation and hyper-mobility; to changes in technology and capital intensity.
2 The nature of consumption and the role of the home as the consumption unit have both been transformed. On the one hand, there has been a significant growth in the amount of consumption and there have been changes in the nature of consumption. On the other hand, a great many activities necessary for the smooth running of the domestic household now require trips to places *outside* the residence (see Chapter 4).
3 The rise of a strongly interventionist state in advanced capitalism has influenced the location and nature of both job opportunities and domestic goods and services; it has altered the urban provision of production, consumption and welfare.
4 There have been changes in the roles and daily lives of urban women (although not necessarily a commensurate alteration in male activities).

Changes in production and the location of paid work
Changes made to the urban macro-structure by shifts in the nature of accumulation have been described for the USA by Gordon (1978). He maintains that US cities carry the legacies of three different phases of accumulation[1]: commercial, industrial and corporate. The commercial city (up to the 1850s) was the marketplace of early capitalism where merchant capital made profits by trading in staples (agricultural, pastoral, fishing, forest, mineral commodities, etc.). The internal character of the cities basically retained the pre-capitalist form, since merchant capitalists were not directly intervening in production and thereby affecting social relations and spatial structure. The organisation of the pre-capitalist city was 'random', although as the commercial port cities grew they developed a simple characteristic form based on a centralised port-district, in which:

> Most establishments remained small, making it possible for nearly everyone to live and work in the same place. People of many different backgrounds and occupations were interspersed throughout the central city districts with little obvious socio-economic segregation. (Gordon, 1978: 33)

Gordon, like Pred, believes that the separation of home and work, occupation and classes comes with industrialisation. The industrial cities (from about 1850–70 to about 1900–20) had centralised factories and adjacent working-class housing districts, carefully separated from middle and upper classes who escaped to suburban outskirts. This is obviously the form of Chicago in the 1920s which Burgess depicted in his classic concentric zone model (Burgess, 1967). For Gordon, the main dynamic which changes this into the corporate city (1900–20 to the present) is the concentration of capital. This led to the decentralisation of manufacturing to peripheral industrial estates, and the emergence of the central city as the locus of power. Administrative and financial activities are spatially and organisationally separate from production in corporate capitalism and locate their headquarters in the central city. Retailing complexes emerge throughout the city, concentrated yet dispersed. There is increasing class segmentation and a scattering of the working class through the metropolitan areas. While Gordon does not refer to the implications for women as distinct from men, they clearly exist. Gordon specifically ties these changes in urban form to the logic of accumulation, specifically the need for social control by capital at each phase.

Just how applicable this generalised model is in the Australian case, is open to question. Mullins (1981) has argued that Australia has not gone through the same phases. Until the 1950s Australian cities typified an advanced form of mercantile urbanisation characterised by high levels of home ownership, low levels of publicly-provided services (notably sewerage) and a consequent need for a degree of domestic self-sufficiency based on household production. For Mullins, the domestic role of women in this situation is equivalent to that of an 'urban peasantry'. The relatively low level of state intervention in service provision and the compensation for this in home ownership and the domestic self-help economy is explained as a direct outcome of the fact that Australia never experienced a true industrial phase of capitalism. The spatial form of the advanced mercantile city and the relations between home and work are not however explored by Mullins.

From the 1950s he argues that Australian cities moved closer to the form of capitalist cities in general under the aegis of the monopoly phase. The characteristics of the corporate Australia city are given as suburbanisation, an even higher degree of home ownership, and the demise of the self-help economy. The analysis is unsatisfying, however, since there is no definition of suburbanisation, nor an explanation for how and why the charges described should necessarily occur in Australian cities. Unlike Gordon, Mullins does not make explicit links between the Australian advanced mercantile city and its corporate form. The problem arises in part because he explicitly focuses on the material form of the city associated with social reproduction, whereas Gordon also traces the changes in production.

If we turn to other evidence relevant to spatial changes associated with the locus of production and paid work, there is some evidence that Gordon's ideas can be applied here. Sydney Central Business District in the 1960s, for example, had an increase in employment in office industries (finance and property; public authority and defence; community and business services) and a fall in manufacturing, wholesaling and retailing jobs (Neutze, 1977: 101). Clerical jobs are the dominant occupational group, making up about two-thirds of female positions and one-third of male jobs. The pattern obviously varies between cities with finance and property relatively more important in Melbourne (the city of head offices) and retail trade still significant in the smaller metropolises, like central Perth. The decline of central city manufacturing is associated with rise of peripheral industrial estates, although some space-efficient manufacturing enterprises such as printing, clothing and footwear and jewellery have remained in the CBD (Neutze, 1977: 98).

Changes in consumption and social reproduction
While changes in production have transformed the location and nature of *paid work*, activities involved in the day-to-day running of a *household* have also changed over the last half-century. Pringle, in her discussion of consumer capitalism (in Chapter 4), argues that the separation of production and consumption reaches a peak under monopoly capitalism not only in response to the aggregate growth of production, but as a result of the introduction of new types of consumption (e.g. the creation and expansion of a market in children's toys). She makes a useful distinction between three phases of consumption: acquisition or purchase; transformation and servicing; and destroying, appropriating or 'using up'. Each phase has undergone different types and rates of change.

One argument which is particularly pertinent to understanding the nature of urban trends is Pringle's belief that the acquisition of goods and services (as for example, in shopping, collecting the drycleaning or taking children to the doctor) takes up a much higher proportion of women's time than it used to: 'As capital removes production from households, it also expands market relations and increases the necessity of purchasing the means of life' (Pringle, Chapter 4). Hence, she holds that there has been a rise in 'ready-made' as distinct from home-made consumer items. This has meant a shift from the production of commodities for use value within the household to the purchase and subsequent transformation of those obtained from outside. Such shifts have led to the demise of the Australian urban vegetable garden, fowl run, fruit trees, and 'do-it yourself' skills in home repair, cooking and sewing (Mullins 1981: 69–70). In some cases, the change has not so much meant the transfer of responsibility for production from the housekeeper to the marketplace or state, but a decline in home-delivery of a service. The decline in visits by the family doctor and home-delivery of groceries are two examples, both of which have forced women to make trips outside the home which were previously unnecessary.

Stacey (1980) takes a different tack on the same general area in her analysis of the relationship between public and private domains. There is no private domain of women left, she says (Stacey, 1983: 3)—a claim which is based first on the fact that many previously domestic services have been removed to the public domain (presumably health, education and general welfare services); and second, on the belief that the private domain of women has been invaded by professionals, bureaucrats, technologists and the like who take over areas of expertise previously in the hands of women.[2] Stacey suggests that many of the domestic activities that have been encroached on in this way are those known as people-work, i.e. activities in which the minds and bodies of people are processed. She finds that since the 'consumers' of such services are as much a part of the 'production' as the teacher, doctor, dentist, social worker to whom they are relating, it is not only difficult to talk about a distinction between public and private domains, it is equally spurious to separate production and consumption.

The public-private dichotomy breaks down when women faced with threats to their own home or residential sphere become involved in urban struggles, as Mullins (1979) has described for women in Brisbane. But this example suggests that there is a pre-existing situation when female activities are, in fact, home-based and privatised and only an overt threat to women will bring them out. Other Australian research attacks this premise at its base. James (1979), for example, examines the behaviour of middle-class women, the wives of retail tradesmen and professionals in a New South Wales country town and shows that:

> far from there being a radical difference between the domestic sphere of the housewife as opposed to the 'public ...world of finance and prestige' ... certain social pressures involve the two spheres so as to make the distinction virtually meaningless. (James, 1979: 41)

The conditions she refer to are for example, a woman's independent wealth and involvement in family businesses; her instrumental role in enhancing the status of the husband or family as in the choice of a prestige home; her role in establishing contacts through club memberships or social network or in engineering her husband's membership of influential organisations such as Rotary. The specific mechanisms employed by women in their 'public' activities may differ between country towns and metropolitan areas, but there is no reason to believe that they do not exist in the bigger cities.

Under this sort of an attack, the differentiation of cities into areas of home/work, female/male, private/public, consumption/production and so on seems increasingly simplistic. Women do not stay home producing the domestic needs of the household. Even women who are not engaged in *paid* work must make frequent trips for a whole variety of reasons. They must purchase or use services for personal consumption or on behalf of other members of the household. Moreover changes like the transfer of activities from the home and backyard to other agencies in the private or public sectors must ultimately reshape the house and city. There may be a lag in time and some changes may accommodate to the existing facilities. Prepared foods, for example, made it easier in the 1950s to cope in small kitchens already introduced under the economic exigencies of the 1940s (Greenbaum, 1981: 59). Eventually, however, there has emerged a discernible shift in the number, type and spatial location of urban facilities and the daily routines of women who use them.

Under the current conditions of economic crisis, the ways of meeting household needs may be changing yet again as they did during the Depression years (Milkman, 1976). Pahl (1980) believes that domestic production which fell away in the face of the mass production of consumer items, is now reviving, albeit in a different form. When faced with a lower real income people may obtain goods and services by making their own *or* by exchanging on a communal and reciprocal basis with neighbourhood people, friends or relatives; *or* by buying them for cash on an illegal or underground basis (so as, for example, to avoid taxes). People seeking an alternative to consumerism, or pursuing a lifestyle based on small-scale, conservation ethics or a celebration of hand crafts contribute to the same phenomena. Pahl argues that at least in Britain, this so-called informal economy is now growing faster than the formal economy. If this is true it will be redirecting household activities, time scheduling, trip behaviour and hence the shape of the city, once again.

Changes in state intervention
The state has had a hand in many of these tendencies affecting the interface between urbanisation, capitalism and patriarchy. For convenience I will treat these in terms of the categories already used, i.e. the state's role in paid work and social reproduction. The well-known growth of the modern state has produced a great number of new tertiary jobs, many of which have been taken by women.

Concentrated as these are in the CBD of Australian capital cities, public service jobs reinforce the pattern already established by the location of the administrative and financial aims of the private corporate world in the central city.

The simultaneous decentralisation of blue-collar jobs has also been underpinned by state policies. Industrial estates are not only located on the periphery as a part of the constraints of town planning, but may be financed wholly or in part by the public sector. The state provision of serviced industrial land is part of what O'Connor (1973) has termed 'social investment'. O'Connor suggests that in order to maintain accumulation in the private sector in the face of current crises the state has progressively socialised some of the costs of monopoly capital by 'social investment' (e.g. harbours, rail, land, industrial services) and 'social consumption' (e.g. housing, health care, and related needs of workers). Examples of state intervention of this type which have transformed Australian cities have been documented by Aungles and Szelenyi (1979) on Whyalla, SA, and Smith (1978) on Kwinana, WA.

But it is the last item—the state's role in the provision of social consumption—which has really captured the imagination of urban theorists like Castells, Dunleavy and Saunders. While the city is still seen by such writers to be an expression of capitalism as the dominant mode of production, it is not the logic of *production* but of *consumption* which is now seen to be the main dynamic in shaping the nature of the city. The state has assumed increasing responsibility for consumption for a variety of reasons not relevant here. This responsibility leads Castells to define 'the urban' in terms of collective consumption—a term which does not refer to the collective *use* of goods and services, but their collective provision, organisation and management (Castells, 1976b :25).

> The scope of the concept can thus be taken to include most aspects of public services provision (including within this category public housing and transport) and urban planning. Collective consumption processes are usually (but not always) services provided by the state apparatus. They stand in marked contrast to, and often compete with commodity forms of commercially organised consumption. (Dunleavy, 1980: 45)

The concept has been severely criticised and remains unsatisfactory despite attempts to refine it both by Dunleavy (1980) and Saunders (1981). Castells has been castigated for his glaring neglect of the position of women in consumption and social reproduction. His concepts and conception of the city are narrowly defined in terms of the capitalist mode of production alone and he treats the relations between men and women as quite unproblematic (Gamarnikow, 1978;

Cass, 1978a; Szelenyi, 1981). Be this as it may, the contributions of the new urban theory are important for highlighting the extent to which the state is seen to be the 'real manager of urban life' and of consumption. Domestic goods and services have not only been moved out of the household into the private sector (i.e. *commodified*); they have equally been taken over by the public sector (i.e. *socialised*). And so as Rose puts it:

> The massive expansion of the social services has meant that the state has increasingly penetrated those areas of social activity which are concerned with the material and ideological reproduction of labour power. Activities which were thus once left to the family, now become the concern of the state. Education, housing, health and social security and the personal social services reach in both material and psychological senses into the lives of the population. (Rose, 1978: 523)

As with commodification, the socialisation of services has not necessarily made the lives of women any easier. Not only must they find the time and means to travel to use particular services as clients, but their ability to do so is constrained by inadequate provision of other services, such as public transport and pre-school childcare facilities. Public transport systems are typically geared to move commuters, not to cater to the requirements of domestic labour. Hence, the state on the one hand forces women out of the home and on the other, immobilises them within it. By the same token there has been a general aversion in the Australian political system to wide-spread provision of pre-school childcare facilities, an aversion which is often justified on the grounds that it will undermine the family. Hence, existing facilities are unevenly spread across the city and tend to advantage inner area residents (who already have some advantage in access to central services) and residents of more affluent suburbs (most of whom do not suffer the same constraints on their personal mobility as poorer households). This pattern has been observed both in Sydney (Freestone, 1974) and in Perth (Houghton, 1979: 72).

Lying somewhere between former domestic activities now commodified or socialised, are those handled by the non-government welfare/charitable/volunteer sector (e.g. pre-school associations, YWCA, Salvation Army, Council of Social Service). The urban theorists struggle with such organisations, making arbitrary decisions as to whether to call them private or public, and whether to include or exclude them from collective or social consumption (e.g. Saunders, 1981: 261). Yet it clearly is a significant set of activities. Graycar and Yates (1981) estimate that 37 000 organisations in Australia provide an enormously varied range of services, of which at least four of the eight broad categories they define are involved in social reproduction (i.e.

agencies involved in some form of physical and mental health; basic material needs; education; family and personal wellbeing and development). Women have traditionally been active as volunteers in charitable organisations (see Baldock, Chapter 14). Hence, in taking account of the need for women to move around the city to fulfil their domestic responsibilities, it is necessary to recognise not only trips made for the purposes of consumption, but equally those made to volunteer labour in the provision of services to others (whether as a part of the informal economy by exchanging babysitting, for example, or in the volunteer sector, as in the case of school lunch or library duty).

The changing role of women, the family and domestic sphere
The traditional female role of woman totally occupied as wife and mother for a nuclear family isolated and privatised in a suburban home, is an increasingly dubious 'norm'. There is little need to dwell on the obvious fact that 45.1 per cent of Australian women are in paid work, including 42 per cent of married women (see Baldock elsewhere in this book). It is now generally accepted that women in paid work have not replaced their domestic responsibilities with employment, but carry a dual role. The constraints imposed on women who fit both roles into their day are reflected in highly fragmented time-space budgets, which contain very little in the way of personal free time (Young, 1980; Palm and Pred, 1977).

Nor can we be content to use the nuclear family as a description of the typical household or consumption unit: only 48.8 per cent of Australian families fit this description. Nor, can we assume that women fulfil their domestic activities as 'dependent' wives: 10 per cent of Australian families are headed by females.[3] Like the shift of women into the labour force, these changes in the structure of households must further alter women's daily use of time and urban space, rendering obsolete the descriptions of industrial time-space budgets and urban form outlined by Pred and others (Figure 1).

The domestic role has itself been transformed by the decline in family size and mechanisation of housework. There is some debate as to whether technology has given women more leisure time as is popularly supposed, or whether it has changed the nature of work and increased time spent in housework (Bose, 1979; Cowan, 1976; Baldock, 1981; Pringle, Chapter 4). In a parallel fashion it is by no means clear that women have more 'free' time as a result of their loss of control over activities now commodified, socialised, transferred to the volunteer sector, or to the communal and cash forms of the informal economy. It seems just as likely that a woman's responsibility for these activities continues and that the main effect has been to substitute time previously spent at home for time now spent on trips to supply or purchase services (Rothblatt, 1979).

It is important to keep in mind that what has been outlined so far is a general model. The tendencies changing the city, society and women have not had an even impact on the built environment or on all social groups. The environment has been shaped by ideologies and practices in which class, gender and race interact. The intervening effect class may have on the way the patriarchal nature of an environment is expressed has been touched on by historians such as Hughes (1978), Cranz (1980, 1981), and Ryan (1975; cited by Hayden, 1980: 928). Women of different ethnic and class blackgrounds have different expectations about what their domestic role entails (see Chapter 4); they operate under quite different constraints. The plight of poor female single parents or of migrant women coping behind language barriers makes this an obvious point. Life-cycle stage is another important intervening variable. In fact, the extent to which women are satisfied with their housing environment and a woman's general sense of psychological wellbeing appears to have more to do with marital status, age, and number of children than it does with class or cultural background (Rothblatt, 1979: 156-62).

The urban non-residential domestic sphere

It is useful at this point to introduce the notion of the non-residential sphere to account for those activities in which women are engaged outside the home as mothers, wives and housekeepers in the course of social reproduction. To the extent that they are engaged in domestic labour the term obviously relates also to men. As in the case of home-based domestic activities, the non-residential domestic sphere may involve consumption—where women go out to acquire, transform or use necessary services and commodities (food, clothing, etc.). It may equally be called production when women create goods and services for use-value either for household consumption or for informal exchange. Production of this type is, however, quite distinct from the production of goods and services for exchange in the formal market.

The organisation of both time and space can then be described using not two, but three basic categories. The home-work dualism is replaced by: (1) home (residential-domestic); (2) non-residential domestic; and (3) paid work spheres.

The non-residential sphere includes wholesale and retail outlets distributing commodities for household consumption; public agencies and facilities providing socialised services used by the household (from parks to post offices); non-governmental and volunteer agencies either aided by women or used to obtain their domestic needs; and finally other residences in the city, when these are part of an informal economy used to support another household.

Leisure activities are still ambiguous in this schema. It is common to distinguish between a woman's 'non-free' time involved in paid work and domestic labour and her 'free' time which may be devoted to leisure (e.g. Palm, 1981). Yet it is very evident that not all so-called leisure activities are 'free' (Baldock, 1981). Certainly those involving children are often obligatory parental activities especially in societies which place a high value on sports and recreation as a means of socialisation and on health care. Hence, both the domestic spheres (residential and non-residential) may be further subdivided according to the degree to which any activities are voluntary or obligatory; discretionary or non-discretionary. What we now think of as leisure may fall anywhere along this scale. So also may shopping. While many writers see marketing as a necessary part of housework (e.g. Pringle, 1981; Palm, 1981), others classify shopping as a leisure activity (e.g. Preston, 1981). This type of confusion is obviously rooted in the limitations of dichotomous categories which restrict women's work to consumption, implicitly devalue its contribution and hence mistakenly imply it as dispensable (as is assumed for all 'leisure').

We are now in a better position to describe the patriarchal basis of cities modified by the logics of monopoly capitalism and the welfare state, and to consider the effects on daily lives of women living in these cities. Most of the discussion is framed in terms of trip behaviour, because this is where we have a small amount of evidence. In looking first at the domestic role, I am assuming for reasons already given that there has been a shift in the use of women's time in the domestic sphere from residential to non-residential with obvious effects on the nature and distribution of urban services and facilities. That women spend a good part of their time making trips for domestic purposes is clear from evidence scattered through the literature on trip behaviour. Hanson and Hanson (1981: 173) for example, compare Swedish male and female frequency of travel for five purposes: work, social, recreation, shopping and personal business. The last two might be considered to include many obligatory non-residential domestic trips. In these two categories women, regardless of whether they are employed or unemployed, consistently made more trips than men—many more in the case of shopping. Preston's study points out that it is the period when women's home care responsibilities are *greatest*, i.e. when they have pre-school children to care for, that they are more frequently engaged in activities like shopping, visiting parks, and helping other people—all activities which contribute to their own or others' support for social reproduction (Preston, 1981, Table 2: 22).

Four hypotheses about female trip behaviour for non-residential domestic purposes under monopoly capitalism now seem tenable. In fact, some of these have already emerged as the findings of empirical research.

1 There has been an increase in the total number of trips made by women.
2 Longer individual trips are being required.
3 Conversely, however, women are spatially and temporarily restricted in how far they can travel and how long they can be away at particular times during the day.
4 There has been an increase in the number of multipurpose trips.

Longer trips are caused by the concentration of capital infrastructure in the private sector, of which the decline of the corner store in the face of reqional shopping complexes is the classic example. But long trips may equally have been inspired by the centralisation and institutionalisation of public services—illustrated, for example, by the massive building programs of medical complexes in Australian cities in the 1970s. In some neighbourhoods it is the uneven distribution of facilities and services and inadequate public transport systems which necessitate long or roundabout trips—*or* preclude them altogether. In a New Zealand study, Forer and Kivell (1981) make it abundantly clear how the interaction of the demands of a housewife's role, her common lack of a car, combined with the uneven distribution of services and facilities between neighbourhoods make it nigh impossible for some women to use the services they need. The problems are particularly acute for women such as single parents who are housed in peripheral state housing areas, located so as to take advantage of cheaper land, but which impose severe social costs on inhabitants.

The concentration, centralisation or uneven distribution of services comes in sharp conflict with the restrictions placed on women's ability to go far from the home base. The recurrent demands of childcare, housekeeping and a common need to rely on public transport all contribute to this restriction. Hence it is not surprising to find that women travel shorter overall distances than men, whether it is to work or for other purposes (Hanson and Hanson, 1980, Table IV: 297; Manning, 1978).

The multipurpose trip is a logical outcome of the need for women to make more trips or longer trips and yet still manage to fit them into the time limits imposed by a finite day and the coupling constraints of children, work demands, closing hours and so on. There is some evidence to suggest that the multipurpose trip has, in fact, changed the nature of the journey to work. Hanson (1980) has shown with a Swedish survey that 56 per cent of *all* trips are multipurpose.[4] Moreover 53 per cent of work trips involved other stops and Hanson concludes that 'personal, social and especially commercial transactions are all frequently linked to the journey to work' (Hanson,

1980: 235). She suggests that some services may be more strongly linked to workplace than home. Virtually all the landuse types she identifies as 'stops' can potentially fill non-residential domestic needs (i.e. they include supermarket, department store, bank, hospital, flower shop, etc.). The radical conclusion to which this leads is that at least some part of the organisation of domestic life and the location of some household services may revolve *not* around the residence as has so long been assumed, but around workplaces. As Hanson says, it is difficult to sort out yet which logic (home, work or any other) governs the location of specific services.

This is a convenient point to turn to working women's own job locations and journey to work. Two factors must be recognised at the outset. The first is the existence of a sex-segregated labour market in which women are concentrated in particular jobs (Collins, 1977; Baldock, Chapter 3.)

On average, women find their job opportunities in different parts of the city from men. Women take the majority of lower-paid tertiary jobs (e.g. as clerks, shop assistants, nurses, bank tellers, receptionists, etc.), whereas jobs in secondary industry are, with obvious exceptions such as those in clothing and textiles, still largely the preserve of males. Under monopoly capitalism and the growth of state employment, tertiary jobs (both private and public) are often centralised, while some industrial sites are decentralised. Hence it is reasonable to expect a higher proportion of working women than of working men to be employed in the central city. The second point to keep in mind is that employed women operate under the special constraints imposed by their dual role (as housekeeper and paid worker) and by their limited mobility. While many Australian households now have two cars, working men are still more likely to have independent transport than working women. Hence it would be logical to find women looking for local jobs in easy reach of their homes and to be using public transport to a greater extent than men.

Empirical research tends to confirm these general patterns, although the findings are not as unequivocal. In a comprehensive study of the patterns in Sydney, Manning (1978) found that while the distribution of job locations for men and women is broadly similar, two differences are evident. Manufacturing areas are generally not concentrated in the CBD, and in some areas (although not all) there are clearly more opportunities for men to work. For example, while women comprised 36 per cent of the metropolitan labour force in 1976, they held only 23 per cent of jobs in South Sydney/Botany and 31 per cent in Parramatta/Auburn (Manning, 1978: 73). On the other hand, the city centre is slightly more important for women than men, having 29 per cent of female employment as compared to 25 per cent of male jobs (Manning, 1978: 76). Manning's maps illustrate the fact that Sydney women more frequently work in the commercial and retailing areas and less often in the major industrial zones. As expected, the spatial distribution of jobs reflects labour market segmentation.

The tendency for women to work locally is also evident with 10 to 30 per cent more women taking nearby jobs than men (Manning, 1978: 86-90). So it is not surprising that the study also confirms that women travel shorter distances; the median straight line journey to work for women is two-thirds of that for men (4.8 km as against 7.5 km). The greater mobility of males is also clear; more than two-thirds of all men travel to work by car, as against a half of the married working women and one-third of single working women.

Howe and O'Connor (1981) have found similar patterns in Melbourne. Their results make it clear that while the female journey to work is, *on average*, shorter than males', women are attracted to the central city from a wider area (or labourshed). Hence some women either can or must sacrifice their need for proximity to the home, in order to obtain a job available in the city centre. Research for Perth by Voysey (1981) does not verify the importance of local work for women. A relatively small proportion of both sexes work locally in that city—an outcome, perhaps, of the city's smaller size and industrial base.

Studies of female time-space budgets provide a micro-view of the daily lives of women in cities. Hanson and Hanson (1980; 1981) have revealed how Swedish women have adjusted their activities, use of time and travel in the city to accommodate their increased participation in the labour force. The time-space budgets of males, which might be expected to change if they shared more of the domestic role, have *not* significantly altered. So while women have gone to work in increasing numbers, the 'implacable array of schedules' and 'unbreakable patterns' which gave them no room to live as individuals in suburbia (Rothblatt, et al, 1979: 13) remain changed but unchanged.

They are unchanged because the need for working women to schedule time for household production still continues. They are changed because now these activities must be arranged around a woman's own working day, and the availability of the services required. As Baldock (1981) points out, doctors, dentists, banks and shops provide their services only during working hours and hence are poorly scheduled in time for working women. We have little evidence on how conveniently they are located in space for working women although it is clear those at home face real difficulties. In an emotional commentary on the issue, Young (1980: 21–22) concludes:

an Australian time-budget survey of one woman's day makes a

mockery of what is termed 'quality of life'. . . . To the degree that women carry dual work loads and function in cities that do not accommodate their (oftentimes) fragmented and disparate activity patterns then terrible assaults are made on their share of time. The result is guilt-ridden women trying desperately to give lie to the old adage 'you can't be in two places at once'.

Further changes: economic crisis, energy crisis and neo-conservatism

Contemporary capitalism is being restructured at an international level (e.g. by technological change; by the effects of OPEC oil price rises; by the international division of labour; and by the various crises of capitalism. It is equally being restructured at national and regional levels, as in the deindustrialisation of the old manufacturing heartlands of Australia, Canada, the USA and Britain. The emergence of neo-conservatism in liberal democracies may be changing the role of the state in social welfare. These changes may affect home, work and the non-residential domestic sphere. They will alter yet again the relationships between male and female roles and urban spatial form in ways which are only hinted at in the three examples given below.

Technological changes, notably in micro-electronics, are altering the scale, organisation and location of production, and the consequent shifts in economic activity are not evenly spread throughout the city, between cities and between men and women. This has altered the traditional understanding of where firms are located both locally and nationally. Technology has further disrupted our understanding of where work is located relative to residential areas, a relationship previously transformed by the deindustrialisation of the city centre and rise of peripheral industrial estates. Micro-electronics may have made it possible to reorganise production in spatially efficient ways. Firms, even large ones, no longer need the quantity of land which attracted them to the outskirts of major cities under monopoly capitalism. Technological change may yet move some production back into the home with sophisticated communication systems allowing for centralised control of a new version of piece-work.

The energy crisis, particularly the high cost of travel by private car, is being seen as a disincentive to long trip patterns, and an incentive for increased urban residential densities and a return to central city living. Rothblatt et al. (1979: 3) argue that the trends in the last quarter of this century will bear striking parallels with the so-called street car suburbs of a century ago in the USA, and the authors call their prophecy 'the once and future suburbia'. They foresee that the stresses on women will be increased, not decreased.

The changing nature of state provision of welfare services under the pressure of neo-conservatism may push welfare provision back to residential care, coinciding with the incentive within households to take on more domestic use production. This has come about with the rise of the informal economy, inspired both by economic necessity and the wish of some individuals for an alternative lifestyle based on less materialism and a conservation ethic. Just how important these tendencies are and how widespread their effects on urban households and city structure will be, remains to be seen. Szelenyi (1981) sees the changes as potentially reuniting home and work, but I remain more sceptical. The changes wrought in female consciousness, in the organisation of the household and in the built environment by the creation of a non-residential domestic sphere, will not disappear overnight. There are infinite prospects for clashes and contradictions between passing and evolving policies, and in a built environment created to meet the needs of one phase of capitalism which now appears to be in the process of being superseded by another phase.

The four phases of the capitalist-patriarchal city

The argument to this point can be roughly summarised in an ideal-type mode (Table 5.1). Like all ideal-types, this is a crude description of the situation for any one city which carries the legacies of its own socio-historical context. It is presented as an evolutionary model but again, particular cities need not move through all phases. Nor is the form of a city and organisation of domestic life necessarily consistent with any one phase. Contradictions are likely to be the norm, not the exception.

Such contradictions may be unintentional. For example, given the uneven nature of capitalist development and the difficulties inherent in transforming the built environment, it is not surprising that neighbourhoods will differ markedly in the same city. Some may have services, facilities and job opportunities distributed on the basis of one logic (e.g. that of the industrial city, replete with corner stores and no secondary industry); while others have been created consistent with a different phase (and lack any retailing at all due to concentration and regionalisation under corporate capitalism).

Other contradictions may be explicitly, if unconsciously, built into our planning practices, or are the outcome of class conflict. Isolated mining towns provide a useful example. Isolated ore bodies as in the north and west of Australia are mined by transnational firms using capital intensive technologies operated by a small, mainly male labour force. Such operations can be efficiently organised on the basis of a fly-in or commuting system built around, for example, six work shifts interspersed with two-week breaks (Centre for Resource Studies, 1979). The workers live in a camp while on site and return to their

Table 5.1 The four phases of the capitalist-patriarchal city

Phase	Form of City	Stage/Submode of Capitalism	Role of the State	Location and Organization of Domestic Sphere	Urban Sites for Production/Workplace
1	pre-mercantile pre-industrial	pre-capitalist	pre-state or laissez-faire state	unity of home and work	home-based crafts or local employment
2	industrial	competitive capitalism	laissez-faire state	separation of home and work; rise of suburbs as domestic sphere	centralisation of work in CBD
3	corporate	monopoly capitalism	welfare state	domestic sphere split into: residential, non-residential (commodification and socialisation of services)	decentralisation of secondary jobs (male); centralization of tertiary jobs (female); diversification of suburbs (local employment: female)
4	neo-conservative	capitalism: in transition; 'in crisis'	neo-conservative state	change in domestic sphere by: emergence of informal economy (decommodification); shrinkage of welfare state (desocialisation); reversion to residential care and voluntary agencies).	loss of local jobs (deindustrialisation); changes in location due to different space needs of technologically advanced firms (implications unclear)

families housed in established urban centres during rest periods. This is not only the standard model for oil rigs, it is the option often preferred by companies operating on land. It has clear advantages for ore bodies with a limited life span and for any isolated site can offer real advantages over the highly expensive and socially troublesome mining towns common in resource rich frontiers of Australia, Canada and elsewhere. Although major companies once saw real value in planning and controlling company towns, they are now increasingly eschewing responsibility for financing, building and governing such settlements (Bradbury, 1980; Thompson, 1981).

Nonetheless, they remain under pressure from governments like that of Western Australia to create towns in isolated regions as a means of developing the areas, establishing infrastructure (and thereby helping to defend the 'vulnerable north'). The modern Australian variants are modelled on suburbia with the typical two- or three-bedroom, airconditioned bungalow with all mod. cons on a fifth- or quarter-acre grassed lot. The company provides all services (via the town manager, company store, maintenance officers, gardeners, etc.).

Company towns are a contradiction for which the women pay the highest price (Williams, 1981; Holden, 1981). Suburbia evolved out of the industrial phase of capitalism and the rise of public transport, as the locus of consumption, and a necessary female role in social reproduction. The company takes over much of this role in company towns having initially found this to be useful (Bradbury, 1980). Women are thereby confined to a built environment but denied their socially necessary role in it (with the obvious exceptions of the satisfaction of male sexual needs and child-sitting). At the same time, women are largely denied jobs in the mine, as much out of the resistance of male workers and unions as from company policy. Hence they cannot even substitute paid employment for their traditional role in social reproduction. It is little wonder they suffer inordinate levels of social and psychological stress. The contradictions take a different form in isolated, non-company mining towns. There Palm (1981) has shown that women must spend more time than their metropolitan counterparts in travel to other places to acquire the goods and services they need, a graphic illustration of the personal tyranny imposed by the organisation of consumption around a non-residential sphere.

A pessimistic postcript

Very few writers have conceived of the capitalist city as liberating for women (MacIver and Page, 1950, are an exception). Most writers who describe the female perspective see the position of women as pro-blematic. Scattered throughout the writings are ad hoc proposals for redesigning the city so as to make life a little easier for women. The proposals range from suggestions that planners redesign residential neighbourhoods to facilitate the traditional activities of wife and mother (e.g. Stretton, 1970), to others proposing that we decentralise jobs so as to provide more local work for women (e.g. Manning, 1978) and improve public transport. Suggestions for reform are handicapped by the fact that the field as a whole is still at the stage of developing a *feminist urban* theory, i.e. one which describes the way women's roles are embedded in urban form. It is a whole new enterprise to construct an *urban feminist* theory, i.e. one which will outline the forms of the city that will help liberate women.[5] Only in radical and Utopian proposals such as those outlined by Hayden is there any suggestion that some fundamental elements of patriarchy, capitalism and physical space must be simultaneously reshaped before women will be much better off. The Swedish experience shows clearly how reforms in favour of women, such as increased job opportunities, can rebound leaving them labouring under an even greater load.

The problem is that urban planners are a long way from realising that a problem even exists, let alone how deep rooted it is. MSJ Keys Young (1975) found in a survey of Australian planners that most did not differentiate between men and women in the city; that there was some sensitivity at the federal level (in the immediate post-Whitlam period) but that even where women were seen as a special concern, they were classed simply as 'disadvantaged' like the poor or ethnic minorities. This is almost worse than perceiving no problem at all since it tends to forestall a serious analysis of the specific causes and nature of the patriarchal city. There has been some suggestion that if only we could get more women into planning, then they would bring a different dimension to the profession (Kennedy, 1981). However, this still ignores the capitalist ideologies embedded in planning and the built environment (Scott and Roweis, 1977). We face infinite difficulties in untying the straitjackets imposed on women by the nexus now forged between urbanisation, capitalism and patriarchy.

Notes

1 Different writers use different terms but there seems to be some general agreement on three main phases variously labelled (a) commercial/mercantile; (b) industrial/competitive; (c) monopoly/corporate/advanced/mature/late capitalism.
2 Ironically, it is the woman who is applauded as the professional homemaker and ultimate consumer in the ideologies carried in advertising and social intercourse. (See Pringle in this book and Rothblatt, 1979: 45.)
3 Source: Australian Bureau of Statistics, 1980c. No. 4101.0.
4 Calculated from Table 1 in Hanson (1980:233).
5 I am indebted to Frances Rowland for pointing this out to me.

6 Women as welfare recipients: women, poverty and the state

LOIS BRYSON

The fact that a meaningful title for a paper can be 'Women as welfare recipients' is itself a comment on the position of women in society and the critical role gender plays in determining life chances. Of course one could construct the reciprocal title 'Men as welfare recipients' but it would appear contrived. Discussions about men and welfare would probably be focused on unemployment or sickness benefits, compensation or invalid pensions, subjects which are specifically juxtaposed to employed status. What is more, as is so often the case in the analysis of social issues, it is most unlikely that the word men would appear in the title: universality would, quite inappropriately, be assumed. For women, the general term 'welfare recipient' is meaningful precisely because it represents an extension of their dependent role in the family situation. This means that my task of considering women as welfare recipients must be recognised to have broad significance, since unravelling values embedded in the welfare system is one way of approaching dominant values in general.

To discuss women and welfare then, raises the whole issue of gender relationships in capitalist society, and to try to explain these relationships we need to look to the conjuncture of two key institutions, the family and the economic system (a point made by many of the contributors to this collection, e.g. Baldock, Cass, Shaver). Women's position in relation to these institutions provides the key to our understanding of why women are likely to be welfare recipients and why, to express a corollary of this, they are likely to be poor.

We must recognise the welfare system as an outgrowth of the capitalist mode of production, though clearly certain values which have shaped the form welfare takes predate capitalism. We must also acknowledge an ambiguity within the situation. Gough (1979) is one of the most recent writers to emphasise this ambiguity, pointing out that welfare on the one hand must be seen as representing a real gain for the working class in general, as people would suffer greater privation without such provisions. At the same time welfare is necessary part of the capitalist system and therefore one of the mechanisms which contribute to working class subordination, that is, the subordination of the very group likely to receive the benefits, and into the bargain it is the working class that largely foots the bill. As Shaver and Walker (1980) point out, benefits tend to be a redistribution from employed workers to the non-employed, or from single workers to married workers, rather than there being a significant redistribution of income downward from the wealthy (cf. Gough, 1979; Westergaard and Resler, 1975; Head, 1980).

Gough (1979) like most other male Marxists does not further examine what I see as a 'double ambiguity' for women. Without welfare measures women would be doubly disadvantaged because they rarely have skills which command high wages in the labour market, their child-rearing responsibilities restrict employment possibilities, and, insofar as they occupy marginal positions in the labour market, their employment opportunities are particularly insecure (cf. Women's Employment Rights' Campaign, 1979; Transnational Co-op, 1980; Chapter 2). This means that welfare provisions represent a crucial form of access to basic economic support. Simultaneously, these welfare measures perpetuate a double form of subordination: within the class system as a whole, working-class women, like working-class men, are subordinate, but additionally at all levels of the class structure, women are subordinated to men. Welfare maintains both forms of subordination but it is with this latter form that I am particularly concerned in this paper. I want to consider the way in which the welfare system reinforces the patriarchal family system and thus helps maintain the subordination and dependency of women. As Wilson puts it, 'social welfare policies amount to no less than the State organisation of domestic life' (1977: 9). I intend to tease out the way in which this is done and the form of domestic life the state is involved in organising.

Much has been written about women's child-rearing role and certainly this is a crucial role, but we must be aware that this is not the only strand of patriarchal ideology, though the separation of female dependency and child-rearing may often be an analytic rather than a real distinction. Bell and Newby have pointed out that:

> a degree of ideological hegemony over women must clearly be maintained if they are to continue to accept their subordinate position as natural and desirable and the superior power of men as legitimate. (1976: 159)

Fundamental to the maintenance of such hegemony is the role of man as economic provider and the role of woman as receiver, a division which developed within the capitalist mode of production with the split between workplace and home, and the relegation of women to the domestic arena which has become identified as secondary to the economic arena. In this way, as Zaretsky has pointed out, 'male supremacy which long antedated capitalism, became an institutional part of the capitalist system of production' (1976: 29).

A number of provisions in the taxation and social welfare systems maintain women outside the labour market in their roles of wife and mother. Taxation policies legitimise women's dependency by providing concessions to married male taxpayers who maintain a dependent spouse. Such policies should be regarded as part of the welfare state, but in this paper I shall be concerned only with some details of income security policies administered by the Australian Department of Social Security which are usually (though I think far too narrowly) understood as welfare policy. Like taxation, these policies also support the right of men to maintain a dependent spouse by incorporating allowances into the various benefits and pensions. The amount made available is of course inadequate but the intention is clear enough and shares the same value underpinnings as the notion of the 'family wage' (cf. Land, 1980; Chapter 3). Dependent status for females is further reinforced by a series of strictly female entitlements based on the notion that if a woman (usually a woman with dependent children) has no man on whom to be dependent, the state is prepared to step into this supporting role.

This automatic legitimacy (subject to income test) of dependent status for females has no direct equivalent for males. Government income maintenance is available to men only when some impediment to paid employment can be demonstrated such as invalidity, sickness, old age, or inability to find paid work, and with satisfactory compliance with the 'work test'. Since the extension of the supporting parent's benefit to fathers, sole responsibility for child-rearing has also become a basis for income provision. While the establishment of this principle is an important one, it has been taken up by very few fathers to date[1] and in any case it does not make male and female situations similar since women are supported by the state not only in respect of their mother role, as will become apparent in our examination of eligibility for welfare payments.

The officially sanctioned dependency of wife on husband is a crucial element of women's oppression, and it is therefore necessary for us to understand the way in which the concept is embedded in social life. The area chosen for examination here is welfare policy, but before dealing with this directly, I shall attempt to demonstrate briefly the overall outcome, by considering women's inferior economic position. Finally the paper raises policy measures which would reduce female dependence and looks at the potential support for these measures and at the lack of support, since what is not supported by government is equally as revealing as what is.

Women's relative economic position

The repercussions of dependence are seen most clearly when women maintain their own households, but married women are also usually relatively poorer than men. I do not intend to pursue the general picture to any depth, but will raise two dimensions which demonstrate the broad parameters. I shall briefly consider personal wealth holdings and relative earning capacity, before moving to a consideration of female-headed families.

The distribution of personal wealth in Australia makes clear the relative disadvantage of women. Although comprehensive statistics are not available, Raskall (1978: 9) has made estimations by extrapolation from estate duty records. As Table 6.1 shows, at no stage of the life cycle are women as a group likely to hold as much wealth as men.

Table 6.1 Estimated distribution of wealth between age groups and between sex groups, 1970: percentage in group owning over $15 000

age group	males	females	total
20–29	10.90	2.30	6.70
30–39	11.38	4.67	8.10
40–49	13.03	6.74	9.90
50–59	16.70	10.28	13.40
60–69	18.80	13.24	15.92
70–79	19.03	13.73	15.86
80 +	19.27	13.64	15.58
all ages	13.75	7.32	10.53

Source: Raskall, 1978: 9.

This discrepancy is most striking in the 20-49 years age categories, that is, during the child-rearing years, before a significant proportion of widows, having inherited from their husbands, increase the proportions of women with higher levels of personal wealth.

When we consider relative earning capacity the picture is confirmed, despite the formal introduction of equal pay in 1974 (Baldock, elsewhere in this book). In January 1980 the weighted average minimum weekly wage rate for males throughout Australia was $175.32, while the equivalent rate for women was $160.89. The discrepancy between the rates was even greater in some states; for example in New South Wales the male rate was $177.09 and the female rate $160.87 (ABS, 1980b: 9). These figures are extrapolated from 'awards, determinations and collective agreements' and thus show that even formal equality has not been achieved. Consideration of other issues suggests that the discrepancy between male and female

arned income can be better described as a 'gulf'. Firstly, as
iotes in Chapter 3, women have higher unemployment rates
i, as well as a higher incidence of hidden unemployment (i.e.
s withdrawal from active job searching and their resulting
ipearance in the ranks of the recorded unemployed).

Secondly, average (mean) weekly earnings are significantly lower
for women: 67 per cent of average weekly earnings for males in
August 1981. While this difference partly reflects the number of
women in part-time employment, the full-time women workers' rate
was still only 79 per cent of the male rate—an increase of only 2 percentage points since the period 1975-77 (New South Wales Premier's
Department, 1980; ABS, 1982d: 4). The significance of women's roles
as wives and mothers can be clearly demonstrated by an examination
of age differences in mean weekly earnings. Amongst young people
(15 to 19 years), women's average earnings represented 86 per cent of
male earnings, but from the age of 19, the proportion dropped to 68
per cent (ABS, 1982d; 9).

In a consideration of relative poverty, it is also important to point
out that lower wages for women are compounded by lower rates of
labour force participation and higher proportions in part-time work
(Chapter 3). Women also earn less from overtime, clearly because of
their reduced opportunities to augment income by working outside
'normal hours', given their domestic responsibilities (New South
Wales Premier's Department, 1980).

Nonetheless we must be aware that this picture of female disadvantage would change dramatically if domestic labour were given
an economic value, rather than being either ignored or in fact
contributing to 'worsening, for wives and mothers, a labour market
position which is already inferior because of other aspects of sexual
inequality' (Gardiner, 1976: 117). As Edwards (1980c) points out,
unpaid domestic work clearly represents value for the income unit.
This can be readily comprehended when the costs expended by
workers on items such as childcare, domestic help, fast foods and
other trade-offs of money for time are considered. The fact that most
economists (usually male) do not assess domestic labour in terms of a
monetary equivalent, highlights the taken-for-grantedness of the
presumption of female dependence. However, it should be noted that
this is a relatively recent phenomenon in advanced capitalist societies.
The occupation of housewife was treated in censuses as an 'economically active' role until 1871, in Australia and England at least
(Land, 1980: 60; Deacon, 1982).

Economic position of female-headed families

In female-headed families, women's precarious financial situation is made dramatically clear. The 1973 survey carried out by the Australian Bureau of Statistics, for the Commission of Inquiry into Poverty (1975a) showed 'fatherless' families to be by far the poorest of the groups categories as 'disability groups'. After housing was taken into account (and housing of course represents one index of 'wealth'), 30 per cent of fatherless families fell below the 'austere' poverty line set by the Commission and a further 20 per cent were only marginally above the line. The next group, with 26 per cent below the poverty line, consisted of 'income units' with 'multiple disabilities', followed by the unemployed (18.7 per cent) and the sick and invalid (17.9 per cent). It is of some relevance to my argument that the next disability group was motherless families (13.2 per cent) which highlights the importance of the 'intact' family structure as a basis for economic wellbeing and supports Edward's assessment of the economic value of unpaid domestic labour. This is further supported by scrutiny of the figures for the aged. Only 3.8 per cent of 'aged couples' formed income units below the poverty line but the figure rose to 8.4 per cent for 'aged females (single)' and 13 per cent for 'aged males (single)' (Commission of Inquiry into Poverty, 1975a: 19).

A 'General Social Survey' of Australian families carried out two years later in 1975 by the Australian Bureau of Statistics for the Family Research Unit of the University of New South Wales, confirmed the Poverty Commission's findings. The survey established that 9 per cent of all Australian families with a child of 17 years or younger were one-parent families, 8 per cent mother-headed and 1 per cent father-headed (ABS 1980a: 6). Samples of approximately 2000 one-parent and 2000 two-parent families were then compared on a series of criteria demonstrating the relative financial deprivation of one-parent families.

Of the one-parent families, 42 per cent were in receipt of government benefits, compared with only 1.4 per cent of two-parent families; 42 per cent had a weekly income of under $80 compared with 2 per cent of the two-parent families, and only 9 per cent were in the top income category ($160 +) compared with 51 per cent of the two-parent families. The date are not disaggregated for male- and female-headed families, but clearly female-headed families constitute the majority of the deprived one-parent families, since they outnumber male-headed families eight to one. In addition, while 76 per cent of fathers in one-parent families were employed full time, only 25 per cent of mothers in one-parent families were in full-time employment (ABS, 1980a).

A consideration of the workforce participation of these families clearly illustrates the basic point of this paper, that it is not the practicalities of domestic and conjugal situations which are decisive, but entrenched sex role definitions. We find, in fact, that the patterns of employment for all fathers and all mothers are very similar irrespective of whether they are in one- or two-parent families (see Table 6.2).

Table 6.2 Labour force status of fathers and mothers (percentages)

	Mothers		Fathers	
	one-parent families	two-parent families	one-parent families	two-parent families
Employed full-time	25	19	76	82
Employed part-time	19	25	12	9
Unemployed	2	1ʰ	5	2
Not in Labour force	53	54	4	5
Not stated	2	2	3	2
Total	101	101	100	100

Source: ABS, 1980a: 10.

Since in 1975 the supporting parent's benefit had not been extended to males, it might not seem surprising that 76 per cent of fathers in one-parent families were in full-time work, not unlike the figure (82 per cent) for fathers in two-parent families. Mothers in one-parent families had a similar (overall) employment pattern to mothers in two-parent families, but were more likely to be in full-time employment. A majority of those not in the labour force were in receipt of government benefits, and it was this group who were, and still are, most likely to be poor.

The extension of supporting parent's benefit to fathers in 1977 has been accompanied by changes in the employment patterns of fathers with dependent children in single-parent families: in June 1981, 83 per cent were employed, 78 per cent full-time and 5 per cent part-time. This represents a contrast with employment rates for fathers in two-parent families (94 per cent; and only 2 per cent working part-time) (ABS, 1982b: 22). It is likely that the existence of an explicit government benefit has enabled supporting fathers to reduce their labour market activity, but the low take-up rates (only 11 per cent of male sole parents) suggests that paid work remains men's favoured means of family support. This clearly protects them from the potential poverty which confronts 80 per cent of women sole parents who were pensioners or beneficiaries in June 1981[1].

A key aspect of the impoverished situation of one-parent families is their vulnerable housing circumstances. The fact that fatherless families remained the poorest group identified in the Poverty Inquiry survey *after* housing had been taken into account, is indicative, and other data confirm this. The 'General Social Survey' of Australian families found that only 37 per cent of one-parent families owned or were buying their accommodation, compared with 72 per cent of two-parent families, and 43 per cent were renting compared with 23 per cent of two-parent families (ABS, 1980a: 16). Lone parents were much more likely to be renting from a state housing authority, and to share accommodation; 11 per cent were boarding (no two-parent families were); and 7 per cent had other arrangements such as living rent-free with parents, relatives or friends (2 per cent of two-parent families). Shared arrangements may well be advantageous for single parents but the evidence suggests that there is often no other choice. The Family Services Committee Report (1978, Vol. 11: 211) summarised the information on housing problems in Australia and concluded that 'the most striking finding is the high housing burden of female-headed families'. Detailed examination of the Victorian housing situation and its failure to meet the needs of low-income families in general and female-headed families in particular has recently been undertaken by the Victorian Women's Refuge Group (1979) in a document entitled *Women and Housing*.

Evidence abounds to demonstrate the financial vulnerability of female-headed families with the sub-group most at risk being welfare recipients. For example, a survey of emergency relief carried out in 1978 in New South Wales, Victoria, Queensland and South Australia, found that persons no longer married formed between 30 and 46 per cent of all clients and that the separated persons are almost ten times as prevalent as in their state population (Commonwealth Department of Social security and ACOSS, 1978: 42).

In view of such evidence, it is not surprising to find that when asked in the 'General Social Survey' to specify their worries, 65 per cent of one-parent compared with 43 per cent of two-parent families specified 'money matters'. The discrepancy between the groups was even larger in relation to 'lack of adult companionship', which was the complaint of 29 per cent of single parents, but only 11 per cent of married couples. This raises another facet of the dominance of the patriarchal family ideology: social interaction patterns are constructed along gender and marital status lines, thus creating barriers to other forms of interaction outside the conventional nuclear family.

Female dependence and income maintenance provisions

Having presented a profile of the economic disadvantage of women in general, and of lone female parents as the most vulnerable sub-group, I return now to the notion of 'dependence' which I am suggesting underpins this situation. I will examine the notion of 'legitimate dependence' as it is embedded in the regulations relating to income maintenance in Australia. I will restrict the discussion to the most salient federal government income maintenance provisions: wives' pensions, dependent spouse allowances, widows' pensions, supporting parents' benefits and a separate discussion of the cohabitation rule. Nonetheless, some provisions that I am unable to include in the discussion are of considerable relevance. Age pensions, for example, embody an age differential between the sexes which is clearly linked to the notion of the dependent spouse and the patriarchal tradition of men marrying younger women. Somewhat paradoxically, family allowances are paid directly to mothers and must be seen at least partly as a redistribution of income directly to women,to some extent mitigating dependence (Chapter 3). However, because the discussion cannot be exhaustive, these relevant issues must be set aside.

Wives' pensions
One of the most explicit expressions of government support for female dependence is in the wife's pension which is paid 'where the wife of an age or invalid pensioner is not qualified for an age or invalid pension in her own right' (Commonwealth DSS, 1979: 12). Here we find the state maintaining the capacity of the husband to support a dependent wife. As there is no stipulation that there be dependent children, the transfer must be seen as having this purpose rather than as a contribution to childrearing. It is of some importance that since 1972 the pension has been paid directly to the wife, since this represents a departure from the traditional arrangement whereby the husband mediates money transactions, even though the wife is still dependent on the husband for her eligibility. In June 1981 a total of 86 333 wives were in receipt of a wife's pension (Commonwealth DSS, 1981a: 35).

Dependent spouse allowance
An allowance for a dependent spouse is payable in respect of unemployment, sickness and special benefit. While this can be in respect of either a male or female, the usual situation is for the allowance to be paid in respect of a wife. The expectations of the Commonwealth Department of Social Security (1979: 7) are prominently displayed in a diagram in its *Annual Report 1978-1979*, indicating the proportion of the Australian population over 16 years receiving various types of payment. One of the cells specifies that 4 per cent of the population were unemployment, sickness or special beneficiaries (including wives).

Again we find the income security provisions explicitly catering for the financial dependence of women, though in recent years the administration of these benefits has come closer to equal treatment in so far as the income of both spouses is aggregated for the purpose of the income test for eligibility. Until November 1977, sickness benefit was the only provision paid to people entirely in respect of their own status, that is without taking account of a spouse's income. However, this was seen as a loophole (cf. Commission of Inquiry into Poverty, 1975a: 288) which was rectified, and now, like other benefits, spouse's income must be included as assessable income.

Widows' pensions

Widows' pensions are based directly on the assumption that women have a right to financial support, though young widows without dependent children are excluded from this, except for the first six months after the husband's death. There are three classes of widow's pensions, Class A, B and C.

Class A widows represent the largest category, with 87 837 in receipt of payments in June 1981. These are widows with at least one dependent child under 16 years or up to 24 years if in full-time study. Class B are older women aged at least 50 if without a qualifying child 'or a women who was aged at least 45 when she ceased to receive a class A widow's pension because she no longer had a qualifying child' (Commonwealth DSS, 1981a: 36). There are slightly fewer women in this category than in Class A (77 700 in June 1981). Class C widows represent a very small group (124, June 1981) not entitled to payment on other grounds, but eligible for a pension for six months after the death of their spouse, as a type of rehabilitation payment.

The pensions apply not only to de jure widows but also to a woman who was the de facto wife of a man for at least three years immediately before his death and for Class A and B widows it also includes:

> a woman who has been deserted by her husband without just cause for not less than six months;
> a woman whose husband is in a mental hospital;
> a woman whose husband has been convicted of an offence and has been imprisoned for not less than six months;
> a woman who is a divorcee. (Commonwealth DSS, 1981a: 36)

Class B is the most contentious category. The Poverty Inquiry pointed out that 'it is difficult to find a consistent rationale for the pension to middle aged widows without children' and recommended its abolition in favour of a provision for breadwinners between 50 and 65 years 'if they are finding difficulty in working for an adequate private income' (1975a, Vol. I: 238). Such a recommendation undermines the assumption of legitimate dependence which probably explains why it has not been adopted. Given its cost-cutting potential, we must assume that it has not been implemented because of its potential unpopularity. Since unemployment benefits, and more recently invalid pensions, have been subjected to greater stringency, the lack of an attempt to do so in respect of Class B widows pensions can be taken as a measure of the strength of support for female dependence. I have not found a similar argument rised in respect of wives' pensions, though presumably Henderson's point in the Poverty Inquiry would apply there as well.

Supporting parent's benefit

The supporting parent's benefit embodies an interesting range of anomalies in respect of gender and income maintenance. After an extensive campaign by single mothers, the supporting mothers' benefit was introduced in 1973 to cover a range of circumstances not covered previously by the widow's pension. Some of these circumstances had been encompassed by the special benefit but changing marital situations indicated new requirements. In 1977 the supporting mother's benefit was extended to include fathers and became the supporting parent's benefit. There had previously been the possibility of a special benefit being paid to a supporting father but this was a discretionary payment and application was rarely made.

The supporting parent's benefit is available to 'a man or woman who has the custody, care and control of a child' and the definition includes:

a male divorcee
a widower
a separated husband or wife or separated de facto husband or wife
a man whose partner is in a mental hospital
a sole parent supporting a child and not eligible for a widow's pension. (Commonwealth DSS, 1981a: 38)

The fact that widowed and divorced men and women are catered for under separate benefits is a clear indication of the appended nature of the male benefit, but it also highlights the change that has occurred and which may reflect some broader changes in attitudes to sex roles. We would, however, need to be cautious about suggesting any general acceptance of the androgynous principle. Henderson, as Chairman of the Poverty Inquiry, when recommending the extension of the supporting mother's benefit to men, expressed quite traditional attitudes (and incidentally ones which foreshadowed cheapness) in assuming that men would be unlikely to wish to become dependent on the state in the interests of fatherhood.

While Henderson might be seen to have been proved generally correct (in June 1981 there were 101 583 female supporting parents and only 5048 males), it is of interests to note that the male take-up rate has increased rapidly since its inception. The number of women supporting parents rose by 52.5 per cent between June 1980 and June 1981, while the proportion of male recipients rose by 32.1 per cent. Proportionally and in absolute numbers there is still an overwhelming preponderance of state-supported mothers, 189 420 in all including Class A widows compared with 5048 fathers who represent just 5 per cent of the single-parent recipients (Commonwealth DSS, 1981a). However, the importance of establishing the principle that childcare is legitimately a male occupation should not be underestimated.

The cohabitation rule
A particularly vexed aspect of eligibility for welfare benefits is the cohabitation rule, a rule which more than any other has precipitated the spelling out of official expectations that a woman will be (in fact must be) dependent on a male with whom she has a sexual relationship and with whom she cohabits. The extension of this rule to allow a man (or woman) to claim as a dependent, a woman (or man) with whom he (or she) lives but to whom he (or she) is not legally married, has proceeded fairly smoothly through the eligibility requirements and now applies to all entitlements. Problems and sometimes formal appeals occur in those cases in which the ruling is used to disqualify people, usually though not invariably, women, from eligibility. There have been recent cases in which men have had their benefit stopped if found to be 'cohabiting', but traditionally widows and supporting mothers have been the target of the rule. Departmental checking of recipients has been a bone of contention for many years, yet all official considerations of the rule have reaffirmed its necessity rather than suggesting serious modification. Both Henderson and Sackville (Commission of Inquiry into Poverty, 1975a; 1975b) investigated the cohabitation rule during the Poverty Inquiry and both, while expressing regret at the distress caused by its application, endorsed it.

In the Second Main Report of the Poverty Commission *Law and Poverty in Australia* (1975b) Sackville pointed out that the 'Cohabitation rule' is based on the

> principle that an unmarried couple living together as man and wife on a bona fide domestic basis should not receive more favourable treatment than a married couple in a similar financial position. (1975: 189)

It is in discussion of this rule that the Commonwealth Department of Social Security has explicitly stated its position that a wife has a right to support and a husband an obligation to provide support: rights and obligations which are extended to unmarried couples on the basis of a sexual relationship and a relatively stable living arrangement. Hayden, in 1974, when Minister for Social Security, was careful to explain that cohabitation did not apply simply on the basis of financial support, but specifically to a male and female in a de facto relationship, not to two siblings or any other combination of singles. As Spalding has pointed out, this merely states anew the proposition that marriage for women is a 'trading off' of financial dependence for domestic services including sex (Spalding, 1977: 351).

Programs the government does not support
This is far from an exhaustive coverage of the way in which female dependence is perpetuated by state provisions and has not analysed areas other than income maintenance. Nonetheless, it provides ample evidence of state support for a patriarchal system which maintains women in their subordinate position. A consideration of measures that would encourage greater female independence, and the lack of official support for such measures, reinforces the general picture. A few of the most obvious include childcare provisions, taxation concessions for childcare, more readily available cheap housing, and payment for domestic services. These are issues which are publicly discussed from time to time but do not receive government support, or, as with housing and the women's shelter movement, do receive some half-hearted support, often with strong overtones of social control. More radical suggestions rarely enter the arena of public debate.

How can we explain women's dependence?

In discussing the legitimate dependence of women we must confront the question of *why* this is maintained, as well as the question of how it is, and to do this, we need to locate our explanation within a broad political economic framework.

Women's dependence, as I pointed out earlier and as is demonstrated also by other papers in this volume, must be seen as an outcome of the inter-relationship between the 'private' sphere of the family and the public sphere of production. In the sphere of production, the wage system allows the appropriation of surplus value from workers.

Women's labour does not attract a wage and in a money economy this clearly restricts one's control in the market situation. However, while this lack of a wage may be disadvantageous for women, it does contribute to the cheap reproduction of labour power. Given current standards of childcare and the general state of the economy, socialisation of domestic services is likely to be more costly for capital and unlikely to be contemplated when the demand for women's paid labour diminishes. Cass has summarised the situation: 'women's unpaid domestic labour supports like an infrastructure the wage structure and profits of the industrial capitalist economy' (1978b: 28). Such an analysis makes it clear that female dependence is important to maintain and shows why a cohabitation rule, which renders the reproduction of labour power the financial responsibility of individual male wage earners, is so significant. Appeals to 'fairness' (in the treatment of non-marital cohabitation vis-à-vis de jure cohabitation) as the rationale for enforcing the cohabitation rule have an underlying logic, as any loosening of the rule would represent an acceptance by the state of major responsibility for the reproduction of labour power. Similar support could then be claimed by de jure couples. Such a costly exercise would clearly undermine the ideology of the patriarchal family and its role in supporting the conditions for capital accumulation.

When women's paid labour has been encouraged, women have typically taken on two jobs, rather than exchanging domestic labour for wage labour. Since this has happened in state socialist as well as capitalist countries, we must seek explanations of women's position additional to that of profitability for capital. The cost of socialised domestic services is certainly raised to counter recommendations for extended childcare services and for substantial cash transfers for parenting. But 'cost' is only a partial explanation, since it does not address the issue of the domestic division of labour—that it is women who care for children. If we assume that reproduction of labour power in a privatised family/household is necessary for the profitability of the capitalist system, it should matter little who remains in the household to carry out the task. Since the task has devolved historically upon women who suffer economic insecurity as a result, it would appear to be in the interests of men to maintain the domestic division of labour. This they are able to do, both in capitalist and state socialist societies, because of their commanding positions in politico/administrative state institutions (cf. Cass, 1981). Of course, in a situation of hegemony, we find that a majority of women also accept this position (Richards, 1978; Harper and Richards, 1979). Hayden, Henderson and Sackville are but representatives of male interests when they publicly assess the case for maintaining policies such as the cohabitation rule and, while expressing regret, conclude that 'in fairness' to married couples it must stand, and that, in the interests of public accountability, the process of scrutiny must continue.

McIntosh neatly summarises the dual function of state policy in maintaining female subordination and ensuring the reproduction of labour power:

> In various and piecemeal ways, then, state policy has sought, sometimes unsuccessfully, to remedy the fact that the family household system is inadequate for mediating the wage and the reproduction of the working class. It has always done so in such a way as to sustain that family system of a male breadwinner, dependent children and a dependent wife responsible for domestic

and child rearing work. Where this would be seriously threatened, the needs have remained unmet. (1978: 274)

Policy implications

This analysis might be read to imply that the provision of income maintenance for women adds to their oppression and should therefore be abandoned. This is certainly not a view which I support. Clearly, in the short run such systems are necessary if women are to survive in a system not of their own making (though one which they constantly help to recreate). In the ambiguous manner of most welfare provisions, income security measures also give women greater independence that they would have without them. At least they are able to exist, albeit with great difficulty, without being dependent directly on a male, and the state is a more remote and less demanding dispenser of income.

Thus current benefits must be maintained and rates raised to mitigate women's susceptibility to poverty. However, urgent emphasis must be placed on programs based on equal status of the sexes; programs which embody the condition that child-rearing is not specifically a female occupation. This latter change is crucial: mere movement into the labour force by women is not enough; men moving out of it (or part way out) seems a more promising method of achieving sexual equality and at the same time a better quality of life for all (see Bryson, 1974). While Engels appears to have been wrong in assuming that full labour force participation by women would produce equality, he was perhaps right in so far as he recognised that some form of equal participation by men and women is necessary. Another condition which Engels postulated as necessary for equality of the sexes was the 'abolition of the individual family {as} ... the economic unit of society' (Marx and Engels, 1970: 501). This also appears to be a necessary, though not a sufficient condition.

Conclusion

Why should we be concerned about the issue of dependence, especially when women are moving into the paid workforce and when welfare provisions also represent a real gain? The reason is that the ramifications of this legitimate dependence are extraordinarily pervasive. They not only affect women in marriage but are woven through the whole fabric of society. The effects are usually expressed via the shorthand phrase 'sex role socialisation', which refers, among other things, to the ways in which girls learn to accept and live a life in which they do not expect full autonomy in the public sphere. Women face the possibility, indeed probability, that a man will be prepared to take financial responsibility for them and this has critical repercussions for the way in which women conceive of their role in the paid workforce as a secondary one.

Men on the other hand expect that they will not only have to be financially independent, but will probably have others dependent on them. The expectation of man's superior, provider status, means that women are unlikely to achieve their full potential, at least in the economic arena. Since in capitalist societies this is the key institutional sphere, the implications of this must not be underestimated. The whole process results, to quote Bell and Newby again, 'in a degree of ideological hegemony over women {so that} they continue to accept their subordinate position as natural and desirable and the superior power of men as legitimate' (1976: 159). Of course, we must not make the mistake of treating this hegemony as complete, it certainly never has been: the feminist movement provides the most obvious example of its limits. It is these limits that we must constantly try to extend.

Acknowledgements

I would like to thank the following colleagues for their helpful comments on this paper: Michael Bittman, Bettina Cass, Bob Connell, Cristina Cordero, Sheila Shaver.

Notes

1   In June 1981, men constituted 5 per cent of all supporting parents beneficiaries. There were 5048 male beneficiaries compared with 101 483 female beneficiaries. This represented approximately 11 per cent of male sole parents with dependent children and 43 per cent of female sole parents with dependent children (of whom an additional 37 per cent were in receipt of Class A Widows pensions). In summary, 11 per cent of male single parents were in receipt of income maintenance, in respect of being a supporting parent, compared with 80 per cent of female single parents (Australian Bureau of Statistics 1982b; Commonwealth Department of Social Security, 1981).

7 Sex and money in the welfare state

SHEILA SHAVER

Social security measures, the 'safety net' of industrial capitalism, are endorsed politically as practical public expression of liberal democratic values guaranteeing individual wellbeing against private economic misfortune. Most benefits are available on grounds formally equal between men and women, the rights of citizens equal before law and bureaucracy. The major exception, the family allowance, has always favoured women as reliable guardians of the interests of children (Kewley, 1980: 93, Chapter 3). It has seemed that struggles around pensions have more to do with poverty than with women's particular demands. However in the discussion to follow I shall argue that Australian social security and the taxation system which supports it are not sex-blind functions of citizenship but rather constitute a systematic mechanism of women's subordination.

The basic elements of Australian social security

The basic framework of Australian social security was established in the 1940s. The foundations of the system had been laid in the early years after federation. The 1907 *Harvester* Judgment created the family wage concept in which the 'living wage' was to enable a breadwinner to support a dependent wife and three children. Legislation enacted in 1908 made an age pension available to men from age 65 and women from 60, and an invalid pension available to persons permanently incapacitated for (paid) work. Both pensions were subject to means tests and funded from general revenue on a non-contributory basis. In 1912 the maternity benefit was introduced. The benefit was paid to the mother on the birth of a child, and was not subject to a means test.

During World War II the remaining planks of the welfare floor were laid on this foundation. Child endowment was established in 1941 for all children after the first, without means test. Initially funded by a payroll tax, the measure was soon integrated into consolidated revenue finance (see Chapter 3) in this volume. Widow's pensions in 1942 provided for widows over 50 years of age, responsible for the care of dependent children, or in otherwise necessitous circumstances. The term 'widow' was defined to include deserted de jure wives and de facto wives who had been living with a man for a minimum of three years prior to his death, and who had been dependent upon him. During the Depression maternity allowances had been made subject to means test, but in 1943 these were restored as a universal entitlement. Unemployment and sickness benefit and a special benefit available at administrative discretion (1944) were introduced. The Commonwealth Employment Service was established in 1945, signalling the beginning of post-war reconstruction predicated on an official full employment policy (see Chapter 8).

Except for child endowment and maternity allowances, all measures were subject to means test; all were non-contributory measures financed from general revenues. These major developments of the social security system were consolidated in 1947 when, after a referendum clarifying the commonwealth's peacetime power to legislate in the social security area, the developments of the war years were systematised in the *Social Services Consolidation Act* 1947. Changes in social security in the 1950s rounded out earlier developments with the establishment of the 'relative needs' principle (Kewley, 1977: 394) in which allowances for dependent spouses and children were made uniform, ensuring a degree of equity among state beneficiaries.

As shown in earlier chapters, the notion of a 'family wage' eventually came under attack on two fronts, its 'needs principle' undermined by that of industry's capacity to pay, and its 'family principle' by equal pay demands. The potential erosion of wage inequality implied erosion also of the patriarchal family structure underlying capitalist production in which a breadwinner engaged in wage labour is serviced by a dependent spouse engaged primarily in unpaid domestic labour (Beechey, 1977).

Built during the war and politically motivated to foreshadow a 'world worth fighting for' (Roe, 1976: 222), the social security system has taken up some of the slack, weaving support for the family of breadwinner and dependent spouse into the mesh of the liberal democratic safety net. The structures of social security and taxation of the Australian welfare state contain a concealed but systematic set of transfers maintaining women as primarily wives and mothers and as wage workers secondarily.

A clue to the way in which social security measures reinforce the sexual division of labour is contained in Hilary Land's (1976) analysis of the benefits provided to women in Britain's contributory system of national insurance. She shows that not only has this system failed to treat men and women equally, but that the rights of women to its social security provisions have been mediated by their marital status in a manner not applicable to men.

Although the discrimination against women is less marked, something similar operates within the Australian social security system. The mechanism is concealed by a structural asymmetry between the taxation system through which revenue is raised and the system of benefits through which welfare monies are paid out. For tax purposes the unit employed is the single individual, the tax due being calculated after a series of rebates taking account of certain dependents and some other personal circumstances. For pensions and benefits, on the other hand, the unit employed to assess entitlement closely approximates the nuclear family. To put it bluntly, when it comes to paying for the welfare state the system treats women as individuals, but in respect of virtually every benefit conferred back on them, social policy measures treat them as somebody's wife or somebody's mother. The basic nexus of women's oppression—the link between family and labour process —is replicated almost literally in the structures of the welfare state.

This asymmetry is made possible by Australia's adherence to a social assistance rather than a social insurance concept as the basis of its social security system. Flat-rate benefits are set at levels presumed to provide for basic needs, and related to income only in the range through which a part pension is paid subject to extra-earnings regulations. With 'need' as the founding principle for entitlement to state support, redistribution from income earners to dependent beneficiaries is an intended effect rather than a breach of actuarial principles. The system confirms the breadwinner and dependent family relation writ large.

Income security and taxation since the 1950s.

Before examining the way in which Australian taxation and social security systems combine to support the sexual division of labour, it is necessary to sketch the major changes made to the social security system since the 1950s and give some background on taxation. Only two wholly new social security payments have been instituted since the post-war consolidation of the system. Supplementary assistance is a small additional pension which was initially instituted in 1958 for single age pensioners paying rent and meeting an additional means test; it has subsequently been extended to all pensioners in similar circumstances. Sheltered employment allowances were instituted in 1967. Provision of income support similar to that available to widows and deserted wives was extended to single mothers in 1972 and to men in similar circumstances in 1977, when it was renamed supporting parent's benefit. In the interim period a tax rebate for single parents was instituted (1975).

The most significant change which has been made to the social security system is a substantial relaxation of the means test applied to age pensions. The Menzies era saw the first liberalisation of the means test for age and invalid pensions in the 'merged means test', which in addition to putting earned and unearned income on a common basis, permitted some pension and significant fringe benefits to become available to persons with considerable private resources. The means test was further liberalised in 1967, and abolished for persons over 74 in 1973. In 1975 the age ceiling was reduced to 69. There has been some reversion since 1976 as pension increases and fringe benefits have been withheld from pensioners over 69 whose income exceeds income test limits. At the same time the age pension was made subject to income tax, and in 1976 unemployment and sickness benefits, widows' pensions and supporting parents' benefits were also made taxable. Of major income support measures, only the invalid pension remains not subject to income tax. In 1976 also most pensions and benefits were made subject to automatic six-monthly cost of living adjustments in line with the consumer price index.

Finally, important changes have been made in cash benefits for dependent children. The 1975 Hayden budget replaced concessional deductions for dependent spouses, children and certain other relatives, the value of which varied directly with taxable income, with flat rate rebates. In 1976 the newly installed Fraser government re-structured benefits for dependent children so that income tax revenues previously forgone in rebates were paid out directly in much larger child endowment payments, renamed family allowances (see Chapter 3 in this volume). Although the change largely rearranged expenditure at existing levels, the measure was of significant benefit to low income families who previously had been unable to gain the full benefit of the rebate due them; and at the same time it removed state provision for children from an arena in which benefits were indexed automatically to one in which adjustments for the effect of inflation depend on budgetary initiative.

The effect of the tax structure on women's dependency has to be understood in the context of the taxation system as a whole. About half of Australian federal government revenues from taxation come from personal income tax receipts (55.1 per cent in 1979/80), and the share has been rising steadily. The picture is complicated by the crude oil levy, which has increased the share of excise taxes in federal government revenues from 14 per cent in 1973/74 (the year when personal income tax first accounted for more than half of government income) to 18.2 per cent in 1979/80. Company tax has been falling in the same period, from 18.6 per cent of federal tax revenue in 1973/74 to 12.5 per cent in 1979/80.

Because personal income tax is applied to individuals, income tax statistics cannot be aggregated to show the incomes and tax burdens of married couples, families or households. To assess the effect of taxation it is necessary to rely on data based on expenditure. Studies based on household survey data for 1966/67 have provided an understanding of the incidence of the total tax structure. These data show that the progressive effects of personal income tax and some excise taxes were largely negated by the regressive effects of property rates, sales and other taxes. Bentley, Collins and Drane (1974) found that the tax structure as a whole was in fact regressive in the low income ranges, proportional at medium levels and progressive only for the top 6 per cent of income recipients. From the same data Podder and Kakwani (1975) concluded that the tax structure as a whole effected little vertical redistribution.

Changes made in the structure of personal income tax in 1975 and 1976 favoured taxpayers with dependents, particularly low-income families on one wage, and taxpayers at both extremes of the income scale. Single taxpayers with average incomes were most adversely affected (Scotton and Sheehan, 1976). Warren (1979) has analysed the effects of all federal taxes for 1975/76, reflecting the change from concessional deductions to flat-rate rebates, but not the subsequent replacement of rebates for children by family allowances. He found that in 1975/76 the incidence of federal taxes was proportional at all income levels except the extreme top and bottom groups. The effect of the shift from child rebates to family allowances in the following year is unlikely to change Warren's findings significantly except at the lowest income levels.

There is reason to believe that the tax structure has become more regressive in the years since 1976. Progressive rates of personal income tax have been flattened and only partially indexed for inflation, with the result that most full-time wage earners now pay tax at the same rate (Sheehan, 1980: 183). The crude oil levy hits low-income families differentially because of their relatively higher expenditure on travel and the large effect of transport costs on food prices. Escalating tax avoidance and the abolition of estate and gift duty have further unequalising effects. Though not all writers agree, Sheehan concludes that the system as a whole is now clearly regressive (1980: 183-6).

Women are the major beneficiaries of such progression as remains in the structure of personal income tax rates. Through labour force segmentation women are employed primarily in low-paid jobs (Collins, 1977; Women's Employment Rights Campaign, 1979). Despite the establishment of equal pay in 1974, the average adult female wage for full-time work was only 79 per cent of the male rate in 1981 (Australian Bureau of Statistics, 1982). Two out of three women in paid work are married; over 40 per cent of these are employed part time. It is also common for married women to work only part of the year (Australian Bureau of Statistics, 1979). Power reports that in 1977 married women in part-time work averaged only 14 hours employment per week (cited in Windschuttle, 1979). Their relatively low tax burden thus reflects their disadvantaged position in the labour market. There is a second order of progression in personal income tax rates provided through family allowances. As tax-free income, family allowances effectively raise the tax threshhold for families with dependent children above that applying to families without children.

Overall, the evidence suggests that Australian taxation achieves little or no vertical redistribution. The major dimension of redistribution is horizontal, from taxpayers without dependents to taxpayers with dependent spouses and/or children. This is, in principle, a redistribution from men to women, though for married women much of the benefit is indirect, paid in tax relief to their husbands on their behalf.

Social security and income redistribution

In the absence of vertical redistribution through the taxation system, the social security system is virtually the only mechanism for reducing income inequality. The Australian system of means-tested, flat-rate benefits has performed relatively well in this regard. OECD data for 1972 show that the bottom quintile of the population received 2.9 per cent of national income after tax but before income transfers, and 6.4 per cent after transfers. Australian social security expenditure is a relatively small share of gross domestic product compared to other OECD countries, but because its benefit system is relatively effective in concentrating benefit at the bottom, it achieves a degree of redistribution comparable with the systems of countries spending considerably larger sums in social insurance programs (Henderson, 1978: 167-8). Some of this redistributive capacity has been lost with the abolition of the means test for aged persons over 69, but there was compensation for these changes to some degree with the taxation of most pensions and benefits. This is primarily a redistribution between the sexes. The extent to which the taxation and social security systems in combination effect a transfer of spending power from men to women can be seen in the fact that women pay only one-quarter of all personal income tax but receive some 65 per cent of the cash welfare payout.[1]

The taxation and social security systems replicate on a larger scale the nexus of women's oppression at the intersection of labour process and family, women's paid and unpaid work, maintaining their subordination by differential treatment in the two spheres. McIntosh (1978) locates the role of the state in the oppression of women in the particular way it constructs the family: the state consistently supports a family household dependent largely upon a male wage and upon female domestic servicing. Australian social policy conveys the ideological construction of women in the vehicle of cold hard cash: transfers embodied in the twin systems of taxation and social security manipulate the incentives and constraints around which women divide their lives between paid and unpaid labour. Lois Bryson's paper in this volume deals substantively with the ideology of family embodied in Australian social security. My concern here will be to supplement her account with an analysis of the way the family ideology is embedded in welfare expenditure and taxation.

The way these incentives and constraints operate is best illustrated in detailed examination of the major cash benefits as they combine to form a set of larger social mechanisms. At this point it is necessary to dissolve somewhat the contrast between social security as state payments to individuals and families, and taxation as receipts from them. Individuals and families receive two types of benefits, those paid out in pensions, benefits and allowances, and those conferred through personal income tax as revenues forgone in deductions and rebates in respect of similar conditions of dependency. Although the latter are not usually recognised as welfare payments, they are in fact part of the same system of transfers. The sole parent's rebate in the tax system, for example, is clearly parallel to the widow's pension and supporting parent's benefit in the transfer system. On the other side, most pensions and benefits are now subject to income tax so that a portion of expenditure is recouped by the state.

In both the tax and the welfare systems the rules used to define entitlements are formally equal in the treatment of men and women, though there have been and continue to be a few interesting exceptions. In practice, nevertheless, the personal circumstances and earning capacities of the persons to whom these largely equal rules are applied are manifestly unequal, so that formal equality of treatment is superimposed upon and avoids contradicting a surrounding logic of patriarchal inequality. For social policy the central assumption of this logic is that of two cohabiting individuals, one will normally be employed in wage work and the other in domestic labour. As couples actually face them, choices about the sexual division of labour are heavily loaded in favour of this pattern. This same patriarchal logic is confirmed in the asymmetries of the welfare state.

Women and cash social benefits

Cash social benefit expenditure through pensions, benefits, allowances and exemption from personal income taxation amounted to $6.7 million million in 1976/77.[2] Of that amount, just over one-third went to expenditure on measures specifically geared to support the family as a social unit. The other two-thirds went to pensions, benefits and tax concessions more closely tied to workforce statuses.

Major cash benefits to families, all of which have primary significance to women, are given in Table 7.1.

Table 7.1 Expenditures on benefits to families in the tax/transfer system 1976/77 ($m)

maternity allowances	6.9
family allowances	1023.3
spouse, housekeeper or daughter-housekeeper rebate	526.3
sole parent rebate	16.7
widow's pension	370.2
supporting mothers' benefit	158.5
less income tax on widows' and supporting mothers' benefit	− 18.7
Double orphans' pension	2.4
Handicapped child's allowance	14.1
Invalid relative or parent rebate	22.0

The last three items are relatively small but signal a trend of particular importance for women.

When they were introduced, maternity allowances were widely believed to be intended to boost the birthrate. Their real value had been declining for some 35 years when they were abolished altogether in 1978 (Kewley, 1980: 21-2, 90). Family allowances are the only other universal benefit of any size in the Australian social security system. Family allowances have always been paid directly to mothers, on the proper grounds that the benefit puts money into the hands of many women otherwise having no source of independent income. At one level, family allowances contradict the thesis which Wilson, McIntosh and others argue, that welfare benefits come with apron strings attached. The allowance is paid without regard to whether the mother is engaged in work outside the home; indeed she may spend it on child-care enabling her to take paid work, though it will not help much. At another level, however, the family allowance also supports the feminist thesis. Bettina Cass's paper in this collection shows that the benefit has served as an instrument to restrain male wages, linked to female wages. The wage reduction effects of the 1976 reconstruction of tax and family allowances repeated this pattern: a significant redistribution of income from men to women worked at the same time to legitimise wage restraint and to allow for minimisation of revenue forgone if child benefits had remained in the tax system (Cass, Keens and Moller, 1981).

Expenditure on family allowances reached a peak of $1038 million in 1977/78 and has been declining since because of a past reduction in fertility. The decline in real value resulting from government failure to index the rates in line with parallel tax rebates for a dependent spouse has been greater: Cass, Keens and Moller (1981) have estimated that the savings to government revenue were $102 million in 1979/80 and escalating rapidly. There is current debate about the proper justification for and most appropriate means of increasing family allowances. On one side it is argued that although family allowances are now formally located in the social security system, they give effect to a tax principle of horizontal equity in the differential capacity to pay between taxpayers with and without children (Gittens, 1981). On the other side it is claimed that the reduction in the real value of family allowances has hit low-income families hardest and that it would be preferable to treat family allowances as a welfare measure subject to means test (Australian Council of Social Service, 1980). The failure to index family allowances has exposed a contradiction between liberal democratic values of equal treatment of individuals and subsistence needs of low wage earners.

The income tax rebate in respect of a dependent spouse, housekeeper or daughter-housekeeper was $500 in 1976/77, amounting to $526 million in forgone revenue. This is a large sum; the same amount of money provided the entire state support of widows, supporting mothers and their children. In 1979 the rebate was increased to $800, at an estimated cost of $860 million for a full year. This large expenditure is advertised politically as support for the family, but since entitlement to the rebate has no necessary connection with the care of children, the claim is doubtful. At the new rate (1982), the state now pays per year almost twice as much for a dependent spouse ($830) as it pays in family allowances for two children ($442.80).[3]

Tax statistics do not show the numbers of men and women claiming the rebate, but recent workforce statistics show that in 1980 only 13000 men were full-time unpaid housekeepers compared with more than 2.5 million women (*Sydney Morning Herald*, 19 November 1980). The rebate is in fact a payment for domestic labour, paid to the husband to recompense him for the cost of reproducing his labour power. It may be significant that the alternative rebate for a daughter-housekeeper is one of the few remaining anomalies in the sex neutrality of welfare and taxation. The benefit may not be claimed in respect of a son (Meredith Edwards, personal communication).[4] Of revenue forgone in this rebate 77 per cent goes to taxpayers in the upper half of the income range (calculated from tax statistics for 1976/77). What this means is that working-class and single taxpayers are paying for the homely comforts of middle-class husbands.

A number of social security benefits support adults solely responsible for dependent children, principally the widow's pension, supporting parent's benefit and the sole parent rebate. Women are the main beneficiaries of these measures. In 1977 single fathers became eligible for supporting parent's benefit, but in 1981 men accounted for only 5 per cent of recipients (see Bryson in this volume).

The sole parent rebate was $350 in 1976/77 and was increased to $580 in mid-1982, and to $713 in mid-1983. This rebate was added to the tax system in 1975 by the Whitlam government in response to pressure to extend the supporting mother's benefit to the small group of men in similar circumstances. The delay in making a parallel provision for single fathers is testimony to the strength of patriarchal assumptions about the proper behaviour of men and women: it had been 34 years since the widow's pension was established. This rebate was clearly a token based on the notion that such men would naturally be wage earners and therefore taxpayers. It was two more years before the supporting parent's benefit was extended to men. Although tax rebates were the only benefit available to supporting fathers in 1976/77, it is likely that the bulk of the revenue forgone went to female family heads. It is the only tax rebate in which the larger share of benefit went to taxpayers having incomes below the median, which is probably a reflection of the poor earning capacities of women. Even at the current rate the measure does not contribute much to childcare expenses, providing little incentive for single parents to take paid work.

In supporting widowed, deserted and single women as full-time mothers, the state must strike a sensitive balance between contradictory effects: to provide a pension releases them from financial dependence on men (and men from responsibility to maintain them), yet not to provide for them would both close a safety valve necessary for the nuclear family and bring into question the ideology of the state's concern for the family and the weak. This contradiction is resolved by structuring benefits for single-parent families in such a way as to replace the absent breadwinner while keeping family structure otherwise intact. Benefit levels are kept low enough that a man cannot improve his wife's financial position by deserting her: a deserted wife must have four children before her pension entitlement plus family allowances exceeds the minimum wage. In principle a deserted wife must seek maintenance from her husband, but the state exercises wide discretionary control over how seriously he is pursued. The cohabitation rule and sexual harassment of widows and supporting mothers must be understood in terms of state protection for the traditional family form: in replacing the breadwinner the state becomes surrogate husband, and naturally a jealous one. Yet again the requirement is contradictory, in that pressure to attach financial responsibility to sexual relations hinders the capacity of these women to re-establish the 'proper' family structure.

Compared with the United States where mothers receiving Aid to Families with Dependent Children have had to enrol for job training to qualify for assistance (Marris and Rein, 1974), there has been little pressure on Australian widows and deserted wives to seek paid employment. When fringe benefits such as free health care and subsidised housing are considered, the security of the pension makes low-paid work comparatively unattractive.

Class B widows are older women, mainly widows whose children have grown up. Their entitlement to pension is proper recognition of their disadvantage in the job market, but the other side of the coin is that the pension also confirms their status as married women who, by virtue of this status, have a right to financial support.

The double orphan's pension, handicapped child allowance and rebate for a dependent parent or relative, are designed to encourage and support the family in extended care functions. These reflect the move to 'community care', reprivatising care of groups otherwise forced to live in institutions. The significance of these benefits to women is that women tend to be the caretakers. The amounts paid, for example $18 per week for a handicapped child, offer no more than token recognition of a whole new realm of domestic labour. In another chapter Cora Baldock considers women's voluntary work in this context.

Workforce-related cash benefits

The remaining two-thirds of cash social benefit expenditure are spent on measures defined by and defining workforce statuses. In 1976/77 half of this was used to provide temporary support for persons of working age. The other half, one-third of all cash benefits, went to retired persons. The principal measures are as outlined in Table 7.2. Whereas benefits directed to support for the family go almost entirely

Table 7.2 Expenditures on other benefits in the tax/transfer system, 1976/77 ($m)

unemployment benefit	618.1
sickness benefit	105.4
special benefit	21.6
less income tax on unemployment, sickness and special benefit	− 35.7
invalid pension	511.0
disability (war) pensions	371.5
national employment and training scheme	31.6
tertiary education assistance scheme	147.6
life assurance, superannuation rebate	26.5
age pension	2484.6
service pension	283.3
less income tax on age and service pensions	− 98.1
funeral benefits	1.5

to women, measures supporting workforce participation are systematically difficult for married women to obtain. Their share of this expenditure is disproportionately small. The most important measure is unemployment benefit, $618 million in 1976/77 and skyrocketing as unemployment rates rose: by 1979/80 it had risen by almost 50 per cent to $910 million. Rates of unemployment are much higher for women than for men. In June 1981 women constituted 48 per cent of the recorded unemployed, and 89 per cent of 'discouraged job seekers' (i.e. persons who have withdrawn from active job searching) (ABS, 1982b; 1982c). Nevertheless, in September 1981, women constituted only 30 per cent of unemployment beneficiaries, as they had in 1976/77 (Commonwealth Department of Social Security, 1981b:2)

Applicants for unemployment benefit are means-tested on the joint income of applicant and spouse, and unless a woman's husband also has no significant income it is rarely worth her while to apply. The same is true of sickness benefits; 80 per cent of those granted go to men. Two-thirds of invalid pensioners are male. The Tertiary Education Assistance Scheme (TEAS) also applies a means test to the joint income of applicant and spouse. In a reassertion of the principle of the family wage, the National Employment and Training Scheme (NEAT) has been restructured to give priority to 'primary breadwinners' (Windschuttle, 1979). Virtually every workforce benefit of significant value is administered according to criteria precluding married women, as second earners, from effective eligibility.

Moreover it must be remembered that the workforce benefit most important to women is denied them: neither the taxation nor the social security system recognises the cost of childcare as an expense in earning income. The Asprey Committee (Taxation Review Committee 1975) recommended some form of tax recognition in 1975. Meredith Edwards (1980, personal communication) estimates that full deductibility would cost $40 million. The government's failure to act on this matter is in large part a consequence of women's political weakness, but it also reflects a contradiction between growing stress on the women to supplement their husbands' earnings. The logic that childcare is an expense incurred in going to work is hard to resist. The benefits of tax deductibility would be doubly biased toward professional and other high income Women, because not only can they afford better care but the tax forgone would vary directly with their earnings: a bias to wealthy women would call into question the assumption that women work primarily for the sake of their families. To provide expanded creche facilities as a welfare measure would entail support for childcare outside the family setting. Family day-care is a response located within this contradiction. (See Chapters 9 and 10 in this book for a fuller discussion of childcare).

The age pension is by far the largest social security expenditure. Of age pensioners, 67 per cent are women; service pensioners are mainly male, but the sexual division of benefit among the elderly as a whole strongly reflects women's greater longevity. Given the proportional structure of Australian taxation, these benefits represent within-class transfers between generations. Supervising these transfers, the state acts as surrogate extended family, helping everybody look after Gran. From the beginning the age pension was a reaction, both attitudinal and financial, to institutional management of the aged poor (Roe, 1975: 137). It may be significant that once their reproductive lives are past, women receive more recognition as individuals; although there are assumptions about marriage built into the age pension[5], this measure is undeniably paid to women in their own right, as citizens as well as wives or mothers. This liberal democratic tendency has been strengthened with the abolition of the means test for persons over 69: women are the major beneficiaries.

Women and taxation revenues

Cash social benefits are largely of two kinds, those geared to family status and dependency conditions and those supporting the workforce. Those of the first kind go primarily to women, treating them as members of the family group. Those of the second kind give more recognition in their conditions of eligibility to their recipients as individuals, nevertheless the system of family unit means tests and allowances for dependents maintains the family group basis of the cash benefit system. With the exception of the age pension, benefits of the second kind go mainly to men because women, as second earners, are excluded from individual entitlement through the means test on joint income of the married couple. Personal income taxation, in contrast, treats men and women as individuals and gives relatively little recognition to marital and parental status. Although the individual basis of personal income taxation is of itself largely sex-neutral, its insertion into the surrounding structures of the sexual division of labour in family and workforce involves it in transfers subordinating married women in patriarchal family relations.

There is a partriarchal logic within the tax structure which effectively increases the tax rates of married women above those paid by their husbands. In principle, it would not seem to matter whether the tax benefits to which a two-income couple are entitled are taken by the husband, by the wife, or split between them. Paid at a flat rate, the rebate has the same value to any taxpayer, whatever the income. In practice, however, it is almost always in the interest of the couple for the available tax relief to be taken on the husband's return. This is particularly true for women who work part time or for only part of the year, who often do not owe enough income tax for full rebates to be taken.

Several tax rebates—most importantly life assurance and superannuation, education expenses, medical expenses and rates and land tax—depend on having total expenditure on rebatable items exceeding a threshhold figure; in 1976/77 this was $1525. It generally requires a high income to support the necessary expenditure (Scotton and Sheehan, 1976), and these measures show a particularly strong class bias.[6] It is easier for a couple to reach the threshhold figure for rebatable expenditure on superannuation, medical expenses, school bills and rates on property if expenditure is consolidated on the return of the highest income earner, almost always the husband. Superannuation is the big item, and it is the only form of rebatable expenditure not freely transferable between husband and wife. The husband is much more likely to have superannuation available as a fringe benefit of employment.

Given the practical incentives for her husband to claim tax relief on her behalf, a married woman's tax return is likely to differ little from that of her single sister. Redistribution in the tax system is thus not simply from single persons to taxpayers with dependants but rather from single men, single women and married women to married men. The welfare state in part reconstructs the asymmetric family of breadwinner and dependent spouse on the model of the old family wage, delivering a part of women's income to men as tax relief in respect of family living costs. The rebate for a dependent spouse has the same effect on women not in paid work. In patriarchal style, the state collects revenues from its taxpayers as individuals and returns it to them as bearers of patriarchal relations.

This has contradictory implications for the sexual division of labour within the family, for it affects women's 'second job' in domestic labour. Housework is increasingly recognised as consumption work (Weinbaum and Bridges, 1979). In constituting a part of women's earnings as joint or family income, married men are given greater control over women's role in consumption. Yet it is likely that this money will be seen as a windfall to be spent for different and more discretionary purposes than regular income. We know too little about how and by whom tax cheques are spent, but it is generally considered that husbands have a bigger part in 'big' than in 'small' decisions (Adler, 1966; Little and Holmström, 1977; Hunt, 1978). With two-earner households becoming more common it is possible that the sexual division of labour in consumption is changing. Chapter 4 in this collection examines the central nexus of sexual and class oppression in changing relations between production and consumption. These changing relations have economic, psychic and social effects.

Sexism in personal income taxation does not arise because the *individual* is taken as the basis for taxation, but it arises from the unequal positions of men and women in the family and the economy. Other forms of income taxation giving more emphasis to the family unit, such as family income aggregation or income splitting between husband and wife, are likely to have much more disadvantaging effects for women. Family unit taxation has larger income pooling effects and creates stronger work disincentives for a second income earner (Edwards, 1980b; 1980d).

Conclusion

Wilson (1977:9) has called social welfare policies a mechanism for the state organisation of domestic life. Before World War II the primary vehicle for state intervention in the sexual division of labour was the family wage. The family component of the male wage was to be redistributed to his wife and children within the private realm of the patriarchal family. With the demise of the family wage the social security system has in part replaced the labour market as the agency constructing the family of breadwinner and dependants: the state has thus become much more directly involved in redistributing the resources of subsistence from men to women. The 'acceptable face of capitalism' smiles on women with a distinctly patriarchal wink.

Social welfare expenditure is a charge on surplus value. A portion of the gross wage is collected from workers in taxation and paid back in the social wage (Ginsberg, 1979: 25-7). Gough subdivides social expenditure into benefits in cash and benefits in kind, confining the definition of the social wage to cash welfare provisions (Gough, 1979: 116). Although this distinction tends to give undue emphasis to the difference between money and services,[7] it is convenient for the purposes of the present analysis.

Because the incidence of Australian taxation is effectively proportional, the social wage works here on an axis tilted slightly downward from the horizontal. It is essentially a mechanism for transferring money from current income recipients to others without income. Three dimensions of redistribution can be identified. Firstly, the state transfers resources for life sustenance from persons in work to those without, due to unemployment, sickness or disability. This is primarily a redistribution among men, as married women tend to be excluded from these measures. Secondly, it rearranges income across generations, from persons of working age to children and the elderly. In these dimensions the state is at once liberal democratic guarantor of minimum personal wellbeing and surrogate extended family: political argument about the conflicting interests of taxpayers and beneficiaries reflects this contradiction. In the third dimension the social wage supports women in full-time housework and childcare. Both second and third dimensions entail redistribution of income from men to women. In all three dimensions the social wage is directly concerned with maintaining the domestic foundations of its workforce in the sexual division of labour, replicating it on a larger scale. It is a circulation of resources from breadwinner taxpayers constituted as individuals to dependent social security beneficiaries constituted as members of the family group. Welfare and taxation come together in a circuit of oppression in which the state collects revenues from its taxpayers as individual citizens and returns it to them as bearers of patriarchal relations.

Much of the theoretical analysis of social welfare now current centres on the argument that the most basic function of the welfare system is to regulate the industrial reserve army of labour (Piven and Cloward, 1971; Wilson, 1977; McIntosh, 1978; Gough, 1979; Ginsberg, 1979). Although the idea clearly has some substance, its formulation tends to bind the analysis into a static functionalism which those who argue the thesis now commonly admit. In commenting on an early version of the present paper, Rosemary Pringle pointed out that we no longer talk of how the family is functional to capital but rather how the state makes it so. She rightly suggests that we must move toward a more open-ended approach, examining how the working class themselves create family structures, but do so within sets of constraints.

The focus on manipulation of labour supply detracts from our ability to see important changes taking place in the basic structure of the Australian 'welfare state'. Social security and taxation are being reconstructed in respect to class with specific effects on women. Although many of its effects are still in the demographic pipeline, alteration of the social security system has already taken place. Reconstruction of the taxation system is also on the political agenda.

Since 1967 the relaxation of means tests on the age pension has extended pension entitlement to persons with substantial private income: in December 1978 part pension was available to a married couple whose other income was approximately equal to average earnings. There is no income limit above age 69. As Kewley has put it,

> ..the character of the means test has been so changed that it is no longer a major instrument of the selective policies followed by Liberal Governments for many years. It is accordingly difficult to determine the rationale of the pensions system today. (1980: 216)

The age pension now supports both persons for whom it (plus supplementary assistance) is their only source of income, and other people for whom it is icing on an already rich cake. The number of age pensioners almost doubled between 1968 and 1978. Although the real value of pensions has increased more rapidly than average weekly earnings (Kewley, 1980: 213), the supplementary assistance payment restricted to those without other income has not been increased since 1974.

The implication of this is a reduction in the capacity of the social security system to redistribute income toward the working class. Since women receive the age pension five years earlier than men and live longer to enjoy it, it is middle-class women who profit most. Except for the age limit, the means test applied to other pensions has been similarly liberalised, with corresponding benefits primarily for middle-class widows, deserted wives and single mothers. In its class dimension this shift parallels the distribution of benefits in the tax rebate for dependent spouse discussed above. There has been no comparable change in the means test applied to unemployment, sickness and special benefits, of which working-class men are the largest number of recipients.

The government's increasing dependence on the crude oil levy will begin to pose problems in 1983/84 when revenues from domestic oil production start to fall. This prospect, and the rising share of personal income tax in total revenue and increasing tax avoidance, are generating pressure for tax reform. The most common proposition is to introduce a broadly based expenditure tax, with corresponding reductions in personal income tax rates (*Sydney Morning Herald*, 20 January 1981). Increased indirect taxation would have inflationary effects, and at the time of writing these were judged too severe (*Sydney Morning Herald*, 24 February 1981), but the pressures for reconstruction of the tax structure along these lines continue. Expenditure taxes are generally regressive in incidence, the more so if they apply to food and clothing (Sheehan, 1980: 204-5). Moreover their incidence is much less visible than the burden of income tax. Changes in the incidence of the tax structure as a whole depend on the whole combination of adjustments, but it is likely that any shift towards indirect taxation will have some regressive impact.

Applied in the course of consumption activity, the broadly based expenditure tax has the household as its source unit. A shift away from personal income towards expenditure taxation would diminish the asymmetry between the individual and family units currently employed to circulate the social wage from taxpayers to beneficiaries. Given the savings possible in shared living costs, the proposal can be seen as a 'family policy' of a very general kind. Moreover, as goods and services produced in the home would not be taxed, the measure would increase the real value of a spouse who has time to spend on cooking, sewing and home improvements. Thus reduced asymmetry of tax and cash benefit is balanced by an incentive to the asymmetry of breadwinner and dependent spouse.

The changes in progress are likely to be more significant for the class structure of the social wage than for its patriarchal functions. *Plus ça change....* Whatever the limitations woven into their structuring, family allowances, widows' pensions, supporting parents' benefits and other welfare provisions are important resources for women. They give women a measure of autonomy otherwise unavailable to many. Feminist considerations of social policy have yet to come to terms with the price women pay for the money they receive. The mesh of the liberal democratic safety net may be supportive, but it is also confining.

Acknowledgements

I wish to thank Chris Walker for energetic research assistance. I am also indebted to Pam Benton, Lois Bryson, Bettina Cass, Bob Connell, Meredith Edwards, Jan Larbalestier, Jeannie Martin, Rosemary Pringle and Claire Thomas for helpfully critical readings of working versions of this paper. Michaela Anderson gave bibliographical assistance.

Notes

1 This estimate is necessarily crude. It may tend to overstate redistribution between the sexes by rough handling of some of the transfers contained within the structure of personal income taxation discussed below.
2 All data provided in the following discussion refer to the year 1976/77 (because of the availability of taxation statistics), unless otherwise indicated (Commissioner of Taxation, 1977).
3 In the budget of 1981/82, the rates of family allowances for third and subsequent children were increased, but this increase benefits only 27 per cent of families (see Chapter 3).
4 For a widow or widower alone, only a daughter engaged in full-time care may be claimed. Where the housekeeper is caring full-time for a taxpayer's dependent children, the claim may be made in respect of a person of either sex.
5 Women become eligible for the age pension five years earlier than men, reflecting assumptions about the appropriate age relation of married couples (Kewley, 1980: 14). The means test assumes that income is shared equally between husband and wife.
6 These rebates serve to redistribute income from the working to the middle class. More than 90 per cent of rebates for education and superannuation expenditure go to taxpayers with incomes above the median; in 1976/77 the $35.7 million taxed from some members of the working class, unemployment and sickness beneficiaries, was enough to finance these two rebates. Only 1 per cent of rebate benefits for medical expenditure and property taxes went to taxpayers below median income.
7 The distinction is based on that between use and exchange values. He terms benefits in kind 'collective consumption'.

8 Population policies and family policies: state construction of domestic life

BETTINA CASS

In feminist sociological accounts of the relationship between women and the welfare state, it is contended that the domestic division of labour lies at the heart of the ideology and practice of the modern welfare state, as essentially as do class relations (Wilson, 1977; McIntosh, 1978; Land, 1978; Land, 1979).

This insight has received little attention in the histories of the Australian welfare state, either as a matter for empirical investigation or conceptualisation. One exception is the work of Jill Roe (1975; 1976) who maps the connections between, on the one hand, colonial and post-colonial voluntarism, charity, residualism and the growth of the 'social services' state from 1942, and on the other hand, the persistent presence in all these periods of women as a major group amongst the 'permanent poor', because of their labour market disadvantages and their enforced dependence.

None of the histories of the Australian welfare state (e.g. Kewley, 1977; Mendelsohn, 1979; Jones, 1980; Dickey, 1980; Watts, 1980; and including Roe, 1976) include an analysis of population policy. They provide descriptions and analyses of employment, wage fixation, income maintenance, and housing and health policies, but no account is given of the ways in which the architects of and commentators on the Australian welfare state conceptualised the desirability and limits of state intervention into the very heart of domestic relations. We have no study which explores the clear connections which have been made in various periods between population policy, social welfare policy and employment policy. The vital connections between the labour market, the tax and social welfare system and the organisation of gender relations in domestic life require identification and investigation.

In a paper on the boundaries between the state and the family in Britain, Land (1979) explores the widely held belief that the state should not intervene in family life. There has not been an explicit 'family policy' in Britain, but there have been policies aimed ostensibly at protecting the inviolability of the family, keeping it outside the realm of state intervention so that it will be able to carry out its major function as a 'haven in a heartless world'. In order to maintain this illusion, social policies are often presented as defending the 'normal' and 'natural' patterns of dependencies and responsibilities already existing within families against the allegedly destructive pressures of economic and social change. Most, if not all, social policies are therefore based on assumptions about the nature and patterns of normal relationships within the family. In other words, they are implicit family policies.

Land's description of the ideology of state non-intervention into family life is analogous with the dominant liberal conservative view of family-state relations in Australia, in which it is held that the state should only intervene in relations between spouses and between parents and children when the 'normal' and expected patterns of dependence and the legitimate exercise of authority have broken down, or when family members, after passing rigorous tests of eligibility, qualify to receive a government benefit. In these cases, social services and cash transfers are seen as substitution for services normally provided by family members and for income normally earned through gainful employment. As has been pointed out by Spalding (1977), Edwards (1980a), Bryson (Chapter 6) and Shaver (Chapter 7), in the Australian context, the processes of the social welfare and taxation systems (as the most obvious forms of state intervention into family life) serve to maintain the sexual division of labour, i.e. assumptions of women's dependence and men's responsibility for the maintenance of women and children. In addition, as Bryson, Shaver, and Roe in this volume make explicit, the interconnected tax and welfare system also tends to maintain class, as well as gender-based inequalities. The implications and effects of the tangled web of tax regulations and welfare provisions have to be teased out by careful analyses, since these implicit family policies are rarely given direct exposure in the arena of political debate.

It is in the context of population policies, in the context of the establishment of national demographic objectives, that direct expression is given to some of the basic assumptions of proto-family policies. It is in the writings and reports on population issues that assumptions are laid bare about the relationship between the family, the state and the labour market, the limits of state intervention, the relationship between men and women, the rights, and more pertinently the obligations, of women, and the obligations of parents to their children.

It has always been considered legitimate for Australian governments to have a vital interest in the subject of population and to deliberate on policies to promote population growth either through 'natural increase' or migration. Sustained population growth has been seen in official policy discourse and in most academic writing (particularly by demographers, economists, and medical practitioners) until the latter part of the 1960s, as the very basis of national security (to defend the 'empty spaces' against the 'threat from the north'), as the means to promote racial purity (to increase the Anglo-Irish stock in the Pacific regions, threatened by but inviolate against Asian and other racial incursions through the exercise of judicious immigration policies), as the necessary adjunct to economic growth (to ensure an expanding workforce with appropriate numbers of consumption units to stimulate demand) and as a force for moral good in society (to promote the stabilising twin institutions of marriage and parenthood).

This chapter examines two reports commissioned by Australian commonwealth governments to examine demographic change and to formulate population policies. The first is the 1944 National Health and Medical Research Council's Report, *Inquiry into the Decline in the Birth-Rate*, commissioned by the Labor government in 1942 to investigate the decline in fertility which had intruded forcefully on to the political agenda as an aftermath of the 1930s Depression. The second is the Supplementary Report of the National Population Inquiry, published in 1978. The genesis of the First Main Report of the National Population Inquiry (1975) owes more to the politics of immigration than to the politics of fertility (Birrell and Hay, 1976; Jupp, 1976), having been commissioned by the Liberal–Country Party government in 1970 to investigate the economic, social, cultural and environmental implications of changes in population growth rates, composition and distribution, so as to formulate future *immigration* policies as a critical and the most readily manipulable component of population objectives. However, in the course of the conduct of the inquiry, it became clear to the demographers from the Australian National University (to whom the inquiry was entrusted) that the post-World War II pattern of marriage and fertility was undergoing a change which required explanation. Once again, as in the 1890s and the 1930s, marriage rates and fertility rates were falling. Thus in the Supplementary Report (1978), which has the benefit of 1976 census data, the issues of fertility decline and positive population policies to counteract it are delineated more *sharply* than in the First Main Report. Although these two reports are separated by 34 years, were commissioned by governments with divergent political ideologies, and are the products of markedly different political and economic conditions, their study demonstrates significant continuities in Australian population thought, and points to the ways in which proto-family policies were and are placed at the very point of intersection of welfare policies and the market economy.

Population policies: 1944

The activities of the Labor government in the 1942–44 period can be summarised as an exercise in the management of aggregate demand, the management of the labour market, the control of inflation by high levels of taxation and the bringing of low income earners inside the tax net, legitimated by the political consensus engendered by mobilisation for the war effort and by the promise of a 'new order' of full employment and social security, the legislative and administrative framework of which was being laid down even before the war was over (Kewley, 1977; Roe, 1976; Jones 1980; Watts 1980). What has *not* been shown, however, is the way in which the *family* was constituted as the legitimate recipient of the rewards of the post-war reconstruction state. Along with the use of government stimulation of the economy to maintain full employment, the introduction of a range of income maintenance measures—unemployment and sickness benefit, widow pensions, allowances for the wives and children of age and invalid pensioners, funeral benefits for pensioners, the universalisation (once again) of the maternity allowance—and the establishment of the National Welfare Fund, went considerable political rhetoric concerned with solving the problem of the falling birthrate.

In 1942, an official inquiry was established by the National Health and Medical Research Council of Australia to investigate the causes of the decline in the birthrate. The interim report of the Eighteenth Session of the Council, published in 1944, defined the steadily falling birthrate of the last two decades as a social problem—a problem 'such as to cause even now, the gravest anxiety about the future of the Australian people' (National Health and Medical Research Council, 1944: 9).

The council, well aware that many women were deliberately limiting their families, or having no children at all, through the use of contraception and abortion, established six 'expert inquiries' on the historical, social, economic, medical, educational and maternal dimensions of the 'problem', invited submissions from interested groups and also invited written statements from women who were limiting their family size, about their reasons for doing so. The Introduction to the Report leaves no doubt as to its ideological genealogy and its dominant assumptions. The Agenda is established with an early reference to and quotation from the NSW Royal Commission on the *Decline of the Birth Rate* (1904) which, 40 years earlier, had officially defined the fertility decline of the previous decade as a grave problem, and had attributed it to the deliberate control of reproduction by women:

'led astray by false and pernicious doctrine into the belief that personal interest and ambitions, a high standard of ease, comfort and luxury are the essential aims of life'. (quote from NSW Royal Commission on the *Decline of the Birth Rate*, 1904, in NHMRC Report, 1944: 9)

But the 1944 report, in its major emphasis, analyses and re-commendations, sets itself against this conclusion. The report of one of the commissioned expert inquiries ('The Population Problem in relation to the Personal Needs of Mothers' by Dame Enid Lyons and Dr Phyllis Cilento) expressed concern that the honourable and noble image of women as mothers had been supplanted by a Hollywood-inspired version of fashionable femininity with little association with maternity. But the pronounced pro-natalism of this report is offset by the gentler pro-natalist prescription for a system of services to help mothers with housework, childcare, maternal and infant welfare services, compiled by Constance Duncan of the Commonwealth Department of Health in a report ('Inquiry into what would constitute a Fair Deal for Mother, Infants and Young Children') which contains the following definition of the modern role of married women:

> The young married woman today wants first to be a good companion to her husband and a good mother to her children. But she also wants some opportunity for the cultivation and expression of her own gifts and powers, and to be able to make a contribution to the life of the community in her own right as it were, and not only as a child-bearing and child-rearing human being. (NHMRC, 1944: 26)

Overall, in a statement of conclusions derived from the collected evidence, the report maintains that the 1904 allegation of women's 'selfishness' was 'far from being the whole story' and the two major factors responsible for the great growth of deliberate birth control were 'the decreasing dependence of women' and 'the increasing sense of insecurity, economic and pyschological, social and international' (p.9). The council also recognised that the limitation of families was often motivated by parents' desire to promote the wellbeing and educational opportunities of their existing children—a motive which the council could not describe as either 'unworthy' or 'selfish'. The major thrust of the report and its appended annexcs might be summarised thus: the instinct for parenthood, or more specifically for motherhood (the existence of which instinct was never doubted), had been thwarted and suppressed by conditions engendering economic and psychological insecurity—conditions which must be corrected by a package of economic, social welfare and medical services to families which would constitute a positive incentive to child-bearing and rearing.

An exemplar of such a diagnosis of the problem and of recommend-ations for its amelioration is provided in the 'Memorandum on some Aspects of Decline in Birth-Rate and Future of Population in Aus-tralia', prepared by an inter-departmental committee of the De-partment of Post-War Reconstruction, the Department of Labour and

National Service and the Bureau of Census and Statistics. (This was presented to the council by H.C. Coombs, Roland Wilson and S.R. Carver.) After a demographic analysis of the relationship between fertility indices and economic conditions, this memorandum concluded that Australia's population growth, due to natural increase, would only start to incline upward with the adoption of wise and effective measures designed to 'encourage a regrowth of family life' and urged the development of a deliberate 'population policy' (pp.21-2). It presented an analysis of the declining birthrate which might well be judged 'sociological' in the mould of Durkheim and Titmuss.

The major social processes and dominant ideas were identified as: the competitive, individualistic value system of an urban society promising rising standards of living and expectations of raised consumption levels; social and geographical mobility isolating the family from kin and neighbourly support systems; within this value structure of raised expectations, a greater awareness of economic insecurity; higher standards of child welfare and increased years of compulsory schooling demanding extra financial maintenance by parents; parents' raised aspiration for their children's occupational future; improved standards of nutrition and hygiene for children which involve greater expense; the improved status of women manifested in women's growing awareness of their right to limit and space their families to maintain their own health and wellbeing; the fall in mortality rates, particularly in rates of infant mortality.[1] Finally, the authors warn against nostalgia for the high fertility levels of the nineteenth century. 'Many of the social and economic changes which have adversely affected fertility have been highly desirable in themselves. Even if it were possible, it would not be desirable to attempt to restore the conditions of the last century' (p.22).

The need for increased fertility is explained as a necessary adjunct to higher levels of employment, increased industrial output and defence security. A social and economic survey of family expenditure and income in Melbourne carried out in the early years of the war is used to show the inadequacy of average male incomes (even with the addition of child endowment) for the nutritional, medical and housing needs of larger families.[2] The 'definition' of a national goal, and the 'discovery' (by means of an academic survey) of the economic hardships suffered by those who would be required to fulfil that goal, are presented as the justification for a social policy designed to encourage increased fertility.

This report's policy prescription for encouraging child-bearing argues against a system of direct cash payments as a pro-natalist inducement ('so as not to encourage the least desirable types of parent') and because families in higher income categories might argue that they required more money than parents in lower income categories to rear their children.

Approval is given to the system of cash transfers available to families at that time: child endowment for children under the age of 16, after the first child, introduced in 1941 in conjunction with income tax concessions for taxpayers with dependent children. Having rejected the possibility of raising tax concessions for children, since this measure would be of greater benefit to taxpayers with higher incomes, this inter-departmental committee found in favour of child endowment because of its underlying principles of universality and uniformity, and canvassed the possibility of extending endowment to the first child and increasing the rate for subsequent children. These heads of commonwealth government departments, administrators and policy-makers of the post-war welfare state, would not advise in favour of a system of cash transfers either downwards (to those who might be 'least desirable parents') or upwards (to those on higher incomes)—but they were prepared to advocate a redistribution of income from the childless and those with small families to those with larger families: horizontal redistribution within income groups and within the family life-cycle. Although they were not explicit on this point, they were, in effect, advocating redistribution of income to mothers.

This report placed more emphasis on the provision of social services rather than on cash transfers: school meals, subsidised production of essential foods; subsidised children's clothing; a housing policy which would give preference to larger families with assistance for home-purchase and rental rebates; the provision of additional kindergartens for preschool children; improved free education; selection by merit for higher education; living allowances for school students after primary school; free medical attention and hospitalisation and the provision of preventive medical services. For the 'housewife' to sustain her in her motherhood it recommended a complex of social services: help in domestic emergencies, communal laundries, housecleaning and family restaurants, kindergartens and nurseries; provision for family holidays; and 'special assistance for the wife and mother in employment' (p.24). The political economic intent of such proposals was clearly to redistribute benefits and opportunities to larger families, and to provide a system of incentives in the form of services (and, in a smaller measure, in cash) to encourage women to bear and rear more children than economic conditions had hitherto allowed them to do. But there is also an emphasis on the resulting *quality* of the population (as well as the desired increase in quantity), a strong belief that health, education, housing and welfare policies would improve the 'health and efficiency of the population'. And the vocation of women as *child-rearers* was never doubted.

As additional 'non-expert' evidence, collected and compiled for the National Health and Medical Research Council Inquiry by J.H. Cumpston, Director-General of Health, there were the written testimonies of 1400 women who responded to a public invitation to state their reasons for limiting their family size. These letters, a proportion of which are quoted in full, provide eloquent documentation of women's hardships and struggles as they attempted to bear and rear children in depression and war, in inadequate, highly-priced, scarce housing, with inadequate wages or soldiers' allowances or without income during periods of unemployment, with the continuing fear of unemployment and income insecurity. It must be remembered, however, that the report compiled by Cumpston is the product of his selection, ordering and categorisation of the letters which were submitted, and as such is a public statement of some of the dominant ideas and values in the context of which he, as head of the Commonwealth Department of Health, viewed the 'problem' of the birthrate (NHMRC Report, 1944: 70-94).

Clearly, what impressed Cumpston most was the economics of family formation: inadequate incomes, housing shortage and high housing costs, job insecurity. He selected letters poignantly and angrily detailing suffering, fear of economic depression, the misery of separation from soldier husbands, the minute details of household budgeting, the difficulties of procuring housing, the experiences of grinding poverty and child deprivation, and, constantly recurring, the unending drudgery and toil of housework and childcare on an inadequate income without any domestic assistance. His summation of these letters was:

> Over and over again as a recurring theme throughout these letters, appears the struggle to maintain a decent standard of living upon the basic wage level.

> The impression left by reading of these letters is that women limit their families for the following reasons:-

> (1) No home
> (2) No help
> (3) No security—natural or economic
> (4) No hope for any change for the better in any of these thing.
> (pp.73 and 70)

Cumpston selected and quoted in full a letter to illustrate his category: 'General distrust of government and present distribution of privilege', adding the caveat that the sentiments expressed in it were an extreme form of those which appeared frequently but in more restrained tones. This letter mounts an angry class analysis of the political and economic situation of that time, locating the misery experienced by the writer and her family within the dynamics of deliberate working-class oppression, and providing a class context for the 'problem' of the birthrate.

> There were thousands in the [Depression] worse than us. Chattels thrown out in the rain. Those same boys have children in this war for what? To give security to big business and monopoly and greed throughout the world .... Stand up any politician who has ten children. You can afford them, why not have them, why look to the proletariat class to have them? ... Give to the people freedom from want, a distribution of Australia's profits to the people (all people) and you will not have to worry about the birth-rate. (p.76)

He also selected and quoted from a letter which mounted a gender analysis of the falling birthrate, but the extract is brief and attracted no editorial comment:

> The falling birth-rate is due to ... the ancient order of master and chattel. To try and apply such a very ancient institution on modern people must and is leading to chaos, and to alter it will mean drastic social reform. Let the state pay the mother a living wage for herself and for each child and so leave her independent of her husband's pay envelope and she will have her family. (p.76)

The theme of the 'selfishness of women' was given a brief airing, only to be discounted as a predominant motive; and the tables were turned by introducing the radical notion of the 'selfishness of husbands'. Cumpston argued that the duty of husbands did not end with the bringing home of income: they also had a duty to share in the upbringing of their children, and to share their pleasures with their wives, rather than seek outside diversion.

The basic assumptions underlying this compilation, selection and ordering of women's testimonies share the pro-natalism of other contributions to the Report, but a pro-natalism tempered by a keen awareness of the economic needs of families with children, the short-fall between needs and income, and the hardships suffered mainly by women. Cumpston chronicles a set of social conditions which, he claims, 'must be profoundly altered if this nation is to survive' (p.91). While there is no attempt to question, in any thoroughgoing way, the domestic division of labour, there is a certain cautionary and bracing shock inflicted by the letter which the Director-General of Health chose to conclude his report:

> I believe you desire the reasons of mothers for only having a limited family. Well, one of them is this: What do we owe to Australia? It starved us and our children after the last war and it will do the same after this *If We Let It*. Therefore, we have decided that there won't be so many of us to starve this time. It is better to gaze on one or

two hungry children then say, eight or nine, and if one can arrange to have none, so much the better. We, the mothers, hold this power in our hands we have a freemasonry among ourselves that is colossal. If we find out any birth control hint, we pass it on. I myself know of an easy, safe method of abortion. I know of hundreds of ideas that have been passed on to me by desperate and despairing mothers of hungry children. Things will have to be mightly attractive in the New World before we consider the inconvenience of big families. (p.91)

It is in the testimonies of these women, as selected and reported by Cumpston, that we have the only clear and unequivocal statement of the class and gender-based inequalities which characterise the material conditions of fertility and in which the 'problem' of the falling birthrate must be located.

The National Health and Medical Research Council's Report on the Decline in the Birth-Rate (1944) presented an analysis of the officially-defined 'problem' of the birthrate, and recommended social policies to promote and support fertility which were embedded in the social welfare concerns of the 1942–48 period of federal politics in Australia. The ideological convictions of most authors of the report are demonstrated in their concern with the economics of family life (rather than with the selfishness and sinfulness of birth-controlling women) and in their advocacy of social services and to a lesser extent cash transfers to counteract the income inadequacies which they saw as the legacy of depression and war and the failure of the basic wage to supply the needs of larger than average families. Their recommended 'population policies' rely on inducement and incentive and not upon the sanction of restricting access to contraception (except in the report by Enid Lyons and Phyllis Cilento which denounced prolonged use of contraception and advocated the salutary restraint of periodic abstinence during the fertile stages of the menstrual cycle)—but the report denounced abortion and called for adequate punishment of violations of the existing law. The report's 'social services orientation' reflected the dominant concerns of the Joint Parliamentary Committee on Social Security, and the Department of Post-War Reconstruction (of which H.C. Coombs was the Permanent Head). Emphasis on the 'family' as the appropriate unit through which social services could be channelled paralleled the interests of Evatt in using an expanded concept of 'family allowances' to circumvent the constitutional restrictions on commonwealth powers to legislate for social services (Kewley, 1977: 173-83). The advocacy of positive population policies based on a social services package to encourage and support family formation fits well within Roe's definition (following Partridge) of Australia as a 'social services state' (Roe, 1976: 219). For Roe, this means 'a state which provides minimal services for the poor', but for the authors of the *Report on the Decline in the Birth-Rate* it meant a state which provides subsidised goods and services to those who serve the state well by bearing and rearing more children than Australians had been bearing and rearing in the previous decade. Housing, health and welfare policies were advocated to inspire a renaissance of intra-marital fertility. Extra-marital fertility was certainly not countenanced (nor even considered) as a source of population increase, and the destiny and status of *married* women as the bearers and hence rearers of future population of 'high quality' was rarely questioned. Indeed, a sex-based domestic division of labour is one of the basic assumptions of the conception of the 'social service state' which the Report encapsulates.

This account has focused on the way in which encouragement of fertility was used as rationale for the direction and scope of social welfare policies. In the post-war reconstruction period, the ideology of the Australian welfare state was consolidated as a system of horizontal redistribution *within classes*, to benefit the period of child-bearing and rearing in the family life-cycle (as age-pensions and their extension in the form of allowances to the wives and children of pensioners represented redistribution to that period of the life-cycle coincident with exclusion from the paid workforce). The system of redistribution was not conceived as one which redressed the inequalities generated by the labour market.

However, it was not really seriously considered in the National Health and Medical Research Council's Report that individual wages alone would create the conditions for a revitalised family formation. Intervention by the state, as the provider of a 'social wage' (child endowment, maternity allowances) and of 'collective consumption' (subsidised housing and health care) was seen as mandatory to compensate for the inadequacies of the individual wage. Within the parameters of Keynesian thought, it was not at all difficult to conceive of the state supplying a supportive infrastructure for expanded fertility, as an essential element in a full employment policy which required high levels of aggregate demand to be enhanced by active family formation. And women's unpaid domestic labour and childcare were assumed as the very basis of welfare, full employment and population policies.

It could be argued that the embeddedness of family policies of this nature in Keynesian economics and social democratic politics, in defining the *family* as the appropriate target for redistributive policies, obscured class-based and gender-based inequalities between and within families. The ideology embedded in the Australian welfare state (parsimonious redistribution to the periods of the life-cycle characterised by exclusion from paid labour) did not explicitly establish either class or gender as the appropriate bases for the formulation of redistributive policies. On the other hand, under the expansionist economic policies of the post-war reconstruction state, the family was defined as the *recipient* of a range of collective provision: it was considered legitimate that public expenditure be directed towards the subsidisation of the market wage so that families could carry out their responsibilities of procreation and childcare.

The National Population Inquiry, Supplementary Report, 1978

The National Population Inquiry was established by the Liberal–Country Party government in 1970 to focus attention on 'matters of particular concern to the government in order to produce results that would contribute usefully to the formulation and application of national policies'. The term 'population policy' was not used, thus continuing with the fiction of non-intervention into personal life. The particular brief was to examine desirable future population levels towards which *migration* (a legitimate area of government intervention) should contribute and to take into account the economic, social, cultural and environmental implications of changes in population growth rates, composition and distribution.

Kathleen Jupp (1976) notes that the establishment of the Australian National Population Inquiry (NPI) had its counterparts in the US *Commission of Population Growth and the American Future* and the UK *Population Panel*, both of which were responses to population debates in the late 1960s in the advanced industrial countries which saw continued population growth as inconsistent with food and energy resources and environmental preservation. The Australian inquiry, however, was promoted by a specific set of political conditions: it was the product of the immigration policy debates of the late 1960s, and surrounding the 1969 election, when strong political differences emerged. Population increase from immigration had reached its peak in the late 1960s, and the brunt of the costs of provision of social infrastructure (housing, schools, social services) had been sustained in Sydney and Melbourne—leading to administrative and governmental disquiet about the social and political costs of migration policies whose major beneficiaries appeared to be the employers of labour. According to Birrell and Hay (1976), senior officers from the Department of Immigration advised the Minister for Immigration that an Inquiry was necessary to lead to a better planned and better argued basis for population growth—rather than an immigration policy which yielded to the intense pressure from employers wanting more immigrant labour.

It seems that the politics of migration policy, as manifested in a conflict of interests between administrative and political elites and business elites, was the major motivation for the establishment of the inquiry. The interests of the labour movement, in relation to the role played by immigrant labour in the labour market, do not enter significantly into the Report's analysis or recommendations.

When the Labor government gained office in 1972, the terms of reference of the Inquiry were extended to include a review of the implications of the government's proposed policies in relation to:

1 Abandoning immigration control based on colour, creed and race.
2 Lowering immigration target levels—especially assisted migration.
3 Decentralisation of metropolitan populations.
4 Providing wider accessability of family planning services.
5 Increasing aid abroad in population matters.

The inquiry was conducted by the Department of Demography at the Australian National University under the chairmanship of Professor Borrie.

While it is clear that immigration policy in relation to projected labour market needs is a major concern of the *First Main Report*, the projection of fertility patterns by a range of social and economic variables allows for an analysis of the report in terms of the implicit and explicit assumptions about the family which can be discovered within it. For the purpose of brevity, I concentrate on the analysis and recommendations provided in the *Supplementary Report* (1978), where fertility decline has been constituted as a *sharper* social issue than was the case in the First Report three years earlier.

What are the Report's basic assumptions in relation to population policy?

> Traditionally—population policy has been thought of as the implementation of measures designed to enable a nation to attain a specific demographic objective, through the manipulation either of national growth rates or immigration, or of some combination of both these elements. (NPI, 1978)

Traditionally, according to the report, government's concern has been most apparent when population trends have tended towards zero or negative growth levels. But it is contended that this concern has been less in evidence in the current conditions of fertility decline—and few countries have responded positively or negatively, except in eastern Europe (Hungary and Poland). This is not so. Kamerman and Kahn (1978) show that what might be called *demographic panic* has been one of the major impetuses towards the implementation of specifically pro-natalist policies in various western European countries, particularly in France, and has informed the introduction or extension of family allowances in various other OECD countries.

What is significant about the report's view of population policy is that it does not pay attention to the politics of policy-construction, where various interest groups compete in a power and decision-making arena to make their position prevail. There is no suggestion that there might be several positions on population policy, not *one* which governments articulate and to which all interest groups adhere, i.e. employers, trade unions, organised ethnic communities, women's groups, church groups. As Birrell and Hay (1976) point out, migration policy as one vital component of population policy should be reconceptualised as the political economy of immigration policy, in which employers and the trade union movement usually express conflicting interests, where well established migrant communities also have interests for which they attempt to mobilise political support.

In the less well researched area of population policy with regard to 'natural increase', feminist writers have demonstrated the politics of fertility control which have been operating. They have pointed out the positive rewards and negative sanctions which have operated to control women's fertility. On the one hand, access to the means or knowledge of the means to avoid unwanted conception and pregnancies has been restricted and only grudgingly conceded after concerted action by women (Gordon, 1976). On the other hand, economic restraints surrounding the costs of family formation and child-rearing have prevented women from having the number of children that they might want (Cass and Radi, 1981). It is now fairly well accepted at government level (and this is endorsed in the NPI), that the right to contraceptive knowledge and means should be protected and extended—though the caveats of age and marital status still constitute a matter of debate and the legal status of abortion has not been unequivocally clarified. But it has not been recognised that the political and economic conditions of advanced industrial capitalism have militated *against* fertility, especially the fertility of working-class women and of working-class migrant women. In the NPI, there is a definition of population policy which takes no account of such conflicting and competing interests in the construction of policy—and which, in fact, perpetuates the fiction that governments (i.e. politico-administrative elites) make policy in some unproblematic way according to their well-intentioned and unchallengeable or unchallenged view of 'the public interest' and national objectives.

The NPI rejects the traditional view of population policy as reaction against demographic trends, advocating instead that population policy should move with the tide of demographic change ('servicing the social and economic needs generated by demographic change rather than trying to alter the course of demographic change'). It does this on the pragmatic ground that there is no empirical evidence to show that governments can intervene successfully to promote fertility.

In the view of the NPI, marriage patterns, age of child-bearing, the small family norm, almost universal acceptance of contraception, cannot be altered and constitute the arena of private life in which the state should not interfere. 'The majority of couples seem able to achieve their objectives without further government assistance, and if this is so, why should governments interfere?'

Whilst this is commendable in its non-intrusive liberalism, this position does not confront the possibility that while governments have adopted the posture of non-interference, they have in fact endorsed or established a whole range of interventions which have had a direct effect on private decisions with regard to fertility. Seemingly private and personal decisions about reproduction have been made in economic and political conditions which considerably constrain and circumscribe the range of possible options and preclude others entirely.[3]

The labour market and government policies provide the conditions under which apparently private/personal decisions about conception, pregnancy, contraception and abortion are made. The NPI adopts the view that social welfare provisions, in the form of cash transfers and social services, should be directed towards the support of families with children—that is, to use public expenditure to support fertility and to subsidise *some* of the costs of child-rearing. The report however does not explicitly recognise that policies at state and business level are also structuring fertility in ways which may in fact run counter to the expressed intention of welfare policies.

The trends in marriage and fertility since 1971 which the National Population Inquiry identifies and attempts to explain are:

1 The rate of first marriages has declined.
2 Higher proportions of marriage end in divorce.
3 Most divorces are followed by remarriage, therefore divorce does not make a significant difference to the total marriage pattern.
4 There has been a probable increase in the prevalence of de facto unions, most likely occurring amongst younger people, which may result in registered marriage at some later date.
5 De facto unions are usually associated with effective contraception and therefore, with no children, or with a very small family.
6 Divorces are much more likely to occur in marriages without children or with a smaller average family size compared with those marriages which have not ended in divorce. (NPI, 1978: 34)

All of these factors point to a reduction in fertility.

Annual marital fertility rates, which have been declining since 1961, were in 1976, age for age, lower than they have ever been since 1921, lower in fact than in 1933 (NPI, 1978: 37). Ex-nuptial fertility rates have also been declining since 1971 (just as ex-nuptial fertility fell in the 1890s and 1930s) and present levels are about the same as those that prevailed in the 1920s. While the decline is evident for all ages, it is particularly marked for women over the age of 25.

The National Population Inquiry Supplementary Report explains the fall in marital fertility since 1971 as the result of the following set of interrelated factors: delayed marriage (which in some cases results in marriage at later ages); postponement of the birth of the first child, sometimes beyond the fifth year of marriage; lengthening of the period between births, but still completion of families usually before the wife reaches the age of 30. The inquiry sees no evidence to suggest that the small family 'norm' of two to three children has been significantly eroded by a shift towards childlessness or the one-child family. The inquiry cites data from a sample survey conducted by the Australian Bureau of Statistics in November 1976, which asked married and formerly married women about their actual and expected family size. The survey shows a marked reduction in total family size expected by the respondents, particularly those aged 20–29, in comparison with actual age-specific family size enumerated in the 1971 census. This is attributed to a compression of family size at two to three children— and a very strong tendency towards the two-child family—but the suggestion that the current postponement of the birth of the first child might result in childless marriages is specifically rejected (NPI, 1978: 42-6). The uncritical acceptance of these responses must be queried. Women may say that they expect to have children because they believe it to be unacceptable to say otherwise; or they may well intend to have children in the future, but circumstances may prevent them from doing so.

What explanations are proposed for the downturn in fertility? The report begins with an economic explanation for the declining rates of marriage and childbirth: the economic boom of the post-war years encouraged new and higher expectations of material living standards which evoked a demographic response of almost universal marriage; earlier child-bearing, but *not* a substantial increase in family size. The economic downturn of the mid 1970s dashed these economic expectations: there was a stabilising or decline in real incomes; higher rates of interest and tighter finance restrictions made home ownership less accessible and more expensive, while the cost of household goods also rose. The demographic response was greater caution before entering a registered marriage; greater caution before having a first child; greater caution in the spacing of children (NPI, 1978: 149).

However, claims the report, other issues must be taken into account apart from 'narrow economic factors'. These are: the extension of education to greater proportions of children continuing in secondary and tertiary education; the increasing proportion of married women in paid employment, particularly young women; the shortening of the period women spend in procreation; and early childcare being offset by the extended period of children's dependence, so that, while family size has been reduced, the period in which parents are financially responsible for their children has extended (NPI, 1978: 150-2). These are elaborations of the theme of the changed position of women and children in the labour market in advanced industrial capitalist society: young people are involved in longer periods of education and training for job certification and married women are involved in the paid workforce to finance home-ownership, household needs and children's education in a two-wage family economy. The NPI's claim that these are not economic factors (narrow or not) must be disputed.

What recommendations are made by the inquiry for intervention into the process of family formation? Like the National Health and Medical Research Council's report on the declining birthrate, 34 years earlier, the major thrust of this report is that the economics of the market have not provided sufficient incentive for high levels of fertility, not even during the 'boom' periods of the 1950s and 1960s, and even less during the economic recession of the 1970s. As a result, state intervention is required to provide a publicly funded support system (in cash transfers and in the provision of services) to maintain and assist family formation. The report demonstrates a re-activation of post-war reconstructionist thought about the 'social services state', pointing out that it is a matter of 'social equity' that transfers in cash and in services he made to families with children. Since the market economy has increasingly required two income-earners in each family to ensure home-ownership, education of children and the high levels of consumption to which families aspire, the state must be used to substitute for the income-earning capacity of the mother, if she is to be enabled to bear and rear children.

It is also important to recognise that even though the 'long boom' did not foster increased fertility, recommendations about the important role of the state in supporting family formation are made *not* in a period of boom, but in a period of economic recession, when the market economy can no longer be relied upon to provide the conditions on which even the modest two-to-three child family of the post-war period was based.

Data from the Household Expenditure Survey conducted by the Australian Bureau of Statistics (1974-75) are used in the report to demonstrate the loss of income sustained by households when the first child is added to the household unit, a loss of income which is recognised as income foregone by the mother who either leaves the workforce or takes part-time or casual work. The pattern which emerges clearly from the figures which the NPI present is one of considerable fall in household income with the presence of children (NPI, 1978: 159-61).

As in the NHMRC Report of 1944, the sexual division of labour in the family is a basic assumption of the NPI report. It is assumed that it will be the woman's income which will be foregone on the birth of a child, because it will be women who continue to leave the workforce to take care of children. It is further assumed that if the state intervenes to provide financial support at the appropriate time (i.e. at the time of rearing the first child) then women's apparent reluctance to bear and rear children will be overcome.

The most expensive child is the first, and being able to have the first child as ideally planned is probably the best assurance that later children will follow until the desired level of completed family is attained. (NPI, 1978: 167)

There is no optimism, however, that social policies will increase fertility, and there is an explicit rejection of the use of such policies as pro-natalist measures. It is held that, short of interfering with basic human rights, family size cannot readily be manipulated to serve the needs of the state: the prime function of the state is seen rather as 'servicing the needs of the family' (p.182).

The legitimate role of the state is defined as furthering *social equity*, not fertility, by supporting family formation at the level of parental desires, not at a level defined by the state as appropriate and desirable. The image of the state as coercive in population policy, e.g. by controlling access to contraception and abortion, is specifically repudiated, in favour of an image of the benign, facilitative state. This is done not only as a matter of policy, but also after a realistic assessment of the past failure of social services to encourage higher levels of fertility. The role of the state is 'to prevent families falling into poverty, enable young people to marry when they wish, and then to plan and achieve the family they want' (p.175). What is left *without adequate explanation* is the apparent failure of the market economy to provide universally for these basic conditions of family formation.

The major explanation given for family limitation in the post-war period (both in boom and in recession) is not poverty, but 'affluence'—the expectations of parents and potential parents that they will be able to enjoy high levels of consumption after the increasingly costly financial needs of dependent children have been met. There is also recognition that certain families fall into the category of 'poverty', particularly when there are young children, but there is no class analysis to show how this poverty is generated. The major assumption is that the loss of income sustained by the family on the birth of the first child is likely to precipitate family poverty, particularly in contrast to the relatively high consumption patterns of the two-income marriage which preceded the arrival of children.

There is even the assumption, stated explicitly in the report, that having more than the average number of children is a major cause of poverty:

There are of course many instances where poverty and other social disadvantages are caused by uncontrolled fertility or where families with many children suffer more than those with few children when unemployment or other economic disaster strikes. (NPI, 1978: 148)

It is interesting to note that in the demographic analysis in earlier sections of the *First Main Report* and of the *Supplementary Report*, it was shown that larger than average family size follows a U-shaped curve, being positively associated with both high income and low income. If 'uncontrolled fertility' causes poverty, why are the big families at the upper end of the income scale not also poor? The absurdity of stating the issue in this way shows how the lessons learnt in the technical, demographic section of the report do not appear to have sufficiently informed the explanatory and policy-oriented sections.

The claim that 'many children' or 'uncontrolled fertility' causes poverty—which can also be discerned as one of the submerged themes in the reports of the Commission of Inquiry into Poverty (1975) and of the Family Services Committee (1978)—serves as an ideology obscuring the real genesis of poverty in the conditions of income and wealth distribution. There is an element here of blaming the victims for their own poverty, since they appear to have eschewed the rational, fertility-controlling behaviour of their fellow Australians and to have reproduced indiscriminately.

The report provides no analysis of class differences in the effects of economic conditions on family formation. The position of families in the class structure is not examined because major analytical emphasis is placed on levels of consumption and on the availability (or not) of two incomes. This leads to the claim and the recommendation that in the situation of 'high' income (in effect, 'two' income) marriages and high consumption-expectations, the loss of income on the birth of the first child must mean the exercise of quite severe constraints, and therefore it is at this point in the family life-cycle that the most substantial cash transfer to the family should be made (p.167). The question of state intervention is seen in terms of compensation for 'parents' (p.162) for income foregone; and of transfer payments to the 'household' (p.161) during the vital years of family formation. The use of the words 'parents' and 'household' shows that neither the position of dependent mothers nor class-based unequal access to income are at issue here.

The report uses the term 'social equity' to describe the objective of cash transfers and the provision of pre-school services to families, but the various meanings of the term social equity are left unexamined. In one section, in a discussion of the new provisions for family allowances introduced by the coalition government in 1976, the report states that augmented cash transfers and the abolition of tax rebates for dependent children: 'introduced a significant income redistribution in favour of women with dependent children and with little taxable income' (p.164).

This is the only point at which it is suggested that it might be *women* who are financially disadvantaged by their rearing of children and the only point at which the role of the welfare system in redistributing income and resources to mothers is explicitly confronted. However, that family allowances are paid to women rather than to men remains an unexamined legacy of Australian history. (Certainly, there are several European examples which show that there is no universal acceptance of the payment to women of cash transfers for children. In fact, in a majority of the most 'generous' countries, the payment is made to men: Bradshaw and Piachaud, 1980.)[4]

Redistribution of income to women responsible for the care of dependent children does not appear to be the meaning of 'social equity' used in this report. Rather, the term refers to redistribution of income through the family life-cycle, from income-earners (who are taxpayers) without dependent children to families with dependent children. This view demonstrates the continuity of thought from 1944 to 1978 about the appropriate target of redistributive policies, as previously identified in the analysis of the NHMRC Report. 'Social equity' defined in terms of horizontal redistribution to the period of child rearing in the family life-cycle does not take into account (once again) class inequalities and gender inequalities between and within families.

If we accept the arguments of Jan Pahl (1980) and Meredith Edwards (1981) we cannot assume income is shared and pooled within families. Pahl and Edwards both insist on the necessity for critical scrutiny of the dominant presumption that men's income and men's labour market situation are sufficient basis on which to assess the wellbeing of the women and children in their families. What Pahl calls the possible 'hidden poverty' of family dependants might in some cases be one of the consequences of women's foregone income (foregone for the purposes of childcare).

Family policies in a period of economic recession

This analysis of two major official reports on fertility decline which presented recommendations for a positive population policy demonstrates the significance of population policy in legitimating the scope and direction of redistributive policies in the Australian welfare state. State intervention in the form of cash transfers and social services to the child-rearing stage of the family life-cycle is seen as legitimate compensation for the inadequacies of the individual market wage, which cannot be relied upon to support family formation at a level sufficiently high to promote national economic interests. However, in focusing on 'families' as the most appropriate target for redistributive policies, such population policy documents obscure both class and gender inequalities. The location of families in the class structure and the resulting unequal distribution of resources available to support fertility and family formation are given scant attention. The dependence of women, resulting from the domestic division of labour and women's responsibility for childcare, is not constituted as an issue to be analysed. Nor is it explicitly considered that state intervention, in the form of redistributive policies, might be directed towards the goal of promoting gender equality. However, both the National Health and Medical Research Council's report, embedded in Keynesian political economic thought, and the National Population Inquiry's supplementary report, which is embedded in the neo-Keynesian, expansionist political economy of 1972–75, defined the 'family' as the recipient of a range of services and cash transfers of direct benefit to women (as mothers responsible for the care of dependent children).

The latter half of the 1970s and the early years of the 1980s have seen the dominance of contractionist economic policies in a period of labour market recession and high levels of unemployment. Reduction of public expenditure for social purposes (cuts in the provision for public authority housing; the demise of universal health insurance; the redirection of education funding from the public to the private schooling system; the erosion of the children's services program) has been accompanied by an official, government-sponsored campaign to establish 'national family policies' (Council of Social Welfare Ministers of Australia, New Zealand and Papua New Guinea, 1980; Australian Family Association, 1981). The basic ideological thrust of such policies is to re-establish the family as the provider of services for the state (Cass, 1982). Cuts in the value of the social wage to women (the non-indexation of family allowances and the erosion of expenditure on childcare services) and incentives to families to purchase services (e.g. health insurance and education) on the private market, all signify components of an implicit family policy: the reinforcement of women's dependency as non-market workers responsible for housework and childcare, and the reinforcement of men's obligation to provide income by wage work.

Assumptions underlying public policies governing family life in a recessionary period are: that the sexual division of labour in the family is natural and must be supported, and that the problems which beset families must be solved individually rather than collectively (Coussins and Coote, 1981; Cass, Keens and Moller, 1981). An economic strategy characterised by cuts in the social wage is legitimated by a mounting rhetoric in support of private provision by families at the expense of collective provision. What is being activated by the official recourse to promoting the 'traditional obligations and dependencies of families' is an invisible welfare system: the unpaid domestic labour of women who are called upon to provide physical and emotional care of dependent family members (cf. Waerness, 1978).

Unlike the uses of 'population policies' in an expansionary period, when public expenditure was seen as providing legitimately for state support of family life, the uses of open and explicit 'family policies' in a contractionary period are to legitimate a significant retreat from welfare state support through public provision towards a 'small' state ideology of privatised provision, in which individual families bear the costs.

The contradictions inherent in the population policies identified in the official reports of two expansionary periods become clear: on the one hand, an emphasis on the 'family' as the recipient of transfers and services recognises the inadequacy of men's market wage in providing income for child-rearing. On the other hand, the obscuring of class- and gender-based inequalities allows the concept of state intervention into domestic life to be turned on its head in a contractionary period, almost without countervailing critique. Family policies which reinforce women's dependence and men's obligation to provide support, as in the current situation, have their roots in a history of population policies in which women's domestic labour was assumed and class inequalities were obscured. What is required is an emphasis on the uses of public expenditure, through cash transfers and social services in combination with tax policies, which redistribute income and services so as to minimise class and gender-based inequalities. Redistribution to the child-rearing stage of the life-cycle is necessary, but not sufficient to promote social equity.

Notes

1   There are clear parallels in this analysis with Kay and Richard Titmuss (1942), and with Titmuss's later essay on women and the family in industrial society (Titmuss, 1976, first published 1958).
2   This survey was carried out by W. Prest of the Department of Commerce, Melbourne University, from 1941 to 1943, and most of its findings remained analysed and unpublished—although preliminary results were made available to the 'planners of the new social order'. An excellent account of the carrying out of this survey and some preliminary results of an analysis of its findings are presented in G. Davison and J. Lack (1981)
3   As the letters sent to Cumpston eloquently demonstrate (NHMRC, (1944)).
4   Of the nine countries of the European Community, Belgium, France, Luxembourg and The Netherlands provide the most generous family allowances (in relation to average earnings). Of these countries, France, Luxembourg and the Netherlands pay the allowance to the father. Of the less 'generous' countries, all but one pay the allowance to the mother (Bradshaw and Piachaud, 1980).

9 Pater–patria: child-rearing and the State

EVA COX

In most societies, women are construed as taking the major, if not total, responsibility for the care and nurture of the dependent child.[1] The consequent ascriptions of gender roles are arguably the most powerful determinants of women's access to social and economic power. Any volume of readings, therefore, concerned with women, welfare and the state, needs to look at those aspects of state policy which directly affect women in their child-rearing roles. The possibilities women have of sharing the responsibilities for childcare outside the immediate biologically-bonded group depend on acts of omission or commission by the state in providing certain types of services. The availability of childcare services will govern women's access to education, to paid work and to other activities outside the home. This makes the issue of childcare policy a crucial one.

This chapter is concerned with the provision of services which complement or supplement parental care. One of the basic demands of the most recent wave of feminism has been the right of women, and their children, to childcare services. Yet, despite demonstrable need in Australia, such services are totally inadequate. In May 1969, the federal government commissioned its first survey of childcare needs from the Australian Bureau of Statistics (ABS, 1977). This survey estimated that 91 000 women with children not yet at school would have sought paid work if suitable childcare had been available, and 69 per cent of these women wanted centre-based care. Yet, at the time, only 11 per cent of children whose mothers worked away from home were in centre-based care (Fry, 1973: 251-2). By 1977, the percentage had risen only to 16 per cent (ABS, 1977).

Some theoretical considerations

The persistently low priority given to childcare services in the public policies of most developed industrialised countries reflects the assumptions officially held about the role of women. The relationship of women to the state parallels that of women to men; the deficits in the provision of such services derive essentially from the patriarchal aspects of the state, rather than from its maintenance of capitalist class relations. The conventional radical description of the role of the welfare state is that it has two major concerns, the reproduction of the labour force and the maintenance of the non-working population. The welfare state is described as 'continually tending to act on behalf of the capitalist class, to service the effective reproduction of capitalist social relations and the accumulation of capital' (Gough, 1979: 140). This assumes an underlying logic of efforts to maximise the use of labour to produce surplus value, and to minimise labour input into the reproduction of the labour force, and the care of the non-working population.

Such an analysis explains broad economic developments in the use of male labour, wage movements, and the introduction of technology and investment capital. It fails however in economic logic when provisions for the dependent sections of the population are closely scrutinised. In particular the state's lack of involvement in many aspects of the early socialisation and nurture of children, and their care in the home, cannot be adequately explained within the above economic analysis.

In ignoring gender-based interests political economists, conservative economists and conventional analysts of the role of the state share common blind spots. Radical political economists (feminists and others) have argued that women serve the needs of the capitalist state by reproducing the labour power necessary for capital accumulation. Those in the workforce are provided with a range of domestic tasks and emotional supports which make the waged worker produce more surplus value, and which also support those unable to work because of age or infirmity. Therefore, the mobile family unit, although a residue of an earlier system of production, has become adapted to the capitalist mode of production and is now essential to it. The corollary of this is that by undermining the nuclear family and its gender divisions, capitalism will be endangered. This viewpoint is shared by both conservative and radical theorists who are divided only on the values they place on the functions provided.

The family (woman) does serve some of the needs of capitalist industrial societies by providing a range of free services, and therefore limiting the necessity for some of these to be publicly funded. Women's other main function, child-rearing, would arguably be more effectively provided through rearing in communal groups. Expecting one woman to care for one or two pre-schoolers is not an appropriate use of resources, unless she is also caring for an aged relative, and other dependent adults. She does, however, provide a continuity of personal service which can be increased in response to state withdrawal of funds from collective services.

As the household tasks related to child-rearing have been deskilled through technology and professionalism (Chapter 4, in this volume) and decreased through contraception, there has not been any real acknowledgement of the potential release of women's labour power for the accumulation process. Instead, there has been the creation of private emotional servicing, the need for a 'haven' for family members, the extension of 'interpersonal relationships', and the development of 'private identity '. These may well serve the needs of capital accumulation in providing the male with a therapeutic alternative to powerlessness in the workplace and the child with training in individualism and competitiveness. However, they appear more likely to serve the needs of the male within the household, i.e. male interests generally rather than the economic interests of the ruling class. These interests would seem to be better served by access to additional, often cheaper female labour, rather than having to seek this by other means, such as migration.

Developments in the commercial sector have provided a range of household services for profit: catering services, home-help services on a commercial basis, private childcaring centres, boarding schools. All of these, plus servants, have given those with the resources to purchase them alternatives to full-time childcare and its attendant housekeeping responsibilities. Public provision for those with fewer resources has been less well developed.

Although the state intervenes persistently in the affairs of the family, it has reluctantly and rarely provided services for the very young child. The assumption remains that the care of the young child is essentially the responsibility of the immediate family, the voluntary caring networks. Most intervention has been aimed at preventing or limiting access to childcare services, thus placing restrictions on women's opportunities. Intervention by the state in the care of the young child is generally seen as undesirable except where the child's safety or wellbeing is endangered, or the parent is considered to lack the necessary expertise to produce appropriate training and skills. The state has usurped various rights and duties of the family in such areas as health and education, but has left the family with the responsibility for economic support (the father role), and the provision of physical care and emotional and social supports (the mother role).

State policies for children primarily support the adult responsible for the support of the child. The original basic wage decisions posited the male requiring the income to support wife and children (see Chapters 2 and 3). Most income maintenance programs are directed to the male charged with the support of wife and child. Mothers are supported directly only when there is no co-resident male. Apart from a contribution through child endowment/family allowance (which is paid to the adult responsible for the child) there is no direct support of the child unless there is no adult to provide primary care.

Why does the state, which controls both the education received by children over six and the quality of medical care available for the sick child, leave the care of the small child to private provision? The answer lies in the assumption that the state plays the male role, the patriarch, treating early childcare as women's work, outside the sphere of legitimate state activity, so long as women fulfil their obligations.

Some historical trends in childcare policies

There have been expectations that the state, representing the common good, would take responsibility for those children who had no adults to care for them. This policy can be traced to colonial 'charitable systems' and continues with few changes into present state-controlled welfare systems. Although there have been swings from large institutions to boarding out/foster care as the appropriate means of providing care for the orphaned and abandoned child, there have always been some financial provisions made either directly or through grants to charitable bodies (Dickey, 1980).

The intervention of the state on behalf of the child, whose family does exist and can care for it, is more recent. It involved a conceptual shift. The family was no longer seen as being the domain of the father with children as his sole property. The rights of the child to separate protection were recognised. This originally arose through the Chancery Court attempting to protect the property of a minor, but was extended in the nineteenth century to a recognition of the special status of children, and the development of a special jurisdiction. The first children's court in Australia was opened in South Australia in the late nineteenth century. Its role was defined as 'acting in the best interests of children' rather than subjecting them to adult concepts of justice. It invoked the concept of 'parens patriae', the state as substitute parent of the child.

This major shift in attitudes to children occurred during the period of industrialisation and urbanisation. In agrarian and petty commodity production, older children had been economically productive and treated as small adults, hence they were not seen as being different from adults and deserving of special legislative protection. Compulsory education was introduced in most states in the 1870s, limiting children's involvement in paid work and making schooling compulsory, partially with a view to improvement of the working class, so they would become more effective members of the workforce, or better future housewives and mothers.

These changes were implemented on both idealistic and practical grounds. Although children provided even cheaper labour than women, their labour was not cost-effective in terms of necessary skills, and an educated, healthy, older labour force was of longer-term advantage. Once younger children were excluded from the workplace, not only were they no longer productive, they were also a potential source of mischief. Regulations were required to force parents to support their children and control their behaviour. The period 1890 to 1930 has been described as the 'golden age of child welfare legislation' (Burns and Goodnow, 1979: 49). Legislation in this period covered the regulation of custody, adoption, employment of minors, income maintenance payments, child vagrancy, truancy, smoking, child endowment and widows' pensions, as well as a range of requirements and constraints on child behaviour and parental obligations. These included both care and control and embodied views of middle-class mores. Some of the language and charges remain in current legislation in that children can be charged with 'being neglected', or being 'exposed to moral danger'.

The role of the state appears in this context to be primarily punitive. On the one hand, the state accepted the necessity for replacing the family in the formal education of the children, but did not attempt to replace the physical care component. These functions were enforced in the family (i.e. devolved upon women) in a way which suggests that in many cases they were not being adequately provided. Thus the contradictions emerged of a state punishing the parent who failed to send a child to school, and also punishing the parent who failed to provide care for the child in the home.

The woman was seen as the primary source of such care, and her inability to provide it was seen as sufficiently detrimental to suggest that state resources should be made available when husbands had departed. In the NSW Parliament in 1923, a member expressed this as follows:

> This widow, the orphan and the babe in arms are the first call upon us ... little children are our human sunshine ... where a mother is engaged in rearing a family of children, she is doing her duty to the State if she rears that family satisfactorily. If, at the same time, she has to go out in the world to try and earn a livelihood, that work cannot be satisfactorily carried out. The children will suffer and the State will suffer when those children grow up by reason of the fact that the work was not properly done. (Burns and Goodnow, 1979: 50)

Apart from the 'boarding-out' fee paid by the NSW State Children's Relief Board since 1896 to enable destitute widows and deserted wives to support their own children (Kewley, 1977), no other services or cash assistance were provided by governments to assist women with their childcaring role. This contrasted with the comparable situation of the aged and infirm. The old age pension was introduced in 1900 (NSW) and 1908 (federal), invalid pensions in 1908 (federal), but widows' pensions took till 1926 (NSW) and 1942 (federal) (Kewley, 1980). Those women who could not provide the requisite level of care or who did not qualify for state relief were dependent on assistance from the spate of voluntary agencies which also appeared at this time—or lost their children through the courts. Well-baby clinics, kindergartens, residential care centres and day nurseries/creches were initially the initiatives of charity groups of the educated middle classes, not of the state.

The kindergarten movement

Kindergartens were seen as a tool of urban reform and the kindergarten movement emerged in Sydney in the 1890s in a period of philanthropic interest amongst educated women to improve poor living conditions in the inner city slums (Spearritt, 1974). The ideas originated in Germany, through the work of Froebel, who saw social change as being possible through changing the nature of education, starting with the young child, letting it grow and unfold like a flower in the garden. This was viewed as a way of changing the nature of adults, and therefore eradicating behaviour which would prevent the social improvement of the poor.

By 1910, there were 32 kindergartens in Australian cities, but already schisms appeared within the movements concerned with the young child. For the most part, kindergartens ran for mornings only and were aimed at enhancing the child's upbringing, not relieving the parent from daily childcare. The day nurseries were providing care for children whose mothers were employed and thus were seen as a welfare service. This difference in emphasis led to the establishment of the Sydney Day Nursery Association in 1910; it had less general appeal than did the Kindergarten Union, being seen as charity, not social betterment. The kindergarten movement was a product of the era in which social reformers believed that education was to be the main avenue through which social change was to be achieved. The kindergartens spread in working-class areas, charity-funded and staffed by the work of middle-class women, both voluntary and underpaid (Spearritt, 1974).

In the 1930 Depression, these centres served additional purposes. They implemented certain health measures, particularly the provision of adequate nutrition with hot lunches for young children in families affected by unemployment. This combination of what appeared to be effective physical and educational intervention led to the first federal government initiative in this area. In 1938, the Commonwealth Department of Health established demonstration centres in all state capitals to encourage the expansion and upgrading of services. These were the 'Lady Gowries' which still operate under direct common-wealth funding.

These kindergartens, however, worked on part-day programs and were deliberately made unsuitable for use by the employed mother. They were for intervention and education, aimed at the child *and* the mother at home. Not only did the centres question the legitimacy of parental values in child-rearing, mothers were only given minimal relief in terms of time, and also expected, in most kindergartens, to contribute by doing some of the domestic chores.

The attitudes of state governments towards the provision of services for those below school age differed widely. Some states, such as Tasmania, incorporated the kindergarten movement directly into education, providing teachers' salaries as part of the education budget. Others, such as Queensland and South Australia, supported the voluntary sector as the appropriate source of such services, but with a level of state recognition and support.

New South Wales experimented with kindergarten classes as early as the 1880s through the education system, hiring a woman from New Zealand who was experimenting with Froebelian methods at Crown Street School in Sydney. However, children under the age of six were enrolled in the schools from early in the century. Even before compulsion was introduced, three-year-olds were admitted to schools for a range of reasons. In 1880, education was made compulsory at six, but the same year a babies' class was offered at Fort Street, presumably for younger children. The NSW Education Department has a pre-school non-compulsory year, the so-called kindergarten year, which it appears to have offered fairly generally through most of this century. It also had a number of actual separate kindergartens in some inner city locations (Annandale, Balmain, Chippendale, etc.) which operated within the system.

These initiatives were, however, consistent with education policy and not aimed at the provision of surrogate care. Doubtless, they did serve parents who needed time away, just as schools do. This was, however, not their intention. Staff expressed their disapproval of parents using the centres for care by making demands on them for assistance as a condition of attendance, e.g. rostering parents for kitchen duty.

Meanwhile, the day nursery and creche movements were not as successful in enlisting public support. They were seen as residual services, providing essentially for the non-coping parent. The few centres provided were 'charity' centres aimed at the woman who had to work due to extreme circumstances, and had no money to pay for childcare on the commercial market. This market flourished, as there has always been a proportion of women with pre-school children in the workforce, and there have always been those who provide care for children in return for money. In addition to informal, in-home minding, many centres were established to run at a profit.

The role of the state in the provision of such services was minimal. Some grants were provided to the charity organisations, but in similar terms to those grants given to other voluntary organisations, as a gesture of encouragement rather than a commitment to the program. Otherwise, state involvement was regulatory. In some states, the pressure from the growing number of kindergarten teachers and organisations led to regulations being incorporated into statutes defining certain minimum physical and staffing requirements for centres' permission to operate.

Recent developments: pre-schools versus day care

The 1940s brought two changes. There was a shortage of male labour, and a need for women to work in the wartime industries. In 1943, the federal government announced that it would extend the kindergarten system and, where appropriate, fund these to stay open for longer hours so women were available for war work. (The hours were later reduced as the demand for female labour slackened—Spearritt, 1979).

At the same time, middle-class women wanted their children to have access to kindergartens so they could benefit from the programs offered. As they could not get access to the charity centres, and these were in the lower-income suburbs, they began to establish their own. These kindergartens were commonly run by parent/community groups, but there were also commercial centres, usually run by women with some training or experience.

By 1973, there were over 2000 pre-school/kindergartens in Australia, compared with fewer than 100 in 1939. Some states had funded centres through their education system, e.g. Tasmania, and others through the health department, as in Victoria. Proportions of children attending kindergartens ranged from a low of just under 6 per cent in New South Wales to over 21 per cent in the Australian Capital Territory. Proportions of government funding provided by the states varied greatly, with New South Wales providing less than $800 000 per annum while Victoria spent over $5 million for a slightly lower population of children. This included the money for subsidies to non-government centres, but not the cost of those provided within the education system in New South Wales (Fry, 1973: Sec.2).

Whatever the funding problems and variations, there was no doubt that the pre-school movement was established. By the late 1960s and early 1970s, advocacy was concerned with extending services to those without access, not with questions of the value of the service. The 'Headstart' program in the USA, for all its political problems, had enshrined the concept of early intervention as an appropriate means of compensating for what were seen as household disadvantages. However, in most of Australia, pre-school centres were parent-established and, therefore, it was more likely to be middle-class children who had access to the services originally devised for poor and assumedly disadvantaged children. There was pressure mounting from many sources to provide a government-financed, free pre-school year for all children.

The splits which occurred in the early part of the century, between those who saw the priority as education/social change via the child, and those who saw the need to provide child and parent with safe places to leave the child, had grown even wider. The middle class co-opted pre-school/kindergarten provision for their own children, defining it as an education service to enhance the child's school attainments. Thus, the reformist pressure was (at best) to make the service universal, rather than compensatory.

Pre-school was seen as a children's service which was not intended to free the mother for other activities. Centre staff and early childhood development professionals sought to reinforce the mother's role at home as being necessary for the needs of the child. The shortened day, divided into two three-hour sessions, was introduced in many centres in the late 1960s to early 1970s and was justified in terms of the child needing the mother-contact hours to be extended. Children under three were regarded as too young to attend in most centres, and three-year-olds were regarded as vulnerable, needing to be carefully watched in case separation distressed them.

The contrast in government expenditure figures for pre-schools[2] compared with long-day-care illustrates the differences in attitudes. In 1973, the Australian figures for day-care subsidies showed that just over $1 million was spent on long-day-care as against over $14 million spent on pre-schools. New South Wales was parsimonious to both services, partly because the state provided some pre-schools as part of general schooling.

Although Victoria was as stringent with its day-care subsidy, it did provide ten times as much for pre-schools. South Australia and Tasmania spent nothing (Fry, 1973: Sec.2.3). In the whole of Australia there were estimated to be some 867 centres providing long-day-care, and 2472 pre-schools. Most of the long-day-care centres were provided as commercial enterprises, and often lacked any trained staff or programs aimed at developing children's skills. They were more or less child-minding places, charging fees on a profit basis. Some provided good standards of care, others complied with fairly minimal health and building standards but otherwise offered little more.

This was the situation when the federal government began to see the provision of some form of services for the child below school age as requiring attention. This arose through public pressure, political climate and a shortage of available labour. A large influx of women into the workforce contributed to this issue being placed for the first time on the federal government agenda. (Chapter 10 in this volume outlines the political/bureaucratic processes involved.)

Official recognition of the influx of women into the workforce was provided by the establishment of the Women's Bureau in the Department of Labour and National Service in 1964. During the 1960s, the bureau's publications highlighted the growing number of married women moving into paid work, and the problems of childcare which they were facing. The 1969 *Child Care Survey*, was the first attempt by the government, through the Australian Bureau of Statistics, to measure unmet childcare needs. At this time, the Australian economy was booming and migration programs could not provide the labour needed in the expanding service sector industries.

The prime minister, John Gorton, made promises to establish some forms of childcare, aimed at the needs of children of working parents. These were facetiously referred to as 'Gortongartens' and were the first governmental acknowledgement of the need for public provision of services for women in paid work. The money was first set aside in the 1972 budget, under the provision of a federal *Child Care Act*. The responsibility for this was, significantly, placed with the Department of Labour and Immigration. The amount allocated was a mere $5 million, but it was a watershed decision.

The advent of a Labor government in 1972 extended the childcare debate. The Labor platform included no item on services for working women, but had under its education platform a commitment to provide a year's free pre-school for every child who wanted it. This was designed to provide all children with the advantages presumed to flow from this year of pre-school preparation.

However, groups such as the Women's Electoral Lobby had made childcare in its broadest sense part of the political agenda. WEL asked each candidate to complete a questionnaire before the election, and the ratings then given were seen to have influenced the outcome of the election. Women in the Labor Party took up the issue. A concerted campaign cutting across party factions led to a change in policy being adopted at the Party Conference in 1973. This extended childcare policy to include long-day-care and other services, aimed at the needs of women in the paid workforce.

Administration of the federal program, which had not been implemented before the election, had been delegated to the Department of Education. Joan Fry, a woman with a long involvement in the field of pre-school and long-day-care, was appointed to head the newly established Australian Pre-schools Committee. This was asked to report to the Minister of Education on measures necessary to allow all children, by 1980, access to a year of pre-school and to ensure that childcare centres would be established for children below school age to meet the needs of children of working parents and underprivileged families (Fry, 1973: ii).

The report was presented in November 1973, by which time various power and pressure groups had drawn up lines of defence. The report itself was received with loud public criticism. For those who had been advocating the extension of services for the working parent, it was seen as a capitulation to the pre-school movement. The report recommended that 70 per cent of children be provided for in pre-schools but only 10 per cent in day-care centres. There was a strong emphasis on the professionalisation of services, rather than their extension.

The splits between those advocating pre-school and those advocating day-care widened. With the prospect of substantial sums of federal money being made available to children's services, the contest for the larger share of the cake became fairly heated. There was the long established pre-school movement, strongly supported by male professionals in child development and education, who had worked for many years to provide services through voluntary organisations for their own children, or for those they considered to be in need of them. Activists included a large proportion of establishment figures, academics and experts, most of them, if not all, believing that a mother should stay at home while her child was young. Misinterpreted research over twenty years (Cox and Martin, 1976) was used to support their contention that children are best served by the type of care which maximises parent contact, and that they are ill served by substitute day-care.

These attitudes were shaped by literature which made its first appearance in the aftermath of World War II. Studies by John Bowlby (1953) and others of children suffering gross deprivation served as a basis for the invention of the concept of 'maternal deprivation'. Although many women had used day nurseries during the war years, and had been in paid work, there was now a need to convince women that stay-at-home motherhood was more appropriate behaviour, when their paid labour was no longer required.

The popularisation of such findings and the post-war baby boom had effectively limited the participation of women with young children in the paid workforce in the 1950s. Elsewhere by the early 1960s, and in Australia by the late 1960s, various circumstances had increased women's entry into the workforce, and the findings on maternal deprivation were being publicly re-examined (Rutter, 1972).

However, the earlier material, although often refuted, had passed into conventional wisdom and provided ammunition both for politicians wary of emerging women's issues, and for professionals trying to protect and extend the existing pre-school services. There was ample evidence that young mothers were already in the workforce, and over eight out of ten of their children were being cared for in a range of often inadequate private minding situations. However, the debate still raged on whether the provision of such services would encourage women to join the workforce. Although the debate purported to be about the welfare of the child, it seemed to revolve on the work status of the mother, and the damage done to children by lack of appropriate care (Cox and Martin, 1976).

Pushing for the extension of services was a loose and diverse coalition of women who had begun to assert their right to paid work and women already employed and aware of their own disquiet at the quantity and quality of care available. There were also some women in the new Labor government bureaucracies with a commitment to women's issues (official and unofficial) who were determined to fight for childcare allocations to be directed to the areas of most need (see Chapter 10 in this volume).

An effective lobby in and outside the bureaucracy gave the feminists their first victory. The Fry report was answered and devalued by an initial report from the Priority Review Staff under the Special Minister of State. The issue was then referred for a further report to the Social Welfare Commission. This was an independent statutory body under Marie Coleman, established to advise the government on social welfare policy. Their report was issued in 1974, and did much to counter the strong education bias of the first report. A further report by the Priority Review Staff endorsing the main recommendations of the second report was issued in August 1974.

Meanwhile, the pressure had mounted to remove the responsibility for this area of funding from the education portfolio and establish it outside the existing departmental responsibilities. It was felt that the linking of children's services with Labour, Education or Social Security tended to limit the scope of the services. So, a successful lobby by WEL and friends had led to the responsibility being taken by the prime minister with Lionel Bowen, as Special Minister of State, assisting the prime minister in this area. After the 1974 election, an interim Children's Commission was established, as the precursor of a permanent commission.

This lobby sought to convince the government that it should campaign on a commitment to childcare in the snap election called in 1974. The government was asked to allocate a specific and substantial amount of money to children's services and make this a major policy plank. This was successful to some degree as advertisements appeared in the media stating the government's intention to commit increased funds to day-care and pre-schools.

The fight continued in various quarters. As money allocated was not divided between pre-schools and childcare, the first submissions received were likely to receive the greater share of available money.

The pre-school movements had their submissions ready and nearly all the money went to establishing new pre-schools, often in areas of considerable affluence. Long-day-care had for long been the Cinderella of the services, and it was now missing the Ball.

Overworked existing organisations such as the Sydney Day Nursery had neither the time nor the energy to establish new services, though they recognised that they were needed. Women already in the workforce had no time or energy left to attend meetings and write submissions to establish centres which were unlikely to be started in time to replace their current form of care. Women who were intending to go back to work had no contacts which allowed them to initiate the process of establishing a centre.

In 1974, the booming economy of the early 1970s was beginning its downturn. Unemployment was rising, as was inflation, and the pressure had commenced to cut government expenditure. What could be easier than to peg funding of a newly established program, especially when the need for women's labour was no longer so acute.

From 1974 until 1982, the situation worsened. Expenditure was pegged at much lower levels than was promised in the election and the advent of a coalition government committed to cutting public expenditure for social purposes ensured that the overall program lost substantially in real value since 1976. However, although the overall commitment has not increased, certain changes in allocation priorities have occurred, with contradictory results.

The first move of the coalition government was to abolish the interim Children's Commission by failing to proclaim the Act. Responsibility for children's services was then passed to the Department of Social Security, which established a separate Office of Child Care. Marie Coleman, whose own commission had earlier been abolished, accepted the position of director of the new body. The shift to the Department of Social Security signalled the government's intention to see these services as welfare rather than education, or general community services.

The new office had a difficult task ahead of it. Despite good intentions, most of the money spent to that time had tended to go to the pre-school services in areas where people were good submission writers. Employed women and children of disadvantaged families were not faring well. This conflicted with the Liberal belief that government should provide services and subsidies only for those in need, not for all who wanted them. Universal pre-school was no longer seen as a federal responsibility, but services for those in need was seen as a legitimate area of involvement. Most states have already committed extensive funds to pre-schools; all states except New South Wales now provide these free for 60 per cent to 80 per cent of children in the year before they start school.

Therefore, the funding was split. In the 1976 budget and all subsequent budgets, the states have been offered a block grant which has diminished in nominal and real value. This grant is to cover the commonwealth commitment to provide access to pre-school for those who need it but cannot afford it. Other funding is seen as individual state or parental responsibility. The remaining amount which gradually came to be 50 per cent of the $65 million overall grant (1972), has been left for the range of other services, primarily childcare services for the children of employed parents.

This shift under a conservative government was actually closer to women's needs than the unclear priorities of the previous reformist government. Labor politicians, almost entirely male, were always uncomfortable about working women with young children, and were not enthusiastic in supporting the extension of services which would serve their needs. While some Liberals were equally conservative, their concept of needs did tend to separate the pre-school lobby from the childcare lobby. Certainly, the fact that the Social Security portfolio was held by a woman who was a working mother seems to have helped, as did the tenure of the Office of Child Care directorship by another woman. For once, the issues seemed to be clear.

This does suggest, once again, that the problem women face in establishing their legitimate claims to services in this area depends more on combatting male values than contending with those of conventional party differences. Though the gains have been limited, they have been made through a coalition of women in the political and bureaucratic systems, not only those mentioned above, but many others, who have been able to influence policies.

Despite the above victory, there have also been losses. One issue which has emerged strongly over the last few years is the resurgence of acceptance of 'one-to-one' care as more appropriate than group care. Whereas, in its original form, this was used to reinforce pressure on women to care for their own children, it is now being used to reject group care in centres and replace it, where possible, with supervised and supported in-home care—family day care. This form of care was first suggested officially in both the Fry Report (1973) and the report prepared by the Social Welfare Commission (1974).

Both reports saw family day care as a cheap way of upgrading available childcare places, though whether this was to be done by recruiting experienced carers to provide more care, or resourcing and upgrading existing private minding, is obscure. Whatever the reasons were originally, the government rapidly recognised two advantages for family day care: it is cheap, needing little or no capital outlay and much lower running costs; it reproduces the various aspects of in-home care which men would see as desirable. Women can use it to care for their own children, earning some extra pocket money by caring for up to four children.

In New South Wales in 1980 more than 5000 children were cared for in family day care schemes. This was more than were catered for in all the non-profit, long-day-care centres and amounted to nearly a third of those places available for children whose parents were employed. Their care was provided by women at home whose median income from caring for up to four children could range from around $25 per week to $140 gross. Most women who provide this care do so for a range of reasons, often related to their own ambivalence about paid work outside the home. Whether it is to provide company for their own child, or the care they perceive is needed by the child of a 'working mother', they suffer both exploitation and conflicts about their own position as low paid working women.

This highlights again the theoretical problem raised in this paper about the status of caring for children. Because most of it is provided by women within the family structure, it is not seen as legitimate paid work. When it is done for pay, the pay available may be very low, below any award, as in family day care and other private caring situations. Women are socialised into accepting childcare as their responsibility and often promote these male values against other women, by proclaiming women duty-bound to care for their own children.

The state enters very reluctantly into the provision of any services which are designed to relieve women substantially of their child-rearing responsibility. In doing this, it represents male interests, a coalition across capital and labour which sees childcare responsibilities as the main means of maintaining women's domesticity and dependence. Childcare policies in Australia will only reflect the needs of women (and children) for a range of alternatives to parental care when women are in the position to establish such services.

Notes

1   The definitions of dependence will vary between cultures from the child still breast-fed to the late adolescent student.
2   There was always confusion in terminology—'kindergarten' became loosely used for classes in school as well as centres outside, also sometimes for commercial ones open long hours. To clarify this in the text of this article, I use 'pre-school' to cover those services operating three to six hours daily and 'long-day-care centres' for those operating for eight or more hours to service parents in paid employment.

10 The women's movement's fandango with the state: The movement's role in public policy since 1972

SARA DOWSE

Anyone attempting to analyse the role of the contemporary women's movement in the shaping of social policy since 1972 will find it a massive undertaking. I am suggesting that we lack the essentials for any sober examination of the subject: distance and perspective. Anyone interested enough to undertake the task will probably be committed to the aims of the movement and will most likely have been active in their pursuit, and therefore too close for clear focus. The women's movement is ongoing, living, organic. One needs no credentials to join it, other than a belief in the justice of its aims. Its character, emphasis and organisation are constantly changing. One finds it difficult to stand back when the developments about which one is writing are continuing to occur and when the very act of writing such a chapter in a book such as this is a measure of one's involvement.

Have there been significant changes as a result of the efforts of organised feminism? The answer depends upon where one stands, but the ground is continually shifting. This is partly due to the problem of perspective and also to the changing political scene in which the Australian movement operates.

Much of state action directed towards women is termed 'social policy'. What is social policy? This troublesome concept arises from the assumption that economic and social policies comprise two distinct spheres, an assumption that lies at the core of capitalist ideology and roughly parallels a similar division of the world into two separate realms: the public and the domestic.[1]

State operations are often associated, quite falsely, only with public expenditure on social welfare, i.e. income maintenance and service provision. As a result of this ideological construction, our attention is diverted from the vast public resources placed at the disposal of the sphere of 'private' production. Most of the activity, personnel and resources of the commonwealth bureaucracy are concerned with assisting the productive sphere. State governments are chiefly occupied with social services and social control, but even here vast public sector resources are channelled into support of the private sector.[2]

In this ideological separation of the social and the economic, much of the mounting political pressure from women has been siphoned into a narrow range of 'social policy' issues. The women's movement has not always been successful in resisting this process, perhaps because feminists too have been deluded by the ideology. Since there is no real distinction between social and economic policy, I use the term 'public policy' in this chapter, even though it represents a euphemism for the operations of the state. Another difficulty arises from the expectation in the social sciences that discussion of matters of public policy can fit into neat conceptual models. From my own experience, the politics of the women's movement are multi-faceted, multi-dimensional, and resist such treatment. What follows then is a rather descriptive, somewhat discursive and defiantly ragged interpretation of what has happened between women and governments over the last ten years or so, and suggestions as to where we might go from here.[3]

What is the women's movement?

In the early 1970s the term used to describe the resurgence of feminism was 'women's liberation'. 'Feminism' at first was eschewed, probably because our generation learned about the early feminists through history books that portrayed them as quaint, rather fussy and prudish, and largely irrelevant. The suffragists, temperance organisers and dress reformers were figures of ridicule. And they were middle class. Women's liberation, both in the United States and in Australia, was born of other movements whose rhetoric was largely Marcusian-Marxist. Women active in the civil rights and anti-war movements of the 1960s began to apply the rhetoric to ourselves, having been increasingly aware of the extent of our exploitation and the discrimination against us within these movements. Yet while we became articulate about our oppression as women, we still could not quite identify with early feminists. They were seen as inconsequential, misguided failures. What did the vote ever do for us, anyway?

Women's liberation was a term, however, that few but the young and politically active could identify with. In Australia it gradually faded from view after 1972 when, in response to the challenge of coming federal elections, the Women's Electoral Lobby (WEL) was formed. Once feminists got into the business of trying to influence public policy, 'women's liberation' must have seemed inappropriate. WEL wished to distinguish itself from women's liberation in order to attract wider support. Soon after, the term feminism reappeared, possibly as a way of describing a more sober movement, with established historical roots. But it was about that time too that distinctions between different strands of the radical arm of the movement were becoming important; feminism was adopted as the generic term, to be qualified by the adjectives 'radical', 'revolutionary', 'socialist' etc. By 1974 'the women's movement' had emerged to cover what had by then become a broad-based, somewhat protean movement loosely made up of many disparate parts.

But did it include the more conservative women's organisations? One government report (Women's Advisory Body Working Party, 1977) noted that there are over 150 national women's groups in Australia, among which can be numbered organisations like the Country Women's Association, the National Council of Women, the Federated Association of Business and Professional Women, the Federation of Women Voters and the YWCA. Some of these date from the first wave of feminism and all have a substantial history of attempting to influence public policy. At first the new feminists tended to ignore these organisations, as we did the women's auxiliaries of the established political parties. The consequence was often resentment by the old of the new. But by the late 1970s the situation had changed. New reactionary women's groups such as the Women's Action Alliance and Women Who Want to be Women came on the scene and gained influence with the Fraser government. The conservative groups found they had become moderate middle-of-the-roaders, increasingly pushed into alliance with younger feminists. The latter for our part were forced to fight a rearguard action, protecting some of the advances of the mid 1970s from erosion and outright attack, and we welcomed support from respectable quarters.

Thus we can view the women's movement in much the same way as we do the trade union movement, and admit to the various conflicting and ideologically opposed factions within it, feminist and anti-feminist. Or we can take the term 'women's movement' to mean only the various shades of feminism, as the 'labour movement' ranges over the spectrum of socialism. Because I believe the women's movement represents a deeply felt groundswell for social change, I have chosen to use the term in its second sense, stepping forward rather than backwards. But I am conscious of the fact that reactionary women see themselves as very much part of the women's movement. And so, of course, do conservative governments.

Feminism and the election of a Labor government

Ten years ago it was a different story. The resurgence of feminism coincided with the Labor Party coming to office for the first time in 23 years. The 1972 election and the resulting Labor government had a profound effect on the development of the women's movement in Australia. The convergence of the rise of 'new wave' feminism and the election of a social democratic government after so long a period of conservative rule is perhaps unique in contemporary western democracies. It put a stamp on the nature of the involvement of feminists with and in government and indeed determined the parameters of the women's movement itself.

The year 1972 was in a sense the culmination of almost a decade of protest over a number of issues that affected the young in particular. Australia was sending conscripts to Vietnam, to fight a war which could be less and less justified as the decade wore on. Young people were rebelling against the puritanical straitjackets of their parents, against the censorship of books, films and works of art, against the smug narrow-mindedness that characterised the post-war period. Young women began to give vent to their frustration and dissatisfaction with the oppressed conditions of their lives.

This made politicians of all parties more sensitive than ever to issues that might swing votes. Though the ALP had no policy on women and even less of a childcare policy than did the Liberals (see Chapter 9), its egalitarian ideology promised a more favourable reception to feminist demands. In the event it was the centrist Australia Party that topped the WEL questionnaire used to 'rate' the candidates and parties, but its chances of forming a government were negligible. What mattered was that the emergence of an apparently powerful feminist lobby awakened hopes within the ALP that increasing numbers of women voters would vote Labor, that the traditional conservatism of women voters was a thing of the past. That was something for the Coalition to ponder too.

The WEL campaign was based upon the six demands formulated by women's liberation: equal pay, equal employment opportunity, equal opportunity in education, free contraceptive services, abortion on demand and free, 24-hour childcare. Ironically, the coalition government was able to respond quickly to the childcare demand because of work carried out in the Department of Labour and National Service after John Gorton proposed in 1970 to provide federal government support for childcare. The policy had been shelved during the 1971 recession, but was taken down again and dusted in time for the 1972 campaign. In the 1972/73 federal budget $5 million was set aside, and in October 1972 the childcare bill introduced by Phillip Lynch, then minister for Labour and National Service, became an Act.

The ALP, too, was confident that its proposals met women's demands for childcare. Having responded to pressure from the Australian Pre-School Association, the party's policy was one year's free pre-school for every Australian child within six years. There was also a commitment to childcare for working parents. Yet when Labor politicans attempted to explain their policy it became obvious that they did not really perceive the difference between the two kinds of services. Unhappily, this confusion was to become a serious impediment to the development and implementation of the Whitlam government's children's services policy.

In the beginning, however, there was much for Australian women to look forward to. Soon after Labor was elected, the Whitlam-Barnard 'diumvirate' moved to help women. They re-opened the national wage case and intervened in favour of the Conciliation and Arbitration Commission's adopting the principle of equal pay for work of equal value. The 22.5 per cent luxury tax on oral contraceptives was lifted, as was the ban on advertising contraception in the Australian Capital Territory. Shortly after, an Australian Pre-Schools Committee was set up under Kim Beazley, the new minister for Education, to administer the childcare act and its $5 million appropriation. Once the new Parliament went into session the Labor government introduced legislation to establish the supporting mother's benefit and maternity and paternity leave for Australian government employees.

The birth of a federal feminist bureaucracy[4]

In April 1973 Whitlam appointed Elizabeth Reid his personal adviser on women's affairs, a clear response to the impact the women's movement made during the campaign.[5] At the time there was no women's policy function in the federal bureaucracy. The coalition government had established a women's section in Labour and National Service in 1963 and upgraded it to the Women's Bureau four years later, but the bureau was primarily a research unit and had no direct policy input. Moreover, it was only concerned with women's employment. The establishment of the position of women's adviser to the prime minister, on the other hand, was a significant step in the development of a women's policy apparatus within the federal government. Initially, though, few were aware of this. The women's adviser was expected to work as part of the prime minister's team, acting as a catalyst and prod to what the government perceived would be a recalcitrant and unimaginative bureaucracy. Its creators did not anticipate how the occupant of the new position would become the focus of the women's movement's demands on the government. Nor was there much appreciation of how this would increase the adviser's workload far beyond what was expected of other ministerial officers.

Within a year, negotiations were under way with the Public Service Board to establish support staff within the Department of the Prime Minister and Cabinet. The Women's Affairs Section was established in July 1974 and proceeded to handle the adviser's voluminous correspondence and assist her in many other matters. Most importantly, the section monitored cabinet submissions for their impact on women. Thus it was that the 1970s women's movement first became involved in government in Australia. Was it co-option? Certainly. But the circumstances, as always, are more complicated and the problems more complex than such language suggests. In the first place, the process began under a Labor government. We know enough now about the threat of such a government to ruling powers at home and abroad to recognise that much of what happens under a Labor government represents a genuine effort to redistribute resources within the country. The Whitlam government and the women's bureaucracies it established were a serious challenge to the status quo.

Yet the acceleration in the rate of reform has as much to do with the temper of the time—with the build-up of social, economic and political pressures—as it does with the kind of government that holds office. A second MacMahon government would have had to respond in some way to the same pressures that brought in a Labor government. The Labor government made a difference, though more in degree than in kind.

Clearly the Whitlam government was prepared—initially at least— to go further than any coalition in redistributing wealth and resources more equitably in Australian society. Eventually, though, it had to bow to the doctors, the insurance companies, the legal profession and the United States. As well, the Labor government was particularly vulnerable in respect of the economic conditions of the early 1970s. Labor came to office when the economy looked good but the massive influx of foreign capital in late 1972 created inflationary conditions just at the time when the government wanted to carry out its 'mandate'—an undertaking which required increased public spending. In 1973 and again in 1974 the government was prepared to push through its program in spite of Treasury advice to prune the public sector and tighten the money flow, but by 1975 it had yielded and major expenditure cuts were introduced in the Hayden budget. A number of government initiatives were either suspended or cut back before the 1975 coup and the subsequent election.[6] Thus the limits to reform are set by the political economy—not by the particular government in office.

With the advent of a Labor government, debate within the women's movement over revolution versus reform was short-circuited. Feminists of all persuasions began to believe, or at least *act* as if they believed, that social reform was a necessary if not sufficient condition of a revolution in the relationships between the sexes.[7]

International Women's Year and the children's services program

In 1974 two major initiatives of importance to women were introduced. In the 1974 election campaign, the government pledged itself to a $130 million childcare program. Upon its return it attempted to cut back the proposed program to $34 million, but after WEL protested it set aside $75 million in the 1974/75 budget and established, pending legislation, an Interim Committee to a Children's Commission (ICCC). The ICCC was charged with developing and administering the new children's services program—an 'integrated' program of care and education based on a priority of need—and was responsible to the prime minister through Lionel Bowen, his minister assisting. That meant that the new program, with its $75 million appropriation, was no longer under the aegis of the Education Minister or his department, but under the close watch of the prime minister's women's adviser and the Women's Affairs Section.

At the same time—September 1974—the government set up the National Advisory Committee for International Women's Year (IWY), with a budget of $2.2 million and a secretariat in Bowen's Department of the Special Minister of State. The National Advisory Committee, chaired by Elizabeth Reid, was responsible for a program to support women in their creative activities, assist them in overcoming disadvantage and to change community attitudes about the role of women in society.

The feminist bureaucracy and its influence within the Australian government was growing, and enabled a substantial childcare program to be developed and approved by cabinet. The IWY program was conceived by the adviser, who was assisted by the Women's Affairs Section in formulating policy and setting up the National Advisory Committee and its secretariat. The IWY Secretariat itself quadrupled in size and was raised in status as the administrative demands of the program increased.

Without such commitment and expertise within the government neither the IWY program nor the children's services program could have been initiated. For while the demand for childcare came from the women's movement, it took a particular type of activity and concentration of effort for the movement to take advantage of the opportunities the Labor government provided. Elizabeth Reid was able to convince cabinet that the report the Pre-Schools Committee presented in December 1973 was biased in favour of pre-schools at the expense of childcare. It was she who got cabinet to refer the report to the Social Welfare Commission and the Priorities Review Staff before committing itself to the policies the Pre-Schools Committee recommended. Both of those bodies provided Reid with data with which to formulate the 1974 election policy and later to prepare the necessary cabinet documents.

Similarly, it is unlikely that an IWY program would have been developed or approved by the prime minister had there not been a women's adviser on his staff who had surveyed the problems of women for a year, acquired an understanding of the constitutional limitations of the government and its approach to the problems of reform, and obtained his respect and confidence.

There are differences, however, in the etiologies of the two programs and these differences are significant. The IWY program was a 'reform from above', the brainchild of a ministerial officer adopted by a government anxious to be seen doing something for women but not prepared to pay much for it. The children's services program resulted from sustained lobbying by sections of the women's movement which was beginning to evolve its own ideas about childcare. The fact that committed feminists were influential in translating these demands and views into government policy was important but not, as we shall see, conclusive.

For much of 1974 and 1975 the energies and attention of the women's movement were focused on IWY. The National Advisory Committee received and processed about 700 submissions, but over two financial years was only able to support just over 150.[8] Much of the appropriation went into administrative costs and on projects designed to change attitudes within the community, such as the Women and Politics Conference held in September 1975. The National Advisory Committee's concern about women and politics was appropriate enough since from the beginning it was embroiled in political conflict. Guidelines for funding were set out in the booklet 'Priorities and Considerations' tabled in Parliament in December 1974, but the question of who should be funded involved more than just meeting the guidelines. The Advisory Committee was worried that if too many submissions from the left were funded, the government would get flak from the right. On the other hand, if the Committee approved too many applications from conservative or 'apolitical' women's groups, the attack from radical and left-wing feminists could be very bitter. Such tensions became manifest in a public meeting held in Balmain Town Hall in January 1975 and were present throughout the year.

The National Advisory Committee was beset with other problems too, not the least of which was the battle with Treasury over which women's projects would be funded under the program. Treasury was arguing that *all* expenditure on women should come out of the $2.2 million appropriation, including projects that should have been funded under other programs. Relations with the media were at best strained but for the most part the media treated IWY in much the same way as it had the women's movement in general. The IWY program was portrayed as trivial and an unnecessary waste of money, and throughout 1975 became a focus for all that was supposedly wrong with the Labor government. Naturally, the media reception had its repercussions, especially as the year wore on and the government began reacting more and more as if it were under siege.[9]

The women's movement seemed unaware of or unconcerned by these pressures. The National Advisory Committee was criticised about how the program was being handled and where the money was going. In many cases the objections were all too valid, but there was very little airing of what would appear to have been wider questions: whether the committee should have disbursed funds at all, whether there was any other kind of financial support available or whether there would be once the government funds dried up. Or, finally, were we getting our priorities right?

Unfortunately the controversies surrounding IWY almost completely eclipsed the far more significant drama concerning childcare. It is only now that the women's movement, armed with more sophisticated analyses of the sexual division of labour and the maintenance of patriarchy by women's predominant role in child-rearing, is turning once again to the childcare issue.[10] From this perspective there is a strange hiatus between the concerns of the early 1970s and the present interest, and it does seem that IWY is to some extent responsible. When one compares the stakes—in concrete terms $75 million compared with $2.2 million in the first financial year—that the flea should have obscured the elephant seems scarcely credible. Yet it is not hard to see how this happened. Because so much was at stake the opposition to feminist control or even a feminist orientation to the children's services program was tremendous. The Australian Pre-Schools' Association was smarting from what it felt to be an unjustified slap in the face from the government. The Education Department had suffered the loss of an important policy function. Both institutions sought to undermine the new policy and were assisted to some extent by the inexperience of the government feminists, who had won the first battle but certainly not the war. From the start there was a deep contradiction between childcare and pre-school education within the children's services program. The policy of 'integration', devised to short-circuit this contradiction, did nothing of the kind. It only served to push the conflict underground—within the government instead of open to public debate. And while the Pre-School Association was able to step up its pressure, the childcare lobby was uncoordinated and weak. The women's movement was able to react quickly when the returned Labor government announced a $96 million cut in the proposed children's services in its mini-budget of July 1974. But come September the movement, under the impression that the new ICCC and its $75 million program would look after childcare, turned to IWY, planning a wide array of innovative projects for funding.

Mention too should be made of the problems inherent in the type of funding arrangement developed under the Whitlam government. This is not the time to go into the complexities of Section 96 specific purpose funding, but it is relevant to point out that the constitutional limitations on the federal government encouraged the development of funding by grant of individual organisations, after consideration of applications from the community. This was in keeping with the current emphasis on community development and participation.

The problem with this method of funding, however, soon became evident—only those organisations with the knowledge and resources to prepare acceptable submissions received government money. That left the disadvantaged more than ever so. To assist people desperately in need of childcare—particularly in migrant and working-class areas—the plan was to appoint workers, or 'catalysts', from within these communities to help develop local services. The appointment of these workers, however, was strongly resisted by the professionals represented on the ICCC. This, and the absence of any concerted childcare lobby, meant that comparatively few submissions for childcare could be completed before the end of the financial year. So some $30 million were left unspent. The bulk of the $45 million that was spent—80 per cent of it in fact—went to pre-schools, which unlike the childcare projects were funded in block through the states. Once this happened the balance of the program was heavily weighted in favour of the massive development of sessional pre-schools (which had been demonstrated to be of little assistance to working mothers or their children, who because they needed other forms of care were unable to attend). What's more, the Australian Pre-School Association, itself in receipt of children's services funds for its operating costs, actively propagandised Bowlby's theories of maternal deprivation, sending home leaflets pinned to children's jumpers exhorting mothers not to go out to work. And all this because feminists fought for and got $75 million from the government.

The history of the children's services program is a fascinating case study in government decision-making, an object lesson in what not to do when devising government policy. The full complexities of the program must be dealt with elsewhere. My reason for touching on them here is to highlight some of the problems facing feminists working for social change. With hindsight it is clear that the movement was fobbed off with a poorly funded public relations exercise that deflected its energies and obscured what was happening in an area involving substantial structural change and redistribution of resources. The divisiveness engendered by the availability of IWY funds could not have been more effective if it had been cynically instigated by an actively hostile government. But the fact is that this occurred through the good intentions of a sympathetic government advised and assisted by committed feminists—a sobering experience.[11]

The state of the women's movement also contributed to the divisiveness. Feminists of the early 1970s believed that the lesson to be learned from the mistakes of the early feminists was 'never put all your eggs in one basket', or 'we must fight on many fronts'. Feminists resisted developing priorities or selecting one issue to the exclusion of all else. We were prepared to evaluate specific reforms and examine them in relation to each other, but would go no further. The ubiquity of patriarchy required many focuses of resistance.

Feminist action reflected this thinking. Feminist caucuses developed in many spheres of activity; networks of feminists developed and could be mobilised quickly and quite often effectively. It is not surprising that the movement should have responded to the IWY program as it did: in a very real sense IWY did arise from the movement and was appropriate to it. The children's services program, on the other hand, posed challenges the movement was not able to meet, either organisationally or ideologically.

The feminist bureaucracy after 1975

The dilemma of whether to concentrate effort on one or two important issues or insist on having a voice in decisions affecting women in almost every conceivable sphere of activity, was an important question for the developing feminist bureaucracy in the federal government. The feminist bureaucrats were part of the growing women's network, but the very fact that they were bureaucrats made communication with the rest of the movement difficult, even if means of communicating were more readily at their disposal. This difficulty was compounded after 1975 by the Fraser government's emphasis on secrecy and the polarisation that occurred as a result of the events of that year. Consequently, the feminists in government suffered acute isolation.

In October 1975 Elizabeth Reid resigned from Whitlam's staff. Shortly after the Women's Affairs Section in the Department of the Prime Minister and Cabinet was upgraded to a branch. To understand what this meant one must be aware of the changes occurring in the prime minister's bureaucracy. By 1974 Whitlam realised that a strong advisory capacity within his office was not enough to ensure the implementation of the Labor government's policies. He needed a stronger department to deal with the rest of the public service. Moreover, the government, increasingly conscious of its own vulnerability, sought to secure the permanency of some of its reforms by embedding the appropriate apparatuses in the bureaucracy. The Women's Affairs Branch was ideally situated in these circumstances, and after the 1975 election its influence continued to grow, since Malcolm Fraser was disposed towards relying heavily on his department for advice and accelerating the momentum towards centralisation.

Throughout 1975 the women's adviser, the Women's Affairs Section, researchers in the Royal Commission on Australian Government

Administration (RCAGA), and other public servants, had been considering future administrative arrangements in women's affairs. The general consensus had been that the Women's Affairs Section should be strengthened, to operate as the hub of a network of women's units to be set up in key government departments.[12] The idea behind this system was that women's affairs could not be isolated in a separate department—as were, say, Aboriginal affairs—but involved the entire range of government activity. The objective was to attain a workable balance between integrating the work of government feminists with that of other departments and concentrating resources sufficiently so that women's issues would receive high priority and would not be submerged under other departmental matters. In other words, what government feminists had been saying was that there was a 'fight within' each government department, but that these battles could not be conducted without the leadership of a central policy body. As such they were hoping to replicate, formally, the structure of the women's movement at large.

It was a novel approach to administration and was consciously shaped by feminist concepts of organisation.[13] Nevertheless, the proposal was endorsed by both the outgoing and incoming governments and on 4 March 1976 prime minister Fraser wrote to six of his ministers asking that they consider setting up women's units within their departments.[14] In August he established the Interdepartmental Working Group on Women's Affairs, chaired by the Women's Affairs Branch, as the coordinating mechanism—or network—for existing units, such as the Public Service Board's Equal Employment Opportunity Section and the Women's Bureau, and the new ones in the making. By June 1977 four of the six ministers approached by Fraser had taken up his suggestion and women's units had also been established in the Schools Commission, the Australian Development Assistance Bureau and Telecom. All were represented on the Interdepartmental Working Group, which was meant to marshall effectively all available government resources advising on major policy in women's affairs.

The development of the women's units also has to be seen in the context of the traditional role the Department of the Prime Minister and Cabinet of 'nurturing' new federal government functions. Both the Office of Education and the Office of Aboriginal Affairs were initially situated in that Department and eventually became departments in their own right. As we have seen, a similar move for women's affairs was not recommended. However, a kind of bureaucratic imperative operates which prescribes the growth of certain functions in very conventional ways. This imperative was reinforced by the appointment at the end of 1976 of a new permanent head, Alan Carmody, who was unsympathetic to feminism and wanted to divest his department of all 'non-essential' functions, such as the arts and women's affairs. It was also given written support in ambiguous recommendations of the RCAGA, that the Prime Minister's Department be streamlined and that the Women's Affairs Branch be maintained (RCAGA, 1979). Early in 1977 the Women's Affairs Section was upgraded again and renamed the Office of Women's Affairs. Though it was still a branch of the department, there was a suggestion that the new name heralded its imminent 'hiving off', either as a departmental outrider or to another department. The office, of course, wanted to stay in that department because being there strengthened its hand in relations with other departments, particularly in chairing the Interdepartmental Working Group on Women's Affairs. Moreover, as an integral part of the department, the Office of Women's Affairs continued to monitor Cabinet submissions and could select and decide which submissions required comment. In this way it wielded some influence over the direction of government policy, especially in matters of government expenditure. In at least two areas—childcare and women's refuges—its intervention was crucial.

The Office of Women's Affairs became something of a nuisance, initially to other departments but eventually to its own. The Prime Minister's Department's evolving role as the central policy body was rubbing departments the wrong way: they resented its incursions into their domains. By the end of 1977 the department was looking for ways to minimise the growing conflicts and tensions. From the government's point of view, the Office of Women's Affairs was ripe for shaking off the departmental tree and in December 1977, shortly after the federal elections, it was transferred to a newly created Department of Home Affairs (Dowse, 1981).

The downgrading of the Office of Women's Affairs reflected both the shift in community priorities and the state of the women's movement at the time. Many feminists, embroiled in IWY and disillusioned by the Whitlam government's performance, were nonetheless shattered by the happenings of November 1975, which exacerbated the tensions within the movement. Again, the experience of dealing with state and federal governments on the funding of projects—refuges and health centres in particular—made the radical arm of the movement more than ever suspicious of the bureaucracy. Feminists were divided over the question of funding and a host of other issues. Factionalism and sectarianism made communication between different groups almost impossible, or fraught with bitterness. Needless to say, there was considerable animosity towards women in government and they were left to fight enormous battles in isolation from the rest of the movement.[15]

In fact the movement was in a state of transition, a painful stage of

growth. Until 1972 the second wave of Australian feminism was embodied in women's liberation. Then there appeared two relatively
discrete, if overlapping, feminist alignments. By the mid 1970s instead
of two large bodies there were a number of groups in different areas
working on different issues with only very loose connections with each
other, if that. The movement was certainly less visible, partly because
the media had decided that after IWY women were no longer news,
but that was probably not the main reason. It became visible again
after 1978, when the fruits of its activity in the universities, the trade
unions and the political parties, began to appear. Until then, and
especially in 1977, it looked as if governments and political parties
could with impunity overlook women as a political force.

The women's movement and the monetarist ascendancy

That the government desired to ignore the women's movement had
much to do with changes in the management of the economy. From
the beginning of 1975, when Professor Milton Friedman paid his first
visit to Australia, government at the federal level increasingly
abandoned social reform as a priority, and concentrated on controlling wages and the money supply and cutting back the public
sector.[16]

The connection between economic and social issues, while apparently hidden to economists, politicians and government policy-
makers, became increasingly obvious to women. Apart from the
effects on employment and government services generally, economic
policy dictated that funds for a number of women's programs were
cut. Of all the programs introduced during the Whitlam years to
benefit women, only the women's refuges increased their budgets in
real terms. A number of women's health centres had to close down;
the working women's centres, first funded under IWY, had to find
additional sources of financial support. The IWY program itself had a
limited life span and no funds were committed under it after 1976. The
Women's Film Fund, set up by the Fraser government in 1976,
consisted principally of returns on IWY film investments. The NEAT
scheme was tightened so that very few women could afford to avail
themselves of its training opportunities. Maternity leave was made
more difficult for federal employees, and paternity leave was
abolished.

An examination of the children's services program points up with
great clarity the economic aspects of an ostensibly social policy. The
program was introduced in the 1974/75 budget—the Cairns social
contract budget—drafted in August 1974 as an alternative to the de-
flationary budget proposed by Treasury. Cabinet, faced with a recession, adopted the classic Keynesian approach of 'spending our way

out'. It was for this reason that there was $75 million for children's services instead of the $34 million announced by Treasurer Frank Crean in the mini-budget of 23 July, though admittedly there would have been less had WEL not protested.

Because of the forced double dissolution and the May 1974 election, in the 1974/75 financial year there were only nine months in which to set up the program and spend the appropriation.[17] Yet as we have seen, there was no organised base within the community which could submit proposals in time whereas the State governments had their pre-school submissions ready. To prevent cuts in appropriation the following year, the ICCC spent the money where they could—on sessional pre-schools. The move was doubly disastrous in that it did not stop the appropriation from being cut in 1975/76—and steadily reduced over subsequent financial years. And while at first the Fraser government committed itself to greater emphasis on childcare by freezing expenditure on pre-schools, it later extended its definition of childcare to cover programs such as the family support scheme and promoted the most exploitative, and therefore cheapest form of care, family day-care, at the expense of other types.

It should be understood that the shift in government policy coincided with the removal of Office of Women's Affairs to a junior department, where it became exceedingly difficult for it to make an impact on policy. For one thing, the Home Affairs minister was not a cabinet member, and access by the office to the full range of cabinet submissions was threatened. Though it was able to retain access, the procedure for retaining submissions and commenting on them became more complicated. Most significantly, it ceased to have a guaranteed voice in the budget cabinet process. In its relations with other departments it had to operate from a position of weakness and for all practical purposes the Interdepartmental Working Group was moribund. In other words, stripped of the structural advantage of being in the Department of the Prime Minister and Cabinet, the effectiveness of the Office of Women's Affairs depended almost solely on the bureaucratic politicking of its director. Inexorably, its functions were restricted to developing and influencing increasingly elusive 'social' policies. Moreover, the impact of these developments was obscured by the more superficial and visible activities of the Fraser government's National Women's Advisory Council.[18]

The Office of Women's Affairs perseveres in resisting pressures to confine its area of responsibility to a limited range of 'women's' issues, but the pressures continue. Furthermore, a good deal of its time and resources is spent in reacting to attacks from militant right-wing women's groups. These have increased since 1975, and their influence under the Fraser regime cannot be underestimated. The Fraser government was particularly sensitive to their lobbying, which was clearly out of all proportion to the extent to which their thinking represents that of women in Australia. But it seems that as long as there is a vacuum in the women's movement, that is, as long as the movement's energies are tied up in a broad front of disparate activities, the movement—and its arms in government—will be, for the most part, merely reacting to the reaction.

Where to now?

We have come to an important juncture in the development of women's affairs. Though from our present vantage point the efforts of the past decade often seem to have been a string of failures, we should not forget our very real accomplishments in an arena where few of us had operated at all as little as ten years ago. The women's movement has succeeded in changing people's notions about the place of women and IWY contributed significantly to that change. If the movement has been less successful in changing the structure of power relationships between the sexes, that is hardly surprising, but there have been cracks in the surface. In a way, the strength of the reaction against feminism is a measure of the threat it poses to the foundations of society. And even where our failures have seemed, to this writer at least, most catastrophic, we have been able to salvage something from the ruins. In spite of reductions in the children's services appropriation since 1975, the childcare portion of the appropriation has more than doubled in that period, a development that can only be attributed to the feminist bureaucracies at federal and State level.

Since 1975 feminists have achieved standards of excellence in a variety of fields. The sophistication and expertise within the movement have grown immeasurably since the early 1970s. Feminist concepts are permeating the institutions of society, and through them to an ever-widening public. But there are liabilities here—as more and more women excel in the arts, in politics, in the trade unions and the professions, there is the risk of co-option and the dilution of feminist aims.

Therefore, I think we should re-examine several articles of faith that have influenced the movement so far. To begin with, we might look again at the struggle for the vote. Certainly the gaining of the franchise was a qualified victory, but was it really a pyrrhic one? We can be alert to the opportunism and militancy that soured the winning of female suffrage without belittling the achievement that it was. We can see how it used up so much of the energy of first-wave feminism without forgetting how well it mobilised support. We can see its limitations as a reform without ignoring its historical appropriateness.

Looking at the question of the vote in a new light should enable feminists to modify our resistance towards organising primarily around any single issue. We have contributed immensely to contemporary radicalism by emphasising the relationship between different aspects of the social, economic and political structure.[19] Yet contribution to the development of such important perspectives should not plunge us into an uncritical, undifferentiated holism where one gain is just as good as another. It also puts those women at the face of policy-making in an impossible position, where they are forced to react willy-nilly to a seemingly endless chain of demands on their time and limited resources. In other words, perhaps we should begin thinking of no longer 'fighting on many fronts' but taking the knowledge, skills and expertise gained from our various theatres of operation and concentrating them in one major thrust. What may be advantageous at one stage may be disadvantageous at another, and such a broad approach may now be holding us back—a Gulliver tied down by Lilliputians.

At the same time we should be resisting more than ever the pressure to limit feminist activity to 'social' policy, and renew our efforts to demonstrate the relationship between social and economic policy and the importance of economic policy to women. We shall actually be making an impact on the direction of social change in a way which we cannot do if we ared confined to the 'soft' issues of what is seen as social policy. The distinction between social policy and economic policy should be shown for what it is, a convenient fiction. Is there a contradiction here? I am asking that we begin to think about developing priorities while at the same time our challenge is to push forward with an alternative analysis of the total social structure, in which social, political and economic factors are demonstrably interlocked. And perhaps this can best be done by sharpening our focus.

In the present decade a few central issues are emerging. A broad spectrum of women's organisations have worked in concert with the feminist bureaucracies[20] towards the reform of rape laws in the states and territories. Such moves and attention to related issues such as domestic violence and child abuse are the practical expression of the women's movement's analysis of the operation of the patriarchy in contemporary society, and its exposure through documentation by the rape crisis centres and women's refuges set up in the mid 1970s. These moves have gained support within the community and among governments, though there has been a backlash.

Adequate anti-discrimination measures have been more difficult to achieve, even though three of the six states have had sex discrimination legislation for at least four years and the commonwealth's discrimination committees have been functioning since 1974. The relative difficulty can be attributed to the fact that in the campaign for anti-discrimination measures the women's movement has been taking on organised vested interests in a way that they have not with rape law reform or women's refuges.[21] The campaigns against discrimination attack the cause and not the symptoms of women's powerlessness—principally, our lack of equal opportunity in employment and the barriers to economic and political power.

But while campaigns against discrimination and for the right to work are important, particularly in the current restructuring of the Australian economy, and while they are based on a sound and increasingly sophisticated theoretical framework, I cannot see how the acceptance by governments of the right of women to work will improve the position of women if there is no material basis for taking advantage of the gains.

Which brings us, in a way, to where we started, only with a difference. Today our understanding of the crucial role childcare plays in the socialisation process is far better than it was ten or so years ago (Dinnerstein, 1978). We would argue now that it is society which has a responsibility to children, not only women. Recent writings are beginning to break the hold of Bowlbyism on attitudes to child-rearing (Cox, 1978a; Langford and Sebastian, 1979). At both federal and state level, the machinery exists to handle a renewal of commitment and expansion of policy in this area.[22] Most importantly there appears to be a rekindling of interest in the women's movement, with the broader implications of childcare also being considered: how, for example, isolation in the nuclear family produces the self-centred, consumer-oriented, politically acquiescent individuals of advanced capitalist societies. To this writer at least there is no doubt that the question of children remains the central issue for women (Rich, 1977), and even the limited objective of providing cheap, good quality community care for our children would make a significant change to women's lives. Such a goal is a necessary condition of women's liberation, and the pursuit of it exposes the contradictions of patriarchal capitalism as no other campaign can.

Conclusion

My use of the term 'childcare' has been imprecise, but deliberately so. I wanted to avoid using it in too narrow a sense but I did not want the discussion to be academic: I have been trying to think strategically. I am aware, though, of the problem of attempting to influence a program of action through mere intellectual formulation. People act politically out of their experience; that, indeed, is what the women's movement has been about and why it alone perhaps of the 1970s movements of social protest still wins converts and changes lives.

But what is this experience? Much to the horror of the anti-feminist, reactionary forces in this country, the birthrate has been falling over the past decade. Considerable pressure is on women to reproduce: there have even been suggestions that the current depression can be attributed to women's neglect in this area (Commonwealth Parliamentary Debates, 1979). On the other end of the spectrum, some feminists are calling for a birth strike. To hear either of these points of view, one could get the impression that the problem of childcare is solving itself, or can, as if it were a question of the quantity rather than the quality of life. But the fact is that while there are proportionately fewer births today than there were in the early 1970s, the number of adults who become parents has increased, with less than one-tenth of women now bearing no children, compared with one-fifth in the 1930s (Royal Commission on Human Relationships, 1977). The Human Relationships Commission calculated that in 1974, 40 000 unwanted pregnancies out of an estimated 100 000 went to full term (Deveson, 1978). Any way you look at it, there are a lot of people involved. And a lot of children.

Who will look after them, why and how remain crucial questions, and the answers will determine the shape of our society.

Notes

1   Contributors to Rosaldo and Lamphere (1974) have made an important if controversial contribution to the analysis of patriarchy in widely diverse societies. The principal, Marxist criticism of the concept of a public/domestic dichotomy, that it is static and therefore firmly situated in liberal-bourgeois consensus analysis, is I think incorrect. That the dialectic can be used in conjunction with the concept has been demonstrated in a lecture by Julia Ryan given to students of the ANU Women's Studies course on 27 March 1978. My objection to the use of terms such as 'economic' and 'social' in connection with policy is not that two separate spheres do not exist—they do—but that the division is a false one and serves to mask relationships of power. The Rosaldo—Lamphere thesis seems to demonstrate that a similar bifurcation underpins patriarchal relationships and structures.

2   Even a cursory examination of the Commonwealth Government Directory and federal and State budgets bears out this contention. The point can be made stronger, however, if the factor of orientation is included in the analysis. For example, while a large proportion of State government finance goes into education, one may argue that, as well as being community services, schools are powerful agents of social control and one of their primary functions is to prepare children for their future place in the labour force.

3   When writing this paper I was often struck by how difficult it was to find the standard documentation for some of the views expressed. I began to realise that this problem stems from two, perhaps three sources. Firstly, my experience of the movement has been the experience of the Canberra movement, which for various reasons has had a distinct flavour of its own. Related to this is the sorry fact that the minutes of Canberra Women's Liberation have disappeared and even if I were so inclined I have not been able to use them to check the accuracy of many of my interpretations. But other women who were involved 'back then' have endorsed much of what I claim.

Secondly, at the onset of the indigenous women's movement, very few of us had realised the importance of what was happening sufficiently to try to record it. In a sense, the movement itself was afflicted with a classic case of the female inferiority complex. The most significant effect of the movement on the women participating in it at the time was the simple discovery that individual problems had their source in patriarchal, capitalist structures. It was heady stuff, and the first steps, though characterised by bravado, were tentative and exploratory. But the few who wrote about the phenomenon ran into trouble from the start and the trouble shows in their writings, even though they may not have been conscious of it. They were forced to use concepts and terms that could not accurately reflect the feelings and/or understanding of women in the movement. Our baggage was the rhetoric of the anti-war and civil rights movements of the 1960s, the economism of the old left and a host of other crude analytical tools. Blessed with the advantage of hindsight, the geographic immobility and longevity of many Canberra feminists, and maybe even a good memory for conversations, utterances and the subtleties of group dynamics, I have come to trust my own experience. Later, as a feminist bureaucrat I had, once more, access to the kind of information not usually recorded but which profoundly influences the course of events.

4   'Feminist bureaucrat' or 'femocrat' has been used pejoratively by both the left and the right. And although there is some argument as to whether a feminist can be a bureaucrat (and vice versa), I have chosen to use the term in much the same way that US Negroes took the name 'black' as their own and divested it of shame. For despite the fact that bureaucrats can often given expression to only the mildest forms of feminism, in the context in which they work they are feminist indeed.

5   The influence of the ACT branch should be seen here. It played an important part in organising the WEL lobby of parliamentarians. ACT members thus gained a working acquaintance with a number of the new ministers and their staff, an acquaintance they could cultivate because of their continual presence in the national capital.

6   Closest perhaps to Whitlam's heart was the National Rehabilitation and Compensation Scheme which was postponed due to the entrenched opposition of the legal profession and the insurance companies, but there were others. Cabinet decided to abolish the Social Welfare Commission, and the Children's Commission Act was not proclaimed because of wrangling over Commission appointments. The Australian Government Insurance Office never got off the ground because of the same pressures affecting the proposed compensation scheme. As well there were substantial cuts to a number of programs, the result of the work of the Expenditure Review Committee set up early in 1975.

7   Though, as I indicated before, much of the writing about the movement would hardly suggest this. See for example Jan Mercer's chapters on the history of WEL and reform or revolution in (1975): *The Other Half* which she edited. While it was evident that by 1972 the women's movement had radical and reformist wings, it is not so clear that women in WEL had solely reformist aims or that women's liberationists eschewed reformist activities. On the contrary, many original WEL members were imbued with revolutionary consciousness but saw the need for basic reforms as part of a strategy to enable wider numbers of women to participate in the struggle. This kind of view was articulated in Helen Shepherd's paper circulated at the 1973 Feminist Theory Conference held in Mount Beauty, Victoria, and was behind such moves as the WEL intervention into the 1974 national wage case which secured the adult minimum wage for women. Further, many women who were attracted to WEL because of its comparative moderation soon became radicalised through the experience of acting politically. Women's liberationists, on the other hand, plunged into apparently piecemeal reforms when they petitioned the Labor government for funds to set up health centres, refuges and rape crisis centres. In short, what distinguishes revolutionary activity from reformism is consciousness, and many feminists did assert that acquiring a revolutionary consciousness was an ongoing process resulting from the interaction of theory and practice (praxis).

When Thelma Hunter delivered a paper at ANU on reform versus revolution in the women's movement, Canberra Women's Liberationists were highly critical of her attempt to impose what was seen as a false dichotomy on political activity or, at least, on the activity of the women's movement. See Hunter (1973); Haley (1973); Summers (1973), and Sawer (1973).

8   The IWY Secretariat referred a number of these projects to other departments for funding, some of which were successful, most notably the women's refuges and health centres.

9   The fact that Margaret Whitlam was an active and enthusiastic member of the committee made the government all the more paranoid about media criticism.

10   The UN announcement that 1979 was to be the International Year of the Child was a stimulus to the renewed interest, especially on the theoretical and ideological planes. Australian feminists feared, with some justification, that the Year would be used to attack recent gains and in buttressing the stereotypical woman's role. WEL countered by launching a campaign for tax deductions for childcare, but to many feminists this was an unsatisfactory approach, so long as there was a shortfall in childcare services. In the 1981/82 budget, the federal government allocated no money for new childcare programs and, at the same time, reviewed options such as vouchers for places in commercial centres and a common means test based on full cost recovery for day-care users. (See Australia, Parliament, 1981a, *Review of the Children's Services Program,*—the Spender Report.) The response to these moves was renewed action on WEL's part (with a shift in emphasis away from tax deductions and towards the continued provision of non-profit services) and the appearance of a range of groups focusing on federal government policy. The basis was set for a nationally coordinated children's services lobby; by mid 1982 such a lobby was under way.

11   But we must acknowledge that though the opportunity to develop good, inexpensive and widely available childcare on a national basis was lost, there are many more quality services operating today than there were in 1972. Though there has been a contraction in funding and high unemployment accompanied by an ideological backlash against women working outside home, we are not back where we were before the children's services program was introduced. The need for childcare has been demonstrated and gained some community acceptance. More than ever questions as to the kind of care as well as the extent of its availability should occupy feminist attention. And if IWY was a penny-ante affair, many valuable things have come out of it. The explosion and thrust of feminist activity within the trade union movement is directly attributable to it, as are the developments in counter-sexist education within State education departments and the teacher's federations. Through IWY feminist ideas reached and awakened many women in the community who might otherwise have been untouched. The ripple effect of IWY has yet to be determined, but it would be unwise—and unrealistic—to underestimate it.

12   From the start, this proposal was objected to by the Women's Bureau and its department, which resented the intrusion of new, more powerful policy bodies into its bailiwick.

13   Under the category 'Power in Institutions' at the 1975 Women and Politics Conference I gave a paper entitled 'Power in the Public Service' which articulated these concepts and, in rather oblique terms, our plans for administration. The paper was not included in the edited version of the papers Australia (1977) *The Women and Politics Conference (1975),* but can be found in the full set deposited in the National Library of Australia.

14   Aboriginal Affairs; Immigration and Ethnic Affairs; Environment, Housing and Community Development; Education; Social Security; and Attorney-General's.

15   To me the nadir of the movement was the Women and Trade Union Conference held at Sydney University in 1976. Women were divided along ideological lines,

union lines, even state lines. But we survived and the Working Women's Charter was born there in spite of it all.

16   Women came in for their share of the blame for the economic ills. Not only were married women accused of taking other people's jobs, but equal pay was cited as a major cause of inflation and unemployment (see in particular Statement No.2, Australia, Parliament, 1978, Budget Papers, 1978). Meanwhile unemployment among women, particularly working-class women, rose throughout the late 1970s while employment opportunities shrank, due to a combination of structural maladjustments in the Australian economy, the government's monetary and fiscal policies and the wholesale introduction of labour-saving technology into traditional areas of women's employment.

17   The budget was brought down in the middle of September instead of the middle of August.

18   In 1978 the Fraser government appointed the National Women's Advisory Council (NATWAC), serviced by a secretariat in the Office of Women's Affairs. The second NATWAC, appointed in 1980, was considerably more conservative. As the terms of members are staggered, sets of appointments have been made in each subsequent year. For more on NATWAC and its relationship to the Office, see Dowse (1981). See also Connors (1981). In 1981 the Review of Commonwealth Functions recommended, and the government decided, that the Office of Women's Affairs and the Women's Bureau would continue but that other departments were 'to integrate their women's units functions with their departmental functions'. As of mid 1982 all women's unit positions had been, theoretically, abolished, though some had slipped through the net. The Interdepartmental Working Group had not met since before the Review began.

19   Starting with Millett's *Sexual Politics* (1972), contemporary feminist theory had consistently explored the implications of 'the personal is political', and exposed the connections between private and public relationships. The most recent expression and development of the potential contribution of feminists concepts and methods to the left can be found in Rowbotham, Segal and Wainwright (1979). I realise, too, that I tend to conflate radicalism and socialism here, but notwithstanding the distinctions, the women's movement has been affected by and has in turn affected all shadings of the spectrum of social protest.

20   The growth of feminist bureaucracies at state level has developed since 1974 and the appointment of the first state women's adviser to the South Australian Premier. There are now women's advisers to all but two state premiers and women's education advisers in all states.

21   This is not to say that there is no organised opposition there, but that the opposition is comparatively weak and gets tangled in an ideological web. Who can argue against rape law reform without appearing to be in favour of rape? Likewise, it is hard to argue against the extension of facilities and reforms to protect battered wives and children.

22   The Interim Committee for the Children's Commission was disbanded in 1976 and replaced by the Office of Child Care. The Office of Child Care became a division of the Department of Social Security in June 1976, headed by Marie Coleman, former Social Welfare Commission Chairman.

11 Legislating for the right to be equal: women, the law and social policy

JOCELYNNE A. SCUTT

Australia has a long tradition of sex discrimination and an equally long tradition of female activism. Throughout two hundred years of immigrant history, laws and practices discriminating against women have been fought by women (and by some men). The fight has been multifaceted: sometimes it has taken the road of agitation for repeal of unjust laws; sometimes laws have been amended after concentrated feminist lobbying to include women in male strongholds; sometimes new laws have attempted to establish equal rights for women and men. The 1970s saw a resurgence of political protest on the part of women —or perhaps a willingness on the part of the media and the authorities to acknowledge that feminist protest was real, and must be taken into account.

In addition to lobbying for policies acknowledging women's priorities—equal pay for work of equal value; childcare in the community and in the workplace; equal access to education; the right to contraceptive education and abortion; the right to be employed; equal access to credit—feminists demanded legislation to eliminate discrimination on grounds of sex and marital status. This demand was premised on the view that unless discrimination was clearly stated to be not only unacceptable but indeed illegal, Australians would fail to acknowledge it as illegitimate.

In 1981 three states—South Australia, New South Wales and Victoria—had anti-discrimination or equal opportunities legislation in operation. A commonwealth *Sex Discrimination Bill* was introduced into the Senate in 1981 by the opposition Labor Party—with real prospects of success in that House at least (Scutt, 1982). The remaining states appeared, for the time, to be a lost cause (Mills, 1981; Ronalds, 1979a, 1979b; Scutt, 1977; Flick, 1981). In the private sphere, equal rights vis-à-vis divorce, property, maintenance and custody of children have been introduced nationally with the passage of the *Family Law Act* 1975.

In fighting for legislation to establish women's equal rights in public and private spheres and in identifying discrimination and making it unlawful, the feminist movement has acknowledged the frustration of a piecemeal fight against sexist laws and administrative practices. Yet the question is whether seemingly equal divorce laws, anti-discrimination legislation and the mere exposure of sexism are sufficient. So long as our society is designed to serve patriarchal ideals—through the current organisation of the family, through the style of corporate organisation, through the nature of bureaucracy, through patterns of employment precluding women from full participation, through the organisation of a parliamentary system ill-designed to suit the needs of women—sex-based equality will remain elusive.

Equality in public: twentieth-century demands

From 1788 until the early twentieth century women were unable to undertake the practice of law in this country. They were, of course, precluded from most other public positions: especially during the late nineteenth century, women fought to be admitted to universities, to professions, to political office, and for the right to vote.

The Australian women's movement during the twentieth century continued its demands for equal rights for women in the public sphere. One of the major concerns was that of equal pay[1]:

> Equal pay was 'won' in 1969 and again in 1972 and yet again in 1974. It was won in NSW in 1958 and in Queensland in 1916. What is the nature of the victory which has to be won again and again: in 1916 and 1958 ineffective legislation; in the later instances decisions by the Conciliation and Arbitration Commission which by 1974 brought only theoretical equality in male and female wage rates . . .
> The Queensland Act had required 'the same wage shall be paid to persons of either sex performing the same work or providing the same return of profit to their employer'. The extent of its application is unknown. The NSW Act did not apply in areas of work 'essentially or usually' performed by women. Tasmania had passed similar legislation for its public servants. By 1969 when the first 'equal pay' case was before the Conciliation and Arbitration Commission, other states had equal pay legislation restricted in application to work not essentially or usually performed by women. (Gaudron and Bosworth, 1979: 161)

Work was not 'essentially or usually performed by women' in many instances because legislation and regulations outlawed women from participating. For decades the Australian government discriminated against women: women were excluded from selection tests for admission to the Third Division of the Public Service from 1915 to 1949, by way of the *Public Service Act* and Regulations. Until as recently as

1966 the Act prohibited married women from permanent employment. In 1958 a Committee of Enquiry into Public Service Recruitment recommended the repeal of the prohibition against permanent
employment of married women, but this failed to prevent the passage
of the *Commonwealth Banks Act* 1959, which contained just such a
prohibition (Taperell et al., 1975). States were not immune from
similar discriminatory provisions, and in 1932 the *Married Women
(Lecturers and Teachers) Act* took away from women, married or not,
an existing right to remain in permanent employment in the New
South Wales teaching service (Mackinolty, 1979; Daniels and
Murnane, 1980).[2] Arguments used to support legislation restricting
the right of women to work were that young, newly trained teachers
had a prior right to employment in the service, and that as most
women retired upon marriage, not many would be affected. By
creating a number of positions for new teachers, the measure would be
justified. The bill had:

> many of the aspects of an emergency measure. If times were normal
> and the Government desired to introduce a bill of this character, it
> would not draft it ... in such a way as to affect the rights of any
> existing officer. *(NSW Parliamentary Debates* Vol.84, 1932: 103)

Thus the government of the day was prepared to run directly counter
to the rights of women who had trained for teaching and taken up
positions on the understanding that they were entering life-time
careers (Heagney, 1935; Power, 1980). Its actions caused single
women and married women to be placed in opposition to one another,
the former seen as deserving of permanent employment, the latter as
greedy parasites depriving others of their rightful due.

More indirect but equally discriminatory legal barriers exist by way
of 'protective' measures. The New South Wales *Factories, Shops and
Industries Act* specifies the weights that women, whatever their age
and physical capabilities, are allowed to handle, thereby precluding
them from some occupations. Special regulations may be made for
female employees and special facilities for women are required under
the regulations and under similar regulations in other states. Some
legislation requires job applicants to be of a particular height, weight
and chest measurement—although these dimensions have no relationship to tasks to be performed. Women cleaners in government stores
are limited to 33 hours of work whilst men work 40 hours per week;
women are temporary employees whilst men are permanent (Anti-
Discrimination Board, 1978 and 1979; Wilenski, 1978). Such dif-
ferentiations effectively bar women from occupations and may bar
promotions and advancement; they bar women from the receipt of
higher income, and from lucrative overtime payments and other
benefits gained by unions for their (male) membership.

Discrimination resulting from entrenched attitudes has also been identified. Beliefs that men are suitable for some occupations and professions, women suitable for others, are little disturbed, if at all, in many fields of employment. These beliefs are sometimes enforced by rules drawn up by employers, or are continued by the application of standards that are steeped in implicit (or explicit) sex stereotyping. Some of these rules are outlined in the Review of New South Wales Government Administration:

> The Department's outdoor workforce, which is engaged essentially on manual work involving at times considerable physical exertion, is not a suitable field for female employment. . . . (Wilenski, 1978: 200)

> . . . There should be no pairing of a policewoman constable with a male in a patrolling car doing duty and operating on a shift basis. The performance of this duty all night might lead to misgivings in the families of both male and female police. (ibid, 1978: 200)

> An abattoir is not normally the type of environment in which women seek employment . . . (ibid, 1978: 201)

In 1974 a study of women in the Commonwealth Public Service found no women employed in the categories of tradesperson, ranger, mechanic, meat inspector, health inspector, carpenter, surveyor, metallurgist, district telephone or postal manager. No men were employed as speech therapist, accounting secretary, punch-card operator, dental assistant, or steno-secretary. The study concluded that this illustrates well

> the importation of traditional roles of men and women to the Service; women tend to be in the personal service and supportive roles, and men predominate in positions which involve dealing with the 'world outside' for example, legal officer, journalist, engineer, industrial relations officer. (Taperell et al., 1975: 23)

(Chapter Two provides an extended account of the sex-based division of labour in the workplace.)

Recognising the pervasiveness of sex-discrimination and the need for an overall approach to combat it, women's organisations in the 1970s, in particular the Women's Electoral Lobby (WEL), began lobbying for legislation to end discrimination against women in employment, education, the provision of goods and services, accommodation, credit, sporting and recreational facilities (e.g. Faust, 1976; Glezer and Mercer, 1973; WEL Sydney, 1973–1974). At the federal level, it appeared in the early years that lobbying was successful: on 17 November 1972 Senator Lionel Murphy, later Attorney-General, promised that a Labor government would legislate against discrimination on the basis of sex:

Australia does not need a Royal Commission to tell us how to improve the status of women. The need for legislation to remove discrimination against women is obvious, and will have early priority from a Labor government. (WEL, ACT, 1973: 2)

In June 1973 the Labor government established the National and State Committees on Discrimination in Employment and Occupation, comprising representatives of unions, employer organisations and government. Not having any powers to enforce their decisions, the committees were never envisaged as a 'solution' to sex-based discrimination, nor indeed as providing an adequate channel for complaints. Rather, they were seen as a forerunner to a more comprehensive attack upon the problem.

Despite such a propitious start, an apparent lack of seriousness on the part of government was soon detected. Sex-based discrimination was given lower priority than other forms of discrimination and other problem areas. In August 1973 WEL wrote to the Attorney-General requesting information on the proposed anti-discrimination legislation. No reply was received. In November 1973 a *Human Rights Bill* and *Racial Discrimination Bill* were introduced into the federal Parliament. In commenting upon the terms of the bills in a submission to the government, WEL demanded, amongst other things, that the *Racial Discrimination Bill* should be amended to include sex along with race, colour, descent or national or ethnic origin in each of its clauses, and that the *Human Rights Bill* should be amended to outlaw sexual hatred in addition to national, racial and religious hatred, and that marriage and maternity should be included in the Human Rights Bill definition of discrimination (WEL, ACT 1973: 3-4). In the event, the *Racial Discrimination Act* passed through the Parliament without the sex-based discrimination provisions urged by WEL and the *Human Rights Bill* languished.[3]

The next move hinting at anti-discrimination legislation came in August 1975, when the office of the Attorney-General circulated a memorandum, *Proposed Bill to Prohibit Discrimination Against Persons by reason of their Sex or Marital Status: Outline of Provisions*. The bill exempted employment where 'it is a genuine occupational qualification that a person be of a particular sex'; where discrimination occurred in conditions of employment 'solely attributable to a lack of adequate sanitary or other accommodations or facilities that is likely to embarrass members of either sex in circumstances where it is not reasonable to expect those facilities to be altered'; and single sex schools and tertiary institutions 'other than those which confer, or examine for, any professional or other qualifications ...' (WEL Records). WEL raised objections to the wide exemption provisions of the proposed legislation and the mechanisms for enforcement; the government proposed that the *Sex Discrimina-*

tion Bill should, when passed, be enforced by way of resort to the (also proposed) Human Rights Commission.

As a result of WEL lobbying, an Office of Equal Employment Opportunity was established in the Public Service Board in 1978, but hopes for acceptable, effective sex-discrimination legislation were abandoned when the government was dismissed summarily from office in November 1975.

WEL began lobbying the new Liberal-National Country Party government. Both the prime minister and the attorney-general, Mr. R.J. Ellicott, issued frequent press releases stating that sex discrimination was recognised and that legislation providing for redress was imminent. There was, however, no consultation with representatives of those discriminated against and whom the legislation was ostensibly intended to serve, although the government consulted with employer and employee organisations. WEL also became aware that some unions were opposing the introduction of anti-discrimination legislation. In addition, the recently appointed Employment Discrimination Committees (EDCs) were actively working for their own perpetuation by way of legislative backing and against effective commonwealth sex-discrimination legislation. They had also been part of a lobby against a proposed Tasmanian sex-discrimination law (WEL, Canberra, 1979). Concerned at this negativeness in an area where women's rights were being inadequately safeguarded not only in the workplace but in all other areas untouched by unions, WEL wrote to all unions to determine their position on the matter. Despite the ACTU Working Women's Charter, in the ACTU hierarchy the problem of sex-discrimination was not given high priority, and women could well suspect that the ACTU was more concerned about preserving a place for union representatives on EDCs than about discrimination. EDCs might have employee representatives, but they would exercise little real power, being matched by employer representatives and two appointees of government. To add to this, the ACTU had taken a strong position against affirmative action principles (ACOA, 1980), despite explicit recognition in Australia and elsewhere that without affirmative action, 'equal opportunity' is a meaningless phrase.

The demise of the Fraser government means that after ten years of continuous lobbying, women now stand with a possibility that commonwealth anti-discrimination legislation drafted by the minister for women's affairs, Senator Susan Ryan, and the attorney-general, Senator Gareth Evans, may be passed.

There can be some confidence then that commonwealth legislation rendering illegal discrimination on grounds of sex will come into effect in the near future. The issue still to be faced is whether the lobbying has been of value, or has the expectation held out for so long been merely a diversion, holding the women's movement back from direct gains? Has the lobbying resulted only in women's energies being tied up in battle for legislation which, when introduced, may well fail our hopes?

These questions may find an answer in the context of achievements at state level. In 1975 a *Sex Discrimination Act* was placed on the South Australian statute books as a result of women's movement agitation and the efforts of women in governmental and advisory positions. New South Wales and Victoria followed suit in 1977 with an *Anti-Discrimination Act* and *Equal Opportunities Act*, respectively. In most regards the three acts are similar (Fristacky, 1977; Thornton, 1982). Each, however, has certain exemptions limiting its effectiveness. The New South Wales act has the greatest number of exclusionary rules regarding employment. The politics of its passage, resulting in these exclusions, raise important issues for the women's movement.

After much torrid debate and amendment upon amendment, the New South Wales Act emerged watered down: '. . . to render unlawful racial, sex and other types of discrimination in certain circumstances and to promote equality of opportunity between all persons'. Partnerships involving more than six persons were originally covered (although those with less than six escaped), but were saved from the act by way of amendment: no partnerships were brought within its terms. Yet discrimination is practised in a pervasive manner in partnerships of many kinds, and in particular in law firms. The schizophrenic nature of law is thus revealed: lawyers drafted and redrafted the bill, and a number of lawyers led the attack in the Upper House, yet this sits ill with a profession which alleges to be equity orientated.

Where a 'genuine occupational qualification' is found to exist, discrimination will be lawful under the act, such as where the 'essential nature of the job' calls for a man for reasons of physiology excluding strength or stamina. This is an easy 'out' for those choosing to continue their old patterns of employing a man where a woman could do the job. If a woman were truly precluded by reason of her physiology from undertaking a particular job of work, there would be no point in her applying, and thus there need be no exemption provision about it. It is difficult to imagine what job a woman would be physiologically precluded from doing—unless it were that of personally supplying a sperm bank with its 'riches'. Similarly, a man would be precluded from taking on the job of wet nurse—but why have a law about it?

It remains legal under the act to discriminate where the job is required to be held by a man (or a woman) 'to preserve decency or privacy' because it involves the fitting of clothing. Yet already the law makes provision for activities which, presumably, this exemption was designed to cover. Thus, if a man fitting women's clothing, or a woman fitting men's clothing interfered sexually with the customer during the exercise, tort law and criminal law provide a proper avenue of redress. If those laws are not effective, the answer is to make them so, not to clutter a so-called anti-discrimination act with discriminatory clauses. As the act stands, women joining the Bar in Sydney continue to be told by a large department store that they cannot be fitted for bar-jackets, and must go elsewhere, for all the tailors are male: a 'respectable' organisation could not possibly condone a man taking a woman's chest measurement!

The act also provides that where the holder of a job provides persons of the opposite sex with personal services relating to their welfare or education, and they or a substantial number of them might reasonably object to the job being carried out by a person of the opposite sex, discrimination in employment will be lawful. Once more the act gives support to ideas and attitudes that sit ill on a society seeking to create equal opportunity. It refuses to face reality: for many years female nurses have dealt with male patients; as a matter of course numerous female patients attend male doctors and some male patients attend female doctors. In the provision of what are intimate services, the community has accepted practices which are not sex-biased. Certainly more women practitioners should be available so that the choice between a male or female practitioner may be made on a more equal basis, but this is reason for extending all areas of medical training on a non-discriminatory basis to women, rather than writing discriminatory provisions into a purportedly anti-discrimination act.

One of the most tedious arguments used against the employment of women in hitherto 'male' fields relates to the provision of lavatories. Bolstering the idea that employers may use this excuse to keep women out, the act provides that discrimination is legal where employment requires living at premises provided by the employer and no separate accommodation or sanitary facilities 'may reasonably be provided'. It is difficult to understand why employers should not be required to divide those facilities they have, so that women and men are able to use them. If extra facilities have to be built, the cost should be borne by those who in the past discriminated against women. They should not be allowed to escape by asserting the cost is too great.

The effect of sex-discrimination legislation is difficult to assess. Publicity has been given to a small number of cases involving women as complainants. Thus the *Deborah Wardley case* became a cause célèbre, the Australian Federation of Business and Professional Women leading an effective boycott against Ansett Transport Industries (Operations) Pty Ltd. Ansett's profits were noticeably down throughout the period of the boycott. By refusing to travel by Ansett Airlines, women and supporters showed that they had power sufficient to harm an employer who refused, for undeniably sexist 'reasons', to take on a skilled woman pilot.[4] The case went to the Victorian Equal Opportunity Board, the Supreme Court of Victoria and the High Court of Australia before being finally resolved in Deborah Wardley's favour. In New South Wales Deidre Harrison brought the Department of Technical and Further Education before the Anti-Discrimination Board, and won. It was held that the Department had treated her, a technical college teacher with 22 years' experience, less favourably than a man would have been treated under the same circumstances. Although to feminists the problems faced by Deidre Harrison and the grounds upon which her claim was based were readily apparent, the issues were more diffuse than those in the Victorian case. Deborah Wardley had been refused the job of a pilot on grounds that she might become pregnant, and therefore unable to fly for some length of time. The Equal Opportunity Board took the view that it would be 'unlikely' that legislation proscribing discrimination in employment on grounds of sex 'would then open the way to that discrimination against members of the female sex because of their child bearing potential which is the very essence of the distinction between the sexes' (Equal Opportunity Board, 1979).

Deidre Harrison became a victim of discrimination because she was an assertive woman, a characteristic the department saw as a 'personality defect' rendering her as a person (not as a woman) 'unfit to discharge the duties she would be required to perform were she promoted after being placed on the promotions list'. Deidre Harrison was of the opinion that had she been 'a non-aggressive personality of the type expected by the Department', she would not have been discriminated against.[5]

Though both complainants won in formal legal terms, both cases show the limitations of complaints-based legislation. Deborah Wardley got her job as a pilot. Deidre Harrison was placed on the promotions list. Nevertheless the personal toll for both was great, as would have been the legal expense had not in Wardley's case the women's movement undertaken to raise funds, and in the Harrison case a union been prepared to underwrite the costs. Wardley received no damages. As for Harrison, there was no assurance that she would get what she presumably wanted—a promotion of the type for which she was competent and suited. There was no order for compensation for the damage she suffered from the discrimination, and no order to prevent it continuing. The board assumed that the discrimination would cease, and if it continued, 'the matter will, doubtless, come back before the Board' (Ronalds, 1979b: 191). Such an approach is of little comfort. Would the union have been so willing to pay a second time around? Why should the union use its funds on a second battle, when another individual with a new claim of discrimination might appear? Why should a complainant be required to undergo another bout of litigation? How could a board set up to deal with discrimination presume that discrimination would automatically cease because a finding of discrimination had been made? In a world where sex discrimination is ensconced into policies and practices, it is hardly likely to stop for such mild reasons.

Beyond this lies a broader issue. Both cases represent only the tip of the iceberg. The *Wardley* case resulted in one woman pilot taking to the air on a commercial airline. Yet the sex divisions basic to the operation of that airline continue. In a letter to one organisation which had criticised the refusal of the airline to employ Deborah Wardley, the General Manager of Ansett Airlines stated:

> Naturally we are concerned with what you have written, but feel that it is important that you appreciate that Ansett is not anti-female in employment generally.
>
> The attached statement gives some details of our employment and we believe the figures speak for themselves. (Letter to the Australian Institute of Political Science, May 1979)

The figures indeed 'spoke for themselves': women employees were clustered in the lower paid, service-type jobs; women may have been employed in large numbers, but they did not hold positions of authority and prestige. Had salary levels been included, women would have been at the bottom of the list. The figures showed conclusively that sex divisions in employment were embedded in the organisation.

Ironically a case brought by men under the New South Wales legislation highlighted conditions in the education system in New South Wales. In 1979 three male teachers complained to the board that a policy to appoint women as principals of girls' schools ahead of men on the promotions list was discriminatory against them. As a result, the Premier ordered that the board undertake an inquiry into the appointment and promotion of women in the Education Department. The *Sexism in Education Report* had declared:

> All in all, it is clear that women in executive positions can be classified as an endangered species, and may soon be an extinct species. (Committee on Sexism in Education, 1977)

The Board's inquiry showed that warning not to be exaggerated:

> As the barriers to promotion are greater for women (in the Department of Education), men, in 1978 occupied 93% of all promotions positions in boys' schools, 85% in co-educational schools and 41% in girls' schools ...
>
> While in 1961 approximately 22% of all State high schools had female principals, the proportion has become less than 10% in 1979. It is now likely that, unless the promotional system is

subjected to major change, the point will be reached where no high school in the State education system is headed by a woman. (Anti-Discrimination Board, 1979)

The Board commented that direct discrimination against women—such as required resignation on marriage of female but not male teachers, or placement of married women on the list of temporaries, might have been eliminated, but systemic discrimination operates still in 'direct and indirect, obvious and more subtle forms'.

Whatever the system adopted by the department for promotion, that system as operated favours men. Most promotions are determined under the seniority system, which due to such factors as the permanency requirement and accreditation of leave results in 82 per cent of all secondary promotions positions being occupied by male teachers.[6] Selection by the principal for posts of responsibility such as form mistress or form master results in 73 per cent of positions being held by men. The 'merit' system for inspectors and top administrators '... appears almost incapable of attracting women and in 1979 92% of inspectors were male'. 'Special fitness' is another criterion for discretionary promotion in schools for special purposes. Of the 53 special schools included in the board's research study, 87 per cent had male principals. It was concluded that each method and their combination '... ensure that, in a service where qualifications are equal for the sexes at recruitment level, and where women comprise over half of the total workforce, benefits accrue to men, and women are excluded from positions of power':

> This promotional system not only distributes benefits and power unequally, it contains a further feature—it is designed and applied almost exclusively by men.
>
> The fact that the forces which determine the very nature of the system are not representative of both sexes is the common single factor to which (the poor representation of women) may be attributed. Men dominate the decision-making and men enjoy the greater share of the resulting benefits. (Anti-Discrimination Board, 1979: 97-8)

Deidre Harrison's case before the Anti-Discrimination Board did not result in the extension of such promotion rights to all women in the Department of Technical and Further Education, or in the Department of Education. Rather, it seemed to antagonise men into utilising for their own ends an act that had been introduced to overcome discrimination against women (see also Thornton, 1979a, 1979b). The subsequent report of the Board showed clearly what all women involved in lobbying for the legislation already knew—that women are disadvantaged by reason of sex, even in those professions that attract the highest numbers of female recruits.

Eventually, further lobbying from outside the government and the development of policies by feminists within the bureaucracy initiated a potentially revolutionary change to the *Anti-Discrimination Act*. In 1980 an amendment provided for the 'promotion of equal employment opportunity for women and members of racial minorities' through the preparation and implementation of equal opportunity management plans throughout the New South Wales public service. The Office of Director of Equal Opportunity was created, and the director (a woman) called upon every department and instrumentality to compile a report upon the position of women and racial and ethnic minorities employed by them, and to draw up a program designed to recruit and promote those disadvantaged by sexism and racism (Anti-Discrimination Amendment Act, 1980).

From the start it was clear that affirmative action throughout the public sector would not occur without significant resistance. The principles on which the amending legislation were based were that complaint-based attempts to ensure equal rights for women in employment required action by those discrimination against, but the onus in eradicating discrimination *should* lie with those involved in perpetuating it; and the costs should be borne by government. The major difficulty lies in the fact that rewards accrue to those adhering to discriminatory policies. It is unrealistic to suppose that men who profit from discrimination against women will readily draw up proposals to improve opportunities for women, thus opening up competition for lucrative and powerful positions. The media began recounting stories of departments refusing to draw up affirmative action programs, or being slow in reporting as requested to the Office of Equal Opportunity. When the date for preliminary affirmative action programs drew near, only a handful of departments had complied.

On a positive note, the public service affirmative action policy is an important advance in the fight to open up the ranks of the public sector. The legislation shows an awareness on the part of government that simple statements of support for equal opportunity are insufficient. Employers (and here the government has submitted itself to experimentation) must take some initiative in setting target dates for employing and promoting specified numbers of women and minority groups in positions previously held by men of white, Anglo-Saxon origin. Not only does the government now acknowledge that discrimination is wrong, it is taking positive action to eliminate it. Its success will depend, however, upon its strength in relation to the bureaucracy: governments can be severely hampered by the unwillingness of bureaucrats to accept change. There is already some evidence that there are conflicts between the Office of the Director of Equal Opportunity, the Office of the Counsellor for Equal Opportunity and the Anti-Discrimination Board. Working together, those three offices could form a strong power block. Each office ostensibly has a clearly defined role, the board dealing with research and education, the Counsellor for Equal Opportunity with handling complaints at a conciliation level, and the Director of Equal Opportunity with supervising and implementing affirmative action plans within the public service. However, it is inevitable that at times the strategies adopted by each agency to eliminate discrimination will differ. Such differences are to the advantage of those within the bureaucracy (and the government) who do not wish to see affirmative action implemented and do not believe that discrimination should be eliminated. Certainly it may be a significant advance that this disagreement in strategies is now taking place within government and the bureaucracy itself.

Equality in private

In 1905 the *Sydney Morning Herald* of 22 November carried an account of the activities of the Australian Women's Union:

WIVES RIGHTS. Mrs Parkes moved and Mrs Spencer seconded: 'That the marriage ceremony should constitute the wife joint legal owner of her husband's property and income, he to be the administrator of her share, without the right of disposing of it unless with her written consent.'

The question was also spoken to by Mesdames Sydenham, Hillier, Soane and Fizzel. Miss Montefiore moved that the following words be added to the resolution: 'that when women have an independent income the marriage ceremony should constitute the husband joint owner of her income.'

After it had been pointed out that this would do away with much useful legislation already in existence, and that a wife's position was not the same as the husband's because on his death she was not so well able to earn a living for herself and family as he would be after her death, the amendment was withdrawn.

It was agreed by majority to pass the resolution with the added clause: 'each to have the right to draw an equal sum for personal wants'. (Womanspeak, 1981: 5)

It is apparent that problems arising out of the unequal nature of the marital relationship, particularly regarding property, were perceived by women at the turn of the century to be fundamental to women's position; today the issue remains a critical one.

The Married Women's Property Acts in the late nineteenth century ensured that the property a woman owned at her marriage would remain hers after marriage; they also acknowledged a married woman's right to ownership of her earnings. However if a woman had no property, or if she was not in paid employment, the legislation availed her nothing. Certainly many women were in paid employment, but then as now their husbands' incomes were usually greater. Additionally, women's paid working lives were, and are, often interrupted by child-bearing and rearing and hampered by the fact that social 'attitudes operate to keep women in the home.

Early in the 1970s women began agitating for changes in matrimonial law, most particularly in relation to property distribution during marriage and upon divorce.

In 1959 under the *Matrimonial Causes Act* divorce law became uniform throughout Australia. The basic 'fault' concept of divorce was retained. Fourteen grounds for divorce included the commission of acts of adultery by one of the parties, desertion, brutality, and habitual drunkenness. (The law also allowed for 'no fault' divorce in a restricted way, after separation of the parties for five years.) In formal terms the law treated men and women equally (Nygh, 1978: 557-72)[8]; however, economic, social and political reality rendered women's position less advantageous than men's. Thus, a woman who left her husband due to domestic violence ran the risk of being found in desertion, unless she could establish, to a high level of proof, her husband's cruelty. As well, women faced the inevitable problem of maintenance following divorce and the very real possibility that property built up during the marriage would be classified as belonging to the husband exclusively.

According to property law, whoever purchases property out of money he or she earns, or from money coming as a gift or inheritance to that person alone, is the person who owns it. If a person earns money and uses it for purchase of food and clothing for the children, for entertainment for the family and so on, there is no legal basis upon which a claim for property bought from the income of the other partner can be made. In marriage, frequently the tasks of the two parties are viewed and exercised differently. The man, in the main, maintains a permanent paid job, whilst the woman may have paid employment, but it may be part-time, or irregular, casual work, interrupted by domestic and child-rearing responsibilities. Furthermore, women as carers and nurturers have been accustomed to use any income they might have for household expenses; women have not been taught to think in concrete property terms and to purchase real estate or pay off the mortgage and electricity bills, keeping the records. The *Matrimonial Causes Act 1959* gave little recognition in real property terms to a woman's traditional effort in the home.

In 1975 the *Matrimonial Causes Act* was replaced by the *Family Law Act* which calls upon the court to acknowledge in part the contribution made to acquisition of property during the marriage, by a woman in her roles as homemaker and parent. In supporting the legislation the Women's Electoral Lobby endorsed the idea that women and men should be taken to have equal rights and equal responsibilities in the area of child custody and maintenance. WEL held also that the system should no longer assume that a married woman was dependent upon her husband, this dependence being recognised in maintenance provisions for an ex-wife. The act continues to acknowledge a right of maintenance for either ex-spouse, and enumerates the matters to be taken into account in determining whether spouse maintenance should be ordered, and if so, how much. Such factors include:

(a) the age and state of health of each of the parties;
(b) the income, property and financial resources of each of the parties and the physical and mental capacity of each of them for appropriate gainful employment;
(c) whether either party has the care or control of a child of the marriage who has not attained the age of 18 years;
(d) the financial needs and obligations of each of the parties;
(e) the responsibilities of either party to support any other person;
(f) the eligibility of either party for a pension, allowance or benefit under any law of the Commonwealth or of a State or Territory or under any superannuation fund or scheme, or the rate of any such pension, allowance or benefit being paid to either party;
(h) the extent to which the payment of maintenance to the party whose maintenance is under consideration would increase the earning capacity of that party by enabling that party to undertake a course of education or training or to establish himself or herself in a business or otherwise to obtain an adequate income;
(j) the extent to which the party whose maintenance is under consideration has contributed to the income, earning capacity, property and financial resources of the other party;
(k) the duration of the marriage and the extent to which it has affected the earning capacity of the party whose maintenance is under consideration;
(l) the need to protect the position of a woman who wishes only to continue her role as a wife and mother;
(o) any fact or circumstance which, in the opinion of the court, the justice of the case requires to be taken into account.

Theoretical equality was not, however, entirely written into the act. Two conditions give particular reason for concern: s. 75(2)(1), introduced as an amendment by the opposition Liberal–Country Party during the Bill's passage in 1975, and s. 75(2)(0). The former subsection confuses the issues to be dealt with in the award of maintenance. Firstly, with regard to the provision under (1) once parties are divorced, it is impossible for any woman to 'continue her role as a wife', and secondly, there is no consideration for the man who might wish to take up full-time parenting following divorce, or who might have played that role prior to the marriage breakdown.[9] If the law is to recognise the roles of male and female as being potentially equal, then the emphasis should have been upon 'parenting' rather than upon 'mothering'. The act serves to continue the split between male and female functions in the marriage relationship. As for the second point—the provisions under (o)—this allows judges who wish to reintroduce fault into the system to exercise full rein. Indeed, some judgements (e.g. *Issom*) have endorsed the view that fault may be relevant to the award of maintenance or the refusal of the court to grant it.[10]

If the philosophy underlying the *Family Law Act* is that the rights and wrongs of marital disputes are difficult to assess for the purpose of ending a marriage, then they should equally be so where maintenance is in question. Additionally, the act was drafted with the view that it would be futile for a court to investigate the causes of marriage breakdown, particularly when its time could be better spent on ensuring that custody matters are settled to the benefit of the children, and that all litigants have a chance of having their cases dealt with relatively promptly. In a later case, *In the Marriage of Soblusky*[11], the Full Court did not directly disapprove of the decision in *Issom*, where a woman was refused maintenance under s. 75(2)(o) on the ground that she had become pregnant to a man other than her husband. The danger here for women is readily apparent: where fault returns to any part of matrimonial law, it will operate to the detriment of women.

Due to our sexist inheritance there were grounds for criticising the *Family Law Bill* when it was first introduced. Would the court have regard to two clearly vulnerable periods in women's lives—first, where she has care of dependent children; second, where she is middle-aged and untrained or, due to social pressures, has given up a career and not kept abreast of developments in the field? Would the court acknowledge the problems facing women in returning to the workforce, and keep this in mind when determining maintenance claims? Six years after, an analysis of case histories held by the WEL Family Law Action Group shows that although women are awarded *child* maintenance where they have the care of the children, amounts are small—frequently in the vicinity of $10 or $15 per week—and maintenance for the mother herself is lacking (WEL, Sydney, 1981). The problem here is that the act is being used as an equaliser in a world where women are not possessed of equal legal or social rights, and where necessary facilities such as childcare centres are scarce. A number of women going through divorce and having dependent children have been thrown upon the resources of government, receiving supporting parent's benefits rather than maintenance from the spouse. These benefits are well below the poverty line, and those in receipt are often stigmatised.[12]

As for middle-aged women presently being ill-served: having left the paid workforce upon marriage to conform to the 'socially acceptable' role of full-time mother and homemaker, many are existing on pensions from the state. Although most would be in the middle-class bracket according to the status of the former husband, women in the working class fall into this group not infrequently. Upward mobility demanded of husbands that their wives remain at home full-time; it demanded of women that they attempt to emulate the lives of middle-class men's wives. Thus women of varying backgrounds are left in a position where it is unrealistic to demand that they enter the paid workforce. Here again, in lobbying for the passage of the *Family Law Act* WEL was aware that the legislation might keep women in a position of poverty, but the overriding hope was that retraining schemes, provision for childcare, and the opening up of the job market to women due to passage of equal opportunity and anti-discrimination legislation, would overcome that possibility.

WEL was also mindful of the fact that orders for maintenance to be paid by ex-husbands to their former wives are frequently unenforceable and on average cease within two or three years. To have orders enforced, women are required to go back to court, at considerable expense to themselves[13], with no legal aid, and with no real assurance that the money will finally be paid (e.g. Buddin et al., 1977; Wade, 1978). What good is a right to maintenance if that right is unenforceable? For women requiring maintenance, the state is a miserly payer, but pays nonetheless. The argument supporting the *Family Law Act* is that because women recognise they could not expect adequate payment from ex-husbands after divorce, upon marriage they will retain their independence in the way of full-time paid work, keep abreast of career developments, ensure that the husband participates equally in childcare and homemaking, and thus not be trapped as were women in the past. Thus women are dealt with as if their economic position is akin to that of men's. Women are viewed as responsible to the same degree as men for their own upkeep and for that of their children, yet are not granted the social and economic equality that would allow them to fulfil that responsibility.

That patriarchal attitudes from the past distort law-reforming attempts is nowhere more clear than in the property provisions of the *Family Law Act*. Under Sections 78 and 79, the court has a power to declare what title or rights any party to a marriage has in respect of the marital property and also has power to 'alter' the interests of the parties in respect of the property. The court may order either or both of the parties to transfer property to the other partner. In considering what orders should be made, the court is required under section 79(4) to take the following issues into account (amongst others):

(a) the financial contribution made directly or indirectly by or on be-

half of a party or a child to the acquisition, conservation or
improvement of the property, or otherwise in relation to the
property;
(b) the contribution made directly or indirectly to the acquisition, conservation or improvement of the property by either party, including
any contribution made in the capacity of homemaker or parent;
(c) the effect of any proposed order upon the earning capacity of
either party.

The basic premise, despite consideration being given to woman's
traditional role, is that the party who pays the money owns the property. That is, property of the marriage is usually regarded as property
of the financial contributor or the major financial contributor who is
usually the husband. The party seeking to have property interests
altered—that is, the party not having legal title to the property, most
often the wife—must establish to the court's satisfaction that it is 'just
and equitable in all circumstances' that the court should make an
alteration of property rights. Thus a heavy monetary burden falls
upon the woman seeking to establish her contribution to the matrimonial property: if she does not secure adequate legal representation,
her case will not be properly established. It will be all the more
difficult because the husband as the financially contributing party will
be aware of the financial transactions he has carried out, and will be
appraised of the nature of the property owned. Although some
women will have kept records of purchase of property, and indeed
some women will have purchased property themselves if they are in
the paid workforce, it is usually wives who are at risk due to their lack
of knowledge of the property side of the marriage (WEL, Sydney,
1981).[14]

The very nature of marriage and the ideal of romantic love surrounding it place women in an invidious position. Women are taught
that marriage is a partnership: during the marriage ceremony
statements such as 'with all my worldly goods I thee endow' promote
the idea that husbands and wives are engaged in a joint venture. When
it is decided to begin a family, there is generally an arrangement that
the husband should remain in the paid workforce, for his is the larger
salary, and the wife should have major responsibility for childcare,
for her 'talents' are most suitable in this area. Bolstering this is a tacit
agreement that they are equal partners in the relationship, and that
their contributions, though different, are of equal value. In marriage,
however, many women find they are not treated as equals. Upon
divorce, the wife finds that rather than a partner entitled to an equal
share of the property built up during the marriage, she is a supplicant
who must approach the Family Court for a toting up of her contribution.

In the 'toting up', women are once more faced with entrenched views as to 'wife and mother' contributions and with sexist attitudes as to women's position generally. The court must take into account money paid for repair, renovation or improvement to property, and also indirect contributions such as payment of household expenses which leaves the finances of the other party free for mortgage repayments, and acquisition of other property and the like. However, there are two primary problems for women. First, women as a rule earn less than men. Thus, even if the woman is contributing to the property, either directly or indirectly, her contribution in real terms will not be seen as equal to that of the man on a higher salary. Second, how can payment of the weekly food bill be balanced against payment of the mortgage? Often the court sees women's efforts as less than men's. Our legal system is orientated toward property ownership; to alter that ownership is a radical step to take, in view of the common law tradition. Thus is has been said in *In the Marriage of Todd*:

> We may take it that Parliament (in the *Family Law Act*) recognised that the wife who looks after the home and family contributes as much to the family assets as the wife who goes out to work. The one contributes in kind. The other in money or money's worth.[15]

The cases do *not* say:

> We may take it that Parliament in the *Family Law Act* recognised that the wife who looks after the home and family, and the wife who goes out to work, contribute as much to the family assets as the husband who goes out to work. The one contributes in kind or in money or money's worth. The other contributes in money alone.

There is another danger. Although fault is not generally relevant to property distribution, fault creeps in disturbingly in relation to 'woman's work'. Thus despite agreement that fault in the sense of who caused the marriage to break down is not relevant, in *In the Marriage of Zappacosta* it was said that consistent failure to attend to housekeeping or repairing duties can lead to a diminution of the interest a party might seek to assert in the matrimonial home.[16] Thus the courts may inquire as to the facility with which the wife carried out her duties. Housekeeping standards are variable. For them to become a matter of inquiry by any court can be only to the detriment of women.

Despite the ideology of romantic love, marriage is constructed upon a real economic base. This base presupposes the dependence of the wife and in fact enforces that dependence. Upon divorce, the former wife does not become as independent as her husband, with equal assets and equal economic standing; she remains dependent, frequently upon the state. Research in the United States has shown that her economic standing some seven years after the marriage has ended lowers itself to 7 per cent below the poverty line. The economic standing of men seven years after marriage has ended rises to some 30 per cent above the standard at which income needs would be met—he is 30 per cent above the poverty line (NOW, 1980: 12). The *Family Law Act* was strongly supported by the women's movement with the issue of equality in mind. The interpretation of the act, and some of its substantive provisions, threatens this possibility. Yet it is only when the traditional role of women in marriage is recognised in substance in property terms, as equal to that traditionally played by men, that there will be a legal basis for equality between husbands and wives.

Conclusions

The results of feminist activity in the private and public spheres in Australia are contradictory. On the one hand there are clear statements outlining the unlawfulness of discrimination in the public sphere. Anti-discrimination legislation acknowledges that discriminatory policies and practices are unlawful and cannot be condoned. Family law legislation recognises substantially the equality of women and men in the private sphere, so that whatever happens in practice, in theory there is a belief that marriage is a partnership of equals. These changes in law, in attitudes and the demand that behavioural changes should follow are important. However, despite legislative change, we continue to live in a patriarchal society, based on practices which demonstrate that women and men are not equal, and that discrimination is not always considered wrong.

Those states having anti-discrimination legislation are to be applauded for, amongst other things, demonstrating its lack in the remaining states and thus encouraging women in those states to lobby for similar legislation. However where anti-discrimination legislation exists, governments are often complacent about their own progress. With family law, it is only upon divorce that principles of equality are to be recognised; no changes to marriage itself have been made, the *Marriage Act* remaining substantially unaltered since 1961.

For feminists the lessons of legislative advances are ambiguous. We may pride ourselves on those efforts over the last two centuries, and most importantly over the last ten years, that have brought some formal equality to women on the pages of the statute books. Lobbying efforts have taught women how to go about changing the law, how to persuade politicians that women's demands are relevant and that women have political influence. At the same time, some feminists consider it humiliating for women to be required to lobby male politicians and legislatures in relation to reform of discriminatory practices or to make individual demands in family law through male lawyers to male judges. Although the fight by women can never be negated and the spirit displayed deserves full support and admiration, we should not hide from ourselves the ultimate reality. The Australian Constitution in no way provides for discrimination to be exercised against women; its terms are neutral. It is therefore ironic that we should have to demand the passage of egalitarian and anti-discrimination legislation. Rather, those seeking to enforce a discriminatory approach should have to lobby legislatures for the introduction of elitist and discriminatory laws. Feminist demands have led to greater autonomy for women in private and in public spheres. Our autonomy will be complete only when those demands cease to be necessary.

Notes

1 For a personal description of how one of the first women advocates in the Industrial Court of Queensland presented a case for the Queensland Branch of the Clerks' Union for equal pay for women see Daisy Marchisotti (1980).

2 Periodic purges of married women from the teaching profession appear to have been in order: in Victoria in 1894 married women teachers were dismissed from the service on recommendation to the Governor in Council made by the Minister of Public Instruction, the Honourable R. Baker. Cases were eventually dealt with 'on their merits', when a number of women who received notice appealed to the minister. Ultimately *all* women teachers either being 50 years of age or having 30 years service were dismissed (with exception of a few cases of 'special hardship'), being asked to 'tender their resignations'. Where married women had appealed against their dismissal, in a few cases the dismissal was withdrawn on the understanding that the teacher in question would leave after a period of 12 months' grace. (See Daniels and Murnane, 1980: 247-8.)

3 At this time, members of WEL ACT working in the Anti-Discrimination Action Group included Kay Vernon, Gail Radford (now Director of Equal Opportunity in the Commonwealth Public Service Board) and Jenny Shipley (now Jenny Neary, Director of Equal Opportunity programs in the New South Wales Department of Technical and Further Education).

4 See also Resolution from WEL (Victoria) 1979 State Conference. All feminist women's organisations followed the lead of the Australian Federation of Business and Professional Women in the boycott, and individual women as well as organisations wrote to Ansett and to local and Australia-wide newspapers deploring the actions of the company and making clear their intention of joining the boycott.

5 Although she would no doubt have failed to end up on the desired promotions list had she acted in this stereotyped way: qualities and characteristics necessary for promotion in professions are those pertaining to the male sex, in stereotypical terms. If they are acquired by or naturally develop in a member of the female sex, as in Deidre Harrison's case, they will be viewed in a negative light. Qualities and characteristics seen as pertaining to the female sex, in stereotypical terms, are the opposite of those needed in order to succeed in a male-oriented world.

6 As the board pointed out in its report, breaks in service present difficulties in terms of accreditation: 'While paid work attracts credit, activities typical of women (child-raising and voluntary community service) do not. Penalisation for service interruption has affected older women most severely, but even today women are

disadvantaged and professional value of child-raising to teaching is not formally acknowledged': see *Anti-Discrimination Board, NSW*, 1976: 92. Following the report the New South Wales Government determined that absence of a teacher for one year's maternity leave will be credited to service, thus overcoming the problem of accreditation for those women who break from service to have a child, except where they absent themselves for more than 12 months. This does not, however, come to grips with underlying issues—such as the need for adequate childcare in the community, in schools, etc. and far more fundamental issues relating to discrimination against women and the failure of men to participate equally in childcare and child raising.

7   Before 1960 women held, 'nearly all the top principals' jobs in primary schools' in New South Wales. Now they hold little more than 5 per cent. In high schools, women held only 9 per cent of principals' jobs in 1981, whereas in 1949 they held 21 per cent. In 1981 they held only 7 per cent of deputy principals' jobs, contrasted with 25 per cent in 1949. Today men have a 1 in 38 chance of being promoted to the job of high school principal, whilst women have only a 1 in 274 chance of taking on the same job. Men have a 1 in 18 chance of being promoted to principal contrasted with a 1 in 419 chance for women. See Andrew Casey, 'Equality backfires on women teachers', *Sydney Morning Herald*, 7 August 1982: 1; also 1981 Annual Statistics of the NSW Department of Education.

8   Note, however, that no change was made to the law of domicile, whereby a woman acquired her husband's domicile upon marriage which for the purpose of determining certain legal rights and duties was regarded as her 'permanent home'. This created very great difficulties for women, in that if a woman did not know where her husband lived, or where she was living in a different country from her husband, she was almost in a state of limbo for legal purposes. This was changed under the *Family Law Act 1975* (Com) where section 4(3)(b) provides that the domicile of a married woman should be determined as if she had never been married.

9   On this issue and that of maintenance and the *Family Law Act* 1975 generally, see WEL, 1978a, 1978b, 1979a, 1979b; also Riches, 1979; Graham, 1981.

10   *Issom* v. *Issom* unreported, 12 April, 1976, Fogarty J; see also Nygh, 1976: 119; Riches, 1979; 217-8.

11   (1976) 2 Fam LR 11,528; 12 ALR 699; see also Nygh, 1978: 118-9.

12   See Australian Council of Social Service regular monthly updates of the discrepancy in benefits paid and the poverty line.

13   Legal aid is unavailable for the enforcement of maintenance orders, although the basis upon which maintenance is ordered is that the recipient is in need and cannot exist without payment of the maintenance and also that the person required to pay maintenance is financially able to do so.

14   A common occurrence with women having middle-class fathers is for the women to bring some money or property into the marriage, sometimes by way of inheritance or gift from her family, sometimes savings built up during the paid working life. Unfortunately after some years of marriage it is difficult to ascertain how much she brought in, because records have not been kept, or have been lost. Because there is an assumption that if the property is contributed to by the husband, the husband owns it, it is difficult for women to produce the evidence required to affirm her contribution. In some cases parents of the wife may give the couple a house, or deposit for a house, which becomes the matrimonial home. The husband's money is thus freed to put into a business or to built one already existing. Years after, it is again difficult for the wife to find evidence of the gift of the house to her, or the deposit, freeing the husband's finances. As well, the gift was no doubt made to both, or viewed by the court as made to both, so would be owned equally—and the wife would be seen as having little or no interest in the business assets built up to a large degree as a result of the gift.

15 *In the Marriage of Todd* (No.2) (1976) 1 Fam LR 11, 186, 11, 190, (1976) 9 ALR 401, 406.
16 (1976) 2 Fam LR 11, 214.

12 Social policy, education and women in Australia

PAIGE PORTER

It is unlikely that the images conjured up in the popular mind by the phrase 'social welfare' extend to the undulating motion and steady buzz that is the typical primary school classroom of 30-odd children and their bustling teacher. Yet the provision of compulsory schooling by democratic governments in industrialised countries was, in fact, one of the earliest of the social policies which now, in conjunction with others, make up what many observers call (with varying degrees of approval and condemnation) the welfare state. Education was one of the earliest arenas for the development of state policies in many parts of the capitalist world as compulsory formal schooling was introduced in the nineteenth century in most of western Europe, England and North America as well as Australia.

This paper discusses education as social policy in relation to the position of women. What must be understood from a historical perspective are the relationships between the changing demands of the economy, evolving family structures, the role of the state, and policies concerning educational reform. However, these relationships are extraordinarily complex; very few observers have attempted to delineate the links; and there are virtually no analyses of Australian society which draw these connections. Thus all I can hope to do in this short paper is to point in certain directions and suggest a framework for further work in this area.

Colonial Australia and the emergence of state-supported public education

A first point which must be made, when education in early colonial Australia is considered, is that a remote British garrison containing mainly soldiers and convicts is not likely to be fertile ground for the development or expansion of any form of education. Official British attitudes at the time were quite negative with regard to education for the lower orders. Austin, in describing the views of the day, states that 'Conservative opinion ... agreed wholeheartedly with the Bishop of

London's conviction that it was "safest for both the Government and the religion of the country to let the lower classes remain in that state of ignorance in which nature originally placed them" ... (1972: 2). However, Botany Bay was not England and most of the early governors became quickly convinced that a convict population 'needed' some education. It also became obvious that whatever the condition of the adult population something had to be done to 'rescue' the rapidly increasing numbers of illegitimate children from the 'savagery' of their convict parents (Austin, 1972: 4), not to mention the need to 'correct' the views of the many Irish dissidents marooned on these remote shores.

In the eighteenth and the early nineteenth centuries education was inseparable from religious and moral training, and the churches were expected to make the appropriate provisions. As the 'established' church in England, the Church of England assumed that it also held this position in Australia. However, circumstances again were different. The Catholic Church was much stronger in Australia, as were other non-conformist churches especially the Presbyterians. All the churches in Australia were poor with small congregations and few wealthy supporters. Their capacity to provide education of any sort for any class was quite inadequate. This led to a situation of great competition for whatever funds the colonial governments could provide for schools and contributed to increasingly bitter sectarian rivalry. Eventually a dual system of education emerged in the middle of the nineteenth century which involved colonial government support both for 'denominational' schools and for the establishment of 'national' or public schools.

However, the second half of the nineteenth century saw rapid social change and it soon became apparent that the dual system of education satisfied few. With the discovery of gold at Bathurst in 1851, followed by rich finds elsewhere, the population of the colonies soared from 405 000 in 1850 to 1 140 000 in 1860. This period also saw increasing urbanisation as many farmers left their unviable small selections for the cities and more and more migrants with urban backgrounds arrived. With increasing urbanisation came increasing state involvement in the provision of water, telegraph, roads, railways, hospitals and, eventually, schools.

Ideological and political factors were also relevant to the movement towards state control of schooling during this period and, in particular, a group of factors best described as the 'secularisation of the state'. The significance of this development for education in Australia can be traced in part to the strength of Catholicism in this country. 'Godless' schools run by the colonial governments were entirely unacceptable to the Australian Catholic hierarchy which continued to establish its own schools. This unwillingness to participate in 'common schools' irritated many Protestants who began to see state support for denominational schools as a response to the demands of primarily one church. Thus secularisation of the state in the second half of the nineteenth century in Australia was related to anti-Catholicism and was undoubtedly one ingredient in the eventual adoption of public education.

Between 1872 and 1895 all the colonial governments moved into the provision of public primary education. Those behind the movement argued for 'free, compulsory and secular' schooling, a slogan which did reflect similarities in the eventual colonial legislation. All the early education acts had a number of important features in common. These included the abolition of state aid to denominational schools; the establishment of a system of secular public education which nevertheless usually allowed either some non-denominational Christian instruction, or made some time available for clergy of different faiths to meet with their young flocks; the intent that schooling should be free; the intent that schooling should be compulsory; the establishment of colonial departments of education with final responsibility lying with a minister; and the notion that the provision of education must be controlled and coordinated from these departments based in the capital cities. However, despite this clear move by the state into the provision of compulsory education, the private sector did not disappear but actually continued to flourish, becoming even more the domain of the growing middle class, the wealthy, and the devout. (By 1980, 78 per cent of the school-age population was in government schools and 22 per cent in non-government schools.)

Educational provision for girls

Education for girls during the colonial period in most cases reflected nineteenth century notions of femininity and the role of women in 'pioneer' Australia. Jean Ely has described this as 'fostering families in which the usually conservative wives and mothers ("God's Police" Caroline Chisholm called them) pumped strong doses of "respectability" into both the children and the husbands' (1978: 10). In the early part of the nineteenth century middle-class girls were generally educated by governesses at home. The various forms of public but non-compulsory schooling that developed in the eastern colonies were attended primarily by working-class children. While such schools did admit girls from the earliest days, strict segregation of the sexes was the rule wherever possible and the curriculum was differentiated according to sex. In general girls were taught reading and writing but not arithmetic, and instruction in sewing and needlework was thought essential.

Secondary education in colonial Australia was very limited for both boys and girls and those schools which did exist were private and mainly church-related. Such private boys' schools developed in the 1850s and girls' schools in the 1860s and 1870s. Some of these schools (such as Presbyterian Ladies College in Melbourne with a crusading headmaster, C.H. Pearson) stressed academic education for girls but the majority emphasised the 'feminine' graces, and girls were sent to these schools by middle- and upper-class families for 'polishing' before their marriage to a man of commerce or of the land.

Tertiary education was even more restricted. The University of Sydney was established in 1851 and Melbourne University in 1854, but neither offered matriculation to women until 1882 and 1881 respectively. While a small number of women did matriculate they were often discouraged from actually enrolling at university. As Ailsa Zainu'ddin has put it, 'The general policy adopted was to leave the road open but not to encourage any would-be travellers in their journey' (1975: 8).

Female university graduates became teachers or sometimes set up their own private schools. Despite the fact that females were accepted in the teaching ranks of the state primary schools, and this was seen as a 'genteel' occupation for women, the job itself had little to recommend it. Typically young women (and young men) became 'pupil teachers' at the school-leaving age of fourteen, a position they needed to hold for four years before promotion. Pupil teachers were paid a pittance, not enough to cover the costs of living away from home; had to teach all day under the watchful eyes of older assistant teachers and the headmaster; and had to be coached in the relevant subjects before and after the school day by the headmaster, while at the same time preparing for annual exams on the basis of which a small pay rise might be granted. Once qualified, overt discrimination in salaries and promotion existed, with women not permitted to enter the higher ranks of teaching and with wages fixed at a percentage of those of the men in the same grade. Generally women who married were compelled to resign. Many of these practices actually continued long after World War II.

The movement of the state into secondary schooling in Australia is a twentieth-century phenomenon. Generally the provision of such education for those of 'average' ability, or those who could not afford to pay the fees of the private secondary schools, was a post-World War II development which is still evolving. Australia, in fact, continues to have secondary school participation rates (as well as tertiary education participation rates) which are well below those of many other countries in western Europe and North America.

At the beginning of this century, state-provided secondary education was selective and entry was controlled by a qualifying examination. Initially fees were also charged but these were gradually replaced with scholarships. In general these select state secondary schools were open to both boys and girls and the curriculum was heavily academic and geared towards the entrance requirements of the universities. These rigorous curricula were in many ways not as sex-typed as those of the modern high school yet such institutions were clearly regarded as basically male institutions to which select females were admitted. However, it was expected that the future role of a female student would be that of a wife and mother, albeit an 'educated' one.

It was not until the early 1960s that the idea of universal secondary education provided by the state became a reality in Australia, and secondary schools akin to the English comprehensive schools and the American high schools began to emerge. The expansion of tertiary education did not begin in earnest until the early 1970s. It is significant that in both secondary and tertiary education female students have had, until the latter half of the 1970s, lower participation rates than their male counterparts.

Women and education: theoretical perspectives

In the 1970s, there was a great deal written in Australia about the continued inequalities experienced by girls and women in educational institutions. Much of this work was both descriptive and prescriptive: it documented extensively issues such as lower secondary school retention rates for girls; lower rates of scholarship awards; lower participation rates; lower rates of technical training; the bias towards arts and humanities in the 'female' curriculum; higher rates of female youth unemployment. Policy prescription was then implied by further documentation of bias and discrimination in curriculum materials and practices, classroom organisation techniques, teacher expectations, teacher training methods and the education service as a whole as a career option for women.[1] However, there has been little theoretical analysis on the causes of the situation as described, particularly with reference to Australian history and culture.

As argued throughout this book, the relationship between the family, the labour market and the state may be seen as the reinforcement by state policies of the sexual division of labour in the household and in the labour process. Women, as specialists in childcare and domestic servicing (as an outcome of the history of industrial capitalism) provide not only services for capital in reproducing labour power cheaply, but also provide other services (e.g. care of the sick and the elderly) which allow the costs of state expenditure to be minimised.

There is also a patriarchal logic in these relationships, which defines women as 'dependent', whatever the reality of their individual situation. They are, therefore, typically utilised as marginal labour force participants, whose labour is available cheaply and expendable during economic recessions (at least at an ideological level). In summary, an adequate analysis of the role of women in education needs to take account of the interconnections of women's domestic labour and their wage labour, as mediated by the presumption of dependence.

The concept of the family-education couple

The relationship between the state, the family, and education has been drawn in detail in a useful account by Miriam David (1980). David's central argument is that the family and the education system are used in concert to sustain and reproduce existing relations within the family and social relations within the economy, maintaining the sexual and social divisions of labour. Using Althusser's (1971) term, the 'family-education couple', to refer to this perspective, David notes that this new ideological apparatus had replaced the 'family-church couple' of the past.

Using a historical analysis of educational policies in England, David identifies two dimensions of the family-education couple. One dimension focuses on the growth and specification of parental responsibilities and rights in connection with the development of mass compulsory education, and the other focuses on how schools are expected to implement the political aims of education through teachers and curricula, particularly in relation to their legal responsibility to *act in loco parentis*. She traces the historical development of state intervention in parent-child relations which developed with changes in the economic order and the demand for different kinds of labour.

For example, she argues that early in the nineteenth century the issue of national primary education for working-class children had been debated in Parliament and rejected on the grounds that child labour was an economic necessity and it was not legitimate for the state to intervene in relations between parent and child or between employer and employee. However, by the end of the nineteenth century the economy had become much more diversified, the need for skilled labour much greater, and the demands of the working class for schools more strident. Hence by 1890 a universal and compulsory system of education developed in England provided primarily by the state (1980: 33). With it developed an ideology that not only condemned child labour but insisted that parents have a responsibility to the state with regard to their children's education and health. Furthermore, this responsibility was seen to be the *mothers'* and hence worked to keep women out of the labour market in company with their children. This trend has continued during the twentieth century with increasing responsibilities placed on mothers for various aspects of their children's intellectual and physical development especially in relation to education.

When examining her second dimension, 'family issues in schooling', David looks at both the form and the content of schooling in which children 'learn' about parenting and the sexual division of labour. Hence schoolmistresses must be 'motherly', but schoolmasters, and the structure of the school, must be 'fatherly'. Again, using a historical policy analysis of the English situation, she describes the history of women in the teaching profession and their unequal treatment, as well as the development of curricula intended to teach girls about their role in the division of labour within the family as well as outside. This kind of analysis raises important issues for a study of the relationship between the state, the family and education in Australia.

Exploration of the state-family-education relationship in Australia

In order to understand the current relationship between education and the position of women in Australia it is necessary to take a broad perspective, which explores in depth the relationship between the changing demands of the economy, evolving family structure, the role of the state and policies concerning educational 'reform'. In this section I suggest a few examples of the possibilities and potential of such research.

Examples of issues
Consider the following report from an advisory body to an important investigation into public education in Victoria in 1918. The view of the family and the role of education in relation to it is clearly indicated:

> The problem of dealing with the further education of girls is much more complicated than in the case of boys. It is known that every boy should ultimately play some definite part in the world's activities.... On the other hand, the main sphere of women is centred in their homes and families. The majority of girls marry a few years after leaving school. In the interval, they may take part in industrial or other activities external to the home; but their experience and training in such a direction, unless actually connected with home occupations, are of little or no service to them for the rest of their life. In fact, the time so spent may be a positive disadvantage to them. (Turney, 1975: 325)

By the early 1940s however, there appeared to be a greater emphasis placed on the importance of academic subjects for girls, one argument being that such study would actually make them better wives and mothers. Hence, in 1943 it was claimed that:

> the greatest, if not indeed the most useful accomplishment, is that of home-making. It is the translation of scientific principles into the creation of homes. There is scope for a working knowledge of

psychology, physiology, physics, chemistry, mechanism, domestic economy and more besides. (Turney, 1978: 166)

Thus, at the same time as the drudgery of household work was being lightened by various labour-saving devices, the 'job' of being a housewife was becoming so 'professional' as to require advanced education. A somewhat similar theme in the post-war period can be identified in the influence of child and educational psychologists who took pains to explain the inherent 'need' of children for 24-hours-a-day mothers. These kinds of arguments developed at precisely the time when greater numbers of women and particularly married women with children were entering the labour force.

The concept of the sexual division of labour is also clearly relevant in a discussion of education in Australia. Not only is teaching an occupation which has always employed large numbers of women and is hence regarded as a 'feminine' occupation, but within the education system there is also a sexual division of labour, with more women than men working at the primary level, slightly more men than women working at the secondary level and many more men working at the tertiary level. Men predominate in high administrative positions at all levels.

Ian Birch (1976) describes one of the few cases concerning education to come before a state supreme court, a 1966 case involving the practice of bonding student teachers in Western Australia. The female student concerned was bonded during her training period to the Department of Education and had signed an agreement that, should she marry during training, the course would be terminated and she would be required to repay her allowance. She became pregnant and decided to marry but indicated her intention of continuing her studies. However, the department required her to resign and repay. The defendant argued amongst other things that the marriage provision of the contract was void as it was 'in restraint of marriage'. The judge ruled against the defendant and argued that while the restraint of marriage (or trade) was illegal, the legality had to be tested by reasonableness. Birch comments that:

the Judge applauded the department's refusal to employ married women and asserted that women should devote themselves to domestic duties. He saw nothing unreasonable in the particular condition which prevented any female student from marrying during the time of her studentship and that required for teaching in fulfilment of the agreement. (1976: 62)

Birch also notes that this decision was criticised by some at the time who claimed that it encouraged immorality, as the obvious alternative open to a student interested in continuing her studies would be to 'live in sin' and bear an illegitimate child. The Western Australian legislation has since changed, but it is well to remember that this was only sixteen years ago.

These few examples of the possibilities of an analysis of the relationship between the state, the family and policy concerning educational 'reform' suggest the potential richness of such work.

Schools and the economy

Many observers have commented on the relatively loosely coupled connection between schools and the demands of the economy. Ann Marie Wolpe (Kuhn and Wolpe, 1978) discusses some of the reasons for this 'loose coupling'. They include the contradictory needs of capitalist society to train for both general adaptability and flexibility of labour, and for specific skills; the relatively unclear notion of 'skills' when one considers the kinds of 'skills' learned at school and the demands of the labour force; the 'lag' that exists in the rate with which the education system can react to the demand for new skills; the fact that the acquisition of qualifications does not actually ensure a job, only the possibility of getting a particular kind of job; the contradictory nature of educational goals in general; and the relatively unchanging nature of the ideology regarding the appropriate work of women and hence the education provided for girls.

It is in relation to schools and the economy that one of the most significant contradictions inherent in the present state-family-education link emerges. This is on the one hand the demand by employers for paid female labour reinforced by the economic need for many women to work, in combination with the strong emphasis in schools on individual achievement and the acquisition of skills by all students regardless of gender, in conflict on the other hand with the continuing ideology of the 'proper' domestic role of women as wives and mothers. This contradiction results in schools typically promoting an overt curriculum that stresses universal attainment of skills by both boys and girls, and a covert curriculum that urges girls to use those skills in the home and teaches boys to expect that this will be the case.

The public sector and bureaucratic ideology

Other features of Australian society also require consideration in an investigation of the state-family-education relationship. Important factors are likely to be the large size of the public sector and the dominance of bureaucratic ideology. Boris Frankel's (1978) account of the contradictory nature of the public sector in capitalist societies identifies the public sector's dependence for revenues on the accumulation of private profit, combined with its need to furnish social services for the working class when either a reform party is in office or the conservative parties must respond to electoral pressures. This contradiction is exacerbated by the relatively large size of the public sector in Australia to the point where capitalist class relations are challenged and limits are set on the conditions for capital accumulation.

> The level of class struggle has forced the public sector to meet demands for improving 'the quality of life', which thereby prevents social crises in the *short term* but gives rise to new forms of social relations based on *use values* instead of commodity exchange value. The fact that there are large sections of the population who are not in the relation of wage labor and capital, producing surplus value (e.g. teachers, social workers, students, all people in receipt of government welfare incomes, e.g. widows, pensioners, etc.) has had a significant effect on the *non-reproduction* of capitalist social relations.... The danger (for capitalists) of a larger public sector is related to the overall income volume of goods and services, which may not generate the accumulation of private wealth but may be non-profit-making community goods and services. This situation spells out the parameters of private enterprise production and the point where the public sector ceases to reproduce the dominant capitalist social relations. (Frankel, 1978: 214)

In other words, the relatively large size of the public sector (of which education is a major part) may in itself play an important part in social change. As women are both a significant group of employees in the public sector, and a significant category of recipients of its services, they are contributing to potential change. Whether they benefit from any change remains to be seen.

The pervasive bureaucractic ideology is a related issue. Consider the nature of the relationship between the development of bureaucratic structures in the organisation of schools and the employment of women. Tyack has argued for the United States

> Hierarchical organisation of schools and the male chauvinism of the larger society fit as hand to glove. The system required subordination; women were generally subordinate to men; the employment of women as teachers thus augmented the authority of the largely male administrative leadership. (Tyack, 1974: 60)

Given the dominance of bureaucratic forms on the Australian educational scene, it is likely that the relationship is even stronger in this country. Furthermore, the prominence of bureaucratic structures ensures another contradiction that also contributes to the potential for social change: the universal values inherent in bureaucratic ideology.

The paradox is that bureaucratic norms such as rewards based on performance and merit make inequalities based on sex (and race and religion) theoretically inappropriate.

In summary, the contradictions of the state-family-education relationship include: first, the contradiction between on the one hand, the demand for female workforce participation and the realities of this participation, and the emphasis in schools on the acquisition of skills, juxtaposed on the other hand with the still prevalent ideology of women as dependent. Second, the contradiction between the growth of a large public sector and the demands of the reproduction of capitalist social relations. Third, the contradiction between the bureaucratic norms of impartiality and reward based on performance, and sexist practices in education systems. There are many contradictions which have not been discussed in this short paper. However, as it is within such social contradictions that the possibilities for social change emerge, it is worth examining briefly current educational policies to identify those changes which have occurred in recent years in the position of girls and women.

Present government policies concerned with education and women[2]

All states and the federal government, with pressure from the women's movement, have developed educational policies in the last decade which are concerned with gender-related inequalities in education. There is little doubt that the federal Labor government was active in drawing attention to the problems of sexism in education. The original report of the Interim Committee for the Schools Commission (Karmel Report) discussed 'disadvantage' in schooling due to gender (along with other factors), and the 1973 legislation establishing the Schools Commission required the commission to have regard to the needs of 'students suffering disadvantages in relation to education for social, economic, ethnic, geographic, cultural, lingual or similar reasons'. One of the major reports of the Schools Commission, *Girls, School and Society* (1975), clearly documented the scope of the problem. From 1975 the Schools Commission employed a project officer on a permanent full-time basis to be responsible for the development and implementation of action concerned with the elimination of sexism in education. There are plans at present for a national inquiry to follow up what progress, if any, has been made since 1975.

The Schools Commission has also supported a wide variety of projects in this area. They include: a project on sexism in early reading and instructional materials in South Australia; a centre for non-sexist educational resources in Victoria; a project in Tasmania dealing with improving the understanding of schoolgirls with regard to the effects of sex role stereotyping; a non-sexist career education project for girls in Western Australia; an adviser on sexism in education in New South Wales; a project intended to work towards the development of policies to eliminate sexism in education by the Australian Teachers Federation; a survey of parent opinion regarding the education of girls for the Australian Parents Council and the Australian Council of State School Organisations; the employment of a person to work with parent groups in Victoria; a home-school interaction project in Victoria; a national dissemination project; the production of a series of films; various practical research projects; and support for a number of small school-based projects funded through the Special Projects (Innovations) Program and the Disadvantaged Schools Program.

The Commonwealth Department of Education contains a Women's Unit which was created as a response to a suggestion from the prime minister to the minister for education and exists without a legislative basis. The unit has a staff of two and its approach is generally to overview and advise in the areas of curriculum development, the special needs of women and girls in the technical and further education area, the development of wider employment options for girls, workforce re-entry programs and other relevant research.

New South Wales enacted an *Anti-Discrimination Act* in 1977 and the Education Department has appointed a number of full-time and part-time staff to develop strategies aimed at promoting equality of opportunity between the sexes. This includes the full-time consultant in non-sexist education funded by the Schools Commission. Other officers work with personal development teachers and coordinate activities going on in the various regions. A major project is the Non-Sexist Resource Centre which has a lending library and offers an advisory service to teachers. A task force was also set up to make further recommendations. While the Department of Technical and Further Education employs no personnel to deal with the issue there are a number of people with responsibilities in this area and a small number of initiatives have been undertaken. The NSW Teachers Federation has a Women's Coordinator who facilitates support networks in the regions.

In Victoria, an *Equal Opportunity Act* was passed in 1977 and the Education Department has appointed a coordinator for the elimination of sexism in schools in a full-time professional position attached to the office of the Director-General. The coordinator's responsibilities include developing procedures for the elimination of sexist bias in curriculum materials and school practices. Projects undertaken include the establishment of a Resources Centre for Equal Opportunity; the production of a film on women in non-traditional occupations; and recommendations regarding the establishment of a number of procedures which would deal with the problem in an ongoing fashion. The Technical Schools Division also has several colleges involved in organising relevant programs. In addition, the three teachers' unions have a joint project designed to counter sexism in education.

In Queensland no specific legislation has been enacted which could be used to change the education system in respect of discriminatory practices. There are also no specific projects undertaken by the Department of Education in relation to sexism in education. However, the department does maintain a 'watching brief' by ensuring that officers are aware of the issue of sexism in the development of curriculum materials in general, and the home economics syllabus in particular. In addition two research officers in the Curriculum Branch give special attention to the area.

South Australia passed a *Sex Discrimination Act* in 1975 which is a far-reaching piece of legislation forbidding discrimination on the grounds of sex and marital status in employment, education and the provision of goods and services. The act deals specifically with education by forbidding the limiting of access to educational programs on the grounds of sex and marital status, but it does not exempt institutions established wholly for students of one sex. The South Australian Education Department has set up a Women's Advisory unit with two full-time and two fractional appointments which is responsible for research, advice and curriculum development in the area. There is also a Women's Studies Resource Centre and a Careers and Girls' Project. Particular attention is given to staff in junior primary schools through the Serim Project. The Department of Further Education has a large number of small projects in the area and the South Australian Institute of Teachers has a women's advisor.

There is no specific legislation in Western Australia which is aimed at discriminatory practices within the Department of Education. However there is a coordinator for equal opportunity appointed at the superintendent level. This appointment followed the report of a committee set up to investigate sexist discrimination in education both in terms of schooling and the career structure. The Curriculum Branch is concerned with sexism in curriculum materials and the Guidance Branch with sexism in vocational information. The Technical Education Division has no specific projects in this area. The Western Australian Teachers Union has an advisory committee and has produced several reports on sexism in education: recently it appointed a women's adviser.

Tasmania passed legislation to prevent discrimination on the grounds of sex, marital status, ethnic origin and handicap in 1979. The Education Department supports a project known as Improving Education for Girls which also has Schools Commission funding. The project involved one full-time officer and a number of fractional appointments and is involved in collecting and disseminating non-sexist curriculum materials, working in career guidance, and generally promoting awareness of the issue. A large number of small projects have spun off from this major endeavour. Funding has also been provided for meetings with others working in the same area in other states. An advisory committee has been established to advise the Director of Further Education on the needs of women in this area.

The ACT Schools Authority has a permanent officer working full-time on the elimination of sexism in education and whose responsibilities include reviewing curriculum materials, disseminating information, advising and generally coordinating activities in this area. The ACT Teachers Federation has a committee for the elimination of sexism.

The Northern Territory Education Department has adopted a policy of non-sexist education and there is one officer who devotes part of the time to this area and a committee of support staff who provide assistance.

In addition to these centrally organised initiatives, there are numerous small projects under the auspices of a few teachers or the administration of individual schools in both the public and private sectors. These school-based efforts are extremely important but impossible to summarise or assess.

Thus we can see from this brief review of official educational policy that there is some recognition of the inherent contradictions in the present state-family-education relationship and there are policy initiatives in educational reform which are attempting to deal with the position of women in education. These initiatives are uneven across the states and from school to school. The federal government has clearly been instrumental in encouraging activity in this area with policies initially set up by the Whitlam Labor Government but suffering erosion in the current period of economic recession and cutbacks in public expenditure for educational innovation. These policies reflect the basic nature and style of Australian education bureaucracies, that of cautious compromise and consensus. Even more importantly the impact of these official policies remains unevaluated. However, that they exist at all is undoubtedly due to the activity of the women's movement in the educational arena and does provide some grounds for a modicum of optimism.

Remaining problem areas

While the previously discussed official changes in education policy in this area are extremely important, it should be kept in mind that such policies are still being implemented within social structures which remain basically discriminatory. The women's movement has promoted significant advances in education in Australia but both within educational institutions and in the surrounding society there are still major barriers which girls and women face.

Some examples of existing practical problems which reflect these conservative educational and social structures include the following:

1 The timing of the school day (9.00 am to 3.30 pm) which, without many advances in after-school childcare, still makes it difficult for women even with school age children to work outside the home.

2 The continuing importance placed on volunteers in schools to raise money, run canteens, etc. 'Volunteers' inevitably means mothers and contributes to the reinforcement of women's position in the home (see also Chapter 14).

3 The 'innovation' of greater parental involvement in schools, again, usually means mothers and, despite the rhetoric, seldom involves participation in important policy decisions but does increase pressure on mothers.

4 The continuing negative attitude of many teachers to employed mothers and the assumption that their children are 'deprived' as a result.

5 The continuing conservative view of many parents with regard to their daughters' future in education and employment when compared with their aspirations for their sons.

6 The continuation of sexist 'hidden curricula' in schools which result in the under-representation of girls in mathematics and science, and their discouragement from entering courses of training in the technically skilled trades.

7 The continuation of traditionally limited career paths for many girls in the 'feminine' occupations, despite the realities of high unemployment rates in many of those areas.

8 The relative lack of expenditure and encouragement provided for girls' sport compared with sport for boys.

9 The implicit priority of some state education departments in hiring teachers to favour the 'breadwinner' status of an applicant (which is typically defined by the largest income) and which usually means discrimination against women.

10 The continuing high proportion of female teachers in temporary rather than permanent status jobs which inevitably militates against promotion possibilities.

11 The difficulty of after-school hours, in-service training for many female teachers without childcare services at those times, which makes it hard to acquire extra qualifications for improvement or promotion.

12 The difficulty of some maternity leave provisions which may involve a compulsory leave period, no pay during that period, insistence on resignation after inadequate time lapse such as

eighteen months; and which are usually available only for women, which means that male teachers cannot choose to look after their babies.

13 The problem of promotion in the teaching service and the under-representation of women in positions of authority. This under-representation is the outcome of interrupted career patterns which militate against the acquisition of varied experience and further qualifications.

14 The difficulty of placing the issues discussed above on the agenda for serious consideration by many schools or state education departments.

Concluding remarks

The policy changes which have occurred at both state and federal level in recent years with regard to sex-related inequalities in Australian education reflect the dynamic nature of the situation as well as the strength of the women's movement in the education arena. However, these changes have occurred within social structures which remain basically patriarchal and thus barriers to the equal participation of girls and women remain formidable.

Acknowledgements

In the preparation of this paper I am grateful for helpful comments from Sandra Brown, Cora Baldock, Jane Kenway, Bettina Cass, Janina Trotman.

Notes

1 For example see: Schools Commission (1975); Mercer (1975); Encel et al. (1974); Sampson (1976); Bradley and Mortimer (1972-73); Keeves and Reed (1974); Rowell (1971); Edgar (1974); Winkler (1976); Bessant (1976); Tefler (1978); and *Education News* (1975) 15, 4/5, which is devoted to women and education.
2 The following information was summarised from a description of the present situation collated by the Australian Education Council in 1979, and from a paper presented by Rosemary Richards, Coordinator for the Elimination of Sexism in Education in the ACT, entitled 'Sexism in Education', given at a conference in Western Australia in April 1980.

13　In sickness and in health: social policy and the control of women

DOROTHY H. BROOM

In the early 1980s, feminists and academics investigating the status of women are caught in a double bind: the dilemma is whether to emphasise the similarities between women and men or to focus on those qualities (inherent or acquired) that differentiate the sexes. Each perspective has its own value and also its own traps.

One common humanity

Those who stress the similarities between men and women do so because they recognise that the concept of a distinctive 'female nature' has been used for generations to relegate women to second-class citizenship. Such practices as occupational discrimination, low pay, and even violence against women have at various times been described as natural consequences of the 'inherent differences' between men and women. In response to the 'inherent differences' argument, action and research are emerging which stress social learning as the major source of gender differentiation and emphasise the fundamental humanness of all persons, regardless of sex. Activists focus on the importance of equal rights legislation, equal pay, and other measures designed to give women the same opportunities as men. Although much remains to be done, considerable progress has been made by invoking the common humanity of women and men.

The danger in this point of view is its ironic tendency to define 'humanity' by the standard of males. When male becomes the norm, women's disadvantages are seen as a consequence of their lack of access to the world of men, and solutions consist of enabling women to live as men have. For example, most people agree that women are entitled to equal pay when they have the same jobs, the same career structures ('uninterrupted'), and the same work pattern (full time, year round) as men. But the consequence of the male norm is that if any of those criteria are not fulfilled, low female earnings are supposedly explained; women did not 'measure up' to the male standard. Where inequality persists, it is either a vestige of the past or evidence that women are not yet 'ready for equality' (see for example Poloma and Garland, 1971). The fundamental structure remains unquestioned (Acker, 1978). Male patterns and values remain the norm, and 'liberation' is defined as conformity to that standard.

Substantive differences

The other point of view holds that we must understand and take account of sex differences (whether innate or learned) in order to achieve a fair deal for women. The danger of this perspective is obvious: a variation on the theme has been the traditional ideological tool in the oppression of women. Despite its hazards, proponents of this orientation argue that special consideration of differences is essential to compensate for a history of discrimination and subordination. Social policy must reflect the fact that the legacy of inequality cannot be corrected by the individual efforts of women and men; policies such as affirmative action are necessary to make 'equal opportunity' a reality instead of a hypothetical construct.

There is a second reason for stressing the differences rather than the similarities between men and women. Women's distinctive reproductive processes are potentially relevant to the entire range of their social experience. Thus, an adequate understanding of human society must necessarily include consideration—long omitted from social science— of the personal and social impact of reproduction, including sexuality and fertility control, and, by extension, of arrangements for care of dependent children. Both our intellectual constructions and our social policies must reflect reproduction and childcare as integral elements of the human life course rather than as aberrations in the 'normal' (male) pattern.

Each of these perspectives carries different implications for social policy. The 'similarities' approach directs attention to sex discrimination in policies and calls for its removal. The 'differences' orientation (in either of its versions) would allow that some policies distinguishing between the sexes are necessary, at least for the time being, and in particular cases (such as maternity leave) permanently. These two points of view are not necessarily in conflict, although feminism's detractors have used an over-simplified rendition of the dilemma in an effort to discredit the women's movement. I suggest that a feminist analysis of social policy cannot be based on the question of 'similarities' or 'differences' alone, but must be a more subtle and complex investigation of the implications of social arrangements for the promotion of women's (and ultimately human) autonomy or the perpetuation of female dependence.

This criterion will allow that sometimes autonomy is promoted by giving women access to men's preserves, and that it may also be promoted by encouraging men to participate in 'women's work' (such as unpaid domestic work) or by devising special arrangements to take account of institutionalised gender differentiation. Thus it is the human *consequences* of social arrangements, rather than the *form* of those arrangements, that we must understand. In this chapter I use the 'lens' of dependence and autonomy to avoid prejudging what liberation will look like by declining to accept the false choice between compelling women to conform to androcentric standards *versus* the perpetuation of disadvantage.

This discussion opens with a consideration of the interplay between women's health on the one hand and their general social position (life chances) on the other. I then take a detailed look at one of the major mechanisms in the medical social control of women: the medicalisation of reproduction. Since the overwhelming majority of Australian women have had or will have at least one pregnancy and confinement, it is essential to understand the modern character of this basic feminine process. With these perspectives as background, I turn attention to a major new health policy initiative of State and federal governments, the prevention of disease (or health promotion), and examine how some particular aspects of the policy may affect women. The chapter concludes with an analysis of the health implications of non-market work.[1]

The socially significant body

In a book on women, social policy and social welfare, there are important reasons for giving attention to health.[2] Radical critics have pointed to the social control functions performed by many welfare and health agencies. Indeed, medicine is seen to have acquired many social control functions previously exercised by the law and the church (Illich, 1975; Zola, 1972). In several ways, the social control function of medicine is amplified in the case of women. Deviant women are often seen as 'sick' rather than as 'bad' (see Ehrenreich and English, 1973; Fox, 1978; Gilman, 1899/1973; Levy, 1976). Hiller (1978) and Smart (1977: 96) discuss illness as an alternative to crime for women.

I have argued elsewhere (Darroch, 1978: Chapter 10) that the female body is more socially significant than that of the male; that is, a woman's body has a more powerful effect on her social experience, life chances, and personal alternatives. This is a consequence of two factors: a material factor and a symbolic factor. First, materially, a woman's ability to control her reproduction is essential to her autonomy because of the pervasive influence of maternity on a woman's mobility, earning power, health, and the allocation of her resources. It is clear that a woman's status—her life chances in the broadest sense of that term—depends profoundly and directly on the occurrence, number, and timing of her children. Second, symbolically, women's bodies are more socially significant because women's 'animality is more manifest' (de Beauvoir, 1952: 239). Although both man and woman are animals with culture, woman's natural or bodily aspect is more strongly stressed than man's. Ortner observes that

> ... proportionally more of woman's body space, for a greater percentage of her lifetime, and at some—sometimes great—cost to her personal health, strength, and general stability, is taken up with the natural processes surrounding the reproduction of the species. (Ortner, 1974: 75)

Although both women and men participate in both nature and culture, they are perceived to participate disproportionately and this imbalance is projected into social organisation.

In sum, woman's body is significant both materially or directly, and symbolically or indirectly. Consequently situations where woman's physical nature and its social consequences are defined, modified, affirmed, legitimised, or denied will figure strongly in the social control of women and in their status allocation. Thus, health and medical issues are central to any analysis of women's general situation.

Furthermore, women have a disproportionate exposure to 'things medical'. Their extra exposure has at least five distinct aspects: First, women may be 'sicker' (i.e. have higher rates of morbidity) than men, although some people argue that this comparison is the result of differences in reporting rather than real differences in illness rates (Nathanson, 1977). Second, there is no doubt that women attend doctors more frequently than men, even allowing for the fact that contraception and obstetrics contribute substantially to women's higher rates of attendance. Third, women go to doctors not only for their own medical care but also as the chaperones of the young and the old. Fourth, women take more medicines (both prescribed and over-the-counter) than men, although perhaps not more drugs overall when tobacco and alcohol are counted. Finally, women enter medical settings in health as well as in sickness because of the medicalisation of fertility control and childbirth.

For many reasons, then, medicine is a potent instrument in the social control of women, and there are frequent and routine opportunities for the exercise of that control. The process of medicalisation is one of the central mechanisms of medical social control, and the medicalisation of reproduction is, in turn, a central mechanism in the medical control of women.

The medicalisation of reproduction

One of the most dramatic features of the rise of modern medicine has been the gradual shift of birth and birth control out of the hands of lay people and women into the hands of professional men (Wertz and Wertz, 1977). Despite efforts to regulate such practices, traditional forms of birth control have been used throughout human history[3], sometimes successfully, as we can see from the Australian fertility decline of the 1880s (Caldwell, 1980). With the 'contraceptive revolution' of the mid twentieth century, several major forms of birth control (oral contraceptives, IUDs, surgical sterilisation, and early safe abortion) have been developed as monopolies of the medical establishment. Even paramedical personnel and nurses are not permitted to provide these forms of birth control except in unusual circumstances. Medicine is a high-status male-dominated profession whose practitioners show little awareness of the costs and benefits of contraceptives to women themselves (Darroch, 1978). Yet nearly all Australian women rely, for at least part of their lives, on doctor-controlled contraception (Caldwell, 1980: 18). Thus, women have become dependent on doctors for one of the crucial elements of their life and health. Because the significance of medicalised contraception is well covered by others (Gordon, 1976) I will turn attention to a parallel process: the medicalisation of child bearing.

The medicalisation of pregnancy and birth has several components, beginning clearly with the verification of pregnancy itself.[4] Even women who have been pregnant before and are familiar with the signs often rely on doctors and laboratory procedures to tell them whether they are 'really' pregnant. For the woman who seeks or agrees to routine medical supervision of her pregnancy, the ensuing months will be organised around gradually more frequent visits to the doctor and the use of a range of clinical and laboratory procedures to monitor her and her baby's condition. Medicines may be prescribed. The doctor can become the arbiter of a range of personal decisions such as travel, sexual activity, or whether (or when) to give up paid work. Here is an exchange between a pregnant woman and her doctor which exemplifies the pattern:

Patient: I'm a hairdresser, I only do three days a week—is it all right to go on working?

Doctor: Up to twenty-eight weeks is all right on the whole, especially if you have a trouble-free pregnancy as you obviously have. After that it's better to give up.

Patient: I only work three days a week. I feel fine.

Doctor: Yes, everything is fine, but now you've got to this stage it's better to give up, just in case. (Oakley, 1980: 19)

The medicalised pregnancy is concluded with a medicalised confinement, in most instances conducted in a hospital, supervised by trained (often specialist) medical staff. Even the timing of the confinement may be a technical decision rather than the result of the spontaneous onset of labour (Oakley, 1979). Birth is often medicated, and increasingly involves the intervention of technological and surgical procedures (Cartwright, 1979). Since the majority of women remain in the hospital for several days after the birth, the neonate is incorporated into the medical model, and first days of the mother/infant relationship may be heavily influenced by the perceptions, values, and beliefs of medical staff. Hospital schedules and routines take precedence over the needs or feelings of the mother or baby in such matters as separation of mother from newborn, the timing or frequency of feeds, use of supplementary feeds, encouragement or suppression of lactation, and access of family and friends to the mother or baby.

The physical, emotional, and social distress caused by these practices are now the subjects of heated debate. Critics argue that for every high-risk pregnancy helped by 'the new obstetrics', many more are subjected to unnecessary, unpleasant, expensive and occasionally dangerous procedures (Haire, 1974). From a woman's point of view, there can be a number of problems created by the medicalisation of pregnancy and birth. I will enumerate only some of these. Pregnant women are stripped of their other identities until their pregnancy becomes the only relevant issue. 'Obstetricians define women as pregnant patients and exclude other social and emotional considerations as irrelevant to childbearing' (Oakley, 1980: 28). Admission to the labour ward is preceded by enemas and pubic shaves which many women find degrading and painful, and which diminish the woman's ability to cope with her contractions. For some, having to labour lying down is uncomfortable and slows progress since the woman is working against rather than with the law of gravity. Unwanted anaesthesia deprives the woman of awareness of her contractions and diminishes her capacity to push effectively; and ironically analgesics may be withheld from women who want them as medical staff assert their expertise even in the matter of the subjective experience of pain (Lennane and Lennane, 1977). Once the baby is born, the mother may be distressed if she is only allowed limited or scheduled contact with her infant. Perhaps it is not surprising, then, that some women are electing to deliver their babies outside hospitals, even if occasionally no medically qualified person attends the birth.

Gradually, some hospitals and some doctors are modifying their routines to take account of these concerns, although professional opposition to home birth remains substantially unchanged. Pregnant women are encouraged to take preparation classes at hospitals from professional childbirth educators. Husbands are increasingly permitted or even encouraged to attend the birth of their children and to 'coach' their wives in labour. (Indeed, one midwife I interviewed expressed the concern that couples were being pressured into having the husband present, even when they preferred otherwise.) In some hospitals, home-like birth suites are being built, rooming in has been accepted, and visiting regulations are being relaxed. Some doctors are reconsidering their routine use of intervention and will permit practices such as a 'Leboyer' bath and breast feeding immediately after delivery.

These reforms are welcome. They diminish the association between pregnancy and disease, make hospitals more human places, and for many women improve the quality of the birth experience. All of these gains are important, and I do not discount them. At the same time we must also be aware that while some practices are being altered, the essential underlying assumptions remain unchanged. Pregnancy and birth are still viewed as medical conditions which require management by an expert who retains responsibility for decision making. Doctors are still in charge of childbirth, medical decision-making prevails, and these bodily functions remain confined to medical definition in medical settings.

The guiding principle is still that 'doctors know more about having babies than women do' (Oakley, 1980: 11). When a change occurs, it is because doctors are persuaded that it is of value. For example, empirical research on bonding between infants and mothers is cited to encourage changes in clinical practice such as the routine use of anaesthesia, breast-feeding as soon as possible after delivery, and rooming in. The responsibility for the decision, however, still resides with the doctor, and a patient who is dubious or refuses to accept the doctor's decision is considered misguided at best and mentally disturbed at worst, rather than as a rational adult whose evaluation of an option varies from the doctor's.

Although women have many health and medical experiences unrelated to reproduction, the medicalised reproduction is a crucial link which establishes the doctor as a central source of help and authority in the woman's life, identifies medicine as a relevant institution for the management of life problems, and sets (or confirms) the pattern of deference and dependence.

With that perspective in mind, I turn now to an analysis of one of the major health policy initiatives of modern western governments and medical institutions: 'prevention'.

The new prevention

A significant change in general health policy during the last decade has been the revival of the venerable tradition of prevention (rather than cure) and its extension to the concept of 'health promotion'. Curative medicine is acknowledged to be effective in only a limited number of conditions. Most ill health today is either minor and self-limiting or else chronic and degenerative and the chronic conditions are attracting increased interest. Since diet, exercise, and consumption of tobacco and alcohol are implicated in several of the chronic diseases that are called the 'new epidemics', the potential of prevention has been rediscovered.

Prevention appeals to almost everybody. Private citizens look forward to less illness and employers hope to avoid lost production. Prevention is usually estimated to be less expensive than cure. Only the tobacco and alcohol lobbies appear to be actively opposed to prevention policies and health promotion campaigns, although there are also considerable bureaucratic and ideological constraints on the successful delivery of health promotion in Australia (Davidson, Chapman and Hull, 1979: Chapter 10).

At least one 'preventive' campaign is exclusively for women: breast self-examination for the early detection of breast cancer. But we can raise several questions about the relevance to women of much of the new prevention since several of the target conditions (notably alcoholism and heart disease) are more common in men than in women, although heart disease is a major killer of women as well as men. On the other hand, a health promotion campaign aimed at women's problems would almost certainly include arthritis which was reported by women more often than the common cold in the 1977–78 Australian Health Survey, and afflicts about twice as many women as men (Australian Bureau of Statistics, 1981a: Table 19). Other aspects of the new prevention hold out little promise for women because many women will find it difficult to apply the recommended measures to their own lives.

For example, in modern health promotion breast-feeding is encouraged as beneficial to both mother and child. Ironically, certain social policies developed for other purposes have the unintended consequence of making breast-feeding more difficult. Any 'crackdown' on the terms of maternity leave discourages breast-feeding among women who return to work, whereas generous maternity leave provisions (regarding eligibility and duration of leave) enable employed women to establish and maintain lactation. Paternity leave allowed fathers of newborns to provide support; the cancellation of that program must place added demands on the mother, thus diminishing the personal resources she is able to invest in her infant. A third factor discouraging breast-feeding is the lack of childcare for young babies, particularly creches at the place of employment. Women who return to paid work soon after the birth of a baby (whether because of inadequate maternity leave or for other reasons) must discontinue breast-feeding at that time; and if a woman knows she will have to wean her baby early, she may opt not to breast-feed in the first place. It seems contradictory to publicise the virtues of breast-feeding without at the same time implementing the kinds of policies that would enable women to adopt it.

that preventive health care is at worst harmless and often of value. The point is that there are hidden costs of the new prevention, and just as the benefits are not uniformly accessible, some of the costs of prevention are being borne unequally. Women's liberation notwithstanding, women still do most housework and care-giving (Darroch and Mugford, 1980; Szalai, 1972). Household work is unpaid and thus omitted from the national accounting, so it appears that changes in diet and lifestyle are essentially 'free'. In fact, there may be considerable costs, but because the costs are incurred in the course of unpaid work, they are invisible and difficult to calculate or redistribute.

The expansion of women's responsibilities as unpaid domestic health workers conceals the real cost of health care to the nation (Waerness, 1978), and at the same time it contributes to the 'domestication' of women by diminishing their capacity for paid work, emphasising their household responsibilities, and reinforcing women's tendency to discount their own needs in favour of the needs of others (particularly family).

Furthermore, there are hazards in attributing responsibility for their family's health to women. Competent adult males should not require someone to supervise their health any more than adult females, yet the implication of putting women in charge of their family's health is that the men cannot look after themselves (let alone their children). This is quite a different matter from the sharing of mutual concern and support for another person's efforts to get or stay well. Giving women the exclusive task of nurturance unbalances social relations from infancy onwards (Chodorow, 1978; Rich, 1976). It is important that men as well as women take responsibility for care-giving, in sickness and in health, if the bonds between women and nurturance are not to be tightened.

This discussion of nurturance leads directly to a broader issue of which nurturance is one aspect, namely non-market work in care-giving and housework.

Health problems of nonmarket work: slipping through the safety net

Whether or not they are also in paid employment, most women do substantial amounts of nonmarket (unpaid) work in their own households. Women in a 12-nation study spent between 20 and 80 hours per week on housework, depending on whether they also did paid work. Women's nonmarket work—housework and caregiving[6]—is a source of a number of health issues and health problems for women. These issues and problems arise from three general sources: (i) the domestic typifications of women, that is, the tendency to define women in terms of their domestic situation regardless of the salience of their other roles; (ii) the devaluation of housework and care-giving because they are not market activities; and (iii) the nature of the work itself. Some of the health problems of houseworkers are unique to full-time houseworkers; other difficulties are peculiar to women who combine paid work and housework. However most of the discussion deals with problems to which the majority of women are at least potentially vulnerable simply because, whatever else they do, they do substantial amounts of housework. I will discuss each of the three groups of problems briefly. (For a more extensive treatment of these issues, see Darroch, 1981.)

Domestic typifications
Recent suggestions from government and the press that married women should relinquish their paid jobs in favour of school-leavers are an indication that myths and stereotypes about women's involvement in the labour force persist. Leaving aside issues of practicality (whether school-leavers could do the work currently done by married women) and justice (whether any category of person has more right to employment than any other), this suggestion ignores the fact that most women in the labour force are there for the same reasons that most men are. However, doctors (Darroch, 1978: Chapter 7) and bureaucrats may assume that a woman can 'always go back to being a housewife' if she is unable to obtain paid work. Consequently, when a woman suffers sickness or injury that impairs her capacity for employment, the importance of her paid work may be discounted, and she may be redefined according to her domestic status, real or imagined. A woman injured at work was encouraged by her doctor to apply for a widow's pension (Watson, 1980: 3). This domestic typification also occurs in the under-enumeration of female unemployment and the tendency to discount the significance of unemployment among women (see Chapters 2, 6 and 7).

Devalued domestic work
The social devaluation of housework and the omission of housework from the market where 'real work' occurs is another source of health problems for women. Many of the health policies in contemporary Australia are organised around the labour force. The policies are designed to protect people on the job (occupational health and safety regulations), to support sick and injured workers (sickness benefits) and to return them to jobs (rehabilitation schemes), and to maintain them if they become incapacitated for work (workers' compensation and invalid pensions).[7] Because these policies are developed according to the implicit assumption that male work patterns are 'normal', and because they are often implemented by people with stereotyped views of women, women workers have difficulties obtaining benefits com-

Another element of health promotion is exercise. Exercise and re-laxation are as relevant to a woman's health as to a man's[5], but there are reasons to suspect that certain categories of women will find it especially difficult to undertake exercise programs or find time to relax. Employed women who carry the heavy demands of both domes-tic work and paid work have very little time to spend on themselves. Women with preschool children also have little 'free' time. A study conducted in Melbourne in 1974 found that two-thirds of the women surveyed 'did not participate regularly in *any* outside activities' (Anderson, 1975: 32; italics mine), and the proportion was higher for women in full-time employment and highest among employed women with young children (87 per cent had no regular outside activities). Since 'outside activities' also included such things as craft, club, volunteer and social activities, the proportions of women who did sport or any exercise regularly would have been considerably smaller.

However, even women who apparently have the time may encoun-ter other barriers in the form of attitudes, beliefs, and values about feminine behaviour. The Melbourne study found that women often felt that they had no right to interests outside the home or to engage in activities that were for their own benefit. Apparently people believe that a woman 'could have outside activities only at the expense of her family and consequently they were disapproved.... Women who do follow an interest or activity tend to experience feelings of guilt or selfishness' (Anderson, 1975: 64). Wives of professional men were much more likely to be involved in activities outside the home than others.

The problem of fatigue among employed women, particularly those in low-status occupations, must be mentioned in this context, al-though it has much wider health implications than the inability to undertake healthy exercise. The factory worker who stands for eight hours on a noisy, poorly ventilated shop floor worrying about her children and then goes home to the second shift of domestic work hardly exemplifies the 'healthy lifestyle'. One wonders how much of the new prevention can be relevant to her.

Domestic health workers and prevention

Apart from the fact that certain benefits of the new prevention appear to have little relevance to women, another potential problem with 'health promotion' derives from women's role as 'domestic health workers' (Wallen, Waitzkin and Stoeckle, 1979). This apt term refers to women's activities as the health administrators for their families and as lay care-givers who look after sick family and friends. Ap-parently the nurturant elements of female roles are generalised to put women 'in charge' of family medical care. Women make medical appointments for their husbands and children, and if someone needs to be taken to the doctor it is almost always an adult female who takes them. The dependent elderly living with their children are more likely to live with their daughters than with their sons (Newman, 1976). People with an elderly parent report spending considerable amounts of time in their care. Looking after an ailing husband or child is a common activity for a women (Waerness, 1978).

In addition, responsibility for the family's preventive care now appears to be falling to women, incorporated into their nursing and other domestic tasks. For example, diet is considered to be an important part of the prevention or management of a number of conditions such as hypertension, heart disease, diabetes, obesity, and various disorders of the digestive system. Since women do the meal planning, shopping, and food preparation in most households, the provision of an appropriate 'preventive' diet has become part of the job. (That job, incidentally, is unnecessarily difficult for whoever does it because of the inadequacy of food labelling in Australia.) Meal preparation thus becomes more than an ordinary domestic task; now it is directly implicated as contributing to (or detracting from) the health of the family or a particular person who is 'at risk' or already suffering from a specific condition. It is no longer enough to serve food that a woman believes to be wholesome and 'good' for her family; now she must be educated in the new prevention, perhaps do considerable research as part of regular shopping, and learn a new set of food preparation skills. The diet may not have been prescribed for the woman, but putting the diet into practice and insuring conformity to it is probably going to be her job. The door is left open to blame the woman for the family's ill health if she has not implemented an appropriate health-promotion program. For example, a current television advertisement for the New South Wales north coast 'Healthy Lifestyle' campaign shows a woman inadvertently 'drowning' her innocent, helpless husband and children in cooking fat.

It may even be part of the woman's nurturant responsibility to supervise her husband's daily medication. An American women's magazine instructed its readers:

> See to it that any family member who's been put on antihypertension drugs takes them faithfully. One wife puts her husband's pills by his plate at every meal, while another puts the midday pills in her husband's lunchbox before he goes off to work. A third packs a supply of pills in her husband's suitcase when he goes on a business trip. (*Women's Day*, 8 March 1977)

The same article told the housewife to maintain a calm emotional atmosphere in the household (since stress is a management factor in the new prevention), to encourage adequate exercise and a healthy 'life-style' for the members of her family.

Of course such care-giving can be worthwhile, and there is evidence parable to those of their male colleagues. For example, until 1978 the eligibility criteria of the Australian Government Rehabilitation Service discriminated against women; although the official criteria were then widened, there are so few places in the program that the criteria may not have been changed in practice.

> Given that the service was only able to cater for 6 per cent of those people referred to it before the change in eligibility . . . it is unlikely that significantly more women will now be accepted because they are still less likely to be regarded as priority patients in terms of re-entry into the workforce. (Owen and Shaw, 1979: 86)

Judyth Watson reports that in Western Australia 'no woman has ever been admitted to a rehabilitation programme in sheltered workshop retraining' (personal communication, 1981). Inadequate rehabilitation can only compound women's dependence, relegating workers whose incomes were probably low before disability to even less skilled lower income work or removing them from the market entirely.

Watson also finds that many employed women are reluctant to claim compensation either because they believe they are not entitled to it or because they fear they will lose their jobs. Even when they do lodge a claim, women may have difficulty getting compensation because of doctors' tendency to trivialise women's sickness and injury. Women who make compensation claims 'receive an average of 23 per cent less money than men and cases for women take 13 per cent longer to process to their conclusion' (Owen and Shaw, 1979: 76).

Houseworkers who are not in the labour force are not eligible for the benefits and protections reserved for paid workers, and even women who do paid work as well as housework do not enjoy any of the privileges of 'workers' with respect to their housework. House-workers cannot claim sickness or recreation leave, sickness benefits, or workers' compensation. Furthermore their workplace is not subject to safety standards or inspection other than those applying to the dwelling itself. Similarly, the appliances and chemicals used by houseworkers are approved for general distribution to consumers, but the houseworker 'is usually exposed to these substances more intensively and for longer periods of time than other family members' (Morton and Ungs, 1980: 345).

The disabled houseworkers' situation illustrates the problem. Because their activities are not regarded by the government as work, some of the arrangements for tax relief and disabled persons' subsidies are not available to them. For example, if a disabled person requires a car for transportation to and from work, the car may be exempted from sales tax. A disabled mother is not entitled to this exemption, even though she also requires a car to perform her unpaid, socially important work. Similarly, the purchase of typewriters and other aids to independent function are subsidised for disabled workers who work for pay but not for those whose work is unpaid.

'Occupational' health hazards
Some of the health problems of houseworkers are consequences of the work itself in much the same way that any other occupation has its own health hazards. Reference has already been made to the worker's exposure to hazardous equipment and chemicals. Another health problem is long hours. Full-time houseworkers have a 50–80 hour work week, as long as houseworkers did half a century ago (Vanek, 1974). When paid and unpaid work are combined, the employed woman has the longest week of any worker (Robinson et al., 1972). Hence, it is not surprising that fatigue and depression are common complaints among houseworkers, particularly those who work the double shift of paid and unpaid work. Women caring for children, the sick, and the elderly are typically 'on call' day and night; their sleep may be interrupted as is their performance of housework and other tasks.

Caring for sick family members also exposes women to increased risk of infectious disease which may contribute to women's higher average rates of acute illness compared to men's (Nathanson, 1977). Wives of men in some industries are vulnerable to the same occupational diseases as their husbands, without the meagre comforts of workers' compensation. 'Asbestos and other mineral dusts are absorbed by the workers' clothing' and can cause disease in women who launder the clothes or in other family members (Owen and Shaw, 1979: 54). Similar health hazards may face wives of pharmaceutical workers. For example, Epstein (1978: 227) reports on health problems among employees exposed to dust containing high levels of DES; however, he does not mention whether the wives of plant employees were examined. I assume they were not, although the health hazards to women and their babies from DES exposure are well documented. The same question might be raised regarding wives of many other industrial and agricultural workers.

An ironic corollary of women's responsibility for domestic health work is that when they themselves get sick or old, there is often no one able and willing to care for the care-givers. The norm (that care-giving is women's work) is reinforced by a variety of formal and informal arrangements that render others incompetent or unavailable to provide family care. 'Women who need nursing will more often be dependent on the public health and social services than men' (Waerness, 1978: 203). This is only partly a consequence of demographic factors: the age-specific death rate is higher among men than women, and the pattern that women marry men their age or slightly older resulting in an excess of widows over widowers in the older population. But even husbands who are alive and well encounter barriers to assuming caring roles. Employers are not usually tolerant of workers who seek special considerations to undertake care-giving, especially if it is prolonged (a fact of which women have been aware for some time). A man with a paid job will experience the same burdens as an employed mother if he attempts to add significant care-giving to his labour force work. Furthermore, the expectation that women will do the care-giving deprives males of opportunities to acquire caring skills. We are startled and perhaps a little uncomfortable when we encounter men in nursing, infant schools, or taking major responsibility for their own children; men's capacity for nurturance has been expressed so rarely in recent times that it has required empirical documentation (Russell, 1979, for example).

The dearth of care-givers is compounded for a sick or elderly houseworker because she lives at the place of work. Thus, it is impossible for her to be sent 'home' from work or for her to be officially exempted from her normal role responsibilities as paid workers are. Unless she is hospitalised, the houseworker is liable to remain, to some extent, 'on the job' despite illness or injury. I am aware of no studies investigating directly whether these circumstances exacerbate illness or retard recovery, although at least some doctors in my study implied that they felt women's domestic work prevented them taking proper care of their own health (Darroch, 1978: 175). Gove and Hughes (1979) claim to show that women's obligation to care for others and the absence of reciprocal care (of others for women) contributes to women's 'excess' morbidity.

Conclusion

There is little reason to expect that medical dominance will diminish in the near future. Advocates of the medical model enjoy special authority in modern societies which are heavily influenced by technical experts. The power of experts and medical social control are especially significant to women in light of the centrality of the body and its processes in social definitions of women, and the importance of reproduction and fertility control to a woman's life chances. Hence, the medicalisation of reproduction and the medical control of life are central to an understanding not only of women's health but of their social position more generally.

This chapter has shown that some health policies and patterns of medical care directly or indirectly contribute to women's social subordination. Through the analysis of several specific examples, I have shown how health and welfare policies frequently perpetuate women's dependence rather than promoting autonomy. Particular attention has been given to women's domestic activities (including reproduction) and the movement of women between private (domestic) and public spheres. Social constructions of domestic activities appear to constitute a major stumbling block in the ways of true social welfare. I have sought to identify and examine some of the unanticipated consequences of social arrangements and to make explicit several assumptions about women that are usually tacit; this has permitted an examination of how these arrangements and assumptions relate to women's health and welfare.

I conclude that human wellbeing will remain elusive while major responsibility for non-market domestic and care-giving work are ascribed to women, and while the health of paid workers is purchased, even partly, at the expense of the health of unpaid workers. At a time when governments are seeking to divest themselves of many health and welfare expenses, and thus to enlarge 'the invisible welfare state' relying substantially on women, these conflicts acquire a special urgency.

Notes

1 The focus is on policies that have a latent tendency to impair the health or welfare of women. I do not assume that all of the welfare state arrangements in contemporary Australia have such negative consequences; women's refuges are an example of a welfare initiative with direct benefit to women and children. But since the manifest function of welfare state policies is to promote (or at least protect) health and welfare, and because official documents of the state describe the manifest functions, I direct attention to the unintended outcomes.

2 A variety of definitions of 'health' have been proposed by people attempting to understand health policy and health and illness behaviour. Space does not permit a discussion of the implications of the various possible definitions; in this chapter I use the term health to refer to the capacity to perform one's normal role responsibilities. Such a definition takes account of the fundamentally *social* character of health and illness, and avoids dependence on medical criteria without discounting the relevance of a person's medical condition to his or her health status. The definition does not stipulate who determines an individual's health status, since the right to declare onself or another as healthy or ill can be a subject of dispute.

3 Including abstinence, abortion, and infanticide; barrier methods are considered 'traditional' in modern 'family planning'.

4 I omit from this discussion two related questions: medical management of subfertility and infertility; and 'genetic counselling'. Recent developments in test tube conception, amniocentesis, and other forms of reproductive technology deserve a chapter of their own.

5 Perhaps more so since more women than men report suffering from 'mental disorders, nervous tension, and depression' (Australian Bureau of Statistics, 1981a: 28).

6 I will not discuss other non-market work here; see Baldock's chapter on volunteerism in this volume. I use the term 'houseworker' to refer to the person who does unpaid domestic work for three reasons. First, the term is not sex-specific, so it could be applied to male workers as well as females, although currently Australian men do comparatively little of this work (Krupinski and Mackenzie, 1979). Second, this term does not specify the marital status of the houseworker as 'housewife' does. Third, the term is a non-evaluative reference to what the person *does*—work in a

house—rather than mystifying the actual activities involved as the word 'homemaker tends to do.

7 It is not within the scope of this chapter to comment on the adequacy of any of these programs from the point of view of workers and their families, or on the difficulties experienced by both men and women in claiming their entitlements. The discussion here will be confined to particular problems of women.

14 Volunteer work as work: some theoretical considerations

CORA V. BALDOCK

In this final chapter a number of themes of this book by now familiar to the reader, will reappear. This is not surprising; the work of volunteers in late twentieth century society represents most markedly the features of the capitalist state and of patriarchy.

For the purpose of this discussion I define a volunteer as a person who, on a regular basis, contributes services without receiving remuneration commensurate with the economic value of the services rendered, and as part of a voluntary agency concerned with the provision of social care and/or the development of social policy.[1] I exclude volunteer work done for leisure organisations, religious groups, professional associations and trade unions, except where this volunteer work concerns the provision of social services or social policy formulation for what economists somewhat quaintly describe as the 'common good'.[2]

My definition is deliberately narrow. I am aware that a full understanding of labour market processes under capitalism can be reached only if and when an explanation is given of *all* work activities and the reasons why they are allocated to specific groups on a paid or unpaid basis. However, my definition excludes activities which are not a regular commitment, or are primarily carried out as leisure-time pursuits. Especially, the definition allows a focus on work processes which take place in an important sector of the labour market, that dealing with social welfare, and which generally complement, extend, are identical to, or are even substitute for, work done by paid workers. In this sense the definition functions as an 'ideal type' in that it postulates that such volunteer work consists of: 'those activities which were done by a person outside the market but may have been accomplished by hiring a third-person from the economic market ... (Hawrylyshin, 1978: 4).[3] In this chapter, then, I assume that volunteer work carried out within voluntary agencies in the social welfare sector is *work*, albeit unpaid, and should be studied as part of the labour market in the same manner as the work of paid social welfare personnel.[4]

The crucial question which follows from this thesis concerns the reasons why such work remains unpaid. Some tentative answers to this question are advanced based on my understanding of the economic value of the voluntary sector for capitalism, and of the relationship between patriarchy and capitalism in determining the position of women (and men) in paid and unpaid labour as discussed in Chapter 2 of this book. There I dealt with the interrelationship between domestic labour and paid labour; in this chapter I am concerned with three kinds of labour: unpaid domestic, unpaid volunteer, and paid work.

It is argued in this chapter that volunteer work fulfils an essential economic and ideological function for the state in providing social welfare services which could be provided by governments. These functions become of crucial importance during times of economic crisis when governments reduce welfare spending and the voluntary sector is placed under considerable pressure to increase services in these welfare areas.

It is further argued that voluntary agencies are only able to satisfy the changing—and ever increasing—demands for their services because of the availability of unpaid *female* volunteers who combine volunteer labour with other unpaid work, namely that carried out in the domestic setting.

The term 'volunteer' is a controversial one, which many feminists reject. Hartmann, for example, remarks that few women have a choice about 'volunteer work': 'Women have so few options that we are reduced to working for nothing in order to keep from getting thrown on the scrap heap of a society that does not want us' (1975: 775). Although I agree with such arguments and would prefer to use the term 'unpaid social service worker' I have retained the word 'volunteer' in recognition of the fact that generally women who are engaged in unpaid social service work, and the organisations for which they work (but not those engaged in social action-oriented unpaid work) continue to define their activities as those of a volunteer.

The political economy of volunteerism

Volunteer work as an economic activity
It has been estimated that there are at present in Australia about 37 000 non-governmental welfare organisations with 'in excess of 100,000 employees plus many tens of thousands of voluntary workers' (Graycar and Yates, 1981: 1) As Graycar and Yates report, these organisations receive annually around 900 million in cash, 65 per cent of which comes directly from government, with the remainder derived from donations, bequests, endowments (27 per cent), and fees or

charges (8 per cent). There are no national data available yet on how much these organisations receive in the form of volunteer labour time, 'labour grants' as Boulding (1973) called them, in addition to cash grants, but case studies indicate that the amount of unpaid labour time donated by volunteers may be considerable. For example, a study conducted in the Bendigo area in 1979 shows that 31.2 per cent of all people over 15 years of age out of a population of 12 131 persons, usually do volunteer work, to an average of 6.38 hours per week. It was estimated in that study that the overall amount of time given in volunteer work in that community could add up to 7 500 person-days per week, or the equivalent of 1 500 full-time working persons (Paterson, 1979).[5]

An assessment of the economic value of such unpaid volunteer time for the whole of Australia, for example, by means of an estimate of minimum hourly wage rates of paid workers in equivalent positions, would not doubt reveal that labour grants make a considerable economic contribution. This is substantiated by research conducted in other countries. For example, Hawrylyshin (1978) estimated from several Canadian studies conducted in the early 1970s that volunteers contributed a weekly average of 5 hours per week, to an overall average value of about $830 per volunteer per year, suggesting an aggregate value of volunteer work at between 1.1 and 3.0 per cent of GNP. Studies done in the United States by the Department of Labor in 1965, and by the Census Bureau in 1974, assessed the number of volunteers in 1965 at 22 million, or 16 per cent of the population over the age of 16, contributing 5.3 hours of their time in volunteer work per week; and at 37 million in 1974, for an average of about 9 hours per week (Mueller, 1975; Filer Commission, 1977; Manser, 1979). For 1974, the monetary value of volunteer time in the United States was estimated at US$22.6 million million (Filer Commission, 1977). The American data include a wider range of volunteer activities than I allowed for in my definition and estimates of the economic value of volunteer work are based on rough measures only.[6] It is apparent, though, that even if only activities in the welfare sector be considered, replacement of volunteer labour by 'market occupation equivalents' (Hawrylyshin, 1978: 37) would be a costly affair. Considering the large amounts of money allocated by governments to voluntary agencies in Australia and in other countries, thereby guaranteeing the continuation of a framework in which volunteers can operate, we have to assume that the unpaid labour of volunteers is considered of value, economic or otherwise, to the national political economy.[7]

The voluntary sector and the welfare state
Charitable organisations have been part of the Australian welfare system from the early days of European settlement, even if they were

not equally important in providing public relief in every state (Mendelsohn, 1979; Kewley, 1980). As Jill Roe describes in Chapter 1, Australian development was not one of 'charity to casework', as in the United Kingdom, because of the relatively late development of professional social work. Instead, it was the machine of government, through its departments of social services which first provided parallel, later competitive services. Mendelsohn (1979) argues that by the time of the 1930s Depression 'old-fashioned' charity had faded away, unable to cope with the volume and nature of problems caused by economic crises. However, this was not to be the final demise of the voluntary sector; in fact, after 1945 a new concept of voluntary action began to emerge. In Mendelsohn's summary:

> Charity in the sense of alms-giving for basic support of the disadvantaged has been largely displaced by government income security services. But if anything the volume, and certainly the quality, of charitable endeavour has been augmented. The emphasis has shifted from income support (though not from income supplementation) to provision of service, sometimes at a highly professional level.... (Mendelsohn, 1979: 128)

It is easily shown, however, that the greatest expansion of the voluntary sector took place in the early 1970s with the development of a wide range of quasi-nongovernmental organisations (QUANGOS) and specific purpose service agencies 'sponsored by or directly encouraged by government' (Graycar and Yates, 1981: 29; see also Hamilton-Smith, 1973). At the same time many self-help and consumer organisations have emerged which, like the service agencies, depend heavily on government funding for their existence. The Australian Assistance Plan, created under the Whitlam government, although of very short duration, is an example of a government initiative which strengthened voluntary community agencies in a variety of areas (Jones, 1980).

Two-thirds of the funding received by voluntary agencies in Australia now comes from the government. This trend is accompanied by increased government control over the operation of non-profit, non-governmental organisations, leading to an increased professionalisation and bureaucratisation of volunteer agencies and a blurring of the boundaries between governmental services and those provided by the private, non-profit sector (Graycar and Yates 1981; Kramer, 1981).

The expansion of volunteer action in the last decades in social welfare areas has also occurred in other countries. For example, in 1969 the Nixon administration in the United States initiated a Cabinet Committee on Voluntary Action, with the expressed purpose of developing a national program for voluntary action which could help 'mobilize and strengthen existing volunteer organizations in a harmonious working relationship with each other and the government' (Ericksson-Joslyn, 1973–74: 162). A national centre and a number of regional Offices for Voluntary Action were set up; at the same time the Center for a Voluntary Society was created as an independent research organisation. One of the professed goals of the center was 'to make volunteers and voluntary organizations more effective not only as agencies of service but also as agents of social change' (Ericksson-Joslyn, 1973–74: 167).[8] In Britain, the establishment of the Wolfenden Committee in 1974 for the investigation of the future of voluntary organisations could possibly be seen as the outcome of similar trends toward increased support for, but also increased scrutiny of, voluntary agencies by government in that country (Wolfenden, 1978).

What are the factors responsible for the re-emergence of the voluntary sector in the contemporary welfare state? Some have answered this question by pointing at the symbolic importance of voluntary agencies as embodiments of the ideal of participatory democracy and the maintenance of political pluralism. Others, however, have explained the growth of the voluntary sector as

> a form of manipulation, pressing citizens into unremunerated public service in order to assuage unrest of citizens' groups hardest hit by recession, unequal opportunities, and differential access to resources and political representation. (Ericksson–Joslyn, 1973–74: 161)

Others, again, see the existence of the voluntary sector as an outcome of economic choice behaviour by individual citizens (Weisbrod, 1977). My explanation is one based on a feminist reading of radical theories of the state and social welfare.

The capitalist state and the voluntary sector:

The state and social welfare
It is generally assumed in the contemporary radical tradition that the state, as an agency of capital,

> must try to maintain or create the conditions in which profitable capital accumulation is possible. However the state must also try to maintain or create the conditions for social harmony. (O'Connor, 1973: 6)

In the language of political economy this means that the state is seen to fulfil two basic functions for capitalism, accumulation and legitimation. When applied to the field of social welfare, the radical perspective assumes that 'the key to an understanding of relief-giving is in the function it serves for the larger economic and political order' (Piven and Cloward, 1971: 3). Specifically, the functions of social welfàre are seen as those of regulating labour for the purpose of the reproduction of labour power and of social control (Piven and Cloward, 1971; O'Connor, 1973; Gough, 1979).

The functions of accumulation and of legitimation are to some extent mutually contradictory; the ambiguities resulting from this imply that government policy in the field of social welfare is not by definition detrimental to the working classes (Gough, 1979; Wright, 1979). Organised political action by unions and other pressure groups may lead to genuine concessions representing a real gain for the working classes (see also Chapters 3 and 6).

Unfortunately few if any contemporary political economists have undertaken an analysis of the voluntary sector in this context. As voluntary agencies dispense social welfare services similar to those provided by governments, it may be suggested that their analysis of the welfare state can be extended to include the voluntary sector as an 'agent' of the state in the process of accumulation and legitimation. It may even be argued that capitalists and governments alike recognise the special advantages accruing from the fact that certain welfare services are being dispensed via the voluntary sector.

Voluntary services and the process of accumulation
The provision of welfare services through the voluntary sector appears to further the process of accumulation, especially under the aspect of social consumption as 'the projects and services that lower the reproduction costs of labor, and other factors being equal, increase the rate of profit' (O'Connor, 1973: 7) in that the essentially cheaper services which the voluntary sector can provide because of donations and labour grants, free government monies for other priorities more directly beneficial to capital accumulation.[9] This is likely to be of particular importance in times of fiscal crisis when the demands made on governments are especially heavy.

Galper (1980) has suggested that at such times the state can apply three remedies, that is (1) to increase the level of taxation; (2) to deny services selectively; or (3) to resist pressures for wage demands from its own employees, the public servants. It would appear, however, that the remedies likely to be most successful economically, as well as most expedient politically, are those which involve government saving through manipulation of the voluntary sector such as may occur by selective cuts in funding to voluntary agencies, or by transfer of responsibilities for certain social welfare provisions to the private, non-profit sector, or even by the impact of unpaid volunteer labour on the wage structure.

Government savings by means of reduction or termination of funding to selected voluntary agencies is, indeed, a common occurrence in Australia at the present time. Although the Australian Council of Social Service (1980, 1981) in its publication *Impact* and other organisation have agitated against such cuts, the proliferation of voluntary agencies and the complexities of funding prevent them from coming to the attention of the general public. Because many of the agencies affected by reductions or even the threat of termination of government funding are economically and politically vulnerable (women's refuges, women's health centres, youth centres, services for Aborigines) they have little opportunity of fighting against these measures. It should be remembered that in Australia many agencies are funded only for limited periods and have to negotiate renewal of funding from year to year, on the basis of carefully prepared budgets conforming to precisely set bureaucratic guidelines.

There is also every indication in Australia that the inability of the state to provide adequate goods and services has placed an increasingly large burden on the voluntary sector. Note, for example, the ever-increasing demands made in the last one or two years on emergency relief funds in the voluntary sector, ranging from urgent requests for blankets and food to pressing demands for financial assistance from people who can no longer afford to make their mortgage payments.[10] Such emergency relief funds are, of course, partly financed by government. It appears, though, that the relatively modest funding supplied by the state—that is, especially when compared with other government expenditure, for example on defence or in the provision of infrastructure to private industry—is more than offset by the savings incurred by diverting the provision of such services to the voluntary sector (Hatch and Mocraft, 1979; Graycar and Yates, 1981; Graycar, 1982).

In Australia, government measures meant to increase the responsibilities of the voluntary sector have been introduced quietly, usually without the necessity of 'selling' such policies to the public. Where such need for public justification and ideological elaboration appears more urgent, as for example in the United States, the links between government cutbacks and increased voluntary action can be clearly observed. The encouragement of volunteer action under the Nixon administration and now again by the Reagan government in the United States, both intent on severe cutbacks in public welfare spending, could certainly be seen in this light (Ericksson-Joslyn, 1973–74; Smith and Freedman, 1972; Los Angeles Times, 1982a).[11] President Reagan gave a clear insight into his administration's priorities in his first State of the Union address in early 1982 when he said:

Together we have begun to mobilize the private sector—not to duplicate wasteful and discredited programs but to bring thousands of Americans into a volunteer effort to help solve many of America's social problems.

Was it coincidence that the President continued, as if in one breath: Together we have begun to restore that margin of military safety that ensures peace. Our country's uniform is being worn once again with pride.' (*Los Angeles Times,* 1982b: 14)

Carmel Shute (1980) has argued, in her study of volunteer work during World War II, that the availability of a vast pool of female volunteers 'competing' for work with paid workers had the effect of depressing status and pay of women in the paid labour market during war years. In her words 'voluntarism [sic] helped to stigmatise women's wage labour as being temporary and, hence, expendable' (Shute, 1980: 23). Shute's analysis concerns a unique period and to my knowledge no similar studies about other periods of Australian history have been conducted. Despite this dearth of information it appears plausible that the availability of volunteer labour has some impact on government's ability to resist pressures for wage demands from public servants (Ericksson-Joslyn, 1973–74; Tideman, 1977).

To recapitulate, it appears that the government is helped considerably in its maintenance of the process of capital accumulation by the existence of the voluntary sector: the savings made by selective cuts in funding to voluntary agencies, or by transfer of responsibilities to the private, non-profit sector, allow the state to give priority to those activities which increase the rate of profit and lower the costs of labour.[12]

The voluntary sector and the process of legitimation
As noted earlier, political economists such as Group (1979) and O'Connor (1973) assume that the state has an important role to play not only in the processes of capital accumulation, but also—and crucially—in the processes of legitimation for the maintenance of social harmony and the prevention of any political unrest which may affect the smooth workings of the capitalist economy. Applying this argument again to the phenomenon of volunteerism it can be seen that the contributions of the voluntary sector have a major impact on the ability of the state to maintain social harmony.

This is due, first of all, to the fact that social services carried out by voluntary agencies are removed from public scrutiny. Board members of voluntary agencies are not responsible to the general public; as most agency funding is administered by the government bureaucracy without interference by Parliament, privileges can be given or withdrawn from agencies without the government having to answer to the electorate. Governments are thus able to give selective support to agencies which conform with government policies and which represent ideologically acceptable social causes (Filer Commission, 1977). In Australia, for example, in at least one state traditional women's refuges have been given greater support by government than refuges run by feminists because of the alleged radical stance taken by feminist refuge organisers vis-à-vis the role of women in the family and the society at large (Reiner, 1980).

Board members of many established voluntary agencies are themselves representatives of private capital or of government (Domhoff, 1970; Higley, Deacon and Smart, 1979) and are likely to have a conservative bias (Graycar and Silver, 1982). All this means, then, that the government bureaucracy is able to exercise a subtle form of social control over the kind of social welfare services available to the general public, *especially* because some of these are dispensed via the voluntary sector without being answerable for these services to the voting public.

There are, of course, many workers in voluntary agencies, paid or unpaid, who are not necessarily supportive of government ideologies and who wish to advance social reforms. However, the dependence of most voluntary agencies on government funding makes agency organisers vulnerable to attempts of co-opting them into the system as a cheap remedy by which 'emerging new, radical or politically threatening elements or leaders of opposed groups' (Ericksson-Joslyn, 1973–74: 168) can be absorbed into an organised body in return for certain specified benefits.

Further, the day-to-day involvement of agency personnel in direct services and administration decreases the likelihood of their participation in genuine political action (Kramer, 1977). As Ericksson-Joslyn notes, this may even happen to groups which aim for radical social change and which become involved in alternative services such as free clinics, communal childcare, or women's refuges. Their efforts may differ from those of established charities, but the results of their activities are the same: 'They enable the establishment to withdraw funds from public services without too much outcry and without tax reform or redirection of funds from military spending' (Ericksson-Joslyn, 1973–74: 177).

That the voluntary sector is available to provide the goods and services necessary for the reproduction of labour and the social wage of citizens which governments can no longer provide without being forced to the unpopular measure of increased taxation, is due in large measures to excessive moral pressures placed on volunteer workers. These moral pressures experienced by voluntary agencies are well described in the following comment by a dedicated volunteer worker in the United States:

'Politicians should not use public media for emotional appeals urging citizens to play their part in making the wheels of our society go round—appeals deliberately designed to arouse guilt feelings—when, at the same time funding of the most urgent social welfare programs is drastically cut back by that same administration'. (Loeser, 1974: 31)

The susceptibility of volunteer workers to these moral pressures can in turn be explained by the ideology of volunteerism which pervades our society and which elevates the motive of altruism—allegedly underlying all volunteer effort—to one of the most cherished human traits (this, of course, ironically, in the context of a society where egoism, self-interest and individual profit-making are assumed to determine most economic transactions). This central focus on altruism as the dominating motive for volunteerism explains why there exists a certain reluctance to examine critically the effectiveness and efficiency of voluntary action. It also means that continuous moral pressure can be exercised on members of society to engage in unpaid volunteer work. After all, if people are made to think that the absence of altruism signifies the absence of an essential human trait, then all voluntary work carried out under the motive of altruism must be good, and cannot be refused.

I mentioned earlier that not all welfare state policies are by definition supportive of the class structure. Gains for the workers can be made by concerted political action. I propose that this also applies to the voluntary sector. The women's movement, the peace movement, and the anti-nuclear energy movement are all examples of voluntary organisations which have acted as political pressure groups and which have, from time to time, contributed to major reforms of benefit to the community at large (Worpole, 1981). The potential for even radical reform instigated by voluntary agencies remains. However, it should be apparent from my assertions regarding the role voluntary associations are required to play in the process of legitimation that I consider the potential limited. The large number of voluntary agencies, not unified around a common cause, and without political party affiliation, are unlikely to create the kind of power base from which radical action can be attempted. Graycar and Yates (1981) hope that ACOSS can provide a context for unified volunteer action for reform. It appears though that so long as ACOSS is dependent on government funding, and so long as it is not affiliated with a political party (as is the case with the trade unions), its chances to bring about effective social charge are slim.

In summary then, it appears that an extension of the radical analysis of the role of the welfare state to the voluntary sector would provide a plausible explanation of the existence of voluntary agencies. It helps to explain the growth of the voluntary sector during periods of economic recession and heavy cutbacks in government spending on social welfare issues. It also makes intelligible the increased government interference in voluntary agencies and demands for greater accountability and professionalism in volunteering. After all, voluntary agencies which remain totally autonomous form a potential threat to social harmony. It is interesting to note though that accountability is usually defined in terms of budgeting and compliance with government regulation. Much less attention appears to be given to accountability in terms of agency goals and their effectiveness in meeting the needs of clients. Would it be reasonable to suggest that governmental demands for accountability provide an additional means of social control over agency personnel?

Volunteer work and the labourmarket: A feminist inquiry

The theoretical argument developed so far in this chapter has led to the inevitable conclusion that the voluntary sector fulfils an essential economic and ideological function for the capitalist state in contributing to the processes of accumulation and legitimation.

My analysis of the political economy of the voluntary sector remains incomplete, though, without a thorough discussion of the issue of volunteer work: the unpaid labour of the volunteer is essential to the survival of voluntary agencies. If voluntary associations were staffed only by professional workers, the cost of service would increase to such an extent that at least the function of the volunteer sector for the process of accumulation could no longer be maintained. Whether under those circumstances agencies would be able to retain their voluntary, non-profit status is questionable.

This, then, leads to the crucial question of how such unpaid volunteer labour can be guaranteed. In other words, *which potential members of the paid labour market display the kind of altruism that makes them willing to forgo the economic rewards of paid work and to dedicate their time and skills to unpaid labour?*

Given the structure and ideology of patriarchy, it seems logical to assume that only women, and especially married women, have the characteristics which guarantee their availability for regular volunteer work: their primary responsibilities to society are not defined, as in the case of men, in terms of their position in paid labour, and altruism, the alleged basic requirement for volunteer work, is commonly assumed to be a typical feminine trait (Adams, 1971; Kravetz, 1976; Tormey, 1976; Cantor, 1978).

Women as volunteer workers
Much of the literature dealing with volunteer work makes the implicit or explicit assumption that the volunteer is a woman. This is inter-

esting in itself because the limited data derived from overseas research on volunteer participation by gender suggest that men also volunteer a considerable amount of time even if generally less than women (L. Smith, 1975; Morgan, Dye and Hybels, 1977). Studies conducted in the United States reveal two significant differences, however, between male and female volunteer work: men do volunteer work in addition to paid work while most women do not, and men have higher positions in their voluntary associations than women.

On the first point, it was found, for example, that about two-thirds of women volunteers in a 1969 USA Department of Labor survey were not in the labour force, as compared with only 15 per cent of male volunteers (L. Smith, 1975). There are no data, to my knowledge, to inform us how much volunteer work by men is conducted during working hours, or how much of the out-of-pocket expenses of male volunteers are covered by their employment. One American study reports a total of US$ 760 million in out-of-pocket expenses for wives, but fails to give similar information for their husbands, thereby leaving us to guess whether husbands did not have such expenses, or were not asked the question (Morgan et al., 1977). The crucial issue, though, is that volunteer work for men is much more readily seen as an extension of their paid work, adding to their prestige and power in the community, while in the case of women volunteer work comes instead of, and as replacement for, paid work.

As to the second point, men's higher rank in voluntary agencies, there is general agreement in the research that:

> men's volunteer hours are predominantly in the more visible and glamorous, higher status categories of leadership and professional skills, while their wives contributed the major share of hours in the less visible, supportive activities of clerical and manual jobs, plus all the 'other' activities which are directly related to the purpose of the charity. (Morgan, et al., 1977: 172)

Men, then, appear to dominate the board of directors of most agencies, setting the policies to be carried out by women. (Hardwick and Graycar, 1982).

The ideology of altruism and the woman volunteer

The structure and ideology of patriarchy ensures the continuation of the myth of motherhood and home-making within western capitalist society. It also ensures the myth of altruism as a female preserve (Tormey, 1976; Blum et al., 1976). As I noted earlier, much of the literatures sees the motive of altruism as an essential factor in the availability of volunteer labour. However, in the tradition of western liberal economic thought altruism is part of the private sphere, of the family and the world of women. As Moller Okin (1979) remarks in her book on the history of western political thought:

> the liberal tradition assumes that the behaviour of its political actors will be based on self-interest. Men with certain natural rights, or at least with certain passions requiring satisfaction, come together in political societies in order to defend themselves from invasion or harassment, and to compete with one another in a market environment. . . .

And further:

> Theorists who have assumed a high degree of egoism to determine relations between individuals in the sphere of the market, have assumed almost total altruism to govern intrafamilial relationships. (Moller Okin, 1979: 284)

Thus, however much altruism is cherished as a human trait it has no place in the public sphere, the world of men. It is women who are seen as the embodiment of the altruistic spirit, of the caring and helping mentality needed for the charitable activities of the voluntary sector (Tormey, 1976). It is women who—both because of their position of economic dependence, and because of the feminine traits they are expected to display—are caught in the 'compassion trap' (Adams, 1971) set by the structure and ideology of capitalist patriarchy.

Unpaid domestic, unpaid volunteer and paid work
In Chapter 2 of this book I discussed the issue of labour market segmentation and the place of women in the labour market as flexible and expendable pools of labour primarily employed in the secondary sector where job security and opportunities for advancement are limited and work conditions are poor. It may now by postulated that female volunteers, like most of their sisters in paid work, are also part of a secondary labour market.

It is generally argued in the literature that volunteer work is a middle-class activity. It is logical to assume this because only the 'middle-class' woman is likely to have time and resources (even if in paid work) to engage in volunteer activities and only the middle-class woman who is not in paid work is likely to engage on a 'volunteer career'. However, as Smith and Freedman (1972) observe, all studies conducted of the social class background of women volunteers use traditional measures of social class, based on husband's or father's occupation. Many women whose husbands have middle-class occupations are themselves in working-class jobs with low pay, or low skill level (Cass, 1978b) or would have been if they had been in paid work; also, informal observation suggests that many low-income female heads of household make an important contribution as volunteers in community action groups such as women's refuges, health centres, or childcare centres.[13] Further, the overall unemployment situation which has forced women out of the paid labour force or into part-time employment, is similarly conducive to participation by low-income women in volunteer work. Whatever the social background of the volunteer, it does appear that apart from a few 'Lady Bountifuls', women's position within volunteering generally remains subordinate with tasks of menial and repetitive nature, and subject to the control of paid staff and male volunteer leaders. This implies that the work conditions of female volunteers, even if, as Gold (1971) suggests, they are part of a petit-bourgeois context, are really those of the working classes.

It may further be suggested that, again like their sisters in paid work, female volunteers form flexible and expandable pools of labour. In time of economic expansion and growth of government services it may be assumed that some of the readily available volunteer labour is channelled into the paid labour force. On the other hand, when in times of economic recession and financial crisis greater demands are made on the voluntary sector, it is only because of the availability of female volunteers that such demands can be met (Gold, 1971).

In Chapter 2 I argued that the sexual division of labour in the family and the separation of the public and private sphere provide a structure and ideology conducive to the maintenance of labour market segmentation by gender. I now conclude that the maintenance of a gender-based volunteer pool of labour appended to the secondary labour market is *also* predicated on the existence of the sexual division of labour in the family. Both volunteer work and paid work of women can thus be seen to depend on the continuation of women's position in domestic labour. It is interesting to speculate what would happen to women's incentive to take up volunteer work as a regular, dependable work activity if truly equal opportunities for women existed in the paid labour market, and if the structural and ideological divisions between 'home-makers' and 'breadwinners' were eradicated. If such a situation occurred, however, it would deprive the capitalist state of the contributions toward accumulation and legitimation made by the voluntary sector. There seems much at stake in the preservation of the sexual division of labour.

The future of volunteer work: some contradictions

The trend toward professionalism

In times when volunteers are given more and more responsibilites for major social services and are even asked to provide services which could be carried out by paid professionals, it is important to ensure that their work is seen to be done efficiently and effectively. On the other hand, increased demands for volunteer labour cannot be met unless the work is made appealing and some special incentives are provided to attract potential recruits to the volunteer sector.

Given the fact that most volunteers performing regular, continuing volunteer tasks are women, and that the increased demand for their services comes at a time when more and more women, including married ones, are hopeful of joining the paid labour force, it is interesting but perhaps not surprising that the incentives offered in recent years to potential recruits for voluntary work have come to focus *not* on the motive of the altruism but on the similarities between voluntary work and paid work, and the professional qualities of work done in the voluntary sector. In reality, the work may not be all that elevated—as noted earlier, much of female volunteer labour is repetitive clerical or manual service work; the promise, though, of a volunteer career figures prominently in the literature (e.g. Mueller, 1975). In the United States this has even led to the development of 'volunteer career' planning programs and to a strong focus on training opportunities in the recruitment of volunteers (L. Smith, 1975; Lauffer and Gorodezky, 1977). For example, Lauffer and Gorodezky, in a manual to be used by voluntary agencies in their recruitment practices, note that volunteers should be made aware of the following concrete rewards offered by volunteer work:

> Opportunities to attend in-service and staff development programs for paid staff.
> Structured career ladder opportunities for more responsible and experienced volunteers...
> Letters of recommendation for future employment or educational endeavors.
> Reimbursement for out-of-pocket expenses...
> Insurance cover while on the job.
> A luncheon or dinner at which staff thank volunteers for their efforts....
> (Lauffer and Godorezky, 1977: 37-8)

In the United States this trend toward professionalism, or rather 'occupationalism' in volunteering, has found pragmatic expression in a number of other ways. Volunteers had begun to demand reimbursement for out-of-pocket expenses, and some expenditures made in the course of volunteering such as telephone use, travel and cost of uniforms became tax-deductible items (L. Smith, 1975; Manser and Cass, 1976). Schemes were developed for the possible introduction of policies regarding tax deductions for volunteer *time*, for the establishment of written agreements spelling out rights and responsibilities of volunteers, and for the provision of insurance protection

(Ericksson-Joslyn, 1973–74; Filer Commission, 1977).

Again in the United States, some federal and state government offices introduced credit for volunteer work in calculating training and experience for the purpose of promotion (L. Smith, 1975: 128); some firms allowed their employees paid time off work to participate in community volunteer activities (Loeser, 1974). Some people were granted leave of absence for up to a year from paid work to take on volunteer work, others interspersed volunteer with paid work, or took on volunteer work when temporarily unemployed (Loeser, 1974).

In Australia such an emphasis on occupationalism has not developed to the same extent, although in many voluntary agencies the need for training is now emphasised, and issues such as out-of-pocket expenses are also subject to discussion. There has even been some talk of a volunteer's bill of rights (Rigby, 1979). Informal observation further suggests that women in Australia use volunteer work as an avenue for gaining experience with paid work as a potential outcome. Whether such opportunities for paid work based on volunteer training exist in reality is not known.

Equal opportunity in volunteer work

Where, parallel to the growth of the voluntary sector as an extension and supplement of government, greater emphasis is placed on professionalism and training, this trend may well put an end to 'haphazard or accidental processes of skill acquisition and utilization in voluntary organizations' (L. Smith, 1975: 120). Some people interested in volunteer work may no longer be seen as suitable, especially where leadership positions are concerned, because they lack the necessary qualifications. Note, for example, this comment in a volunteer training manual: . . . volunteers must be carefully selected and trained for their specific roles and should not be placed into positions for which they are not qualified' (Stenzel and Feeney, 1976: 16). However, decisions on recruitment and job placement in the voluntary sector are taken without any reference to equal opportunity or anti-discrimination legislation. This may lead to the ironic situation in which

> unless egalitarian criteria are used in recruitment, training, assignment and distribution of rewards, women will come to have as little access to another source of social rewards as they have to professional, elective and other paid jobs. (Smith, 1975: 120)

Such a trend would constitute a genuine disadvantage for volunteer workers, who expect that volunteerism will help them towards a future career in paid work.

A related issue of potential discrimination is that of the relationship between volunteers and paid professionals. Paid workers are often heard to complain about lack of training, skill, or general aptitude of volunteers (e.g. Euster, 1980; Kramer, 1981)[14], but it is apparent that with the increased emphasis on professionalisation of volunteering, and the heavy cutbacks in government spending on social welfare, paid employees in the welfare section now have reason to fear the competition of unpaid labour for their own careers.[15]

On the other hand the volunteer experiences a sense of inequality when she is not paid for what amounts to essentially similar services to those carried out by paid workers.

In a situation of 'fiscal crisis' when government funding to welfare is cut and volunteers are asked to do more for less funds, it becomes increasingly difficult not to see volunteers in service work as exploited (e.g. Deagan, 1979). In Australia some paid workers in voluntary agencies (women's refuges) have voluntarily cut their own wages, paid out of inadequate government subsidies, for the sake of the agency's survival (Reiner, 1980). Volunteers under pressure do not even have an income to 'negotiate' with. We may well ask how far altruism will go under such circumstances.

Professionalism and altruism

In order to ensure the continuation of unpaid volunteer labour the motive of altruism needs to be emphasised. On the other hand, the need for well trained volunteer labour, able to cope with the demands of contemporary social service work, calls for a professionalism which requires a desire for self-development and healthy self-interest, most likely leading to aspirations for paid employment. As Ericksson-Joslyn notes, 'professionalization subverts the underlying ideological meaning of volunteering' (1973–74: 178).

In these circumstances it is understandable that volunteers become aware of the fact that they are 'in reality underpaid employed workers' (US Department of Labor, 1969, as quoted in Ericksson-Joslyn, 1973–74).

Ericksson-Joslyn predicts that the trend toward 'professionalism' will make volunteers more aware of the distinction between volunteering as *service* and as a means of *effective political participation*, and that eventually volunteer *service* activities will erode altogether. It is interesting in this context to note a resolution passed at a 1974 Conference of the National Organization for Women (NOW), the largest US reformist women's organisation, that women should be 'only change-oriented volunteers'; service volunteerism was seen as 'exploitation of women designated to keep them in a subordinate position' (Manser and Cass, 1976: 59; Gold, 1979).

The future of volunteerism, thus, appears uncertain. If the pressure continues on the voluntary sector to alleviate the financial crisis of the state and at the same time professionalism remains emphasised as an incentive and as a requirement for responsible service, the inevitable outcome I suggest will be the demise of altruism on the part of women, and their increased demand for economic remuneration and entry into paid work. However, if due to government cutbacks unemployment increases (especially in areas concerned with social services), and no opportunities exist for women to move from volunteer to paid work, there is indeed a considerable chance that they will reject service-oriented volunteer work and channel their skills, experience and any remaining altruism into change-oriented volunteerism, i.e. political activism. The workings of capitalism and patriarchy would then have created a contradiction through their emphasis on mutually contradictory motives of professionalism and altruism, which may lead to genuine social change.

Acknowledgements

I acknowledge with thanks the hospitality offered to me while writing this paper by Joelle Juillard, Director, and other Faculty and staff, of the Program for the Study of Women and Men (SWMS) at the University of Southern California, Los Angeles. I continue to be grateful to Anne Bartlett for stimulating my interest in the volunteer worker, and thank Margaret McAllister and her colleagues at the Social Welfare Research Centre, University of New South Wales for helpful information and encouragement with this project.

Notes

1   This definition combines elements of two definitions, one from the Encyclopedia of Social Work, which defines a volunteer as 'the individual who freely contributes his [sic!] services without remuneration, commensurate with the value of the services rendered, to public or voluntary organizations engaged in preventing, controlling, or ameliorating the affects of social problems experienced by individuals, groups, or communities' (National Association of Social Workers, 1973: 1525), and the other by Graycar and Yates, who define voluntary agencies as 'non-governmental, non-profit, formal organisations concerned with the provision of social care and/or the development of social policy' (1981: 6).

2   See also Kramer's (1981) distinction between *voluntary associations* as membership organisations, usually with a social purpose of benefit to their constituency (eg. religious, service and fraternity organisations, political parties and unions) and *voluntary agencies* as structures essentially bureaucratic in organisation, governed by an elected volunteer board of directors, employing professional or volunteer staff to provide a continuing social service to a clientele in the community.

3   Hawrylyshin (1978) aimed to analyse the economic value of volunteer work by classifying volunteer actions as to their economic and non-economic aspects. It may be noted that Hawrylyshin applied a similar analysis to the value of housework (see Hawrylyshin, 1976).

4   See also Baldock (1980).

5   Hardwick and Graycar (1982) in a study published too late for inclusion in this chapter, estimate a total of between 751 388 and 1 436 398 volunteers or between 7 and 13 percent of the population 15 yrs and over. On average these volunteers work

4 hrs per week; converted into full-time equivalent positions, this would equal about 125 000 jobs, with a wage bill of about $ 1,5 billion, or 1.1 % of GDP.

6   In the assessment of market wages for volunteer-work equivalents Hawrylyshin (1978) takes into account problems of measurement due to difficulty of finding paid work equivalents for volunteer labour, and due to the problem of evaluating the relative efficiency of paid and volunteer work. Hawrylyshin's measure is, then, based on a mean wage, derived from minimum and maximum wage rates for market occupation equivalents. The US studies apply a less carefully spelled out methodology.

7   Kramer (1981) provides comparative data to show considerable variations in the number of agencies, their relationship to the state and their relative autonomy, in four capitalist countries, the US, Britain, the Netherlands, and Israel. His analysis, however, does not give much consideration to the volume of volunteer work and its economic value.

8   Earlier I reported estimates of the number of volunteers in the US in 1965 and 1974; the significant growth in numbers may be indicative of the success of the Nixon administration in encouraging volunteerism.

9   I have not dealt specifically with the social investment aspect of the accumulation process, i.e. the 'projects and services that increase the productivity of a given amount of labour power and, other factors being equal, increase the rate of profit' (O'Connor, 1973: 7). This, however, overlaps so much with social consumption that it may be assumed it also benefits from volunteer services.

10   Anne Bartlett, Director, Western Australian Council of Social Service, public address at the State, Capital and Labour Conference, Murdoch University, 1981. See also Los Angeles Times (1982c) for comparable American observations.

11   On another occasion President Ronald Reagan, speaking to a New York volunteer organisation, pronounced that government does not help the nation in the long run, and that the real route to prosperity is for people to help each other and themselves. And then: 'The Rev. Billy Graham estimates that if every church and synagogue in the United States would average adopting ten poor families beneath the poverty line, we could eliminate all government welfare in this country— federal, state and local' (*L.A. Times*, 1982a: 13).

12   There are, undoubtedly, other government policies regarding voluntary agencies that also further the process of accumulation. Among these are tax deductions and tax-exempt status given to charitable organisations, which provide considerable benefits to large corporations and wealthy individuals, not only as tax dodge, but also as avenues for gaining community standing conducive to acquiring economic and political power (Filer Commission, 1977). Another potential factor which ought to be examined is that of the traditional division of labour between charity and government, whereby the voluntary sector takes special (although not sole) responsibility for the 'deserving', that is those who are unable to work due to handicap, old age, sickness, and family circumstances such as single parenthood (Jones, 1980; Mendelsohn, 1979) thus allowing the government to expend the full measure of its coercive power on the control of the undeserving, that is on the regulation of the labour of those able to work.

13   As has been noted in other chapters of this book, female heads of household often find they cannot afford the costs involved in going out to paid employment (childcare, transportation) and thus remain full-time mothers supported by social security. It appears, at least from informal observation that there are many in this category who join in community volunteer activity.

14   Euster reports that 25 per cent of social workers surveyed in his study of occupational prestige said that their prestige was hurt by 'those persons, ineffectively practising social work without sufficient training' (Euster, 1980: 273-84).

15   And this in an area of work which already provides lower than average wages (Tideman, 1977).

Bibliography

Acker, J. (1978) 'Issues in the sociological study of women's work' in A.H. Stromberg and S. Harkness (eds) *Women Working* Palo Alto: Mayfield Publishing, pp.134-61

Adams, C.T. and Winston, K.T. (1980) *Mothers at work: Public Policies in the United States, Sweden and China* New York and London: Longman

Adams, M. (1971) 'The Compassion Trap' in V. Gornick and B.K. Moran (eds) *Woman in Sexist Society* New York: Basic Books, pp.555-75

Adler, D. (1966) 'The Contemporary Australian Family' *Human Relations* 19, (3): pp.265-82

Administrative and Clerical Officers' Association (ACOA) (1980) ACTU policy on anti-discrimination legislation, letter in WEL records, Canberra, ACT dated 4/1/80

Aitken-Swan, J. (1962) *Widows in Australia* Sydney: NSW Council of Social Service in association with the Australian Council of Social Service

Allen, J. (1982) 'The Invention of the "Pathological" Family: Some Historical Perspectives on Domestic Violence in New South Wales' in J. Craney and C. O'Donnell (eds) *Family Violence in Australia* Melbourne: Longman Cheshire

Althusser, L. (1971) 'Ideology and Ideological State Apparatuses' in *Lenin and Philosophy and other Essays* London: New Left Books

Amsden, A.H. (ed.) (1980) *The Economics of Women and Work* Harmondsworth: Penguin

Anderson, G. (1939) 'Industrial Tribunals and Standards of Living' in F.W. Eggleston (ed.) *Australian Standards of Living* Melbourne: Melbourne University Press, pp.65-112

Anderson, R. (1975) *Leisure: An Inappropriate Concept for Women?* Canberra: AGPS

Anti-Discrimination (Amendment) Act 1980 (NSW) (1980) Section 122, 1.

Anti-Discrimination Board, New South Wales (1976) *Report* section 3, part A, Sydney: NSW Government Printer

——(1978) *First Annual Report* Sydney: NSW Government Printer

——(1979) *Report* vol.1 and vol.11, Sydney: NSW Government Printer

Aungles, S. and Szelenyi, I. (1979) 'Structural Conflicts between the State, Local Government and Monopoly Capital—The case of Whyalla in South Australia' *The Australian and New Zealand Journal of Sociology*, 15(1): pp.24-35

Austin, A.G. (1972) *Australian Education 1788-1900: Church, State and Public Education in Colonial Australia* 3rd ed., Carlton, Vic.: Pitman
Australia, Parliament (1978) *Budget Papers, 1978-1979,* Canberra: AGPS.
Australia, Parliament (1981a) *Review of the Children's Services Program* (not tabled)
——(1981b) *Review of Commonwealth Functions* Canberra: AGPS
Australia (1977) *Women and Politics Conference 1975* Canberra: AGPS
Australian Bureau of Statistics (1935) *Labour Report, February*
——(1976) *Social Indicators No.1* Ref.no. 13.16. Canberra: AGPS
——(1977) *Child Care* Cat.No. 4402.0
——(1979) *Population and Dwellings: Cross-Classified Tables* 1976 Census, Cat.No. 2426.0, Canberra: AGPS
——(1980a) *General Social Survey Australian Families, May 1975* Cat.No. 4107.0, Canberra: AGPS
——(1980b) *Monthly Summary of Statistics, Australia* June, Cat.No. 1304.0, Canberra: AGPS
——(1980c) *Social Indicators no.3* Cat.No. 4101.0, Canberra: AGPS
——(1981a) *Australian Health Survey 1977-78: Recent Illnesses* Cat.No. 4318.0, Canberra: AGPS
——(1981b) *The Labour Force Australia, May 1981* Cat.No. 6203.0, Canberra: AGPS
——(1982a) *The Labour Force Australia, February 1982* Cat.No. 6203.0, Canberra: AGPS
——(1982b) *Labour Force Status and Other Characteristics of Families, Australia, June 1981* Cat.No. 6224.0, Canberra: AGPS
——(1982c) *Persons Not in the Labour Force, Australia, September 1981* (Preliminary), Cat.No. 6219.0, Canberra: AGPS
——(1982d) *Weekly Earnings of Employees (Distribution) Australia, August 1981* Cat.No. 6310.0, Canberra: AGPS
——(1982e) *Australian Families 1982* (Preliminary), December, Cat.no. 4407.0 Canberra: AGPS
Australian Council of Social Service (ACOSS) (1980) *Impact* vol.10, Sydney: Australian Council of Social Service
——(1981a) *Impact* vol.11, Sydney: Australian Council of Social Service
——(1981b) 'Poor must have more' P. Smith, letter to the editor *Sydney Morning Herald* 13 January
Australian Council of Trade Unions (1979a) *Draft Guidelines and Negotiating Exhibit on Part-time Work* Melbourne: ACTU
——(1979b) Report of the Working Women's Charter Committee to the 1979 Congress unpublished paper
Australian Department of Labour, Women's Bureau (1974) *The Role of Women in the Economy, Women and Work No. 12* Canberra: AGPS
Australian Family Association (1981) *The Family, Education and Community support* Melbourne: University of Melbourne
Australian Financial Review (1971) 16 March
——(1980) 10 September
Baker, W.A. (1966) 'The Shifts in Basic Wage "Principles" ' *Australian Left Review*: pp.50-7
Baldock, C.V. (1978) *Australia and Social Change Theory* Sydney: Ian Novak

———(1980) The Role of the Volunteer in the Labour market: Some Theoretical Considerations, paper presented at ANZAAS Jubilee Congress Adelaide, August

———(1981) Public Policy and Women's Work: The Issue of Reduced Working Hours, paper presented at 23rd annual conference of the Australasian Political Studies Association (APSA), Canberra, August

Baldock, C.V. and Thiele, B. (1979) Working Women in Western Australia, paper presented at Mid-decade for Women Conference, Perth

Baran, P. and Sweezy, P. (1966) *Monopoly Capital* Harmondsworth: Penguin

Barker, D.L. (1978) 'The regulation of marriage: repressive benevolence' in G. Littlejohn et al. (eds.) *Power and the State* London: Croom Helm, pp.239-66

Barrett, M. (1980) *Women's Oppression Today: Problems in Marxist Feminist Analysis* London: Verso

Barron, R. and Norris, J. (1976) 'Sexual Divisions and the Dual Labour market' in D. Barker and S. Allen (eds) *Dependence and Exploitation in Work and Marriage* London: Longman, pp.47-69

Baudrillard, J. (1975) *The Mirror of Production* St. Louis: Telos Press

Bavin, T.R. (1922) 'The Case Against Motherhood Endowment' *The Forum* (May 24): p.11

Beaton, L. (1980) 'The importance of women's paid labour—based on the study of women at work in the second world war' in The Convenors *Second Women and Labour Conference* Melbourne, pp.67-75

Beechey, V. (1977) 'Female Wage Labour in Capitalist Production' *Capital and Class* 3: pp.45-66

———(1979) 'On Patriarchy' *Feminist Review* 3: pp.66-82

Bell, C. and Newby, H. (1976) 'Husbands and wives: the dynamics of the deferential dialectic' in D.L. Barker and S. Allen (eds) *Dependence and Exploitation in Work and Marriage* London: Longmans, pp.152-68

Benjamin, J. (1977) 'The end of internalization: Adorno's Social Psychology' *Telos* 32 (Summer): pp.42-64

Bentley, P., Collins, D.J. and Drane, N.T. (1974) 'The Incidence of Australian Taxation' *The Economic Record* 50: pp.489-510

Berger, J. (1972) *Ways of Seeing* Harmondsworth: Penguin

Bernard, J. (1973) 'My four revolutions: an autobiographical history of the ASA' *American Journal of Sociology* 78 (January): pp.773-91

Bessant, B. (1976) 'Domestic Science Schools and Women's Place' *Australian Journal of Education* 20(1): pp.1-9

Beyrer, J.B. (1961) 'Family Allowances in Australia' *International Social Security Review* 14, (1-2): pp.45-60

Bielski, J. (1981) Women and Trade Unions, paper presented at WEL National Conference, Sydney

Birch, I.K.F. (1976) *The School and the Law* Melbourne: Melbourne University Press

Birrell, R. and Hay, C. (1976) 'The National Population Inquiry: The Findings and the Political Response' *Current Affairs Bulletin* 52(8)

Blum, L., Homiak, M., Housman, J., Scheman, N. (1976) 'Altruism and Women's oppression' in C.C. Gould and M.W. Wartofsky (eds) *Women and Philosophy* New York: Capricorn Books, pp.222-47

Boon, T. and Jones, A. (1979) 'Aspects of Female Clerical Workers in

Australia' *Women's Sociological Bulletin* 1(3): pp.41-52
Bose, C. (1979) 'Technology and Changes in the Division of Labour in the American Home' *Women's Studies International Quarterly* 2(3): pp.295-304
Boulding, K.E. (1973) *The Economy of Love and Fear* Belmont, California: Wadsworth Publishing
Bowlby, J. (1953) *Child care and the Growth of Love* Harmondsworth: Penguin
Bradley, D. and Mortimer, M. (1972-3) 'Sex Role Stereotyping in Children's Picture Books' *Refractory Girl* 1: pp.8-14
Bradbury, J.H. (1980) 'Instant Resource Towns Policy in British Columbia, 1965-1972' *Plan Canada* 20(1): pp.19-38
Bradshaw, J. and Piachaud, D. (1980) *Child Support in the European Community* London: Bedford Square Press
Brennan, T. (1977) 'Women and Work' *Australian Journal of Political Economy 1* October: pp.34-52
Broom, L. and Jones, F.L. (1976) *Opportunity and Attainment in Australia* Canberra: Australian National University
Bryson, L. (1974) 'Men's work and women's work: occupation and family orientation' *Search*, 5(7): pp.295-9
Bryson, L. and Thompson, F. (1972) *An Australian Newtown* Melbourne: Penguin
Buddin, T., Golding, H. and McCrae, M. (1977) Observations on the Theory and Practice of Maintenance Enforcement with Particular Reference to Legal Aid and Social Services, unpublished paper, University of New South Wales Law School
Bulletin (1970) 7 February: pp.46-7
Burbidge, A. (1981) 'Working people in poverty' in R.F. Henderson (ed.) *The Welfare Stakes* Melbourne: Institute of Applied Economic and Social Research, pp.147-78
Burgess, E.W. (1967) 'The Growth of a City: An Introduction to a Research Project' in R.E. Park and E. Burgess (eds) *The City* Chicago: University of Chicago Press
Burnett, P. (1973) 'Social Change, the Status of Women and Models of City Form and Development' *Antipode* 5: pp.57-62
Burnley, I.H. (1980) *The Australian Urban System* Australia: Longman
Burns, A. and Goodnow, J. (1979) *Children and Families in Australia* Sydney: Allen & Unwin
Cahn, A.F. (1979) *Women in the US Labour Force* New York: Praeger
Caldwell, J.C. (1980) 'Long-term perspectives on the Australian Family' in D. Davis et al. (eds) *Living Together: Family Patterns and Lifestyles* Canberra: Centre for Continuing Education, pp.17-25
Campbell, P. (1927) Family Endowment in Australia, paper read before Economic Society of Australia and New Zealand (New South Wales Branch) (8 November), Sydney
Cantor, A. (1978) 'The Sheltered Workshop' *Lilith (NY), The Jewish Women's Magazine* 5: pp.20-1
Cartwright, A. (1979) *The Dignity of Labour? A Study of Childbearing and Induction* London: Tavistock
Cass, B. (1978a) A Critical Evaluation of the Concept of Consumption in

Urban Sociology, paper presented at Sociological Association of Australia and New Zealand Conference (SAANZ) Brisbane, May

——(1978b) 'Women's Place in the Class Structure' in E.L. Wheelwright and K.D. Buckley (eds) *Essays in the Political Economy of Australian Capitalism* vol.3, Sydney: ANZ Book Co., pp.11-41

——(1981a) Family Policy and the Privatisation of Welfare, paper presented at Australasian Political Studies Association (APSA), Canberra

——(1981b) 'Materializing the Invisible. Women's work and class analysis' in P. Hiller (ed.) *Class and Inequality in Australia* Sydney: Harcourt Brace Jovanovich, pp.164-82

——(1981c) *'Unemployment and the Family'* SWRC Reports and Proceedings No.7, Sydney: Social Welfare Research Centre, University of New South Wales

——(1981d) 'Wages, Women and Children' in R.F. Henderson (ed.) *The Welfare Stakes* Melbourne: Institute of Applied Economic and Social Research, pp.45-77

——(1982) *Family policies in Australia: contest over the social wage* SWRC Reports and Proceedings, No.21 (May), Sydney: Social Welfare Research Centre, University of New South Wales

Cass, B., Keens, C. and Moller, J. (1981) 'Family Policy Halloween: Family Allowances: Trick or Treat?' *Australian Quarterly* 53, (1): pp.56-73

Cass, B., Keens, C. and Wyndham, D. (1983) 'Childrearing: Direct and Indirect Costs' in A. Graycar (ed.) *Retreat from the Welfare State* Sydney: Allen & Unwin

Cass, B. and Pedler, K. (1980) 'Where are they hiding the unemployed?' *Australian Social Welfare, Impact* (10)5 and 6: pp.17-22

Cass, B. and Radi, H. (1981) 'Family, Fertility and the Labour Market' in N. Grieve and P. Grimshaw (eds) *Australian Women: Feminist Perspectives* Melbourne: Oxford University Press, pp.190-204

Castells, M. (1976a) 'Theoretical Propositions for an Experimental Study of Urban Social Movements' in C.G. Pickvance (ed.) *Urban Sociology: Critical Essays* London: Tavistock

——(1976b) *The Urban Question: A Marxist Approach* London: Edward Arnold

——(1978) *City, Class and Power* London: Macmillan

Centre for Resource Studies (1979) 'Employee Relations Initiatives in Canadian Mining' *Proceedings of the Queens University, Ontario*, No.5

Charteris, A.H. (1927) 'Family Endowment in New South Wales' *Australasian Journal of Psychology and Philosophy* 5-6: pp.94-112

Chodorow, N. (1978) *The Reproduction of Mothering: Psychoanalysis and the Sociology of Gender* Berkeley: University of California Press

Clark, M.J. and Lange, L. (eds) (1979) *The Sexism of Social and Political Theory* Toronto: University of Toronto Press

Collins, J.H. (1977) 'A Divided Working Class' *Intervention* 8, March: pp.64-78

——(1978) 'Fragmentation of the Working Class' in E.L. Wheelwright and K.D. Buckley (eds) *Essays in the Political Economy of Australian Capitalism* vol.3, Sydney: ANZ Books, pp.42-85

Comer, L. (1974) *Wedlocked Woman* Leeds: Feminist Books

Commission of Inquiry into Poverty (1975a) (R.F. Henderson, Chairman) *First Main Report, Poverty in Australia* vol.1, Canberra: AGPS
——(1975b) (R. Sackville Chairman) *Second Main Report, Law and Poverty in Australia* vol.2, Canberra: AGPS
Commissioner of Taxation (1977) *56th Report: 1976-1977* Parliamentary Paper 129, Canberra, AGPS
Committee on Education and Labour (1970) *Discrimination against Women* Report of the Special Subcommittee on Education, House of Representatives, Ninety-First Congress, Washington: US Printing Office
Committee on Sexism in Education (1977) *Report* Sydney: NSW Government Printer
Commonwealth Arbitration Court (1937) *Basic Wage Inquiry* Melbourne: AGPS
Commonwealth ·Arbitration Reports (1940) *Basic Wage Inquiry* Canberra: AGPS
Commonwealth Department of Social Security (1977) *Annual Report of the Director-General 1976-1977* Canberra: AGPS
——(1979) *Annual Report 1978-79* Canberra: AGPS
——(1981a) *Annual Report 1980-81* Canberra: AGPS
——(1981b) *Quarterly Survey of Unemployment Benefit Recipients, 4 September, 1981* Canberra: DSS Development Division
Commonwealth Department of Social Security and Australian Council of Social Service (1978) *Emergency Relief—A Study of Agencies and Clients* Canberra: AGPS
Commonwealth Joint Committee on Social Security (1941) *First Interim Report* Canberra: AGPS
Commonwealth Parliamentary Debates (1941) *House of Representatives* (March 12-April 3)
——(1976) *House of Representatives* (May)
——(1979) *House of Representatives* vol.113
Connell, R.W. (1977) *Ruling Class, Ruling Culture* Melbourne: Cambridge University Press
Connors, L. (1981) 'The Politics of the National Women's Advisory Council' *Politics*, 16(2): pp.238-42
Council of Social Welfare Ministers of Australia, New Zealand and Papua New Guinea (1980) *Towards a National Family Policy* Macquarie University, NSW
Coussins, J. and Coote, A. (1981) *The Family in the Firing Line* London: Child Poverty Action Group
Cowan, R.S. (1976) 'The Industrial Revolution in the Home: Household Technology and Social Change in the Twentieth Century' *Technology and Culture* 17, (1): pp.1-23
Coward, R. (1978) 'Rethinking Marxism' *M/F* 2
Cox, E. (1978a) 'Beware the Call of Nature' *Social Alternatives* November, 1(3): pp.69-73
——(1978b) 'Child Care, Who Cares?' *Current Affairs Bulletin* 54(8), January: pp.20-31, Sydney: Sydney University Press
Cox, E. and Martin, J. (1976) *There's No Come In For a Cuppa, Love, For Us* Sydney: NCOSS

Cranz, G. (1980) 'Women in Urban Parks' *Signs* 5(3): pp.579-95
——(1981) 'The Sharon Building: The Transformation of Women's Recreational Needs in the Late Nineteenth Century City' *Heresies* 11, 3(3): pp.77-9
Curthoys, A. (1979) 'Explaining the Sexual Division of Labour under Capitalism' *Refractory Girl* December: pp.61-2
Curthoys, J. and Barbalet, J. (1976) 'Women: Class or Class Determined? A Marxist Analysis of Housework' *Political Economy Conference: Selected Papers* Sydney: University of Sydney Press
Daily Mirror (1981) 9 March
Dallacosta, M. and James, S. (1972) *The Power of Women and the Subversion of the Community* London: Falling Wall Press
Daniels, K. et al. (1977) *Women in Australia* Canberra: AGPS
Daniels, K. and Murnane, M. (1980) *Uphill All the Way* Brisbane: University of Queensland Press
Darroch, D.B. (1978) *Power and Participation: The Dynamics of Medical Encounters* PhD dissertation: Australian National University
——(1981) The occupational health of houseworkers, paper presented to the Conference *Work and Health: Future Issues in Occupational Health*, Centre for Continuing Education, Australian National University, proceedings forthcoming
Darroch, D.B. and Mugford, S. (1980) 'The Division of domestic labour in Australia' *Social Science Quarterly* 60 (March): pp.685-90
David, M. (1980) *The State, the Family and Education* London: Routledge & Kegan Paul
Davidoff, L., L'Esperance, J. and Newby, H. (1976) 'Landscape with Figures: Home and Community in English Society' in J. Mitchell and A. Oakley (eds) *The Rights and Wrongs of Women* Harmondsworth: Penguin, pp.139-75
Davidson, L., Chapman, S. and Hull, C. (1979) *Health Promotion in Australia* 1978-80 Canberra: AGPS
Davison, G. and Lack, J. (1981) 'Planning the New Social Order: The Melbourne University Social Survey, 1941-1943' *The Australian and New Zealand Journal of Sociology* 17, 1: pp.36-45
Deacon, D. (1981) The Employment of Women in the Commonwealth Public Service: the Creation and Reproduction of a Dual Labour Market, unpublished research paper, Australian National University
——(1982) Political Arithmetic? Women and the Census 1861-1891, paper presented at the SAANZ Conference, Sydney, August
Deagan, C. (1979) 'Childcare Workers: Volunteers and Conscripts: Women Working in Childcare' *Refractory Girl* December: pp.6-8
De Beauvoir, S. (1952) *The Second Sex* New York: Alfred A. Knopf, Inc. (first published in French in 1949)
Delphy, C. (1977) *The Main Enemy* London: Women's Research and Resources Centre
Denis, A.B. (1980) 'Women's Labour Force Participation in Australia since the 1930's: A comparison of birthplace groups' in The Convenors *Second Women and Labour Conference* vol.1, Melbourne, pp.52-66
Deveson, A. (1978) *Australians at Risk* Sydney: Cassell
Dickey, B. (1980) *No Charity There, A Short History of Social Welfare in Australia* Melbourne: Nelson

Dinnerstein, D. (1978) *The Rocking of the Cradle: And the Ruling of the World* London: Souvenir

Dixson, M. (1976) *The Real Matilda* Melbourne: Penguin

Domhoff, G.W. (1970) *The Higher Circles: The Governing Class in America* New York: Random House

Douglas, M. (1979) *The World of Goods* New York: Basic Books

Douglas, P.H. (1925) *Wages and the Family* Chicago: University of Chicago Press

Dowse, S. (1981) 'The Transfer of the Office of Women's Affairs' in S. Encel, P. Wilenski, and B. Schaffer (eds) *Decisions: Case Studies in Australian Public Policy* Melbourne: Longman Cheshire, pp.3-20

Dunleavy, P. (1980) *Urban Political Analysis* London: MacMillan

Eadie, J. (1977) Part-time work in the Australian occupational structure, unpublished BA Honours thesis in Sociology, Australian National University

Edgar, D. (1974) 'Adolescent Competence and Sexual Disadvantage' *La Trobe Sociology Papers* 10, Melbourne: La Trobe University

Edholm, F., Harris, O. and Young, K. (1977) 'Conceptualising Women' *Critique of Anthropology* 3 (9 & 10): pp.101-30

Education News (1975) 15 (4/5)

Edwards, M. (1980a) 'Changing family patterns: some implications for social security' *Australian Social Welfare, Impact* 10(4), September: pp.4-8

——(1980b) 'A Critique of Income Splitting Proposals' Sydney: Australian Council of Social Service

——(1980c) 'Economics of home activities' *Australian Journal of Social Issues* 15, (1) February: pp.5-16

——(1980d) 'Social Effects of Taxation' in J. Wilkes (ed.) *The Politics of Taxation* Sydney: Hodder and Stoughton, pp.142-61

——(1981) *Financial Arrangements within Families* Canberra: National Women's Advisory Council

Ehrenreich, B. and Ehrenreich, J. (1974) 'Health care and social control' *Social Policy* (May/June): pp.26-40

Ehrenreich, B. and English, D. (1973) *Complaints and Disorders: The Sexual Politics of Sickness* Old Westbury, N.Y.: The Feminist Press

Eisenstein, Z.R. (1979) 'Developing a Theory of Capitalist Patriarchy and Socialist Feminism' in Z.R. Eisenstein (ed.) *Capitalist Patriarchy and the Case for Socialist Feminism* New York and London: Monthly Review Press, pp.5-40

Ely, J. (1978) *Reality and Rhetoric: an Alternative History of Australian Education* Sydney: Alternative Publishing Co-operative

Encel, S., MacKenzie, N. and Tebbutt, M. (1974) *Women and Society: An Australian Study* Melbourne: Cheshire

Engels, F. (1884) *The Origin of the Family, Private Property and the State* Moscow: International Publishers

Epstein, S. (1978) *The Politics of Cancer* San Francisco: Sierra Club Books

Equal Opportunity Board, Melbourne (1979) *Wardley v. Ansett Transport Industries (Operations) Pty. Ltd.* (unreported) Melbourne, Vic., June, pp.10-11

Eriksson-Joslyn, K. (1973-74) 'A Nation of Volunteers: Participatory Democracy or Administrative Manipulation?' *Berkeley Journal of Sociology*

XVIII: pp.159-82

Euster, G.L. (1980) 'The Occupational Prestige of Social Work' *Sociology and Social Welfare* VII (2): pp.273-84

Evatt, H.V. (1979) *William Holman: Australian Labour Leader* Sydney: Angus & Robertson

Ewen, S. and Ewen, E. (1978) 'Americanization and Consumption' *Telos* 37: pp.42-51

Family Services Committee (1978) *Families and Social Services in Australia* vols.I and II, Canberra: AGPS

Faust, B. (1976) 'Feminism then and Now' *Australian Quarterly* 46, 1: pp.15-28

Filer Commission on Private Philanthropy and Public Needs (1977) *Research Papers* vol.1, Washington, D.C.: Department of Treasury

Fine, P. (1971) Modern Eating Patterns: the Structure of Reality, paper for the American Medical Association Food Science Council Symposium, November, New York

Fitzpatrick, B. (1969) *The British Empire in Australia* Melbourne: MacMillan

Flick, G.A. (1981) *Civil Liberties in Australia* Sydney: Law Book Co.

Foenander, O. de R. (1943) *Wartime labour developments in Australia* Melbourne: Melbourne University Press

Foord, J. (1980) 'Women's Place—Women's Space' *Area* 12: pp.49-50

Foreman, A. (1977) *Femininity as Alienation* New York: Pluto Press

Forer, D.C. and Kivell, H. (1981) 'Space-time Budgets, Public Transport, and Spatial Choice' *Environment and Planning* A, 13,: pp.497-509

Fox, M. (1978) 'Protest in Piety: Christian Science Revisited' *International Journal of Women's Studies* 1 (July/August): pp.401-16

Frankel, B. (1978) 'The State and the Private Sector: Towards a Political Economy of Socialisation in Australia' in F.J. Hunt (ed.) *Socialisation in Australia* Melbourne: Australian International Press, pp.202-22

Frankenberg, R. (1976) 'In the production of their lives, Men (?) .... Sex and Gender in British Community Studies' in D.L. Barker and S. Allen (eds) *Sexual Divisions and Society: Process and Change* London: Tavistock, pp.25-51

Fraser, D. (1973) *The Evolution of the British Welfare State* London: Macmillan

Freeden, M. (1978) *The New Liberalism. An Ideology of Social Reform* Oxford: Clarendon Press

Freedman, F. (1975) 'The internal structure of the American Proletariat: A Marxist Analysis *Socialist Revolution* 5: pp.41-83

Freestone, B. (1974) Location and Allocation: a Geographic Study of some urban services in Sydney, BSc. thesis, Department of Geography, University of New South Wales

Friedan, B. (1963) *The Feminine Mystique* Harmondsworth: Penguin

Friedl, E. (1975) *Women and Men: An Anthropologist's View* New York: Holt, Rinehart and Winston

Fristacky, J.M. (1977) 'Equal Opportunity: The Victorian Bill' *Legal Service Bulletin* 2: pp.205-6

Fry, J. (1973) *Report of the Australian Pre-schools Committee* Canberra: AGPS

Galbraith, J.K. (1973) *Economics and Public Purpose* Boston: Houghton Mifflin

Galper, J. (1980) *Social Work Practice: A Radical Perspective* Englewood Cliffs, N.J.: Prentice Hall

Gamarnikow, E. (1978) 'Introduction' *International Journal of Urban and Regional Research* 2(3): pp.390-403

Game, A. and Pringle, R. (1979) 'Sexuality and the Suburban Dream' *Australian and New Zealand Journal of Sociology* 15(2): pp.4-15

Gardiner, J. (1976) 'Political economy of domestic labour in capitalist society' in D.L. Barker and S. Allen (eds) *Dependence and Exploitation in Work and Marriage* London: Longmans, pp.109-20

Gaudron, M. and Bosworth, M. (1979) 'Equal Pay?' in J. Mackinolty and H. Radi (eds) *In Pursuit of Justice: Australian Women and the Law 1788-1979* Sydney: Hale & Iremonger, pp.161-9

Gilman, C.P. (1973) *The Yellow Wallpaper* Old Westbury, N.Y.: The Feminist Press (first published 1899)

Ginsberg, G. (1979) *Class, Capital and Social Policy* London: MacMillan

Gittens, R. (1981) *Sydney Morning Herald* 8 January

Glezer, H. and Mercer, J. (1973) 'Blueprint for a Lobby: The Birth of WEL as a Social Movement' in H. Mayer (ed.) *Labor to Power* Sydney: Angus & Robertson, pp.169-76

Gold, D.B. (1971) 'Women and Volunteerism' in V. Gornick and B.K. Moran (eds) *Women in Sexist Society* New York: Basic Books, pp.533-44

——(1979) *Opposition to Volunteerism: An Annotated Bibliography* Bibliography No.8, June, New York: Council of Planning Librarians

Goot, M. and Reid, E. (1975) *Women and Voting Studies: Mindless Matrons or Sexist Scientism?* London: Sage

Gordon, D. (1972) *Theories of Poverty and Underemployment* Lexington, Mass.: Heath

Gordon, D.M. (1978) 'Capitalist Development and the History of American Cities in W. Tabb and L. Sawyers (eds) *Marxism and the Metropolis* Oxford University Press, pp.25-59

Gordon, L. (1976) *Woman's Body, Woman's Right* New York: Penguin

Gorney, S. and Cox, C. (1973) *After Forty: How Women can Achieve Fulfillment* New York: Dial Press

Gough, I. (1979) *The Political Economy of the Welfare State* London: MacMillan

Govan, E.S.L. (1942) 'The Social Worker in Public Administration' *Public Administration* (Sydney) IV, (38) March

Gove, W. and Hughes, M. (1979) 'Possible causes of the apparent sex differences in physical health' *American Sociological Review* 44: pp.126-46

Graham, D.L. (1981) 'A Question of Community Property Rights' *Womanspeak* 6(1): pp.4-5

Graycar, A. (1982) *Government officers' Expectations of non-government welfare organisations: A discussion paper* SWRC Reports and Proceedings, no.28, Sydney: Social Welfare Research Centre, University of New South Wales

Graycar, A. and Silver, W. (1982) *Funding of non-government welfare: Agencies serving disabled people in Western Australia* SWRC Reports and

Proceedings, no.17, Sydney: Social Welfare Research Centre, University of New South Wales

Graycar, A. and Yates, I. (1981) Public Policy and the Non-government Welfare Sector, paper presented to the Australasian Political Studies Association, Australian National University: Canberra

Green, V. (1973) 'WEL's Canberra Confrontation' in H. Mayer (ed.) *Labor to Power* Sydney: Angus & Robertson, p.192

Greenbaum, J. (1981) 'Kitchen Culture/Kitchen Dialect' *Heresies II* 3(3): pp.59-61

Hagan, J. (1981) *The History of the ACTU* Melbourne: Longman Cheshire

Haire, D. (1974) *The Cultural Warping of Child Birth* Hillside, N.J.: International Childbirth Education Association

Haley, E. (1973) 'The Long Haul' *Politics* November, pp.330-2

Hamilton, R. (1978) *The Liberation of Women* London: Allen & Unwin

Hamilton-Smith, J. (1973) 'Changing trends in Volunteering' *Australian Social Work* 26(2): pp.15-20

Hancock, W.K. (1961) *Australia* Brisbane: Jacaranda

Hanson, S. (1980) 'The Importance of the Multipurpose Journey to work in Urban Travel Behaviour' *Transportation* 9: pp.229-48

Hanson, S. and Hanson, P. (1980) 'Gender and Urban Activity Patterns in Uppsala, Sweden' *Geographical Review* 70: pp.291-9

——(1981) 'The Impact of Married Women's Employment on Household Travel Patterns: A Swedish Example' *Transportation* 10: pp.165-83

Hardwick, J. and Graycar, A. (1982) *Volunteers in non-government welfare organisations in Australia: A working paper* SWRC Reports and Proceedings, no.25, Sydney: Social Welfare Research Centre, University of New South Wales

Harper, J. and Richards, L. (1979) *Mothers and Working Mothers* Harmondsworth: Penguin

Harper, R.J.A. (1972) 'Family Assistance and the Redistribution of Income' *Australian Journal of Social Issues* 7, (3): pp.177-89

Hartmann, H.I. (1975) 'Comment on M.W. Mueller's "The Economic Determinants of Volunteer Work by Women"' *Signs* 1, (3): pp.773-6

——(1976) 'Capitalism, Patriarchy and Job segregation by Sex' in M. Blaxall and B. Reagan (eds) *Women and the Workplace* University of Chicago Press. (*Signs* 1, (3) spring supplement, pp.137-69)

Hatch, S. and Mocraft, I. (1979) 'The Relative Costs of Services Provided by Voluntary and Statutory Organisations' *Public Administration* 57, Winter: pp.397-405

Higgins, H.B. (1915) 'A New Province for Law and Order' *Harvard Law Review* November: pp.13-39

——(1920) *A New Province for Law and Order* (a Collection of reprinted articles published in Harvard Law Review, 1915-1920)

Higley, J., Deacon, D. and Smart, D. (1979) *Elites in Australia* Boston: Routledge & Kegan Paul

Hill, R. & F. (1875) *What We Saw in Australia* London: MacMillan

Hiller, A.E. (1978) 'Women, illness and deviance' in *Women's Health in a Changing Society* vol.3, Canberra: AGPS, pp.337-41

Holden, A. (1981) Work and Marriage in the Pilbara, unpublished Honours thesis, Murdoch University

Houghton, D.S. (1979) *Perth at the 1976 Census: A Social Atlas* Department of Geography, University of Western Australia
Howe, A. and O'Connor, K. (1981) Travel to work and Labour Force Participation of Men and Women in an Australian Metropolitan Area, unpublished manuscript, Department of Geography, Monash University, Melbourne
Hicks, A., Friedland, R. and Johnson, E. (1978) 'Class Power and State Policy' *American Sociological Review* Vol. 43 (June)
Hawrylyshin, O. (1976) 'A Survey of empirical estimates of the value of Household Work' *Review of Income and Wealth* September: pp.101-31
——(1978) 'The economic nature and value of volunteer activity in Canada' *Social Indicators Research* 5, (1): pp.1-71
Hayden, D. (1976) *Seven American Utopias: The Architecture of Communitarian Socialism 1790-1975* Cambridge, Mass.: MIT Press
——(1980) 'What would a Non-sexist City Be Like? Speculation on Housing, Urban Design, and Human Work' *Signs*, 5(3) (Supplement): S170-87
Hayden, D. and Wright, A. (1976) 'Architecture and Urban Planning' *Signs* 1(4): pp.923-33
Head, B. (1980) 'Inequality, welfare and the state: distribution and redistribution in Australia *Australian and New Zealand Journal of Sociology* 16, (3): pp.44-51
Heagney, M. (1935) *Are Women Taking Men's Jobs?* Melbourne: Milton & Veitch
Henderson, R.F. (1978) 'Social Welfare Expenditure' in R.B. Scotton and H. Ferber (eds) *Public Expenditures and Social Policy in Australia vol.1, The Whitlam Years, 1972-1975* Melbourne: Longman Cheshire for the Institute of Applied Economic and Social Research, University of Melbourne, pp.160-78
Hughes, D.O. (1978) 'Urban Growth and Family Structure in Medieval Genoa' in P. Abrams and E.A. Wrigley (eds) *Towns in Societies: Essays in Economic History and Historical Sociology* Cambridge: Cambridge University Press, pp.105-30
Hunt, P. (1978) 'Cash Transactions and Household Tasks' *The Sociological Review* New Series, 26: pp.555-71
Hunter, T. (1973) 'Reform and Revolution in Contemporary Feminism' *Politics* Vol.8(2) Sept: pp.321-9
Hutson, J. (1971) *Six Wage Concepts* Annandale, NSW: Amalgamated Engineering Union
Illich, I. (1975) *Medical Nemesis: The Expropriation of Health* London: Calder and Boyars
International Journal of Urban and Regional Research (1978), 2, 3: whole issue
Ireland, M. (1928) *A Survey of Women in Industry, Victoria* Canberra: Commonwealth Department of Health
James, C. (1980) *Unreliable Memoirs* London: Jonathan Cape
James, K. (1979) 'The Home: A Private or Public Place? Class, Status and the Actions of Women' *The Australian and New Zealand Journal of Sociology* 15(1): pp.36-42
James, S. (1975) *Sex, Race and Class* London: Falling Wall Press
Jamrozik, A. and Hoey, M. (1981) *Workforce in Transition: Implications for*

Welfare SWRC Reports and Proceedings, No.8, Sydney: Social Welfare Research Centre, University of New South Wales

Jelly, F. (1977) 'Child Endowment' in H. Radi and P. Spearrit (eds) *Jack Lang* Sydney: Hale & Iremonger, pp.88-98

Johnston, R.J. and Rimmer, P.J. (1969) *Retailing in Melbourne* Canberra: Research School of Pacific Studies, Australian National University

Joint Select Committee on the Family Law Act (1980) *Report* Canberra: AGPS

Jones, M.A. (1980) *The Australian Welfare State* Sydney: Allen & Unwin

Jupp, K. (1976) 'The Borrie Report: Background, Findings, Recommendations' *Population and Development Review* 2(1): pp.65-77

Kamerman, S. and Kahn, A.J. (eds) (1978) *Family Policy: Government and Families in Fourteen Countries* New York: Columbia University Press

Keens, C. and Cass, B. (1982) *Fiscal Welfare: Some Aspects of Australian Tax Policy Class and Gender considerations*, SWRC Reports and Proceedings, No.24 (September), Sydney: Social Welfare Research Centre, University of New South Wales

Keeves, J. and Reed, A. (1974) *Sex Differences in Preparing for Scientific Occupations* IEA (Australia) Report, Melbourne: ACER

Kendig, H. (1979) *New Life for Old Suburbs* Sydney: Allen & Unwin

Kennedy, M.I. (1981) 'Towards a Rediscovery of "Feminine" Principles in Architecture and Planning' *Women's Studies International Quarterly* 4(1): pp. 75-81

Kewley, T.H. (1977) *Social Security in Australia: 1900-1972* Sydney: Sydney University Press

——(1980) *Australian Social Security Today: Major Developments for 1900-1978* Sydney: Sydney University Press

Keynes, J.M. (1940) *How to Pay for the War* London: Macmillan

Kilmartin, L. and Thorns, D. (1978) *Cities Unlimited* Sydney: Allen & Unwin

Kingston, B. (1975) *My Wife, My Daughter and Poor Mary Ann* Melbourne: Nelson

——(1977) *The World Moves Slowly* Sydney: Cassell

Kipnis, D. (1980) Technology and Control, paper presented at ANZAAS Jubilee Congress, Adelaide, August

Kramer, R.M. (1977) 'Alternative Futures for Voluntary Agencies in Social Welfare' *Journal of Voluntary Action Research* 6, (1-2): pp.18-22

——(1981) *Voluntary Agencies in the Welfare State* Berkeley: University of California Press

Kravetz, D.F. (1976) 'Women Social Workers and Clients: Common Victims of Sexism' in J.I. Robert (ed.) *Beyond Intellectual Sexism: A New Woman, A New Reality* New York: David McKay, pp.160-71

Krupinski, J. and Mackenzie, A. (1979) *The Health and Social Survey of the North-West Region of Melbourne* Institute of Mental Health Research and Postgraduate Training, Health Commission of Victoria Special Publication No.7

Kuhn, A. and Wolpe, A.M. (eds) (1978) *Feminism and Materialism: Women and Modes of Production* London: Routledge & Kegan Paul

Labour Daily (1924) March, 17

Land, H. (1975) 'The Introduction of Family Allowances: An Act of Historic Justice?' in P. Hall, H. Land, R. Parker, and A. Webb *Change, Choice and*

Conflict in Social Policy London: Heinemann, pp.157-230

——(1976) 'Women: Supporters or Supported?' in L.D. Barker and S. Allen (eds) *Sexual Divisions and Society: Process and Change* London: Tavistock, pp.108-32

——(1978) 'Sex-role stereotyping in the social security and income tax systems' in J. Chetwynd and O. Harnett (eds) *The Sex Role System* London: Routledge & Kegan Paul, pp.127-42

——(1979) 'The Boundaries between the State and the Family' in C. Harris et al. (eds) *The Sociology of the Family: New Directions for Britain* London: Sociological Review Monograph, pp.141-59

——(1980) 'The Family Wage' *Feminist Review* 6: pp.55-78

Lang, J.T. (1956) *I Remember* Sydney: Invincible

Langford, P. and Sebastian, P. (1979) *Early Childhood Education and Care in Australia* Melbourne: Australian International Press and Publications Pty. Ltd.

Larmour, C. (1975) 'Women's Wages and the WEB' in A. Curthoys et al. (eds) *Women at Work* Canberra: Australian Society for Study of Labour History, pp.47-58

Lasch, C. (1979) *The Culture of Narcissism* New York: Norton

Lauffer, A. and Gorodezky, S. (1977) *Volunteers* Beverley Hills: Sage

Lawrence, R.J. (1965) *Professional Social Work in Australia* Canberra: ANU Press

Lefebvre, H. (1971) *Everyday Life in the Modern World* London: Allen Lane

Lennane, J. and Lennane, J. (1977) *Hard Labour* London: Gollancz

Levy, R. (1976) 'Psychosomatic symptoms and women's protest: two types of reaction to structural strain in the family' *Journal of Health and Social Behaviour* 17 (June): pp.122-34

Little, G. and Holmström, E. (1977) 'Family Authority' in A.F. Davies, S. Encel and M.J. Berry (eds) *Australian Society* 3rd edition, Melbourne: Longman Cheshire, pp.176-88

Loeser, H. (1974) *Women, Work and Volunteering* Boston: Beacon Press

Lojkine, J. (1976) 'Contribution to a Marxist Theory of Capitalist Urbanisation' in C.G. Pickvance (ed.) *Urban Sociology: Critical Essays* London: Tavistock, pp.119-46

Los Angeles Times (1982a) 'Reagan Praises Volunteers, Assails Government Waste', 15 January (V): pp.12-13

——(1982b) 'Reagan State of Union', 27 January (I): p.14

——(1982c) 'Fundraising: Givers, Takers find Dilemma Deepening' and 'Government Funds Diminish', 7 March, (V): pp.1, 4, 10

Lynch, L. and Tiffin, S. (1979) 'Maternity Leave 1979: Who benefits?' *Refractory Girl* December: pp.34-40

Macarthy, P.G. (1967) 'Labor and the Living Wage 1896-1910' *Australian Journal of Politics and History* XIII (April): pp.67-89

MacDonald, P.F. (1975) *Marriage in Australia* Canberra: ANU

McDonald, S. and Mandeville, T. (1980) 'Word Processors and Employment' *Journal of Industrial Relations* 22(2): pp.137-48

McIntosh, M.C. (1978) 'The State and the Oppression of Women' in A. Kuhn and A.M. Wolpe (eds) *Feminism and Materialism* London: Routledge & Kegan Paul, pp.254-89

——(1981) 'Feminism and Social Policy' *Critical Social Policy* vol.I, no.(1),

(Summer): pp.32-42

MacIntyre, S. (1981) 'Equity in Australian History' in P.N. Troy (ed.) *A Just Society* Sydney: Allen & Unwin, pp.37-50

MacIver, R.M. and Page, C.H. (1950) *Society: An Introductory Analysis* London: MacMillan

MacKenzie, S. (1980) 'Women's Place—Women's Space' *Area* 12: pp.947-9

McKinley, B. (1979) *A Documentary History of the Australian Labour Movement 1850-1975* Richmond, Vic.: Drummond

Mackinolty, J. (1979) 'To stay or go—Sacking married women teachers' in J. Mackinolty and H. Radi (eds) *In Pursuit of Justice: Australian Women and the Law, 1788-1979* Sydney: Hale & Iremonger, pp.140-7

Mackinolty, J. and Radi, H. (eds) (1979) *In Pursuit of Justice: Australian Women and the Law, 1788-1979* Sydney: Hale & Iremonger

McQuade, N. (1980) 'Making a Drama out of Shopping' *Fortune* 24 March: pp.104-7

Madden, J. (1977) 'A Spatial Theory of Sex Discrimination' *Journal of Regional Science* 17: pp.369-80

Manning, I. (1978) *The Journey to Work* Sydney: Allen & Unwin

Manser, G. (1979) *The Voluntary Sector in Brief* Washington: Academy for Educational Development

Manser, G. and Cass, R.H. (1976) *Voluntarism at the Crossroads* New York: Family Service Association of America

Marchisotti, D. (1980) 'Equal Pay Case, 1951' in E. Windschuttle (ed.) *Women, Class and History—Feminist Perspectives on Australia 1788-1978* Melbourne: Fontana/Collins, pp.423-9

Marcuse, H. (1964) *One Dimensional Man* London: Routledge

Markusen, A. (1980) 'City Spatial Structure, Women's Household Work, and National Urban Policy' *Signs* 5(3) (supplement): S23-S44

Marris, P. and Rein, M. (1974) *Dilemmas of Social Reform* Harmondsworth: Penguin

Marx, K. and Engels, F. (1970) *Selected Works* London: Lawrence & Wishart

Melville, G. (1954) 'Fifty Years of the LWCOC' in *Golden Jubilee Souvenir of the Labor Women's Central Organising Committee 1904-54*, Sydney: ALP

Mendelsohn, R. (1979) *The Condition of the People: Social Welfare in Australia 1900-1975* Sydney: Allen & Unwin

Mercer, J. (1975) 'The History of WEL' in J. Mercer (ed.) *The Other Half: Women in Australian Society* Melbourne: Penguin, pp.395-404

——(ed.) (1975) *The Other Half: Women in Australian Society* Melbourne: Penguin

Mercer, J. and Miller, D. (1975) 'Liberation: Reform or Revolution' in J. Mercer (ed.) *The Other Half: Women in Australian Society* Melbourne: Penguin, pp.447-73

Milkman, R. (1976) 'Women's work and the Economic Crisis: Some Lessons from the Great Depression' *Review of Radical Political Economy* 8, Spring: pp.73-97

Millett, K. (1972) *Sexual Politics* London: Sphere Books

Mills, H. (1981) 'Equal Opportunities' in A. Parkin and A. Patience (eds) *The Dunstan Decade—Social Democracy at State Level* Melbourne: Longman Cheshire, pp.115-26

Mitchell, J. (1971) *Woman's Estate* Harmondsworth: Penguin

Moller Okin, S. (1979) *Women in Western Political Thought* Princeton: Princeton University Press

Monthly Labour Review (1929) 'Family Allowances. Progress of the Family Endowment Movement in Australia and New Zealand *Monthly Labour Review* 28(3)

Morgan, J., Dye, R.F. and Hybels, J.H. (1977) 'Results from Two National Surveys of Philanthropic Activity' in Filer Commission on Private Philanthropy and Public Needs *Research Papers* vol.1, Washington, D.C.: Department of Treasury, pp.157-323

Moroney, R. (1976) *The Family and the State* London: Longman

Morton, W.E. and Ungs, T.J. (1980) 'Cancer mortality in the major cottage industry' *Women and Health* 4(Winter): pp.345-54

MSJ Keys Young Planners Pty Ltd. (1975) *Women and Planning: Planners Attitudes* report prepared for the Cities Commission, November

Mueller, M. (1975) 'Economic Determinants of Volunteer work by Women' *Signs* 1(2): pp.325-33

Mullins, P. (1979) 'Women and the Struggle Against Brisbane's Freeways' *The Australian and New Zealand Journal of Sociology* 15(1): pp.43-9

——(1981) 'Theoretical Perspectives on Australian Urbanization: 1. Material components in the Reproduction of Australian Labour Power' *Australian and New Zealand Journal of Sociology* 17(1): pp.65-76

Nathanson, C.A. (1977) 'Sex, illness, and medical care: a review of data, theory, and method' *Social Science and Medicine* 11 (January): pp.13-25

National Advisory Committee for International Women's Year (1976) *Report* Canberra: AGPS

National Association of Social Workers (1973) *Encyclopedia of Social Work* 16th issue, vol.11, Washington: NASW

National Catholic Welfare Committee (1962) *A Case for Graded Child Endowment and Increased Maternity Allowances* (roneoed booklet)

National Health and Medical Research Council (NHMRC) (1944) *Interim Report on the Decline in the Birth-Rate* Canberra: Commonwealth Government Printer

National Organisation of Women (NOW) (1980) *Legal Defence and Education Fund, Annual Report*

National Population Inquiry (NPI) (1975) *Population and Australia: A Demographic Analysis and Projection* vol.1, Canberra: AGPS

——(1978) *Population and Australia: Recent Demographic Trends and their implications, Supplementary Report* Canberra: AGPS

National Women's Advisory Council (1979) *First Annual Report* Canberra: AGPS

Neutze, M. (1977) *Urban Development in Australia* Sydney: Allen & Unwin

Newman, S. (1976) *Housing Adjustments of Older People* Ann Arbor: Institute for Social Research, University of Michigan

New South Wales Parliamentary Debates (1920) *Legislative Assembly* 22 December

New South Wales Parliamentary Debates (1932) vol.84, September 2

New South Wales Premiers Department, Women's Co-ordination Unit (1980) *Facts about women in the New South Wales workforce structure* Statistical Bulletin, No.1

New York City Commission on Human Rights (1970) *Report on Women's*

Role in Contemporary Society New York: Discus Books

Nieuwenhuysen, J. and Hicks, J. (1975) 'Equal Pay for Women in Australia and New Zealand' in B.O. Pettman (ed.) *Equal Pay for Women: Progress and Problems in Seven Countries* Bradford: MCB Books, pp.63-83

Nygh, P.E. (1978) *Guide to the Family Law Act: 1975* 2nd ed., Sydney: Butterworths

Oakley, A. (1974) *The Sociology of Housework* New York: Pantheon

——(1976) *Housewife* London: Pelican

——(1979) *Becoming a Mother* Oxford: Martin Robertson

——(1980) *Women Confined: Towards a Sociology of Childbirth* Oxford: Martin Robertson

O'Brien, L. and Turner, S. (1979) *Establishing Medical Social Work in Victoria* University of Melbourne: Department of Social Studies

O'Connor, J. (1973) *The Fiscal Crisis of the State* New York: St. Martin's Press

Ortner, S.B. (1974) 'Is female to male as nature is to culture?' in M.Z. Rosaldo and L. Lamphere (eds) *Women, Culture and Society* Stanford: Stanford University Press, pp.67-87

Owen, A. (1976) 'Psychotropic drugs: psycho-social aspects' in M. Diesendorf (ed.) *The Magic Bullet* Canberra: Society for Social Responsibility in Science, pp.44-8

Owen, M. and Shaw, S. (eds) (1979) *Working Women: Discussion Papers from the Working Women's Centre, Melbourne* Carlton, Melbourne: Sisters

Pahl, J. (1980) 'Patterns of Money Management within Marriage' *Journal of Social Policy* 9(3): pp.313-35

Pahl, R. (1980) 'Employment, work and the Domestic Division of Labour' *International Journal of Urban and Regional Research* March: pp.1-20

Palm, R. (1981) 'Women in Nonmetropolitan areas: A Time-Budget Survey' *Environment and Planning* 13A: pp.373-8

Palm, R. and Pred, A. (1977) 'A Time-Geographic Perspective on Problems of Inequality for Women' Institute of Urban and Regional Development, University of California, Berkeley, Working Paper 236

Paterson, H.M. (1979) *Voluntary Workers: Special Report No.3* Bendigo: Bendigo Labour Force and Community Survey

Piddington, A.B. (1921) *The Next Step: A Family Basic Income* London: MacMillan

——(1922) 'The Case for Motherhood Endowment' *The Open Platform* (May 24)

Piven, F. and Cloward, R.A. (1971) *Regulating the Poor, The Functions of Public Welfare* New York: Vintage

Podder, N. and Kakwani, N.C. (1975) 'Distribution and redistribution of household income in Australia' Taxation Review Committee, *Commissioned Studies* Canberra: AGPS

Poloma, M.M. and Garland, N.T. (1971) 'The Married Professional Woman: a study in the tolerance of domestication' *Journal of Marriage and the Family* 33 (August): pp.531-40

Power, M. (1974) 'The Wages of Sex' *Australian Quarterly* 46: pp.2-14

——(1975a) 'The Making of a Woman's Occupation' *Hecate* 1(2), July: pp.25-34

——(1975b) 'Women's Work is Never Done by Men—A Socio-Economic Model of Sex-Typing in Occupations' *Journal of Industrial Relations* September, 17(3), pp.225-39

——(1976) 'Cast-off jobs: women, migrants, blacks may apply' *Refractory Girl* pp.27-31

——(1979) 'Women and Economic Crisis: The 1930s Depression and the Present Crisis *The Journal of Australian Political Economy* 4: pp.3-12

——(1981) Employment Prospects for Women, paper presented at WEL National Conference, Sydney

Pred, A. (1981a) 'Production, Family and Free-time Projects. A Time-Geographic Perspective on the Individual and Societal Change in Nineteenth Century U.S. Cities' *Journal of Historical Geography* 7(1): pp.3-36

——(1981b) 'Social Reproduction and the Time-Geography of Everyday Life' *Geografiska Annaler* 63B: pp.5-22

Preston, V. (1981) Family Roles and the Leisure Activities of Women, unpublished manuscript, Department of Geography, University of Kansas

Pringle, R. (1979) 'Feminists and Bureaucrats—the last four years' *Refractory Girl* December: pp.58-60

——(1981) 'The Dialectics of Porn' *Scarlet Woman* 12, March: pp.3-10

Prosser, B. (1981) *Families at Work. Family Information Bulletin* 1, Melbourne: Institute of Family Studies

Public Service Board (1978) *AEQUA—Equal Employment Opportunity Newsletter* supplement to Issue 3, June, Canberra

Radi, H. (1974) '1920-29', in F. Crowley (ed.) *A New History of Australia* London: Heinemann, pp.357-414

Rainwater, L., Coleman, R.P. and Handel, G. (1959) *Working Man's Wife: Her Personality, World and Life Style* New York: Ocean Publication

Raskall, P. (1978) 'Who's got what in Australia' *Journal of Australian Political Economy* 2: pp.3-16

Rathbone, E.F. (1924) *The Disinherited Family: A Plea for the Endowment of the Family* London: Edward Arnold

——(1940) *The Case for Family Allowances* Harmondsworth: Penguin

Reed, J. and Oakes, C. (1977) *Women in Australian Society, 1901-1945: A Guide to the Holdings of Australian Archives Relating to Women, 1901-1945* Canberra: AGPS

Reich, M., Gordon, D.M. and Edwards, R.C. (1973) 'Dual Labor Markets: A Theory of Labor Market Segmentation' *American Economic Review* 63(2): pp.359-65

Rein, M. (1980) 'Women and work—the Incomplete Revolution' *The Australian Economic Review* 3rd Quarter: pp.11-17

Reiner, C. (1980) Women's Refuges as a Feminist Alternative, Success or Failure?, unpublished Honours thesis, Social and Political Theory Programme, Murdoch University

Rich, A. (1976) *Of Woman Born: Motherhood as Experience and Institution* New York: W.W. Norton

Richards, L. (1978) *Having Families* Melbourne: Penguin

Riches, A. (1979) 'The Family Law Act' in J. Mackinolty and H. Radi (eds) *In Pursuit of Justice: Australian Women and the Law 1788-1978*, Sydney: Hale & Iremonger, pp.212-24

Richmond, K. (1974) 'The Workforce participation of married women in Australia' in D. Edgar (ed.) *Social Change in Australia* Melbourne: Cheshire, pp.267-308

Rigby, N. (1979) 'The Contribution of Volunteers in Programs for Aged and Disabled Persons' *National Rehabilitation Digest* 3(3/4): pp.23-6

Robinson, J.P., Converse, P.E. and Szalai, A. (1972) 'Everyday life in twelve countries' in A. Szalai (ed.) *The Use of Time* The Hague: Mouton

Roe, J. (1975) 'Social Policy and the Permanent Poor' in E.L. Wheelwright and K. Buckley (eds) *Essays in the Political Economy of Australian Capitalism* vol 1, Sydney: ANZ Book Co., pp.130-52

——(ed) (1976) *Social Policy in Australia: Some perspectives 1901-1975* Sydney: Cassell

——(1981) 'Old Age, Young Country: The First Old Age Pensions and Pensioners in New South Wales' *Teaching History* July: Vol.15(2): pp.23-42

Ronalds, C. (1979a) *Anti-Discrimination Legislation in Australia* Sydney: Butterworths

——(1979b) 'To Right a Few Wrongs: Legislation Against Sex Discrimination' in J. Mackinolty and H. Radi (eds) *In Pursuit of Justice: Australian Women and the Law 1788-1978* Sydney: Hale & Iremonger, pp.190-201

——(1980) 'Discrimination—Federal Industrial Award and State Anti-discrimination Legislation' *Legal Service Bulletin* pp.71-3

——(1981) 'Employment discrimination committees don't work' *Legal Service Bulletin* 6(1): pp.17-21

Rosaldo, M.Z. and Lamphere, L. (1974) *Women, Culture and Society* Stanford: Stanford University Press

Rose, H. (1978) 'In Practice Supported, in Theory Denied: An Account of an Invisible Urban Movement' *International Journal of Urban and Regional Research* 2(3): pp.521-37

——(1981) 'Rereading Titmuss: The Sexual division of Welfare' *Journal of Social Policy* 10, 4: pp.477-502

Rothblatt, D.N., Carr, N.J. and Sprague, J. (1979) *The Suburban Environment and Women* New York: Praeger

Rowbotham, S. (1973) *Women's Consciousness, Man's World* Harmondsworth: Penguin

Rowbotham, S., Segal, L. and Wainwright, H. (1979) *Beyond the Fragments: Feminism and the Making of Socialism* London: Merlin Press

Rowell, J. (1971) 'Sex Differences in Achievement in Sciences and the Expectations of Teachers' *Australian Journal of Education* 15(1): pp.16-29

Royal Commission on Australian Government Administration (1976) *Report* Canberra: AGPS

Royal Commission on the Basic Wage (1920) *Report* Melbourne: Govern Printer

Royal Commission on Child Endowment or Family Allowances (1929) *Reports* Canberra: Government Printer

Royal Commission on the Decline of the Birth-rate and on the Mortality of Infants in New South Wales, (1904). *Vol.1, Report and Statistics* Sydney: Government Printer

Royal Commission on the Status of Women in Canada (1976) *Report* Ottawa: Information Canada

Rubery, J. (1980) 'Structured Labour Markets, Worker Organisation and Low Pay' in A.H. Amsden (ed.) *The Economics of Women and Work* Harmondsworth: Penguin, pp.242-70

Russell, G. (1979) 'Fathers: Incompetent or reluctant parents?' *Australian and New Zealand Journal of Sociology* 15(March): pp.57-65

Rutter, M. (1972) *Maternal Deprivation Reassessed* Harmondsworth: Penguin

Ryan, E. (1980) 'Paid Maternity Leave for all' *Womanspeak* 5(2)

Ryan, E. and Conlon, A. (1975) *Gentle Invaders: Australian Women at Work 1788-1974* Sydney: Nelson

Ryan, M.P. (1975) *Womanhood in America: From Colonial Times to the Present* New York: New Viewpoints

Ryan, P. and Rowse, T. (1975) 'Women, Arbitration and the Family' in A. Curthoys et al. (eds) *Women at Work* Canberra: Australian Society for the Study of Labour History, pp.15-30

Saegert, S. (1980) 'Masculine Cities and Feminine Suburbs: Polarized Ideas, Contradictory Realities' *Signs*, 5(3) supplement: S96-S111

Safilios-Rothschild, C. (1976) 'Dual Linkages between the Occupational and Family Systems: a Macro-Sociological Analysis' in M. Blaxall and B. Reagan (eds) *Women and the Workplace* Chicago: University of Chicago Press, pp.51-60

Sahlins, M. (1976) *Culture and Practical Reason* Chicago: University of Chicago Press

Sampson, S. (1976) 'Egalitarian Ideology and the Education of Girls' *Australian Journal of Education* 20(1)

Saunders, P. (1981) *Social Theory and the Urban Question* London: Hutchinson

Sawer, M. (1973) 'Consensus and Patriarchal Values' *Politics*, (November): pp.332-33

Sawkins, D.T. (1933) *The Living Wage in Australia* Melbourne: Melbourne University Press

Schlesinger, B. (1979) 'The Client Speaks' *New Zealand Social Work* 3, June

School of Behavioural Sciences (1980) The White Goods Industry: The Labour Process and the Sexual Division of Labour, unpublished report, Macquarie University

Schools Commission (1975) *Girls, School and Society, Report* Canberra: Schools Commission

Scott, A.J. and Roweis, S.T. (1977) 'Urban Planning in Theory and Practice: A Reappraisal' *Environment and Planning* A9: pp.1097-119

Scotton, R.B. and Ferber, H. (eds) (1980) *Public Expenditures and Social Policy in Australia vol.II: The First Fraser Years 1976-78* Melbourne: Longman Cheshire

Scotton, R.B. and Sheehan, P. (1976) 'Recent changes in personal income tax' *Australian Economic Review* 2: pp.13-24

Scutt, J.A. (1977) 'The Anti-Discrimination Act (NSW) 1977' *Law Society Journal* 15(4): pp.241-5

——(1982) 'Commonwealth Sex Discrimination Bill' *Australian Law Journal* 56(6)

Sekuless, P. (1978) *Jessie Street: A Rewarding but Unrewarded Life* St. Lucia: Queensland University Press

Shaver, S. and Walker, C. (1980) Sex and Money in the Welfare State, paper presented at ANZAAS Jubilee Congress, Adelaide, August

Sheehan, P. (1980) *Crisis in Abundance* Melbourne: Penguin

Shepherd, H. (1973) Reformism: How Necessary—How Possible—How Dangerous, unpublished paper

Short, K. (1979) 'Women Workers, Multinationals and Asian Industrialisation' *Refractory Girl* December: pp.25-8

Shute, C. (1980) 'From Balaclavas to Bayonets: Women's Voluntary War Work, 1939-41' *Hecate* VI(1): pp.5-26

Signs (1980) 5: whole issue.

Smart, C. (1977) 'Criminological theory: its ideology and implications concerning women' *British Journal of Sociology* 28 (March): pp.89-99

Smith, C. and Freedman, A. (1972) *Voluntary Associations* Boston: Harvard University Press

Smith, D. (1980) Women, Class and Family, paper presented at SSHRC workshop on *Women and the Canadian Labour Force* University of British Columbia

Smith, H. (1978) Urbanization in Contemporary Australian History: An Historical Materialist Perspective, unpublished honours thesis, Murdoch University

Smith, L.M. (1975) 'Women as Volunteers: A Double Subsidy' *Journal of Voluntary Action Research* 4, (3-4): pp.119-36

Smith-Rosenberg, C. (1972) 'The hysterical woman: sex roles and role conflict in 19th century America' *Social Research*, 39 (Winter): pp.652-78

Social Welfare Commission (1974) *Project Care* Canberra: AGPS

Social Welfare Policy Secretariat (1981) *Report on Poverty Measurement* Canberra: AGPS

Spalding, B. (1977) 'Women and Welfare' *Legal Service Bulletin* 2(10): pp.355-8

Spearritt, P. (1974) 'The Kindergarten Movement: tradition and change' in D. Edgar (ed.) *Social Change in Australia*, Melbourne: Cheshire, pp.583-596

——(1979) 'Child care and Kindergartens in Australia, 1890-1975' in P. Langford and P. Sebastian (eds) *Early Childhood Education and Care in Australia* Melbourne: Australia International Press, pp.10-38

Stacey, M. (1980) The Division of Labour or Overcoming the two Adams, paper presented at the 30th Annual Conference of the British Sociological Association, April

Stenzel, A. and Feeney, H.M. (1976) *Volunteer Training and Development: A Manual* revised edition, New York: Seabury Press

Stilwell, F.J.B. (1980) *Economic Crisis Cities and Regions* Sydney: Pergamon

Stone, J. (1976) 'Women in the Metal Trades' *Frontline* 5, International Socialists, December: pp.9-17

Street, J. (1966) *Truth or Repose* Sydney: Australasian Book Society

Stretton, H. (1970) *Ideas for Australian Cities* Melbourne: Georgian House.

Summers, A. (1973) 'A Radical Political Currency' *Politics* (November): p.333

——(1975) *Damned Whores and God's Police* Melbourne: Penguin

Sydney Morning Herald (1980) 19 November

——(1981a) 20 January

——(1981b) 24 February

Szalai, A. (ed.) (1972) *The Use of Time* The Hague: Mouton

Szelenyi, I. (1981) 'Structural Changes of and Alternatives to Capitalist Development in the Contemporary Urban and Regional System' *International Journal of Urban and Regional Research* 5(1): pp.1-14

Taperell, K., Fox, C. and Roberts, M. (1975) *Sexism in Public Service* Canberra: AGPS

Tax, M. (1970) 'Woman and Her Mind: The Story of Daily Life' *Bread and Roses* Somerville: NE Free Press

Taxation Review Committee (1975) (Chairman K.W. Asprey) *Full Report* Canberra: AGPS

Tefler, R. (1978) 'Decision Congruence and the Sex of School Administrators' *Journal of Education Administration* 61(1) May: pp.39-45

Thame, C. (1974) Health and the State: The Development of Collective Responsibility for Health Care in Australia in the First Half of the Twentieth Century unpublished PhD thesis, Australian National University

Thane, P. (1978) 'Women and the Poor Law in Victorian and Edwardian England' *History Workshop* 6: pp.29-51

Thompson, E.P. (1967) 'Time, Work-discipline, and Industrial Capitalism' *Past and Present* 38: pp.56-97

Thompson, H.M. (1981) ' "Normalisation": Industrial Relations and Community Control in the Pilbara' *The Australian Quarterly* 53(3): pp.301-24

Thornton, M. (1978) 'Women Teachers and the New South Wales Anti-Discrimination Act' *Australian Current Law Digest* DT pp.341-3

——(1979a) 'Board's First Decision' *Legal Service Bulletin* October: pp.180-7

——(1979b) 'Women Teachers and the New South Wales Anti-Discrimination Act: A Postscript' *Australian Current Law Digest* DT 3(4), pp.3-4

——(1981) Anti-discrimination Legislation in Australia: Straws and Strategies, paper presented at WEL National Conference, Sydney

——(1982) 'Perspectives on Sex Discrimination Legislation in Australia' in *Third Women and Labour Conference Papers 1982* vol.2, Adelaide: Salisbury Education Centre, pp.382-92

Thornton Merle (1980) 'Work and Consciousness' in P. Boreham and G. Dow (eds) *Work and Inequality* vol.2, Melbourne: Macmillan, pp.198-229

Tideman, T.N. (1977) 'Employment and Earnings in the Non-profit Charitable Sector' in Filer Commission *Research Reports* vol.1, Washington: Department of Treasury, pp.325-31

Titmuss, R. and Titmuss, K. (1942) *Parents Revolt: a Study of the Declining Birth Rate in Acquisitive Societies* London: Secker & Warburg

Titmuss, R.M. (1974) *Social Policy* London: Allen & Unwin

——(1976) 'Industrialization and the Family' in R. Titmuss, *Essays on the Welfare State* London: Allen & Unwin

Tormey, J.F. (1976) 'Exploitation, Oppression and Self-Sacrifice' in C.C. Gould and M.W. Wartofsky (eds) *Women and Philosophy* New York: Capricorn, pp.206-21

Trans National Co-operative (1980) 'Women and Work' *Trans National Brief* 3 November

Tulloch, P. (1979) *Poor Policies* London: Croom Helm

Turner, I. (1974) '1914-1919' in F. Crowley (ed.) *A New History of Australia* Melbourne: Heinemann, pp.312-56

320   *Women, social welfare and the state*

Turney, C. (ed.) (1975) *Sources in the History of Australian Education 1788-1970* Sydney: Angus & Robertson

Turtle, A. (1979) 'Superannuation and the Sexes' in J. Mackinolty and H. Radi (eds) *In Pursuit of Justice* Sydney: Hale & Iremonger, pp.149-59

Tyack, D.B. (1974) *The One Best System: a History of American Urban Education* Cambridge, Mass.: Harvard University Press

United Front Committee of the Unemployed (1932) *Lang, Piddington and the Fight for Child Endowment* mimeoed brochure: Sydney

United States Department of Transport (1978) 'Women's Travel Issues: Research Needs and Priorities: Executive Summary' September

Vadakin, J.C. (1958) *Family Allowances, An Analysis of their Development and Applications* Miami: University of Miami Press

Vanek, J. (1974) 'Time Spent in Housework' *Scientific American* 231 November: pp.116-20

——(1978) 'Household Technology and Social Status: Rising Living Standards and Status and Residence Differences in Housework' *Technology and Culture* 19(3): pp. 361-75

Victorian Select Committee on Child Endowment (1940) *Report* Melbourne: Government Printer

Victorian Women's Refuge Group (1979) *Women and Housing* Melbourne: VWRG

Voysey, E. (1981) Women and the Journey to work, unpublished paper, School of Social Inquiry, Murdoch University

Wade, J.H. (1978) 'Maintenance Orders and Causes for Non-Payment' *Australian Journal of Social Issues* 13(3): pp.232-49

Waerness, K. (1978) 'The Invisible Welfare State: Women's Work at Home' *Acta Sociologica* vol.21, supplement on 'The Nordic Welfare State': pp.193-207

Wallen, J., Waitzkin, H. and Stoeckle, J.D. (1979) 'Physician stereotypes about female health and illness' *Women and Health* 4 (Summer): pp.135-46

Warren, N.A. (1979) 'Australian tax incidences in 1975-76: Some preliminary results' *Australian Economic Review* 3: pp.19-30

Watson, J. (1980) Adding insult to injury, paper presented to the Medical Anthropology section of the Australian Anthropological Society Annual Conference: University of Queensland

Watts, R. (1980) 'The origins of the Australian Welfare State' *Historical Studies* 19(75): pp.175-98

Wearing, B. (1981) The Ideology of Motherhood, unpublished PhD thesis, University of New South Wales

Weber, M. (1923) *General Economic History* London: Allen & Unwin

Weinbaum, B. and Bridges, A. (1979) 'The Other Side of the Paycheck: Monopoly Capital and the Structure of Consumption' in Z.R. Eisenstein (ed.) *Capitalist Patriarchy and the Case for Socialist Feminism* New York: Monthly Review Press, pp.190-205

Weisbrod, B.A. (1977) *The Voluntary Non-Profit Sector: An Economic Analysis* Lexington, Mass.: Lexington Books

Weisman, L.K. (1981) 'Women's Environmental Rights: A Manifesto' *Heresies II* 3(3): pp.6-8

Wertz, R.W. and Wertz, D.C. (1977) *Lying in: A History of Childbirth in America* New York: Free Press

Westergaard, J. and Resler, H. (1975) *Class in a Capitalist Society* London: Heinemann

Whalley, P. (1972) Child Endowment in Australia as an Inducement to Fertility, unpublished seminar paper delivered in Department of Demography, Australian National University, Canberra

Whelan, D. (1979) 'Women and the Arbitration System' *Journal of Australian Political Economy* 4: pp.54-60

White, M.J. (1977) 'A Model of Residential Location Choice and Commuting by Men and Women Workers' *Journal of Regional Science* 17: pp.41-60

Whiteside, T. (1978) 'Din-Din' in J.D. Gussow (ed.) *The Feeding Web: Issues in Nutritional Ecology* Palo Alto: Bull Publishing

Wilenski, P. (1978) *Review of Government Administration: Directions for Change* Sydney: NSW Government Printer

Williams, C. (1981) *Open cut* Sydney: Allen & Unwin

Williams, P. (1981) 'Economic Processes and Urban Change: An Analysis of Contemporary Patterns of Residential Restructuring' Urban Geography Section of IAG Conference, Bathurst

Williams, R. (1976) *Keywords* Harmondsworth: Penguin

Williamson, J. (1978) *Decoding Advertisements: Ideology and Meaning in Advertising* London: Marion Boyars

Willis, E. (1971) 'Consumerism and Women' in V. Gornick and B.K. Moran (eds) *Women in Sexist Society* New York: Basic Books, pp.658-64

Willis, S. (1980) 'Made to be Moral—at Parramatta Girls' School, 1898-1923' in J. Roe (ed.) *Twentieth Century Sydney: Studies in Urban and Social History* Sydney: Hale & Iremonger

Wilson, E. (1977) *Women and the Welfare State* London: Tavistock

Windschuttle, E. (1974) 'Should the Government pay a Mother's Wage?' *Social Security Quarterly* Winter: pp.12-17

——(ed.) (1980) *Women, Class and History* Melbourne: Collins

Windschuttle, K. (1979) *Unemployment* Harmondsworth: Penguin

Winkler, A. (1976) 'Sex and Student Stereotypes in Australian University Students' *Australian Journal of Education* 20(3): pp.285-91

Wolfenden, J. (1978) *The Future of Voluntary Organisations* London: Croom Helm

Womanspeak (1981) 6(1): p.5

Women's Advisory Body Working Party (1977) *Report: Women's Advisory Committee to the Prime Minister* Canberra: AGPS

Women's Electoral Lobby ACT (1973) *Human Rights for Women, submission to the Department of the Attorney-General, Australian Government* ACT: 19 November

——(1979) *The Need for Anti-Discrimination Legislation in Australia* Canberra

——(undated) *WEL Records* Canberra

Women's Electoral Lobby, NSW (1975) *When Will We Get A Fair Go Under Aussie Rules? Women and the Law* September

Women's Electoral Lobby, Sydney (1973-1974) *The WEL Papers* Sydney

——(1978a) *WEL Submission on Family Law to the Commonwealth Attorney-General* June

——(1978b) *WEL Submission on Family Law to the Parliamentary Joint Select Committee on the Family Law Act* December

——(1979a) *WEL Submission to the Enquiry into the most appropriate form and structure for a scale of costs under the Family Law Act and Regulations to Mr. Justice L.H. Williams, Australian Conciliation and Arbitration Commission* Sydney, September

——(1979b) *WEL Submission on Superannuation and the Family Law Act 1975 to the Parliamentary Joint Select Committee on the Family Law Act and to the Family Law Council* May

——(1981) *WEL Family Law Action Group Records*

Women's Employment Rights Campaign (WERC) (1979) *Women and Unemployment* Sydney: WERC

Worpole, K.K. (1981) 'Volunteers for Socialism' *New Society* 29: pp.199-200

Wright, E.O. (1979) *Class, Crisis and the State* London: NLB

Young, C. (1974) 'Demographic patterns in the life cycle of Australian Families' *Search* 51: pp.306-8

Young, S. (1980) '... "you can't be in two places at once ..." ' *Social Alternatives* 1(8): pp.17-22

Zelinsky, W., Mont, J. and Hanson, S. (1981) 'Women and Geography: A Review and Prospectus' April (forthcoming in *Professional Geographer*)

Zainu'ddin, A. (1975) 'Reflections on the History of Women's Education in Australia' *Education News* 15(4/5): pp.4-13

Zaretsky, E. (1976) *Capitalism, the Family and Personal Life* London: Pluto Press

Zola, I.K. (1972) 'Medicine as an institution of social control' *Sociological Review* 20 (November): pp.487-504

Index